The
WILEY
advantage

Dear Valued Customer,

 W9-BMP-314

We realize you're a busy professional with deadlines to hit. Whether your goal is to learn a new technology or solve a critical problem, we want to be there to lend you a hand. Our primary objective is to provide you with the insight and knowledge you need to stay atop the highly competitive and ever-changing technology industry.

Wiley Publishing, Inc., offers books on a wide variety of technical categories, including security, data warehousing, software development tools, and networking — everything you need to reach your peak. Regardless of your level of expertise, the Wiley family of books has you covered.

- For Dummies – The fun and easy way to learn
- The Weekend Crash Course –The fastest way to learn a new tool or technology
- Visual – For those who prefer to learn a new topic visually
- The Bible – The 100% comprehensive tutorial and reference
- The Wiley Professional list – Practical and reliable resources for IT professionals

The book you hold now, *Red Hat Linux Firewalls,* is the Red Hat–reviewed and approved guide to constructing firewalls on a Red Hat server. When you want to lock out intruders and defend your network against attacks, this book provides everything you need to learn firewall design, implementation, and administration. Beginning with a foundation in security technology, you are guided through designing, implementing, testing, and operating packet-filtering firewalls, as well as implementing bastion hosts and detecting network intrusions. Not just another Linux book, *Red Hat Linux Firewalls* is your official Red Hat guide to securing your Red Hat Linux system with state-of-the-art firewalls.

Our commitment to you does not end at the last page of this book. We'd want to open a dialog with you to see what other solutions we can provide. Please be sure to visit us at www.wiley.com/compbooks to review our complete title list and explore the other resources we offer. If you have a comment, suggestion, or any other inquiry, please locate the "contact us" link at www.wiley.com.

Finally, we encourage you to review the following page for a list of Wiley titles on related topics. Thank you for your support and we look forward to hearing from you and serving your needs again in the future.

Sincerely,

Richard K Swadley

Richard K. Swadley
Vice President & Executive Group Publisher
Wiley Technology Publishing

15 HOUR WEEKEND CRASH COURSE

V **Visual**

Bible

DUMMIES

WILEY
Independent Thinkers

*more information
on related titles*

The Next Level of Red Hat Press Books

— Available from Wiley Publishing —

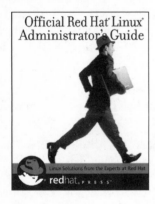

Red Hat® Linux® Firewalls

Red Hat® Linux® Firewalls

Bill McCarty

WILEY

Wiley Publishing, Inc.

Red Hat® Linux® Firewalls

Published by
Wiley Publishing, Inc.
10475 Crosspoint Boulevard
Indianapolis, IN 46256
www.wiley.com

Copyright © 2003 by Red Hat, Inc.

Published by Wiley Publishing, Inc., Indianapolis, Indiana

Published simultaneously in Canada

ISBN: 0-7645-2463-1

Manufactured in the United States of America

10 9 8 7 6 5 4 3 2 1

1O/RV/RR/QT/IN

For general information on our other products and services or to obtain technical support, please contact our Customer Care Department within the U.S. at (800) 762-2974, outside the U.S. at (317) 572-3993 or fax (317) 572-4002.

Wiley also publishes its books in a variety of electronic formats. Some content that appears in print may not be available in electronic books.

Library of Congress Cataloging-in-Publication Data: 2002112138

Ⓦ Wiley Publishing, Inc. is a trademark of Wiley Publishing, Inc.

Credits

ACQUISITIONS EDITOR
Debra Williams Cauley

PROJECT EDITOR
Eric Newman

RED HAT TECHNICAL EDITOR
Mark J. Cox, Senior Director
of Engineering, Red Hat

RED HAT PRESS LIAISONS
Chris Grams, Manager
of Marketing Services
Lorien Golaski

SPECIAL RED HAT ASSISTANCE
Kathleen Langhi
Jonathan Opp
Jeremy Hogan

COPY EDITOR
Rebecca Whitney

EDITORIAL MANAGER
Mary Beth Wakefield

VICE PRESIDENT & EXECUTIVE GROUP PUBLISHER
Richard Swadley

VICE PRESIDENT AND EXECUTIVE PUBLISHER
Bob Ipsen

EXECUTIVE EDITORIAL DIRECTOR
Mary Bednarek

PROJECT COORDINATOR
Maridee Ennis

GRAPHICS AND PRODUCTION SPECIALISTS
Amanda Carter
Sean Decker
Brian Drumm
Melanie DesJardins
Jackie Nicholas
Jeremey Unger

QUALITY CONTROL TECHNICIAN
Laura Albert
John Greenough
Andy Hollandbeck
Susan Moritz
Angel Perez
Dwight Ramsey

PROOFREADING AND INDEXING
TECHBOOKS Production Services

COVER DESIGN
Michael J. Freeland

About the Author

Bill McCarty is an associate professor of information technology at Azusa Pacific University, Azusa, California, where he teaches Linux system and network administration; information security; JavaScript, PHP, and ColdFusion programming; Web site development; and e-commerce. Bill earned a Ph.D. in Management of Information Systems from The Claremont Graduate University, Claremont, California. The author or co-author of more than a dozen technical books, Bill is a Red Hat Certified Engineer and has worked with Linux since 1993.

Foreword

I'd be lost without my firewall.

Gene Spafford, of the Center for Education and Research in Information Assurance and Security, once said, "The only truly secure system is one that is powered off, cast in a block of concrete, and sealed in a lead-lined room with armed guards – and even then I have my doubts." If you can't encase your computer in concrete, you need a firewall as your first line of defense. A properly configured firewall can greatly increase the security of your network – just don't expect a firewall to be the miracle cure that will instantly make you immune to security problems.

My firewall protects me from attackers. (Well, at least from some of them.)

The Internet is a door connecting you with the rest of the world. When that door is left unguarded, others can and will find their way in. Worms like Code Red, Ramen, and Nimda exploited known software security flaws, with disruptive and costly results. As long as networks are connected, security threats won't go away. Vulnerabilities in software are being found and disclosed every day, and it is becoming increasingly harder to keep up to date with them. Every new security vulnerability requires time to analyze it: Does it directly affect you or your organization? Is the vulnerability being actively exploited? Is a workaround available? Are patches available? Do the patches have side effects?

My home network has a firewall with only one open port to the outside world, port 80, to allow incoming Web traffic. I trust my firewall and I care about remote attackers only, so I can effectively ignore vulnerabilities in other software such as lpd, the printing service, or OpenSSH. I still have to watch out for vulnerabilities in the firewall code or in TCP/IP or Apache, but fortunately they don't occur that often.

My firewall protects me from myself. (Without my firewall I'm doomed.)

I run the security response team at Red Hat, so I'm always playing with the latest OS releases, the latest versions of Apache, and many other random network and security applications. I don't want to worry about what network services might have been opened by some new application I'm testing. I don't want to remember to secure everything I set up on my network with strong passwords. My firewall stops me from making simple or silly mistakes that could jeopardize my security.

It doesn't matter that my girlfriend still uses Microsoft Windows on our home network – the firewall protects it. We didn't need to worry when serious remote exploits were found in the new Netbios protocol; the firewall was already blocking packets to the vulnerable Netbios port. When we added our TiVo onto the local network, we didn't care about securely configuring it; the firewall rules stop remote attackers from gaining access. The worst-case scenario would be to return home to find that a remote attacker had deleted all our saved episodes of "Cops."

An effective firewall is one that is correctly configured and maintained. Once an attacker is inside your firewall, it is basically useless. A badly configured firewall will give you a false sense of security. So when it comes to deploying a firewall, you need to understand how it works, how it protects you, what its limitations are, and, most important, how to configure it correctly. That is where *Red Hat Linux Firewalls* comes in.

You could buy one of a hundred different complete commercial firewall solutions, but you'd still have to understand how they work and how they protect you. All the technology you need to make your own firewall is included in recent Linux distributions, so this book concentrates on how to create a firewall yourself using open-source software. With the knowledge in this book, you can quickly set up a firewall that rivals commercial solutions at a fraction of the price, without compromising security.

Lots of books and Internet resources tell you how to design, build, and maintain a firewall. What I particularly like about this book is that everything you need to know is in one place and explained in a consistent manner. It gives you the background, tells you why a particular technology is relevant, explains how to use it, and provides code and configurations that will work first time out of the box. The best part: The book and all the examples have been tailored to Red Hat Linux.

So go make a pot of tea, sit back, relax, and let Bill McCarty show you how to make a firewall using Red Hat Linux and other open-source software. You'll learn how to protect your network not only from evil attackers but also from yourself.

Mark J. Cox
Senior Director of Engineering, Red Hat

Preface

Red Hat Linux is a relatively secure operating system. Properly installed and configured, a Red Hat Linux system can be highly resistant to attack. However, the level of threats now emanating from the Internet is considerable. Anyone who administers a Red Hat Linux computer connected to a public network generally should protect that computer with a properly configured firewall. This book will help readers protect computers and computer networks by using Red Hat Linux firewalls.

Who Should Read This Book?

This book presumes a general knowledge of Red Hat Linux system and network administration. Therefore, the book's primary intended audience is experienced Red Hat Linux system and network administrators who plan to implement Red Hat Linux firewalls. However, those familiar with a Linux distribution other than Red Hat or a Unix-like operating system other than Linux will have little difficulty understanding the material and using it to implement firewalls based on Red Hat Linux or another Linux distribution.

This book primarily addresses the needs of professional system administrators, who must support multiple servers providing a variety of network services. However, those who operate personal networks can also use the tools and apply the techniques presented here.

This book does not discuss commercial hardware or software firewalls in depth. Instead, it focuses on the IPTables facility, a standard component of Red Hat Linux. The flexible and sophisticated stateful firewall facility IPTables has features and a performance that compare quite favorably with those of commercially offered firewalls. Moreover, organizations having limited budgetary resources will appreciate the low out-of-pocket costs associated with IPTables firewalls. The book also presents the older Red Hat Linux IPChains firewalls facility. Though the IPChains facility does not permit the construction of stateful firewalls, some people prefer using it for the sake of compatibility and familiarity.

Implementing a Red Hat Linux firewall demands a significant functional understanding of the TCP/IP protocol family. However, purchasing a commercial firewall appliance does not permit you to escape the need for such expertise. You cannot properly configure and operate even a commercial firewall appliance without a functional understanding of TCP/IP. This book provides both the necessary foundation in TCP/IP networking and the details of IPTables and IPChains firewall implementation necessary to configure and operate Red Hat Linux firewalls.

How This Book Is Organized

This book is organized into three parts, plus a glossary. It also includes several appendixes useful for reference.

Part I: The Network Security Context

The first part of this book explains why network security is important and the role firewalls play in protecting computer networks. It also presents details of the TCP/IP protocol family that are important to firewall design.

Part II: Firewall Design and Implementation

The chapters in Part II cover the design and implementation of IPChains and IPTables firewalls. The chapters present basic firewall architectures, the elements of firewall policy design, and the particulars of the IPChains and IPTables facilities used to construct Red Hat Linux firewalls.

Part III: Firewall Operation

The third part of this book focuses on managing and administering deployed firewalls. The chapters explain how to strengthen hosts to resist attack, how to test and troubleshoot firewalls, and how to monitor operational firewalls.

Glossary

The book concludes with an extensive glossary of terms related to firewalls.

Appendixes

The book concludes with appendixes that identify potentially useful Web resources; summarize commonly used ports, protocol numbers, and ICMP messages; present sample firewall code; and provide an overview of virtual private networks (VPNs).

How to Approach This Book

Readers unfamiliar with computer security and the TCP/IP protocol family should read Part I before Parts II and III. Part I will help them understand why network security is important and how firewalls should be used in combination with other defensive measures. Part I also explains the details of the TCP/IP protocol family necessary to implement Red Hat Linux firewalls. Readers already conversant in these topics can freely ignore familiar material from Part I or even skip immediately to Part II.

Parts II and III can be read in any order. Readers who have already deployed Red Hat Linux firewalls may prefer to read Part III before reading Part II. Those who plan to implement IPChains firewalls should read Chapter 7, "IPChains Firewalls." Those who plan to implement only IPTables firewalls can skip that chapter. Otherwise, the chapters in Part II should be read in sequence because subsequent chapters build on material introduced in earlier chapters.

The chapters in Part III can be read in any order and can be read before or after the chapters in Part II. In particular, those who are implementing a firewall for the first time may benefit from reading Chapter 11, "Bastion Host Implementation," before other chapters in Parts II and III. That chapter gives useful guidance in securely installing and configuring Red Hat Linux.

Conventions Used in This Book

Each chapter in this book begins with a heads-up of the topics covered in the chapter and ends with a summary of what you should have learned by reading the chapter.

Throughout this book, you will find in the margins some icons that highlight special or important information. Keep an eye out for these icons:

 A Caution icon indicates a procedure that could cause difficulty or even data loss; pay careful attention to Caution icons to avoid common pitfalls.

 Cross-Reference icons point to additional information about a topic, which you can find in other sections of this book.

 A Note icon highlights interesting or supplementary information and often contains extra bits of technical information about a subject.

 Tip icons draw attention to handy suggestions, helpful hints, and useful pieces of advice.

In addition to the icons listed previously, the following typographical conventions are used throughout the book:

- Code examples appear in a `fixed width font`.

- When a segment of code is too long to fit on a single printed line, the line has been broken and the character ⊃ inserted, indicating that the line break does not appear in the original.

- Other code elements, such as data structures and variable names, appear in `fixed width`.

- File names and World Wide Web addresses (URLs) also appear in `fixed width`.

- Package names appear in `fixed width`.

- The first occurrence of an important term in a chapter is highlighted with *italic* text. *Italic* is also used for placeholders — for example, `ICON` *icon file name*, where *icon file name* represents the name of a bitmap file.

- A menu command is indicated in hierarchical order, with each menu command separated by an arrow. For example, File → Open means to click the File command on the menu bar and then select Open from the menu that appears.

- Keyboard shortcuts are indicated with the following syntax: Ctrl+C.

What Is a Sidebar?

Topics in sidebars provide additional information. Sidebar text contains a discussion related to the main text of a chapter but not vital to understanding the main text.

Acknowledgments

First, I'd like to acknowledge and thank you, the reader, for reading these acknowledgments. As a teacher, I know that readers rarely take the time to learn who's responsible for a book, even one they like or find useful. I appreciate your interest in learning about the team that built this book.

Debra Williams Cauley, the acquisitions editor, worked with me to hone and polish a book concept to a point where the stakeholders agreed it was viable. She closely monitored the nascent manuscript and sent helpful comments at every stage.

Eric Newman, the project editor, kept me on track and organized. He regularly detected problems that had slipped past me and offered or even effected – bless him – solutions that spared me significant embarrassment and improved the quality of the book.

Mark Cox, the senior director of engineering for Red Hat, Inc., and the editor of *Apache Week,* reviewed the manuscript for technical accuracy, completeness, relevance, and a multiplicity of other important characteristics. Mark's keen eye found many defects and gave me the opportunity to correct them. Whenever I've failed to properly do so, the responsibility is mine alone.

Rebecca Whitney, the copy editor, made it seem as though I write clear, concise English. As my students would eagerly attest, hers is an accomplishment of inestimable scope and value.

Margot Maley-Hutchinson of Waterside Productions, Inc., my literary agent, brought this writing opportunity to my attention and ably shepherded me through the business aspects of the project, as always.

My family – Jennifer, Patrick, and Sara – tolerated my writing yet another technical book, cheerfully undertaking tasks and responsibilities that I was unable to perform because of the demands of authorship.

Finally, I thank Jesus Christ, whom I profess as the author of all that is good, for His promise of sanctification and salvation.

Contents at a Glance

Contents

Part I

The Network Security Context

Chapter 1

What's a Firewall?

THIS CHAPTER BRIEFLY EXPLAINS WHAT FIREWALLS ARE and why they're useful. It also describes several types of firewalls. Finally, it explains some drawbacks presented by firewalls and describes other security measures that can be used with, or in place of, a firewall.

Why Firewalls Are Useful

Firewalls protect networks. But, the reasons that a network requires protection may not be immediately clear. More specifically, because the term *network* is somewhat abstract, it may not be clear what about a network requires protection or what a network should be protected from.

From a business standpoint, the valuable aspects of a network are:

- ◆ The confidentiality of data residing within and traveling across the network
- ◆ The integrity of data residing within and traveling across the network
- ◆ The availability of the network and the associated computing resources

These three aspects are sometimes referred to as CIA, for *confidentiality, integrity,* and *availability.* The following subsections explain them in more detail.

Confidentiality

Some data are valuable because they're not widely known. For instance, if you had advance knowledge of tomorrow's closing price of a stock, that information might

3

be valuable. If the information were accompanied by a guarantee shielding you from any losses entailed by acting on it, the information might be worth a great deal.

But suppose that everyone had access to the same information and had the same guarantee. In that case, the information would be worthless. Public disclosure of the information compromises its value. Therefore, the confidentiality of the information must be protected.

Many companies possess confidential data, which may reside in computer files. For instance, details of product formulas and manufacturing processes are often a source of competitive advantage. The disclosure of this type of information might weaken the market position of the company that owns them. Therefore, the computers that hold confidential data must be protected against attack, unauthorized use, and other events that might lead to the unplanned disclosure of confidential data.

Integrity

The integrity of a person or institution is the degree to which the person or institution can be relied on. Similarly, the integrity of data is the degree to which one can be confident that the data are complete and accurate – that is, the degree of confidence that the data have not been inappropriately modified, whether by criminal malice, negligence, or act of nature.

Data integrity is important because the value of data is generally diminished if the data are changed and therefore become inaccurate. In the worst case, an entire data set can be changed to a random series of bits. In that case, whatever value was associated with the data set is entirely lost. More subtly, an unauthorized person might insert a fraudulent transaction into a data set representing purchases awaiting shipment. The loss of value in such a situation might vary from nominal to catastrophic, depending on the monetary value of the related goods and the likelihood of the fraud's being detected before the goods are shipped. Because the integrity and value of data are closely linked, information systems must be protected against events that might result in unauthorized modification of data.

Availability

A few information technology systems, such as strategic planning systems, support non-operational aspects of businesses. However, most information technology systems and associated networks support business operations. Therefore, a disruption of these systems may affect the conduct of business, perhaps catastrophically.

For instance, Yahoo! and other online vendors have been the victims of *denial of service* (DOS) attacks that seek to disrupt the ability of customers and potential customers to access vendors' Web sites. Because much of the Yahoo! revenue stream is tied to online purchases, the interruption of these purchases is costly to Yahoo!. Sufficiently effective and prolonged DOS attacks could cause Yahoo! – or any similarly situated online company – to lose revenue to the point of ceasing to be a viable business.

How Networks Are Threatened

Events that threaten the confidentiality, integrity, or availability of data can arise either accidentally or through intent, usually malicious intent.

Accidents that threaten data run the gamut from avalanche to zoological infestation. Firewalls are not generally effective in protecting data from accidental compromise. Instead, firewalls are a tool for protecting data against intentional attacks.

Most organizations have deployed Internet hosts only recently. Before the advent of the Internet, organizations that used computer networks generally maintained private networks that were closed to outsiders. Attacking a computer or network required the attacker to be in close physical proximity to the target. So, the attacker had to be authorized to access the target computer or network, or the attacker had to defeat physical security measures. Physical security measures can be quite difficult to defeat by all but the most capable and determined attacker. Thus, most attacks were performed by disgruntled employees and consultants who were authorized to access computers and networks. Consequently, such attacks were relatively uncommon.

The use of dial-up modems provided a new potential avenue to attackers, who could simply dial in from remote locations rather than breach physical security measures. However, modems were not generally intended for public use and therefore were relatively easy to secure from outside attack. For instance, modems with a callback feature could be accessed only from authorized telephone lines. Such modems complete a connection by calling back a user, whose telephone number must be included on a programmed list of telephone numbers of authorized users. However, many companies failed to implement adequate defenses against unauthorized modem use and therefore became the victims of attacks.

The popularity of the Internet raised the threat level tremendously. Many companies now operate Internet hosts that are intended to be accessed by the general public. Often, these hosts contain data requiring protection. In other cases, the hosts reside on networks alongside other hosts that contain sensitive data. An attacker who compromises a publicly accessible host may be able to use the resources of that host to successfully attack other hosts on the same network. From a security standpoint, the Internet potentially provides would-be attackers with a convenient means of gaining access to an organization's network.

Why Access Is Problematical

Of course, mere access to a host doesn't compromise the host. Access is a necessary but not a sufficient condition leading to compromise. It may seem that access could be controlled in a manner that prohibits the unauthorized use of a system. However, this view fails to account for the existence of software defects, which are commonly called *bugs*.

Modern computer software is humanity's most complex artifact. Software is so complex, in fact, that it reflects the imperfections of its makers, who find their limited cognitive capabilities insufficient to identify and eradicate their errors. A complex software system may include a million lines of source code or more. And, the source code may contain one bug for every thousand lines of code. Indeed, a modern software system may contain more bugs than the lines of code included in software systems of fifty years ago.

A primary strategy for attacking a computer system is to identify software bugs that affect it and then transmit data that capitalize on those bugs to achieve *privilege escalation*. In a common privilege-escalation scenario, an attacker feeds a system more data than the system's programmers expected. The programmers' error causes the system to accept and execute an arbitrary command supplied by the attacker, who thereby gains administrative privileges. The attacker can then freely access or modify data residing on the system.

What Firewalls Do

The firewall of an automobile is designed to prevent a fire in the engine compartment from spreading to the passenger compartment. Its purpose is containment. A network firewall is also a containment device. A firewall works by dividing a network into multiple zones and containing activity within them — that is, by preventing unauthorized traffic from entering or leaving a zone. If properly configured, a firewall may prevent an attack from reaching its intended victim.

Figure 1-1 shows a simple but typical firewall configuration. The firewall enables certain users to access a protected Web server and denies that privilege to others. To access the Web server, an attacker who is not an authorized user must first defeat the firewall.

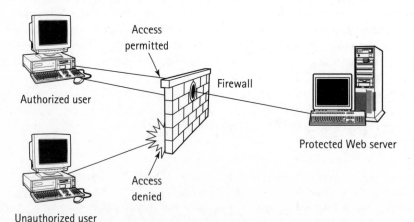

Figure 1-1: A firewall screens hosts from unauthorized traffic.

However, a firewall does more than merely block unauthorized access. A firewall has two principal roles: prevention and detection.

Security policy specifies the operations a user or host is authorized to perform. A firewall prevents attacks by filtering traffic in support of security policy. That is, the firewall accepts traffic that is consistent with the security policy and blocks other traffic. A firewall also detects attacks. It logs attempted and actual accesses to hosts and networks and alerts administrators to suspected attacks. Obviously, a firewall cannot prevent an attack that it fails to detect. So, detection precedes prevention. But, it's important – when possible – to prevent an attack rather than merely detect it. Hence, prevention is more important than mere detection.

A firewall can filter traffic in a variety of ways. The most common are via

- ◆ IP address

- ◆ Service

Network traffic is tagged with a pair of IP addresses indicating the source and destination host. Network traffic that entails access to a service is tagged with a port number that, along with the destination IP address, identifies the service. As Figure 1-1 shows, a firewall can be configured to block traffic bound for a host running a Web server unless the traffic originates from a host with an authorized IP address. More sophisticated firewalls can inspect other traffic characteristics, such as the URL of a requested Web page.

However, firewalls are not entirely immune to attack and compromise. Therefore, they're often deployed in combination. Figure 1-2 shows a pair of firewalls protecting a Web server and a local-area network (LAN) inhabited by clients. The outer firewall, which has somehow been breached, protected the Web server. The inner firewall, which is intact, continues to protect LAN clients from attack via the compromised Web server.

In the preceding examples, firewalls protect internal computers – that is, computers not directly connected to the Internet – from attack by computers on the Internet. They do so by filtering inbound traffic. However, firewalls can also protect computers on the Internet from attacks by local hosts. Doing so may seem unimportant, but consider the damage to an e-commerce site's reputation, not to mention its continued existence, that might occur if its computers were compromised and used to attack, say, a military site. In the aftermath of such an event, customers might understandably be reluctant to share their credit card information with that vendor. To protect against such a possibility, you can configure a firewall to filter both inbound and outbound traffic.

Often, the role of firewalls in preventing attacks overshadows their role in detecting attacks. However, an analysis of actual and attempted accesses logged by a firewall can identify many sorts of attacks. Moreover, such analysis need not be deferred but can be performed in near–real-time, affording administrators time in which to respond to an attack before it gets out of hand.

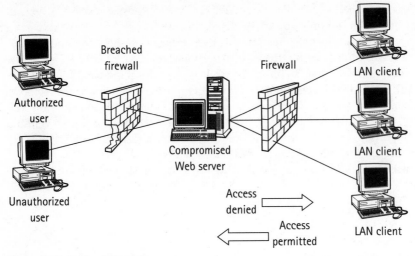

Figure 1-2: A pair of firewalls

Types of Firewalls

Roughly speaking, three types of firewalls exist:

◆ *Personal firewalls* generally protect a single computer or a small network of computers. Personal firewalls are often used to protect computers and networks attached to DSL or cable modem lines. This book doesn't emphasize personal firewalls, though the information in this book could be used to construct a personal firewall. Most home and small-office computer users would likely be better served by a firewall appliance rather than by a firewall they design and implement. Such appliances, widely available at costs as little as US$75, consume little power and generally have no moving parts. Consequently, these appliances are highly reliable and trouble-free. However, the optimal use of a firewall appliance requires an understanding of network security and firewalls, such as that provided in Part I of this book.

◆ *Departmental firewalls* generally protect more computers than a personal firewall does. Moreover, the computers protected by a departmental firewall are likely to provide a greater variety of services than those associated with a personal firewall. Departmental firewalls must also generally handle higher traffic volumes than do personal firewalls.

Departmental firewalls tend to be deployed as combinations of multiple firewalls in order to provide enhanced security beyond the typical concerns of the home and small-office user. This book focuses on the design, implementation, and operation of departmental firewalls.

- *Enterprise firewalls* consist of multiple instances of departmental firewalls and generally also include one or more firewalls that filter and log traffic inbound to and outbound from departmental firewalls. Enterprise firewalls are unlike departmental firewalls in that they require more care and effort in operation. Because they typically handle larger traffic volumes than departmental firewalls, enterprise firewalls require automated processes for the monitoring and analysis of the associated logs. Moreover, their design and implementation are generally more challenging than those of departmental firewalls. A skilled Linux system administrator can craft highly effective and efficient enterprise firewalls by using the tools and methods explained in this book. However, enterprise contexts tend to be highly idiosyncratic. Therefore, this book emphasizes departmental rather than enterprise firewalls.

Disadvantages of Firewalls

Firewalls present several disadvantages. In most circumstances, the benefits of firewalls outweigh their disadvantages. However, you should know the potential disadvantages of firewalls so that you can minimize or overcome them.

A firewall cannot effectively filter network traffic if traffic can bypass the firewall. Therefore, inbound and outbound traffic must traverse the firewall. The disadvantages of firewalls arise because a firewall often becomes a bottleneck in any one or more of three ways:

- Reliability

- Performance

- Flexibility

A firewall can decrease the reliability of a network by presenting a single point of failure. Because traffic cannot bypass a firewall, the failure of a firewall generally entails unavailability of the network it protects. This potential problem can be avoided by configuring multiple firewalls so that traffic must traverse one firewall or the other but need not traverse all firewalls. The firewalls can operate concurrently or be configured so that the failure of one firewall activates another. Figure 1-3 shows a dual-firewall configuration.

Similarly, a firewall can decrease the performance of a network. If all network traffic must traverse the firewall, the capacity of the network is limited by the throughput of the firewall. This problem can be solved in much the same way as the problem of reliability – namely, by the deployment of multiple firewalls. To improve network throughput, the firewalls must be configured to operate concurrently. The capacity of the associated network is then limited by the sum of the firewall capacities rather than by the capacity of a single firewall.

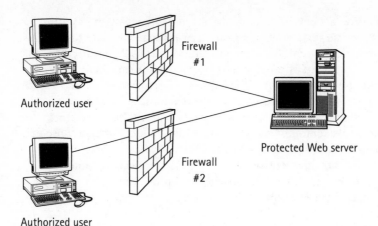

Figure 1-3: A dual-firewall configuration

A firewall can also decrease the flexibility of a network. A firewall is configured to handle authorized traffic. If a new type of traffic is authorized, the firewall must be reconfigured to accommodate it. Reconfiguring the firewall may require time and resources. In extreme cases, reconfiguring the firewall in a timely manner may not be possible.

However, a lack of flexibility is characteristic of security measures generally, not merely of firewalls. An organization's security policy must strike a careful balance between the flexibility demanded by users and the protection of information technology assets and resources that is the responsibility of the information technology staff. Consequently, the development of an organization's security policy requires the informed and active participation of senior management, which is responsible for striking the optimal balance between these competing concerns.

Other Security Measures

Despite the disadvantages of firewalls, most organizations have deployed – or should deploy – them as part of their network security architecture. The strength of a network's defenses is determined by the depth and variety of defensive measures that are employed more than by the strength of any one particular countermeasure. Consequently, firewalls are generally used alongside other security measures.

Security measures are applied at either of two levels:

◆ Individual hosts

◆ Entire networks

Most networks include both host- and network-based security measures.

Firewalls can be applied to individual hosts or to entire networks and can also be applied at both levels. Deploying both host- and network-based firewalls adds depth to the security of a network. To compromise a host, a would-be intruder must compromise both the firewall protecting the network and the individual host firewall. This situation requires the attacker to expend more time and effort, increasing the likelihood that the host's administrators will detect the attack and shut it down before it has effect. Even if the host's administrators fail to detect the attack, the host's resistance to attack may frustrate an attacker and lead the attacker to break off the attack and seek a more vulnerable target.

Other host-based security measures often used with firewalls include

◆ TCP wrappers

◆ Host-based intrusion-detection systems, such as Tripwire

◆ Application-based security measures

For example, the Apache Web server can be configured to deny access to all hosts other than those specified in its configuration file.

Firewalls are often used in combination with network intrusion detection systems (NIDs). NIDs generally inspect network traffic in much the same way as an antivirus system inspects program and data files. An NID that detects traffic matching the signature of a known attack generates an alert to inform network administrators of the event. Some NIDs can also initiate defensive responses, such as terminating a TCP connection between an attacking host and its victim.

Summary

This chapter has briefly described how firewalls work and how they protect hosts and networks. The chapter also presented some alternatives to firewalls, such as TCP wrappers and intrusion detection systems. The remainder of the book elaborates on the network security role of firewalls, explaining how you can use Red Hat Linux to build firewalls to help protect your data and computing resources.

Chapter 2

TCP/IP Quick Start

IN THIS CHAPTER

◆ TCP/IP terms and concepts

◆ Content and structure of TCP/IP datagrams

◆ Tools for TCP/IP networking

◆ Configuring TCP/IP networking

◆ Troubleshooting TCP/IP

CREATING AND OPERATING FIREWALLS that protect the perimeter of your network isn't rocket science. But, doing so does demand a more detailed and comprehensive grasp of TCP/IP networking than that required for most other system and network administration functions. This chapter reviews common TCP/IP networking terms and concepts and explains less commonly used terms and concepts that are important in the context of firewalls. For example, the chapter covers in some detail the processes of establishing and tearing down TCP connections. So, even if you're a TCP/IP expert, you're likely to find this chapter a helpful refresher and reference.

The chapter also explains some software tools often used in configuring and troubleshooting TCP/IP networking, including `ifconfig`, `ping`, `route`, `traceroute`, `host`, `dig`, `nslookup`, `netstat`, `tcpdump`, `tcpshow`, and `iptraf`. In addition, the chapter explains the principal files that specify the TCP/IP configuration of a Red Hat Linux system, including `/etc/sysconfig/network`, `/etc/sysconfig/static-routes`, `/etc/sysconfig/network-scripts/ifcfg-ethn`, `/etc/nsswitch.conf`, `/etc/hosts`, and `/etc/resolv.conf`. Finally, the chapter presents a simple TCP/IP troubleshooting procedure that will help you pinpoint firewall-related problems.

TCP/IP networking is the most popular type of networking. Because the Internet itself uses TCP/IP networking, systems that connect to the Internet must be TCP/IP-capable. Although other types of networking, such as IPX and Appletalk, still exist, their use is confined mostly to local-area networks and private wide-area networks. Consequently, firewalls seldom operate on any type of network traffic other than TCP/IP traffic. Indeed, firewall tools are generally designed to work only – or at least primarily – with TCP/IP traffic. Therefore, this chapter addresses only TCP/IP. If you're concerned about some type of networking other than TCP/IP, you can likely extrapolate from the information presented here. However, you need to be careful to select firewall tools that support non-TCP/IP networking.

TCP/IP Terms and Concepts

In the context of networking, the term *protocol* refers to a specification that determines how computers exchange data. Simply put, a networking protocol defines how computers communicate via a network. A networking protocol resembles the grammar that prescribes how humans communicate using a written language. The grammar provides the rules that govern such characteristics as person and number, inflections that indicate verb tenses, and the use of punctuation. Of course, humans follow the grammars associated with their languages less strictly than computers follow network protocols.

As mentioned, TCP/IP is the dominant networking protocol. More accurately, TCP/IP is the dominant protocol family because TCP/IP is a family of related protocols rather than a single protocol. Let's look more closely at several members of the TCP/IP protocol family.

Protocols

Table 2-1 summarizes the principal low-level protocols that make up the TCP/IP protocol family. In addition to the listed protocols, the TCP/IP protocol family includes dozens of higher-level protocols, referred to as *application protocols*. These include such familiar protocols as SMTP (Simple Mail Transfer Protocol), IMAP (Internet Message Access Protocol), POP (Post Office Protocol), FTP (File Transfer Protocol), HTTP (HyperText Transfer Protocol), and SSH (Secure Shell Protocol).

TABLE 2-1 PRINCIPAL LOW-LEVEL TCP/IP PROTOCOLS

Abbreviation	Name and Description
ARP	Address Resolution Protocol. Used to map between hardware and IP addresses.
ICMP	Internet Control Message Protocol. Used to send error messages and tests.
IP	Internet Protocol. Used to transfer data over the network.
TCP	Transmission Control Protocol. Used to reliably send data streams.
UDP	User Datagram Protocol. Used to quickly send small amounts of information.

The workhorse of the TCP/IP protocol family is the IP protocol. Every TCP/IP message is sent via the IP protocol through a means known as *encapsulation*. To see how it works, suppose that a TCP message is to be sent. The TCP message, which is referred to as a *segment,* is built according to the rules of the TCP/IP protocol. Then, the segment is inserted into an IP message, which is referred to as a *datagram,* for network transmission. You can think of the IP datagram as an envelope that contains the TCP segment. Like a postal envelope, the datagram is marked with the address of the sender and the recipient.

The concept of encapsulation can be extended in two directions. Messages of higher-level protocols travel the network inside TCP segments. And, IP datagrams themselves ride inside Ethernet frames or another vehicle more suited to transmission over the local network. Figure 2-1 shows how encapsulation works.

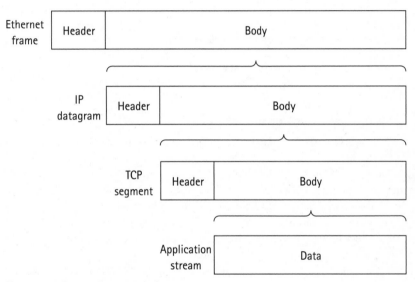

Figure 2-1: Protocol encapsulation

Figure 2-1 shows that network messages, commonly referred to as *packets,* consist of two components: a header and a body. The *header* of a packet contains information about the message. For instance, the header may specify the message sender or receiver, or the message length. The *body* of a packet contains the message itself. Several network messages may be exchanged during the transmission of a message. In particular, long messages are often divided into several network messages, for reasons to be explained shortly.

A typical network packet may contain several nested messages. For instance, a packet containing an HTTP message may be nested within a TCP segment that's nested within an IP datagram that's nested within an Ethernet frame. You can think of each layer of nesting as providing a distinct function. Such a scheme is shown in Figure 2-2. Let's examine the layers, beginning with Layer 1.

4	**Application layer: Stream** Provides services (Telnet, FTP, SMTP, HTTP, etc.)
3	**Transport layer: Segment** Provides reliable or connectionless datagram delivery (TCP, UDP)
2	**Internet layer: Datagram** Provides routing and error messages (ARP, IP, ICMP)
1	**Network layer: Frame** Provides access to the physical network (Ethernet)

Figure 2-2: Architecture of the TCP/IP protocol family

LAYER 1: THE NETWORK LAYER

Layer 1 is known as the *network layer*. The primary function associated with Layer 1 is access to the physical network. Most modern networks are based on Ethernet. So, Layer 1 frequently consists of a software driver that provides access to an Ethernet network adapter. However, other technologies, such as Token Ring, continue to be used and so a variety of Layer 1 technologies exists.

A Layer 1 packet is referred to as a *frame*. The largest possible Ethernet frame contains only 1,514 bytes. Therefore, longer messages must be broken into two or more frames, each less than 1,514 bytes in length.

Layer 1 technologies require that messages be chopped into frames for two main reasons. Sending messages in frames makes it possible for several processes to share a network interface. If messages were sent all at once rather than as frames, a process sending a very long message might block other processes from having access to the network interface for an unacceptably long time. Moreover, sending messages as frames facilitates error detection and recovery. If a frame is garbled during network transmission, only the faulty frame must be re-sent. Sending a long message all at once over a less than perfectly reliable network might require many long retransmissions before a perfect copy arrives at the destination.

LAYER 2: THE INTERNET LAYER

Layer 2 is known as the *Internet level,* and Layer 2 packets are known as *datagrams.* Layer 2 provides functions that make it possible for messages to move between a local network and a larger network, such as the Internet. In particular, Layer 2 is concerned with routing, the process whereby a message finds its way from its source to its destination. Layer 2 also provides mechanisms for delivering error messages that inform a message sender of problems in delivering messages. Most data switches are Layer 2 devices.

Layer 1 and Layer 2 messages use hardware addresses for the source and destination hosts. The hardware address of an Ethernet device is commonly known as a *MAC address*. The acronym *MAC* stands for *media access* control. A MAC address is a 48-bit number, generally written as 12 hexadecimal digits – for example, 00-03-47-91-63-E5.

The Institute for Electrical and Electronic Engineers (IEEE) assigns manufacturers blocks of numbers within the MAC address space. In turn, manufacturers assign MAC addresses to network interfaces as they're manufactured. The address of a device is supposed to be unique. But, manufacturers sometimes release network adapters that have non-unique MAC addresses. Fortunately, the MAC address of an adapter can be overridden by configuration items.

LAYER 3: THE TRANSPORT LAYER

Layer 3 is known as the *transport level,* and Layer 3 packets are known as *segments.* Whereas Layers 1 and 2 are concerned with the network itself, Layer 3 provides functions necessary to sending useful data over the network. When programmers write network programs, they write function calls that create and send UDP or TCP segments.

TCP segments provide end-to-end error detection and recovery, so programmers don't need to be much concerned with the routine jostling that messages commonly undergo when traversing a network. For instance, some packets of a message are commonly delayed in transit and arrive after packets that were actually sent later but were not delayed. TCP smooths over this problem and similar ones. For example, TCP reassembles the packets in their proper sequence before presenting them to the recipient.

However, packet reassembly and other TCP functions require resources; therefore, considerable overhead is associated with the convenience of TCP. Therefore, TCP/IP includes the UDP protocol, which provides a way of sending messages without the overhead entailed by TCP. Some wags refer to UDP as "Unreliable Datagram Protocol" because UDP doesn't guarantee that packets are received in the order in which they were sent. However, it's not entirely accurate to style UDP as unreliable. Instead, it's better to view UDP as placing responsibility for reliability on the application. An application that uses UDP can check for missing or out-of-sequence packets and handle the situation in whatever way deemed appropriate by the application's programmer.

To see how UDP might be useful, consider an Internet video application. If a packet of a video message is garbled or lost, requesting that the missing packet be retransmitted might be a waste of time. It might not even be possible to obtain a replacement packet in time to display it. It's sometimes better simply to press ahead. UDP is well suited for such applications, which benefit from UDP's lower overhead.

Layer 3 messages are sent using IP addresses. An *IP address* is a 32-bit number that is generally written as a series of four decimal numbers, one for each byte of the IP address, separated by dots. The decimal numbers can range in value from 0 to 255. For instance, 192.168.1.1 is a valid IP address. This format is sometimes called *dotted quad.*

IP addresses are explained more fully in the next section. They follow two basic rules. Each network interface of a host may have one or more associated IP addresses. And, no two interfaces or hosts may have the same IP address, with certain exceptions explained in the next section. In principle, IP addresses are unique across the entire Internet. Like MAC addresses, IP addresses are used to identify hosts. However, IP addresses can be used anywhere on the network or Internet, whereas MAC addresses can be used only on the local network on which the addressed host resides.

LAYER 4: THE APPLICATION LAYER

Layer 4 is known as the *application layer.* Applications that operate at Layer 4 don't have to cope with the division of messages into packets because Layer 3 has reassembled the packets into a complete data stream or message.

Layer 4 data is sent and received using compound addresses known as *sockets.* One component of a Layer 4 address is an IP address. The other is a number known as a *port,* ranging from 0 to 65535. However, most TCP/IP implementations disallow the use of port 0. So, ports are commonly numbered from 1 to 65535. A Layer 4 address is commonly written by following its IP address with a colon and port number – for instance, 192.168.0.1:25, which denotes port 25 of the host known as 192.168.0.1.

Ports are classified in several ways. Ports numbered 1023 and below are referred to as *system ports.* Under some operating systems, including Linux, a process must be running as `root` in order to initiate access to a system port. Ports numbered 1024 and above are referred to as *ephemeral ports* because they can be used by any process. However, after a process has opened a port, it owns the port until it closes it. Processes are not generally free to access ports owned by other processes.

Operating systems associate ports with *services,* which wait for and process requests transmitted by clients. Perhaps the most familiar service is that provided by a Web server, which processes requests transmitted by Web browsers.

By convention, certain services are run on standard ports, known as *well-known ports.* The Internet Assigned Numbers Authority (IANA) maintains a list of well-known ports, which you can view at `http://www.iana.org/assignments/port-numbers`. The IANA also publishes a list of reserved ports that identifies common uses for ephemeral ports numbered from 1024 to 49151. On a Red Hat Linux system, the file `/etc/services` contains a directory of well-known and registered services. You can view this file by using a text editor or grep; however, you should not modify the file arbitrarily because the correct functioning of several services depends on the correctness of their entries in the file. Table 2-2 presents some of the most commonly used ports.

TABLE 2-2 COMMON SERVICES AND THEIR PORT NUMBERS

Protocol	Port Number	Service
TCP	21	FTP, file transfer protocol
TCP	22	SSH, secure shell protocol
TCP	23	Telnet, telnet protocol
TCP	25	SMTP, simple mail transfer protocol
TCP/UDP	53	DNS, domain name services
TCP/UDP	67–68	DHCP, dynamic host configuration protocol
TCP	80	HTTP, hypertext transfer protocol
TCP	109–110	POP, post office protocol
TCP	113	AUTH, authorization service also known as IDENTD
TCP/UDP	123	NTP, network time protocol
TCP	143	IMAP, interim mail access protocol
TCP/UDP	161	SNMP, simple network management protocol
TCP	443	HTTPS, secure hypertext transfer protocol
UDP	514	SYSLOG, system logging
TCP/UDP	515	LPD, remote printer

Only convention requires that a service run on a well-known port. For example, HTTP (Web) servers are sometimes run on port 8080 rather than on the well-known port 80. Running a service on a well-known port merely makes it easier for users to find the service.

A client communicating with a service contacts the server host by sending a special packet to the port on which the service runs. To do so, the client uses a port on the local system. By default, most client applications choose an available ephemeral port for this purpose. The conversation between the client and server is therefore associated with a pair of sockets, as shown in Figure 2-3.

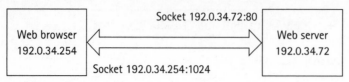

Figure 2-3: A socket pair

IP Addressing

Both Layers 3 and 4 use IP addresses to specify source and destination addresses. Originally, IP addresses were of one of three types: Class A, Class B, or Class C. Today, a greater variety of IP address forms is used. However, the original terms are still in widespread use. Let's look at the original address forms before dealing with the more modern forms.

CLASS A ADDRESSES

Recall that an IP address is a 32-bit number. Networks function efficiently when all hosts on a given network have part of their 32-bit IP addresses in common. The common part of the IP address is referred to as the *network address*. The remaining part of the IP address is referred to as the *host address*. Separating network and host addresses makes it possible to determine quickly whether a given IP address refers to a local host or to a host outside the network.

A Class A address is one in which every host on the local network has the same value for the first byte of its IP address. That is, the network address consists of one byte, and the host address consists of three bytes. The IANA, which assigns IP addresses, denotes a Class A address by assigning a value less than 128 as the first byte of the IP address. Consequently, relatively few Class A addresses exist and therefore only the largest organizations have been assigned Class A addresses. On the other hand, a Class A address can have many associated host addresses because three bytes are available to represent the host. More than 16 million host addresses are associated with each Class A address. Figure 2-4 shows a Class A IP address. Notice that the bits are numbered beginning with zero, as is customary when numbering bits within words.

Several methods are used to specify how an IP address is divided into a network and host address. A common technique is the specification of a *network mask* value, a 32-bit number having a 1-bit in positions occupied by the network address and a 0-bit in positions occupied by a host address. A Class A network has an associated network mask value of 255.0.0.0 because 255 is the decimal value of a series of eight 1-bits. Often, a network mask value is referred to simply as a *netmask*.

A more modern way of specifying a network address associated with an IP address is by following the IP address with a slash and the number of bits that make up the network address. Because a Class A network address consists of one byte

(8 bits), you can recognize a Class A address by the appearance of a /8 after an IP address. For instance, 10.1.2.3/8 specifies a host on the Class A network having the address range 10.0.0.0–10.255.255.255. Sometimes, this method of specification is referred to as CIDR (Classless Internet Domain Routing) because of its use in Internet routing schemes.

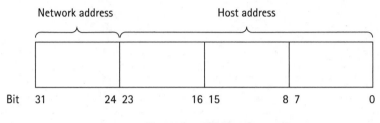

Network mask: 255.0.0.0

Example network address: 10.0.0.0/8

Example address range: 10.0.0.0–10.255.255.255

Figure 2-4: A Class A address

CLASS B ADDRESSES

Figure 2-5 shows a Class B IP address. The IANA assigns values of 128–191 to the first byte of a Class B IP address. As the figure shows, a Class B address consists of a two-byte network address and a two-byte host address. A single Class B network can include more than 65,000 hosts.

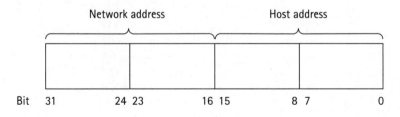

Network mask: 255.255.0.0

Example network address: 192.168.0.0/16

Example address range: 192.168.0.0–192.168.255.255

Figure 2-5: A Class B address

CLASS C ADDRESSES

The most common IP address class is Class C, as shown in Figure 2-6. The IANA assigns values of 192–223 as the first byte of a Class C IP address. A Class C network address has 256 associated host addresses. However, several of these values must generally be reserved. A Class C network address is generally associated with fewer than 254 hosts. Many networks having Class C addresses contain only a few hosts.

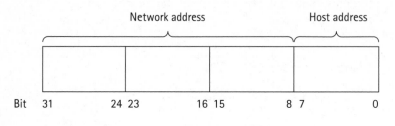

Network mask: 255.255.255.0

Example network address: 192.168.100.0/16

Example address range: 192.168.100.0–192.168.100.255

Figure 2-6: A Class C address

SUBNETTED CLASS C ADDRESSES   A convention known as *subnetting* splits a Class C network into two or more *subnetworks,* often referred to simply as *subnets.* As shown in Figure 2-7, a subnetted Class C network has a network address longer than three bytes (24 bits). In the figure, the network address consists of 25 bits. Nonsubnetted netmasks have values of 0 or 255 for each netmask byte. Subnetted netmasks can have other values, such as the value 128 that appears in the figure.

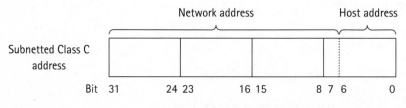

Network mask: 255.255.255.128

Example network address: 192.168.100.128/25

Example address range: 192.168.100.128–192.168.100.255

Figure 2-7: A subnetted Class C address

Splitting a Class C network by using a 25-bit network address yields two subnets. One has hosts numbered from 0–127; the other has hosts numbered from 128–255. A network can have a network address of more than 25 bits. For instance, a 26-bit network address splits a Class C network into four subnets: 0–63, 64–127, 128–191, and 192–255. The number of subnets in a split network is always a perfect power of 2: 2-, 4-, and 8-way splits are common.

It's possible to subnet a Class A or Class B network address. Whenever a netmask byte consists of mixed 0- and 1-bits, the associated network address is a subnetted address. If you prefer, you can think of a subnetted Class B address as a *supernetted* Class C address. That is, you can consider the network address to be unusually short rather than unusually long. After you understand that a network address can have lengths other than 8, 16, or 24 bits, you see that the terms Class A, Class B, and Class C are no longer exhaustive; some networks fit none of these categories. However, they continue in common use for the special cases to which they apply.

SPECIAL IP ADDRESSES

Several forms of special IP addresses are in common use, including RFC 1918, broadcast, multicast, and loopback IP addresses.

Version 6 of the IP protocol (IPV6) uses a somewhat different scheme to specify host addresses, one providing 128 bits and therefore capable of referring to many more hosts than IPv4. IPv6 is expected to replace IPv4 only gradually, as much of the Internet's infrastructure is not yet compatible with IPv6. However, some organizations are already using IPv6 internally.

RFC 1918 IP ADDRESSES   Obtaining an assigned block of IP addresses from the IANA requires time. Some hosts may not require a unique IP address. In particular, hosts that act only as clients may not require a unique IP address. A technique called *network address translation* (NAT) enables several such hosts to use a single IP address.

Chapter 5, "Firewall Architecture," explains how NAT is used.

Several blocks of IP addresses, referred to as *RFC 1918 addresses* or *private addresses,* have been reserved for private use. Table 2-3 identifies these address blocks. You can freely assign these addresses to networks and hosts. However, these addresses must be translated to assigned addresses if the associated hosts communicate via the Internet. Most routers are programmed to drop packets bearing RFC 1918 addresses.

Despite the fact that most routers are programmed to drop packets bearing RFC 1918 addresses, your firewall should also be configured to drop inbound packets having RFC 1918 addresses so that a misconfigured router won't jeopardize your network's security.

TABLE 2-3 RFC 1918 IP ADDRESSES

Network address	Netmask	Range of IP addresses
10.0.0.0/8	255.0.0.0	10.0.0.0–10.255.255.255
172.16.0.0/12	255.240.0.0	172.16.0.0–172.31.255.255
192.168.0.0/16	255.255.0.0	192.168.0.0–192.168.255.255

BROADCAST IP ADDRESSES   Sometimes, sending a single message to all hosts on a particular network is efficient. Some operating systems, including Linux, support this capability. A broadcast address has a 1-bit in each position corresponding to the host address. For instance, consider the network 192.168.1.0/24. This network has a 24-bit network address and an 8-bit host address. The corresponding broadcast address is 192.168.1.255. Broadcast addresses of subnetted networks are a bit more difficult to compute. The reason is that the division between the network and host addresses occurs inside an address byte rather than between bytes, but such broadcast addresses are formed in the same way as nonsubnetted broadcast addresses.

Broadcast messages can generally be sent only by hosts on the same network as the intended destination hosts. Routers are generally programmed to drop packets having a broadcast address as the destination IP address.

MULTICAST IP ADDRESSES   The *multicast* technology somewhat resembles broadcast, but it occurs on the Internet rather than on a local network. Multicast enables a sender to transmit a single packet that is received by multiple Internet hosts. Multicast, which is not widely used, is an efficient means of broadcasting video via the Internet.

Multicast employs a reserved set of IP addresses, each having a first byte value of 224–239. Each assigned number represents a multicast network, and all hosts on the network use the same IP address. So, the network mask associated with a multicast IP address has a length of 32 bits.

LOOPBACK IP ADDRESSES   Human languages include an objective first-person pronoun – in English, *me* – that is a convenient way for a speaker to refer to himself or herself. Computer networks use the *loopback IP address* for the same purpose. The IP address 127.0.0.1 refers to the local host – that is, the host sending the packet. The associated network address, 127.0.0.0, is commonly considered a Class A address. So, the corresponding netmask value is 255.0.0.0.

Generally, a network adapter has one associated IP address. However, it's possible to associate multiple IP addresses with a network adapter. Such addresses are called virtual IP addresses. An interface having virtual IP addresses is called a virtual interface. Virtual IP addresses are often uses to permit Web servers to host multiple domains by associating each domain with a virtual IP address.

Domain Name Service

Humans find it cumbersome to recall and use IP addresses. The Domain Name Service (DNS) makes it possible to refer to hosts by name rather than by IP address. For instance, the host `example.com` has the IP address 192.0.34.72. Other common names for DNS are name service, named, and bind.

A DNS server enables clients to resolve a host name to an IP address, a process known as *forward name resolution*. Properly configured DNS servers can also perform *reverse name resolution,* which determines a host name given an IP address.

The sections titled "Nslookup" and "Dig" explain the `nslookup` and `dig` commands, which you can use to query a DNS server. Firewalls generally inspect IP addresses rather than host names. Consequently, this book doesn't deal with the operation of DNS, except to the extent that a firewall must permit the correct operation of DNS clients and servers.

For more information on DNS, see *Red Hat Linux Networking and System Administration,* by Terry Collings and Kurt Wall (Red Hat Press/Wiley, 2002).

Routing

Hosts typically can send packets directly to other hosts on the same network. However, hosts outside the local network can be reached only by a process known as *routing.* Routing is performed by *multi-homed hosts* — that is, hosts with two or more network interfaces. Such hosts can function as *routers* or *gateways* by forwarding packets received on one interface to another interface.

Figure 2-8 shows a typical gateway configuration. In the figure, the hosts named client1, client2, and gateway reside on a local network. These hosts can communicate freely via the local network. The multi-homed host named gateway is also connected to the Internet and therefore can communicate with Internet hosts, including the host named webserver. However, client1 and client2 can communicate with Internet hosts only if gateway is configured to forward packets on their behalf.

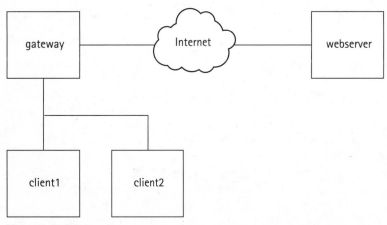

Figure 2-8: A gateway

Routing is a fairly simple process in practice. Each host maintains a *routing table* that identifies the networks to which it's directly attached. In addition, the routing table can list other networks and hosts and identify local gateway hosts that will forward packets to them. The routing table also generally identifies a *default gateway* — that is, a host that forwards packets to networks and hosts not explicitly identified in the routing table.

One complication of routing is that a packet may traverse several networks before arriving at its destination. Each network may employ any of a variety of technologies; Ethernet is the most common. Each network may have distinctive characteristics, including a *maximum transmission unit* (MTU). The MTU of a network is the largest frame the network can accommodate. The MTU of Ethernet, for instance, is 1,514 bytes. Because the Ethernet header occupies 14 bytes, the largest data packet that can be sent via Ethernet is 1,500 bytes.

If a packet having a size larger than the MTU of a network arrives at a gateway of the network, either of two events occurs. First, the frame can be blocked and an error returned to the sender. Alternatively, the frame can be split into several smaller frames, known as *fragments*. As explained in Chapter 9, "IPTables Firewall Implementation," fragmented frames pose special problems for firewalls.

TCP/IP Datagrams and Segments

Now that I've reviewed protocols, addresses, and networks, let's look at packets in more detail. Recall that TCP/IP packets are known as datagrams. TCP and UDP datagrams are known more particularly as segments. In this section, we study the structure of IP, ICMP, UDP, and TCP datagrams. Because firewalls filter packets, you'll find a detailed knowledge of packet structure helpful in designing effective firewalls. In particular, firewalls can test the value of fields within datagrams and accept or reject packets according to their contents.

IP Header

Recall that every TCP/IP message travels inside an IP datagram and that IP datagrams have two main components: a header and a body. Figure 2-9 shows the fields that make up an IP header. Notice that the header consists of six or more 32-bit words and that the bits and words are numbered starting with zero. Let's survey the fields one by one.

IP VERSION
This four-bit field indicates the version number of the IP protocol. IP version 4 is currently in widespread use. A few organizations have deployed IP version 6; however, hardware and software support for IPV6 (as it's known) is not widespread.

HEADER LENGTH (IHL)
This 4-bit field indicates the length, in 32-bit words, of the IP header. An IP header has a minimum length of 20 bytes. Therefore, the minimum value of this field is 5.

TYPE OF SERVICE (TOS)
This eight-bit field is not commonly used except within networks. There, it is used to indicate datagrams that should receive expedited forwarding or other special handling.

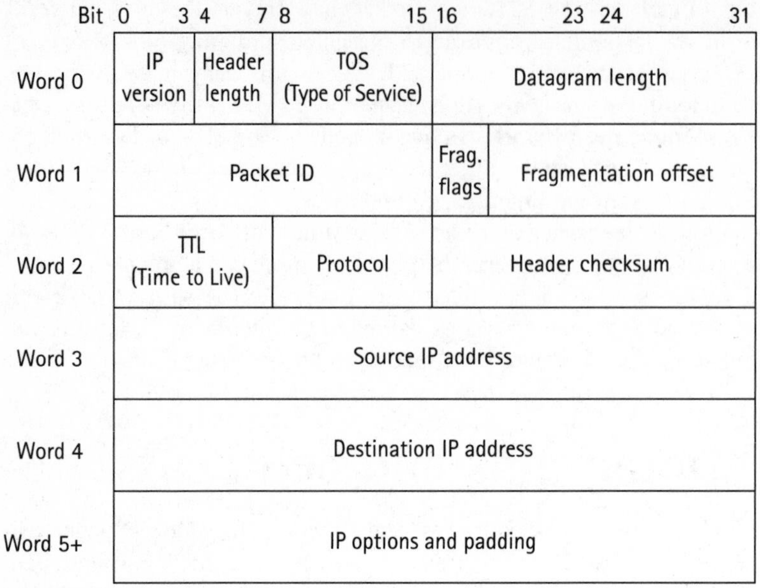

Figure 2-9: The IP header

DATAGRAM LENGTH

This 16-bit field indicates the length of the IP datagram in bytes, including the header and body.

PACKET ID

This 16-bit field is also known as the fragment identification, or simply the identification. All fragments created from a given datagram must share the same packet ID value so that they can be efficiently reassembled.

FRAGMENTATION FLAGS

This three-bit field includes two flags. Bit 0 of the field, the high-order bit, is reserved and should have the value zero. Bit 1 is termed the Don't Fragment flag (DF). If a datagram's size exceeds the MTU of a network, the network should not fragment a datagram having the DF flag set. Instead, the network should return an ICMP error message.

Bit 2 is termed the More Fragments (MF) flag. When a large datagram is fragmented, each resulting datagram except the last has the MF flag set. The receiving host tests the MF flag to verify that all fragments have been received and are ready for reassembly.

FRAGMENTATION OFFSET

This 13-bit field gives the offset in double words (64 bits) of the current fragment within the original oversized datagram.

TIME TO LIVE (TTL)

This 8-bit field provides a simple way of avoiding datagrams that endlessly circulate throughout a network. Each time a datagram traverses a router, the router decrements this field. When a router obtains zero as the result, it does not forward the packet. Instead, it returns an ICMP error message to the sender.

PROTOCOL

This 8-bit field indicates the type of data contained within the body of the IP datagram. Common values are 1 (ICMP), 6 (TCP), and 17 (UDP). The file /etc/protocols lists other valid values.

HEADER CHECKSUM

This 16-bit field is a checksum used to verify the integrity of the IP header. It does not verify the integrity of the IP body.

SOURCE IP ADDRESS

This 32-bit field gives the IP address of the host that sent the datagram.

DESTINATION IP ADDRESS

This 32-bit field gives the IP address of the intended destination of the datagram.

IP OPTIONS AND PADDING

This variable-length field can indicate a variety of IP options. It is always padded out to a 32-bit word boundary for alignment. For more information on IP options, see Internet Request for Comments (RFC) 791, available at http://www.rfc-editor.org.

ICMP Datagrams

Figure 2-10 shows the fields that make up an ICMP datagram. Recall that ICMP datagrams are used primarily to return error codes or perform network testing. They're not intended as a means of sending application data. Also recall that ICMP datagrams are sent within IP datagrams as the body of the IP datagram. The ICMP datagram does duplicate the source IP address of other fields contained within the IP datagram. See RFC 792, available at http://www.rfc-editor.org, for more information on ICMP datagrams.

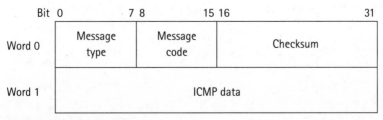

Figure 2-10: An ICMP datagram

MESSAGE TYPE

This eight-bit field indicates the type of ICMP message. Table 2-4 summarizes the available message types. The `ping` command, explained in the section titled "Ping," sends a Type 8 ICMP message. A host configured to respond to a ping transmits a Type 0 ICMP message. Type 3 ICMP messages are sometimes sent when hosts are down or have been configured not to respond. In particular, firewalls can be configured to respond to unauthorized traffic by sending a Type 3 ICMP message. Type 11 ICMP messages are sent when a TTL is decremented to zero.

TABLE 2-4 ICMP MESSAGE TYPES

Type	Description
0	Echo Reply
3	Destination Unreachable
4	Source Quench
5	Redirect
8	Echo
11	Time Exceeded
12	Parameter Problem
13	Timestamp
14	Timestamp Reply
15	Information Request
16	Information Reply

MESSAGE CODE

This 8-bit field is used to provide more detailed information about the ICMP message type. For instance, the Type 3 ICMP message indicates that the destination host is unreachable. The message code of a Type 3 ICMP message can take any of the values shown in Table 2-5.

CHECKSUM

This 16-bit field contains a checksum used to verify the integrity of the ICMP message.

TABLE 2-5 MESSAGE CODES USED WITH ICMP TYPE 3 MESSAGES

Code	Description
0	Network unreachable
1	Host unreachable
2	Protocol unreachable
3	Port unreachable
4	Fragmentation needed and DF flag set
5	Source route failed

ICMP DATA

The length and contents of this field vary according to the ICMP message type. See RFC 792 for details.

UDP Datagrams

Figure 2-11 shows the structure of a UDP datagram. Like ICMP datagrams, UDP datagrams travel inside IP datagrams. For more information on UDP datagrams, see RFC 768.

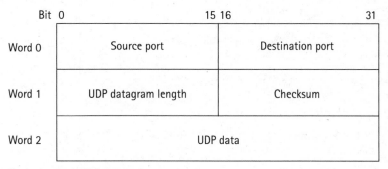

Figure 2-11: A UDP datagram

SOURCE PORT

This 16-bit field gives the source port.

DESTINATION PORT
This 16-bit field gives the destination port.

UDP DATAGRAM LENGTH
This 16-bit field gives the length in bytes of the datagram, including the header and data.

CHECKSUM
This 16-bit field verifies the integrity of the IP header, UDP header, and UDP data.

UDP DATA
The length and contents of the UDP data field vary according to the needs of the application.

TCP Datagrams

Figure 2-12 shows the field of a TCP datagram. Like ICMP and UDP datagrams, the TCP datagram resides within the body of an IP datagram. RFC 793 describes the TCP datagram.

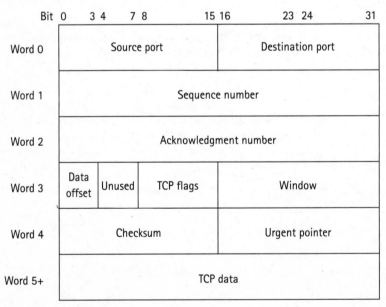

Figure 2-12: A TCP datagram

SOURCE PORT
This 16-bit field gives the source port of the TCP datagram.

DESTINATION PORT
This 16-bit field gives the destination port of the TCP datagram.

SEQUENCE NUMBER
The sequence number field indicates the position of this datagram within the data stream. TCP uses the sequence number to reassemble datagrams in their proper sequence and to detect missing datagrams.

ACKNOWLEDGMENT NUMBER
The acknowledgment number field informs the recipient that the sender has processed datagrams up to the indicated point within the data stream. The acknowledgment number is used in ensuring the reliable delivery of datagrams.

DATA OFFSET
This 4-bit field gives the length of the TCP header, in 32-bit words. The TCP data follows the TCP header.

TCP FLAGS
TCP employs flags that indicate various conditions and events. Table 2-6 summarizes the TCP flags. The SYN and ACK flags are particularly important in firewall design. The next section of this chapter explains how they are used.

TABLE 2-6 TCP FLAGS

Bit Position	Flag	Description
0	SYN	Indicates a request to initiate a TCP connection. The flag requests that the recipient synchronize TCP sequence numbers with the sender.
1	ACK	Indicates that the datagram's acknowledgment sequence number specifies the sequence number of the next stream data byte that is expected.
2	RST	Indicates that the sender has abruptly closed the connection.
3	PSH	Indicates that the recipient should immediately make the data available to the application layer rather than wait for subsequent datagrams.
4	URG	Indicates that the datagram's urgent pointer is set, identifying data that the recipient should process ahead of any other data buffered from the connection.

Continued

TABLE **2-6** TCP FLAGS *(Continued)*

Bit Position	Flag	Description
5	FIN	Indicates that the sender has completed its communication and plans to close the connection.
6-7	RES	Two bits of the TCP flags are not generally used and have the value zero. Some TCP/IP implementations use this flag to signal network congestion.

WINDOW

This 16-bit field indicates the number of bytes the sender of this datagram is willing to accept. The window is used to synchronize communication between hosts having differing data rates.

CHECKSUM

This 16-bit field is used to verify the integrity of the TCP header and data.

URGENT POINTER

This 16-bit field is used when the URG flag is set. It indicates the position within the TCP data at which urgent data resides.

TCP DATA

The length and contents of the TCP data field vary according to the application.

Establishing a TCP Connection

The UDP protocol is a connectionless protocol. TCP, in contrast, is a *connection-oriented protocol,* in which communication occurs in well-defined phases. Hosts exchange special datagrams to establish and terminate TCP connections. These special datagrams are indicated by the values of the TCP flags.

Figure 2-13 shows how a client establishes a TCP connection with a server. Three steps are involved:

1. The client sends the server a datagram with the SYN flag set.

2. If the server is willing to communicate with the client, the server sends the client a datagram with the SYN and ACK flags set.

3. The client sends the server a datagram with the ACK flag set.

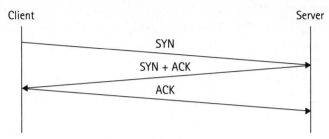

Figure 2-13: Establishing a TCP connection

 The process of establishing a TCP connection is sometimes called the TCP three-way handshake. You must understand how the SYN and ACK flags are used in the three-way handshake. For instance, firewalls that restrict access to services generally enforce their policies by testing the SYN flag of incoming datagrams.

After a connection has been established, either participating host can send a datagram to the other. Each host acknowledges datagrams received from the other so that the hosts remain synchronized. To acknowledge the receipt of a datagram, a host sends a packet having its ACK flag and acknowledgment fields set. Hosts need not individually acknowledge each datagram. The acknowledgment field specifies the sequence number of the most recent datagram received. By properly setting this field, a host can send a single datagram that acknowledges multiple received datagrams.

Closing a TCP Connection

Figure 2-14 shows the process of closing a TCP connection, which involves a four-step process:

1. Either the client or server can terminate the connection. The host wishing to terminate the connection is identified as Host A in the figure. This host sends its counterpart a datagram having the FIN and ACK flags set.

2. Host B acknowledges the request to terminate the connection by sending a datagram having its ACK flag set.

3. Host B then sends a datagram having its FIN and ACK flags set.

4. Host A acknowledges the datagram by sending a datagram having its ACK flag set. At that point, the connection is deemed to have been terminated.

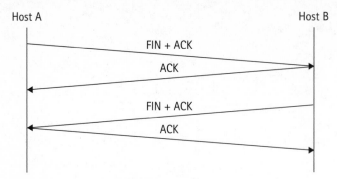

Figure 2-14: Closing a TCP connection

 A connection can be abruptly terminated by sending a datagram having its RST flag set.

TCP/IP Tools

This section surveys some software tools that are helpful in configuring and troubleshooting TCP/IP networks. The material emphasizes only certain features of each command, those that are especially useful in working with firewalls. For a more comprehensive treatment of this topic, see *Red Hat Linux Networking and System Administration,* by Terry Collings and Kurt Wall (Red Hat Press/Wiley, 2002). You can also learn more by consulting the Linux man pages for each command. In the section "TCP/IP Troubleshooting," later in this chapter, you learn more about using some of the commands described in this section.

ifconfig

The ifconfig command is used to configure, or report the status of, a network interface. Under Red Hat Linux, interfaces should be configured by tweaking the appropriate ifcfg-ethn file or by using a tool that does so. Otherwise, configuration changes are lost when the system is booted.

Issuing the ifconfig command and giving the name of an interface as a parameter causes the command to report the status of the specified interface. Issuing the ifconfig command with no parameters causes the command to report the status of each installed network interface. A typical report of the interface status of an Ethernet host follows:

```
[root@host root]# ifconfig
eth0      Link encap:Ethernet   HWaddr 00:02:B3:5E:9D:4F
          inet addr:192.0.34.7  Bcast:192.0.34.255  Mask:255.255.255.0
          UP BROADCAST RUNNING MULTICAST  MTU:1500  Metric:1
          RX packets:159707882 errors:0 dropped:0 overruns:0 frame:0
          TX packets:118176825 errors:0 dropped:0 overruns:0 carrier:0
          collisions:0 txqueuelen:100
          RX bytes:476737229 (454.6 Mb)  TX bytes:568792793 (542.4 Mb)
          Interrupt:11 Base address:0xa000

eth1      Link encap:Ethernet   HWaddr 00:02:B3:5E:9D:4E
          inet addr:10.0.0.7  Bcast:10.255.255.255  Mask:255.0.0.0
          UP BROADCAST RUNNING MULTICAST  MTU:1500  Metric:1
          RX packets:92761938 errors:0 dropped:0 overruns:0 frame:0
          TX packets:77263594 errors:0 dropped:0 overruns:0 carrier:0
          collisions:0 txqueuelen:100
          RX bytes:2416046221 (2304.1 Mb)  TX bytes:3392159563 (3235.0 Mb)
          Interrupt:11 Base address:0xc000

eth2      Link encap:Ethernet   HWaddr 00:30:48:11:71:45
          inet addr:192.168.1.7  Bcast:192.168.1.255  Mask:255.255.255.0
          UP BROADCAST RUNNING MULTICAST  MTU:1500  Metric:1
          RX packets:13818869 errors:0 dropped:0 overruns:0 frame:0
          TX packets:6593040 errors:0 dropped:0 overruns:0 carrier:0
          collisions:0 txqueuelen:100
          RX bytes:3496028396 (3334.0 Mb)  TX bytes:1459030679 (1391.4 Mb)
          Interrupt:9 Base address:0x9000

lo        Link encap:Local Loopback
          inet addr:127.0.0.1  Mask:255.0.0.0
          UP LOOPBACK RUNNING  MTU:16436  Metric:1
          RX packets:386554 errors:0 dropped:0 overruns:0 frame:0
          TX packets:386554 errors:0 dropped:0 overruns:0 carrier:0
          collisions:0 txqueuelen:0
          RX bytes:44071142 (42.0 Mb)  TX bytes:44071142 (42.0 Mb)
```

The name of the interface (eth0, eth1, eth2, or lo) appears at the left margin. The interface named lo is the loopback interface. Table 2-7 summarizes the contents of the report.

TABLE 2-7 OUTPUT OF THE ifconfig COMMAND

Field	Description
Link encap	The type of frame associated with the interface – for example, Ethernet.
HWAddr	The MAC address associated with the interface.
inet addr	The IP address associated with the interface.
Bcast	The broadcast address associated with the interface.
Mask	The network mask associated with the interface.
UP	Indication that the interface is configured to be enabled.
BROADCAST	Indication that the interface is configured to handle broadcast packets.
RUNNING	Indication that the interface is operational.
MULTICAST	Indication that the interface is configured to handle multicast packets.
MTU	The maximum transmission unit for which the interface is configured.
Metric	The value of this configuration item can be used to control which interface a packet is forwarded to, when multiple interfaces could be used to reach the packet's destination.
RX packets	The number of packets received via the interface.
RX errors	The number of damaged packets received.
RX dropped	The number of packets dropped because of reception errors.
RX overrun	The number of received packets that experienced data overruns.
RX frame	The number of packets that experienced frame errors.
TX packets	The number of packets transmitted via the interface.
TX errors	The number of packets that experienced transmission errors.
TX dropped	The number of packets dropped because of transmission errors.
TX overrun	The number of transmitted packets that experienced data overruns.
TX carrier	The number of transmitted packets that experienced loss of carrier.
TX collisions	The number of transmitted packets that experienced Ethernet collisions.
TX txquelength	The configured length of the transmission queue.
RX bytes	The number of bytes received via this interface.

Field	Description
TX bytes	The number of bytes transmitted via this interface.
Interrupt	The IRQ associated with this interface.
Base address	The IO base address associated with this interface.

ping

The ping command sends an ICMP echo request packet to the specified host. The host can be specified by IP address or by host name. When an IP address is specified, the -n flag should appear so that the command does not unnecessarily attempt to resolve the IP address as though it were a host name.

If the specified host is operational and configured to respond, it replies to ICMP echo requests. The ping command prints each reply, along with the TTL of the reply packet and the round-trip time required by the echo request and reply. Under Linux, the ping command continues its operation indefinitely unless the -c option is used. To cancel execution of the command, press Ctrl+C. The command then prints a summary of the activity, including the number of packets transmitted and received and the average round-trip time:

```
[root@host root]# ping -n 192.168.1.5
PING 192.168.1.5 (192.168.1.5) from 192.168.1.7 : 56(84) bytes of data.
64 bytes from 192.168.1.5: icmp_seq=0 ttl=255 time=787 usec
64 bytes from 192.168.1.5: icmp_seq=1 ttl=255 time=221 usec
64 bytes from 192.168.1.5: icmp_seq=2 ttl=255 time=198 usec
64 bytes from 192.168.1.5: icmp_seq=3 ttl=255 time=215 usec
64 bytes from 192.168.1.5: icmp_seq=4 ttl=255 time=199 usec
64 bytes from 192.168.1.5: icmp_seq=5 ttl=255 time=212 usec
(Ctrl-C pressed here)
--- 192.168.1.5 ping statistics ---
6 packets transmitted, 6 packets received, 0% packet loss
round-trip min/avg/max/mdev = 0.198/0.305/0.787/0.216 ms
```

route

The route command is used to configure, or report the status of, a host's routing table. Under Red Hat Linux, the /etc/sysconfig/network and /etc/sysconfig/static-routes files should be used to configure routing. Changes made via the route command are lost when the system is rebooted.

To obtain a report of the routing table, issue the `route` command. The `-n` flag causes the report to show IP addresses rather than host names:

```
[root@host root]# route -n
Kernel IP routing table
Destination     Gateway         Genmask         Flags Metric Ref    Use Iface
192.0.34.0      0.0.0.0         255.255.255.0   U     0      0        0 eth0
192.168.1.0     0.0.0.0         255.255.255.0   U     0      0        0 eth2
10.0.0.0        0.0.0.0         255.0.0.0       U     0      0        0 eth1
127.0.0.0       0.0.0.0         255.0.0.0       U     0      0        0 lo
0.0.0.0         192.0.34.1      0.0.0.0         UG    0      0        0 eth0
```

Table 2-8 summarizes the content of the routing report.

TABLE 2-8 OUTPUT OF THE route COMMAND

Field	Description
Destination	The destination IP address. The entry 0.0.0.0 is used to specify the default gateway.
Gateway	The IP address of the gateway host for reaching the destination. The entry 0.0.0.0 indicates that the destination is reachable via a local network.
Genmask	The network mask associated with the destination.
Flags	U = The interface is up.
	G = The destination is reachable via a gateway.
	H = The destination refers to a host.
	N = The destination refers to a network.
	Other flags sometimes appear; see the man page for details.
Metric	Used to optimize routing.
Ref	Not used by the Linux kernel.
Use	The number of route cache misses.
Iface	The name of the associated network interface.

traceroute

The traceroute command enables you to determine connectivity to a remote host. The command shows each intermediate host traversed in reaching the remote host and the round-trip time of a UDP packet sent to each intermediate host. Some hosts may be configured not to respond to traceroute requests. The command tries several times to access such a host, printing a series of asterisks if all attempts fail.

Typical output of the traceroute command follows:

```
[root@host root]# traceroute www.example.com
traceroute to www.example.com (192.0.34.72), 30 hops max, 38 byte packets
 1  sbm1.example.com (192.0.34.1)  1.088 ms  0.440 ms  0.411 ms
 2  attlink.example.com (192.0.34.250)  0.756 ms  0.690 ms  0.777 ms
 3  12.125.102.13 (12.125.102.13)  1.925 ms  1.998 ms  1.805 ms
 4  gbr1-p55.la2ca.ip.att.net (12.123.28.177)  2.293 ms  1.839 ms  1.932 ms
 5  tbr2-p013502.la2ca.ip.att.net (12.122.11.145)  3.626 ms  3.574 ms  33.541 ms
 6  ggr1-p3100.la2ca.ip.att.net (12.122.11.222)  1.890 ms  1.963 ms  1.937 ms
 7  p4-1-3-0.r02.us.bb.verio.net (129.250.9.185)  2.166 ms  2.287 ms  2.082 ms
 8  ge-1-1-0.a02.us.ra.verio.net (129.250.29.131)  2.329 ms  2.303 ms  2.120 ms
 9  d1-1-2-2.a02.lsanca02.us.ce.verio.net (198.173.172.146)  3.164 ms  2.594 ms
10  192.0.33.1 (192.0.33.1)  3.258 ms  3.274 ms  3.394 ms
11  * * *
12  * * *
```

The traceroute command is a privileged command available only to the root user.

host

The host command lets you perform forward and reverse DNS lookups. For example, here's a typical forward lookup:

```
[root@host root]# host www.example.com
www.example.com. has address 192.0.34.72
```

And, here's a typical reverse lookup:

```
[root@host root]# host 192.0.34.72
72.34.0.192.in-addr.arpa. domain name pointer www.example.com.
```

You can specify the IP address or host name of the name server to be used. Simply append the identity of the server to your command. For example, the command host www.example.com dns.example.com uses the server dns.example.com to attempt to resolve the host name www.example.com.

dig

The dig command also lets you perform forward and reverse DNS lookups. However, it can report additional DNS information as well. Here's the output of a typical forward lookup:

```
[root@host root]# dig www.example.com

; <<>> DiG 9.1.3 <<>> www.example.com
;; global options:  printcmd
;; Got answer:
;; ->>HEADER<<- opcode: QUERY, status: NOERROR, id: 781
;; flags: qr rd ra; QUERY: 1, ANSWER: 1, AUTHORITY: 2, ADDITIONAL: 2

;; QUESTION SECTION:
;www.example.com.                IN      A

;; ANSWER SECTION:
www.example.com.        172729  IN      A       192.0.34.72

;; AUTHORITY SECTION:
example.com.            21529   IN      NS      a.iana-servers.net.
example.com.            21529   IN      NS      b.iana-servers.net.

;; ADDITIONAL SECTION:
a.iana-servers.net.     172729  IN      A       192.0.34.43
b.iana-servers.net.     172729  IN      A       193.0.0.236

;; Query time: 2 msec
;; SERVER: 10.0.0.6#53(10.0.0.6)
;; WHEN: Sat Jun  1 09:24:15 2002
;; MSG SIZE  rcvd: 129
```

Notice that the output reports the name server used in resolving the query, 10.0.0.6. The output also reports a variety of other DNS-related information. You can specify the DNS server to be queried by using an @ sign, as follows:

```
dig @10.0.0.7 www.example.com
```

This line specifies that the DNS query should be addressed to the server residing at 10.0.0.7 rather than to the default name server. The `dig` command has many additional features; consult its man page to learn about them.

nslookup

The `nslookup` command is an old command that performs essentially the same functions as the more modern `dig` command. Because `nslookup` remains in wide-spread use, it's worth a quick example. Here's a typical forward DNS lookup, performed using `nslookup`:

```
[root@host root]# nslookup www.example.com
Note:  nslookup is deprecated and may be removed from future releases.
Consider using the `dig' or `host' programs instead.  Run nslookup with
the `-sil[ent]' option to prevent this message from appearing.
Server:        10.0.0.6
Address:       10.0.0.6#53


Non-authoritative answer:
Name:   www.example.com
```

Notice that the output suggests using the `dig` or `host` command rather than `nslookup`.

netcat

The `netcat` command, sometimes known as `nc`, is not part of the standard Red Hat Linux distribution. However, the command is handy for a variety of purposes. `netcat` lets you read and write UDP and TCP data much as the `cat` command lets you read and write ordinary data. You can obtain netcat via the Web at http://www.atstake.com/research/tools/. It is not distributed as an RPM package, so you must compile and install it manually.

Following is netcat's usage output:

```
[root@host netcat]# ./nc -h
[v1.10]
connect to somewhere:    nc [-options] hostname port[s] [ports] ...
listen for inbound:      nc -l -p port [-options] [hostname] [port]
options:
        -g gateway              source-routing hop point[s], up to 8
        -G num                  source-routing pointer: 4, 8, 12, ...
        -h                      this cruft
        -i secs                 delay interval for lines sent, ports scanned
        -l                      listen mode, for inbound connects
```

```
-n                          numeric-only IP addresses, no DNS
-o file                     hex dump of traffic
-p port                     local port number
-r                          randomize local and remote ports
-s addr                     local source address
-u                          UDP mode
-v                          verbose [use twice to be more verbose]
-w secs                     timeout for connects and final net reads
-z                          zero-I/O mode [used for scanning] port numbers
                            can be individual or ranges: lo-hi [inclusive]
```

For example, you can configure netcat to listen on a TCP port and send received data to a file. Here's a command for doing so, using port 1234 as the port on which to listen:

```
nc -l -p 1234 > output
```

If you specify a host name or IP address and port, the command accepts packets only from the specified IP address or source port:

```
nc -l -p 1234 10.0.0.6 4321 > output
```

To send data to a remote host, use a netcat command such as the following, which sends data to port 1234 of the target host:

```
nc -w 3 target.example.com 1234
```

You can establish two-way TCP communication with a host by simply providing the host's name or IP address and the port to which you want to connect. For example, the following command lets you type commands to an SMTP server running on port 25 and view the server's replies:

```
nc mail.example.com 25
```

For more information on netcat, see the Read Me file included in the netcat distribution file.

tcpdump

The tcpdump command lets you view packets arriving at a network interface. You can optionally capture such packets to a file and subsequently view them. The tcpdump command provides many flags and options. It even implements a small language known as Berkeley Packet Filters (BPF) for specifying packets of interest. The command understands many common TCP/IP protocols and provides formatted output that helps you interpret packet contents.

The `tcpdump` command is a privileged command, available only to root.

Here's a simple `tcpdump` command that reads from the interface named eth2. The flags `-n` and `-nn` specify that IP addresses and ports are to be displayed numerically. The command ignores packets other than TCP and UDP packets:

```
[root@host root]# tcpdump -n -nn -i eth2 tcp or udp
tcpdump: listening on eth2
09:31:01.477327 10.0.0.7.44743 > 10.0.0.6.873: . ack 212571 win 49265
<nop,nop,timestamp 922525100 256688417> (DF)
09:31:01.477570 10.0.0.6.873 > 10.0.0.7.44743: P 212571:212579(8) ack 311 win
6432 <nop,nop,timestamp 256688418 922525100> (DF)
09:31:01.481476 10.0.0.7.44743 > 10.0.0.6.873: . ack 212579 win 63712
<nop,nop,timestamp 922525100 256688418> (DF)
09:31:01.481884 10.0.0.7.44743 > 10.0.0.6.873: P 311:315(4) ack 212579 win 63712
<nop,nop,timestamp 922525100 256688418> (DF)
09:31:01.482195 10.0.0.6.873 > 10.0.0.7.44743: P 212579:212587(8) ack 315 win
6432 <nop,nop,timestamp 256688418 922525100> (DF)
09:31:01.515832 10.0.0.7.44743 > 10.0.0.6.873: . ack 212587 win 63712
<nop,nop,timestamp 922525104 256688418> (DF)
09:31:01.516837 10.0.0.6.873 > 10.0.0.7.44743: P 212587:212603(16) ack 315 win
6432 <nop,nop,timestamp 256688422 922525104> (DF)
09:31:01.516928 10.0.0.7.44743 > 10.0.0.6.873: . ack 212603 win 63712
<nop,nop,timestamp 922525104 256688422> (DF)
09:31:01.517428 10.0.0.7.44743 > 10.0.0.6.873: P 315:319(4) ack 212603 win 63712
<nop,nop,timestamp 922525104 256688422> (DF)
09:31:01.518887 10.0.0.6.873 > 10.0.0.7.44743: F 212603:212603(0) ack 319 win
6432 <nop,nop,timestamp 256688422 922525104> (DF)
09:31:01.521781 10.0.0.6.514 > 192.0.34.10.514:  udp 77 (DF)
09:31:01.546271 10.0.0.7.44743 > 10.0.0.6.873: F 319:319(0) ack 212604 win 63712
<nop,nop,timestamp 922525107 256688422> (DF)
09:31:01.546998 10.0.0.6.873 > 10.0.0.7.44743: . ack 320 win 6432
<nop,nop,timestamp 256688425 922525107> (DF)
09:31:01.558887 10.0.0.7.50814 > 10.0.0.6.53:  63885+ MX? example.com. (25) (DF)
09:31:01.560213 10.0.0.6.53 > 10.0.0.7.50814:  63885 2/4/6 MX mail2.example.com.
20, (262) (DF)
09:31:01.560968 10.0.0.7.50814 > 10.0.0.6.53:  63886+ A? mail.example.com. (30)
(DF)
09:31:01.562580 10.0.0.6.53 > 10.0.0.7.50814:  63886 1/4/4 A 192.168.237.153
(208) (DF)
```

```
09:31:01.564497 10.0.0.7.50814 > 10.0.0.6.53:  63887+ PTR? 7.97.107.199.in-
addr.arpa. (43) (DF)
09:31:01.568209 10.0.0.6.53 > 10.0.0.7.50814:  63887 1/2/2 (141) (DF)

342 packets received by filter
0 packets dropped by kernel
```

Notice that each packet is listed with the time of its arrival, in microsecond precision. Next come the source IP address and port, if applicable, and the destination IP address and port. P and F indicate the TCP PSH and FIN flags, respectively. The output also shows TCP sequence and acknowledgment numbers, window size, and options. Learning to read packet dumps requires considerable time and study. However, mastering this skill is a worthwhile endeavor for designers of firewalls.

To write packets to a capture file, use the -w flag, which is followed by the path. To read packets from a capture file rather than from an interface, replace the -i flag and the name of the interface with an -r flag and the path associated with the capture file.

tcpshow

The tcpshow command can help you interpret the output of the tcpdump command. The tcpshow command displays its results in a more verbose and descriptive fashion than the tcpdump command. An easy way to use tcpshow is to pipe the output of tcpdump into it. Several tcpdump options must be properly specified in order for this technique to work:

```
[root@host root]# tcpdump -s 1518 -lenx -i eth2 tcp or udp | tcpshow -pp -
cooked|less
tcpdump: listening on eth2
Packet 1
        Timestamp:                  09:34:50.141668
IP Header
        Version:                    4
        Header Length:              20 bytes
        Service Type:               0x10
        Datagram Length:            148 bytes
        Identification:             0x502A
        Flags:                      MF=off, DF=on
        Fragment Offset:            0
        TTL:                        64
        Encapsulated Protocol:      TCP
        Header Checksum:            0x66CD
        Source IP Address:          192.168.1.5
        Destination IP Address:     192.168.1.7
TCP Header
        Source Port:                222 (<unknown>)
        Destination Port:           44618 (<unknown>)
```

```
        Sequence Number:              0429154412
        Acknowledgement Number:       0437233800
        Header Length:                32 bytes (data=96)
        Flags:                        URG=off, ACK=on,  PSH=on
                                      RST=off, SYN=off, FIN=off
        Window Advertisement:         8576 bytes
        Checksum:                     0xB9DF
        Urgent Pointer:               0
        <Options not displayed>
TCP Data
        .29...v....3o0..q..".......u"I..]..M..c.........o..".T/.....3.M.:...-...qD
..2...$6...............
```

Notice how easily you can read the output of tcpshow in comparison with output of tcpdump. However, the output quickly becomes voluminous. To reduce the volume somewhat, you can use the tcpshow -terse flag:

```
[root@host root]# tcpdump -s 1518 -lenx -i eth2 tcp or udp | tcpshow -pp -cooked
-terse |less
tcpdump: listening on eth2
Packet 1
TIME:    09:38:52.529163
  IP:    192.168.1.5 -> 192.168.1.7 hlen=20 TOS=10 dgramlen=180 id=6866
         MF/DF=0/1 frag=0 TTL=64 proto=TCP cksum=4E71
  TCP:   port 222 -> 44618 seq=0429802524 ack=0437234328
         hlen=32 (data=128) UAPRSF=011000 wnd=8576 cksum=10C6 urg=0
DATA:    ..,2.Y...N;+.j.`-.R.w6y.~
         ..nb...3..d....WS..l'F.7.7d.G'5.0.E.r
         .Np..?E#_.D..:R?G w..X.h...x^....;...(.O..._.7.C.E/........N)..A
```

 The tcpshow command is not included in the Red Hat Linux distribution. You can obtain it from http://www.tcpshow.org/ or from the Red Hat contributed library.

iptraf

The iptraf command is useful for measuring the volume of traffic flow into or out of a network interface. The command uses a character-mode menu as its user interface. To view the menu, issue this command:

```
iptraf
```

The menu appears, as shown in Figure 2-15. Use the arrow keys to navigate the menu and press Enter to make a selection.

Figure 2-15: The iptraf menu

The General Interface Statistics function is one of the most useful. Figure 2-16 shows the related output. The report shows, for each interface, the number of packets received and the data rate. You can return to the main menu by typing the letter *x*.

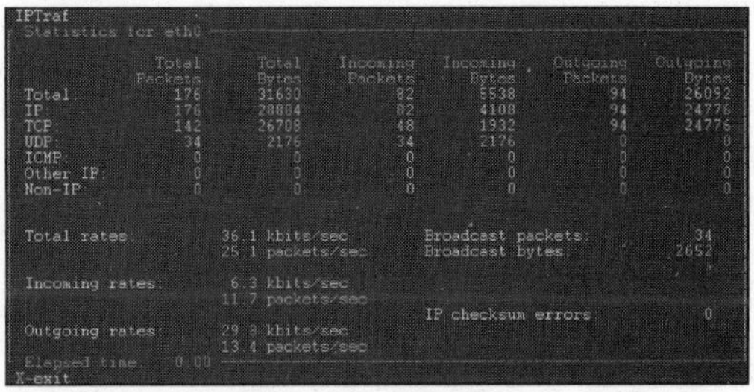

Figure 2-16: Iptraf interface statistics

TCP/IP Configuration

This section describes the key TCP/IP configuration files used in Red Hat Linux. It provides tools, such as netconfig, that modify the contents of these files on your behalf. However, the tools and their user interfaces change between releases, whereas the configuration files and their structure have remained relatively constant over many releases. Consequently, many system administrators prefer to tweak their existing configuration files with a text editor rather than use configuration tools. Certainly, understanding the configuration files helps you develop better mental models of how systems work.

As is true of the preceding section, this section does not attempt to be comprehensive. It focuses on the files and configuration items most important in the context of firewalls. For a more detailed and comprehensive treatment, see the book by Collings and Wall, cited earlier in this chapter, in the "Domain Name Service" section.

/etc/sysconfig/network

The `/etc/sysconfig/network` file is used to determine whether a host is attached to a network and to specify the name of the host and the default gateway. Here is a typical example:

```
[root@host sysconfig]# more /etc/sysconfig/network
NETWORKING=yes
HOSTNAME=myhost.example.com
GATEWAY=192.0.34.1
```

Notice that all lines within the file have the form of shell assignments, in which an environment variable is given a value. You can use the text editor of your choice to modify the contents of the file. However, changes do not become active until networking is restarted.

/etc/sysconfig/static-routes

The `/etc/sysconfig/static-routes` file is used when a host has access to gateway hosts other than the default gateway. Otherwise, the file does not exist. Here is a typical example:

```
[root@host /root]# more /etc/sysconfig/static-routes
any net 199.199.199.199 netmask 255.255.255.255 gw 192.0.34.1
```

The file consists of one or more lines, each containing the following fields:

- ◆ **Interface:** The name of the network interface or the word `any`, which indicates that the specification applies to every installed interface.

- ◆ **Host or network:** The word `host` or `net`, indicating whether the following IP address is the address of a host or that of a network.

- ◆ **IP address:** The IP address of the destination host or network.

- **Network mask:** The word `netmask`, followed by the network mask of the destination host or network.

- **Gateway:** The letters `gw`, followed by the IP address of the gateway host.

As is true of the `/etc/sysconfig/network` file, you can use the text editor of your choice to modify the contents of the `/etc/sysconfig/static-routes` file. However, changes do not become active until networking is restarted.

/etc/sysconfig/network-scripts/ifcfg-ethn

Multiple `/etc/sysconf/network-scripts/ifcfg-`ethn files may exist, one for each network interface, unless the network interface is virtual. The ethn part of the file name represents the name of the associated interface – for example, eth0. Here is a typical `ifcfg` file:

```
[root@host network-scripts]# more ifcfg-eth0
DEVICE=eth0
BOOTPROTO=static
IPADDR=192.0.34.31
NETMASK=255.255.255.0
GATEWAY=192.0.34.1
HOSTNAME=myhost.example.com
DOMAIN=example.com
```

As with the `/etc/sysconfig/network` file, the contents of this file consist of shell assignments. The variables used in the example include those most commonly used. However, other variables exist. The included variables are

- `DEVICE`: The name of the device, which should be consistent with that specified as part of the file name.

- `BOOTPROTO`: The word `static` if the network configuration is fully specified by the file, or the word `dhcp` or `bootp` if the network configuration is obtained from a DHCP or BOOTP server.

- `IPADDR`: The IP address of the interface.

- `NETMASK`: The network mask of the interface.

- `GATEWAY`: The gateway used by the interface, if a gateway other than the default gateway specified in `/etc/sysconfig/network` is appropriate for this interface.

- ◆ HOSTNAME: The host name associated with this interface, if a host name other than that specified in /etc/sysconfig/network is appropriate for this interface.

- ◆ DOMAIN: The domain name associated with this interface, if a domain name other than that specified in /etc/sysconfig/network is appropriate for this interface.

 As is generally true of network configuration files, you can use the text editor of your choice to modify the contents of the interface configuration files. However, changes do not become active until networking is restarted. Occasionally, changes to interface configuration files require that the system be rebooted.

/etc/nsswitch.conf

The /etc/nsswitch.conf file is a rather lengthy file. Like most of the configuration files described in this section, it consists mainly of comments, identified by a hash mark as the first non-whitespace character of a line. Here is a typical example:

```
[root@host /etc]# more nsswitch.conf
#
# /etc/nsswitch.conf
#
# An example Name Service Switch config file. This file should be
# sorted with the most-used services at the beginning.
#
# The entry '[NOTFOUND=return]' means that the search for an
# entry should stop if the search in the previous entry turned
# up nothing. Note that if the search failed due to some other reason
# (like no NIS server responding) then the search continues with the
# next entry.
#
# Legal entries are:
#
#       nisplus or nis+       Use NIS+ (NIS version 3)
#       nis or yp             Use NIS (NIS version 2), also called YP
#       dns                   Use DNS (Domain Name Service)
#       files                 Use the local files
#       db                    Use the local database (.db) files
```

```
#       compat                  Use NIS on compat mode
#       hesiod                  Use Hesiod for user lookups
#       [NOTFOUND=return]       Stop searching if not found so far
#

# To use db, put the "db" in front of "files" for entries you want to be
# looked up first in the databases
#
# Example:
#passwd:    db files nisplus nis
#shadow:    db files nisplus nis
#group:     db files nisplus nis

passwd:     files nisplus nis
shadow:     files nisplus nis
group:      files nisplus nis

#hosts:     db files nisplus nis dns
hosts:      files nisplus nis dns

# Example - obey only what nisplus tells us...
#services:  nisplus [NOTFOUND=return] files
#networks:  nisplus [NOTFOUND=return] files
#protocols: nisplus [NOTFOUND=return] files
#rpc:       nisplus [NOTFOUND=return] files
#ethers:    nisplus [NOTFOUND=return] files
#netmasks:  nisplus [NOTFOUND=return] files

bootparams: nisplus [NOTFOUND=return] files

ethers:     files
netmasks:   files
networks:   files
protocols:  files
rpc:        files
services:   files

netgroup:   nisplus

publickey:  nisplus

automount:  files nisplus
aliases:    files nisplus
```

Unless you're using Network Information Services (NIS), a topic beyond the scope of this book, the only line of interest is this one:

```
hosts:      files nisplus nis dns
```

This line indicates the order in which various means are used to resolve host names to IP addresses. The word `files` indicates that the system first consults the `/etc/hosts` file, which is explained in the next section. Unless NIS is used, the words `nisplus` and `nis` have no effect. The word `dns` indicates that the system consults a DNS server only if the `/etc/hosts` file contains no pertinent information about a host name.

You can revise this line in any of several ways. For example, you can specify that the `/etc/hosts` file should not be consulted:

```
hosts:      dns
```

Or, you can specify that the system should attempt to resolve host names via DNS before consulting the `/etc/hosts` file:

```
hosts:      dns files
```

/etc/hosts

The `/etc/hosts` file is a simple means of associating a host name with an IP address. It has the advantage of not requiring a network connection to a DNS server, so the `/etc/hosts` file can be used to resolve the host names it contains even if the network is down or you're using someone else's DNS server and can't configure it to resolve local hosts or aliases.

The file contains one of more lines, each consisting of an IP address, followed by one or more associated host names. Often, the names are given in fully qualified form (that is, including a domain name) and in nonqualified form. In such cases, the fully qualified name should be given first. Here is a typical `/etc/hosts` file:

```
[root@host /etc]# more /etc/hosts
127.0.0.1           localhost.localdomain localhost
192.0.34.193        myhost.example.com
```

/etc/resolv.conf

The `/etc/resolv.conf` file specifies the IP address of the name server or servers used in resolving host names. It also specifies the domain name assumed when a host name does not appear to be fully qualified. Here is a typical `/etc/resolv.conf` file:

```
[root@host /etc]# more /etc/resolv.conf
search example.com
nameserver 192.168.237.168
```

The file specifies that the default domain is example.com and the default DNS server's IP address is 192.168.237.168. Multiple DNS servers can be specified by separating each one from the next by one or more whitespace characters. The servers are queried in the order given. However, each server must time-out before the next one is tried. So, failover to a secondary server is not rapid, generally requiring tens of seconds for each query.

 The Red Hat Linux DHCP client automatically updates the /etc/resolv.conf file with the IP address of the DNS server identified by the DCHP server.

Modifying the Network Configuration

When you revise a TCP/IP network configuration file, the changes generally do not take effect immediately. Instead, you must reload the network configuration. To do so, issue the following command as root:

```
service network reload
```

If you prefer, you can stop networking and then restart it. To do so, issue the following two commands:

```
service network stop
service network start
```

TCP/IP Troubleshooting

This section presents a simple, three-step TCP/IP troubleshooting procedure. The procedure is generally adequate for localizing the sorts of problems that occur when working with firewalls. However, a more sophisticated troubleshooting procedure is appropriate in contexts that may include hardware failure or other complications:

1. Test connectivity to the default gateway.

2. Test connectivity beyond the gateway.

3. Test host name resolution.

If a test fails, you have succeeded in localizing the problem. You can then pinpoint the problem by using one or more of the TCP/IP tools described earlier in this chapter. Network problems tend to be idiosyncratic; that is, the next one tends to differ significantly from those that preceded it. Moreover, network problems tend to manifest differently depending on the network configuration. Therefore, a comprehensive, cookbook approach to TCP/IP troubleshooting is not possible. However, based on your knowledge of the structure of your own network, you may be able to construct your own cookbook procedure.

When you're working with firewalls, an incorrect firewall rule is often the cause of a network problem. Check your firewall's operation before considering more serious problems.

Test Connectivity to the Default Gateway

A good first test is to use the ping command to test connectivity to the default gateway. Be sure to use the -n flag and specify the IP address of the gateway rather than its host name. Otherwise, a host name resolution problem may manifest itself as a connectivity problem.

If you're able to ping the gateway, move on to the next troubleshooting step. Otherwise, try pinging other nearby hosts to determine the scope of the problem.

This troubleshooting step depends on the gateway's being configured to answer echo requests from its client hosts. If an overzealous network administrator has configured the gateway to ignore such requests, you have to work out another way to test connectivity.

Test Connectivity Beyond the Gateway

Next, test connectivity to hosts beyond the gateway by pinging them. It's handy to perform this test before you run into a problem and thereby identify several remote hosts that are configured to respond to echo requests. Many Internet hosts gladly do so, but some are configured to ignore echo requests.

If possible, try pinging hosts beyond the gateway but under local administrative control. If you're able to access such hosts but not Internet hosts, you should suspect that your Internet link is down.

If you're able to ping a variety of local and Internet hosts beyond the gateway, move on to the third and final troubleshooting step.

Test Host Name Resolution

Finally, use the host command to perform forward and reverse lookups of hosts within your domain and outside it. If the host command fails, explicitly specify the DNS server to be used. This action helps you determine whether your primary DNS server has failed.

If all three troubleshooting steps work okay, your TCP/IP networking configuration is probably in good working order. If TCP/IP operations do not work properly, your firewall configuration may be at fault.

Many ISPs provide open DNS servers that you can access to test host name resolution. Check with your ISP to see if one is available to you.

Summary

In this chapter, we've surveyed TCP/IP networking terms and concepts. We've looked in some detail at protocols, addressing, and packets. We've described some popular TCP/IP networking commands and the key TCP/IP configuration files used in Red Hat Linux. Finally, we've presented a simple troubleshooting procedure suitable for localizing TCP/IP problems. In the next chapter, we look at some common network security threats and how to defend against them.

Chapter 3

Threats and Principles of Defense

IN THIS CHAPTER

- ◆ Who is attacking your network and why
- ◆ What harm attackers can do to your network
- ◆ What sorts of attacks you can anticipate
- ◆ Principles for defending your network

TO EFFECTIVELY DEFEND YOUR NETWORK AGAINST THREATS, you must understand the sorts of threats you face. You should also know something about the opposition: who they are, what they know, and why they're launching attacks against your network.

This chapter describes two categories of attackers: blackhats and script kiddies. It explains what motivates the typical attacker. It describes the general categories of attacks being used and the potential effects such attacks can have on the target network. Finally, the chapter provides ten general principles that should guide you in designing your defenses.

This chapter aims at presenting the big picture, so it doesn't specifically mention firewalls. An effective firewall must be part of a larger array of defensive measures. Subsequent chapters – especially Chapter 5, "Firewall Architecture," and Chapter 6, "Firewall Design" – show how firewalls fit into the big picture, explaining what firewalls can – and can't – do to defend your network.

This chapter consists of two main sections. In the first section, you learn about the threat environment. In the subsequent section, you learn about some principles that should guide you in designing your network's defenses.

Threats to Network Security

Certainly, an effective network defense strategy must be capable of dealing with novel attacks. However, the vast majority of attacks are relatively crude and predictable. By ensuring that your network is immune – or at least highly resistant – to these attacks, you're free to focus energy and attention on less familiar threats.

The Threat Level

Historically, the greatest threat to an organization's information security has come from within the organization itself. Disgruntled and dishonest employees have been responsible for most computer-related crime. Measured by the dollar value of the loss, crimes perpetrated by insiders may continue to be the biggest threat. However, if the crimes are measured by the number of attempted and successful attacks, outsiders seem to have become the numerically greatest threat.

It's necessary to write *may* and *seem* because computer crimes are often not reported, lest public knowledge of them reflect poorly on the victims. As a result, statistics on computer crime are considered incomplete and regarded as not accurately reflecting the true level of this type of behavior. However, such statistics show unmistakably that reported computer crime, at least, is on the rise.

Table 3-1, which presents statistics on incidents reported to the Computer Emergency Response Team (CERT) of Carnegie Mellon University, shows that the volume of incidents is roughly doubling each year. During 2002, this trend appeared to continue. You can view these and other statistics on the Web at http://www.cert.org/stats/.

TABLE 3-1 COMPUTER INCIDENTS REPORTED TO CERT

Year	Incidents
1999	9,859
2000	21,756
2001	52,658

One reason for the increase in reported computer crime is, of course, the advent of the Internet. Before the Internet, a would-be attacker required physical access to an organization's information resources in order to inflict damage. The information resources of many organizations are now available globally via the Internet and the Web. Sensitive information may be protected by passwords and other devices so that it's not publicly accessible. However, a skilled attacker may be able to circumvent such protective measures. Such an attacker can reside and wreak havoc from anywhere in the world. Recently, many computer attacks on U.S. organizations have arisen from such countries as

◆ People's Republic of China

◆ France

◆ Germany

- South Korea

- Pakistan

- Romania

As this book was being written, the U.S. Central Intelligence Agency (CIA) had published warnings of anticipated widespread and concerted attacks by Chinese attackers on U.S. information resources. Concurrently, U.S. authorities were expressing concern about U.S. vulnerability to computer attacks potentially conducted by terrorists. Computer crime is no longer typified by the criminal acts of the lone disgruntled or greedy insider. Now that attacks can originate from any place on the globe, computer crime has clearly become a global problem.

Attacker Categories

Another sea change in computer crime concerns the backgrounds and skills of attackers. The popular media have tended to extol the skills of computer attackers, sometimes even glamorizing the attackers, as seen in films such as *Sneakers* and *Swordfish*. The news media have often followed suit by focusing on young attackers, adding a human interest angle. For instance, one often sees stories of "15-year-old computer geniuses" thwarting the security of some well-known organization.

In contrast to the prevalent media image of young expert attackers, security experts broadly recognize two categories of human attackers: blackhats and script kiddies. The categories are distinguished based on level of expertise and method of attack, not on age, with blackhats having a higher degree of expertise than script kiddies.

Blackhats, because of their greater expertise, are capable of mounting a wide range of attacks against a wide range of systems. A skilled and determined blackhat poses a serious threat to even a well-defended network.

However, most attacks are mounted by script kiddies, who are far more numerous than blackhats. *Script kiddies* attack by using programs that they download via the Internet. Often, they don't understand or care how the programs work. They don't need to because the programs tend to operate in a "fire and forget" manner that requires little or no expertise on the part of the attacker.

Script kiddies use several types of programs. *Scanners* probe hosts and networks for known vulnerabilities. When a script kiddie finds a vulnerable host, he or she can run a program known as an *exploit,* which breaches the security of the victim host. Some programs, known as *autorooters,* combine both capabilities. An autorooter can scan a network for vulnerabilities and automatically breach the security of vulnerable hosts. Once a host has been compromised, a script kiddie usually installs a set of programs known as a rootkit. A *rootkit* masks the intrusion and presence of an attacker and provides the attacker with a means for controlling the victim host.

Blackhats too may use such tools as these, but the blackhats tend to use them in a more sophisticated manner. Script kiddies tend to attack indiscriminately, like a would-be cat burglar who rings the doorbell before trying the back window.

Unfortunately, most network administrators receive no warning that their network is under attack, because they haven't implemented network intrusion-detection mechanisms. It's as though their doorbell, helpfully rung by the cat burglar, were inoperative. Blackhats generally attack in a more disciplined, organized manner. For instance, whereas a script kiddie may attack every host on a network, a black-hat may first determine which hosts are more likely to be vulnerable and attack only the softer targets.

A growing number of attacks are conducted automatically, by programs known as *worms*. During 2001, the worms referred to as Nimda and Code Red infected hundreds of thousands of systems.

One such worm exploits a vulnerability in Microsoft's SQL Server to take over victim hosts. The worm, once in control of its victim, uses the victim's resources to attack other systems. In a short time, the worm infects thousands of systems. Moreover, the worm creates a backdoor whereby a human attacker can take control of an infected system. A popular activity of script kiddies is seeking out such systems that have already been compromised, occupying them, and using them for their own purposes.

Attacker Motivations

Criminal acts are often intended to financially benefit the perpetrator. However, criminals may be motivated in a variety of ways. Computer attackers too are motivated in a variety of ways, including financial gain. The motivation of an attacker is relevant to the design of defensive countermeasures. An attacker who discerns that he or she is unlikely to achieve his or her goal by attacking your network may break off the attack and seek another target.

FINANCIAL OR PERSONAL GAIN

Both conventional criminals and computer attackers are sometimes motivated by financial gain. Computer attackers frequently target computer databases that hold credit card information. An attacker who succeeds in compromising such a database can obtain access to hundreds or thousands of credit card records.

The gain sought by an attacker is not always financial. For instance, students have been known to break into databases that hold transcript information and modify their records and those of others. At least a few enterprising attackers have sold their services to fellow students, offering an improved grade-point average in exchange for a fee.

Attacks motivated primarily by financial or personal gain are more likely to be conducted by blackhats than by script kiddies. However, script kiddies are adept at perceiving and seizing opportunities. A script kiddie might successfully attack a system holding financial data without initially realizing the nature of the system. But, once such a system is compromised, a script kiddie might exploit the break-in in much the same way as a blackhat, selling credit card numbers or other valuable information on the black market.

Most modern businesses own data that must be kept confidential from outsiders, particularly competitors. Such organizations should pay careful attention to the design and administration of firewalls and other measures intended to thwart computer attacks. A traditional principle of defense is to make the network so resistant to attack that the cost of successfully attacking it exceeds the potential financial gain. However, as is explained later in this section, this principle has become less appropriate as a guide to network administrators because of the activity of script kiddies and other nontraditional criminals who are not primarily motivated by financial gain.

ACCESS TO COMPUTING RESOURCES

As explained in the preceding section, attackers often seek access to information residing on target systems. However, sometimes all they want is access to the computing resources of target systems. Attackers can use these resources in a variety of ways.

For instance, a blackhat seeking to compromise a given system may first attack several unrelated systems. The blackhat uses these compromised systems to mask his or her identity, in much the same way that a bank robber typically uses a stolen car rather than his or her personal vehicle. A compromised host can provide an attacker with anonymity.

Attackers often use compromised systems to launch *denial of service* (DOS) attacks. In launching a DOS attack, an attacker intends to deny the use of a target system. During 2001, several major on-line retailers, such as Amazon.com, were the targets of DOS attacks. Typically, DOS attacks operate by overtaxing the resources of the target system. For instance, if an attacker who controls dozens of Internet hosts directs them to continuously access a target host, the target host may be unable to handle the traffic volume. The target host may even lock up or otherwise fail. Because successful DOS attacks generally require the participation of many compromised hosts, would-be DOS attackers are eager to add new hosts to their collection.

Attackers may also intend to use a compromised system as a point of distribution for illegal or illicit software or data. Pornography is often distributed by this means. Illegal copies of commercial software applications, known as *warez,* are also made available via compromised systems.

RECREATION AND MISCHIEF

Some attackers, script kiddies in particular, are intrinsically motivated by the challenge of attacking systems. Moreover, they may enjoy enhanced peer esteem based on the number of systems they've successfully compromised. These factors can lead them to expend enormous amounts of time and energy seeking out and attacking vulnerable systems.

These attackers, because they view their attacks as sport, often have no particular intention other than to compromise the target system. Sometimes, such attackers leave a compromised system largely undisturbed, perhaps leaving only a backdoor to facilitate reentry. Other times, they deface Web pages on the system, leaving behind a sort of digital graffiti announcing their skill.

Attackers not in search of personal gain present difficulties in the design of countermeasures. The traditional approach of making a system costly to attack in comparison to its value to an attacker typically does not thwart recreational attackers, who aren't much concerned with earning a return on the time they invest in attacking a system. However, the threat posed by such attackers cannot be dismissed. As mentioned earlier, an attacker initially motivated by desire for recreation may seize the opportunity to profit from a successful attack on a valuable system.

A more effective approach is to employ sufficient countermeasures to make a network relatively less susceptible to attack than similar networks. However, this criterion fails on two counts. First, if applied universally, it would lead to an unchecked escalation of defensive measures that eventually entails overexpenditure. Second, it fails to take into account the irrational, opportunistic behavior of recreational attackers. Such attackers may not break off an attack in search of easier prey. Instead, they may be attracted to the challenge posed by novel countermeasures and therefore devote additional resources to the attack until they achieve success. Notwithstanding the inadequacies of this criterion, it remains a useful rule of thumb for determining the appropriate scope of defensive countermeasures.

POLITICAL AGENDAS

Some attackers have a political agenda. They may seek to embarrass public figures who hold opinions differing from their own, or public agencies or companies they despise. For instance, many blackhats hate the commercial security industry and therefore seek to embarrass or even disrupt the business of security companies, particularly those that claim that their products are highly resistant to attack. Denial-of-service and Web defacement attacks are popular among attackers having a political agenda. Like recreational attackers, those whose motivations are political may devote effort out of proportion to the possible financial or personal gain resulting from a successful attack. Consequently, such attackers are relatively difficult to thwart.

Computer Attackers and the Law

Until now, I have referred to blackhats and script kiddies as attackers rather than as criminals. Clearly, some activities they engage in are crimes. Yet, the laws governing computer attacks are not well developed, so separating the criminal from the noncriminal is generally difficult.

Criminal law often rests on the notion of *criminal intent* — that is, the criminal must have reasonably foreseen his or her actions as leading to harm and must have acted without regard to the consequences. However, as actual cases make clear, criminal intent need not be the provenance of computer crime. In one such case, Randal Schwartz, a respected author and software developer, was convicted under Oregon law of three felony counts of computer crime. You can read on the Web the appellate court decision that upheld Schwartz's conviction, at http:// www. publications.ojd.state.or.us/A91702.htm.

Briefly, the facts of the case are these. Schwartz, employed as a consultant by Intel, was involved in assessing the security of the Intel computer network. In particular, he tested the security of user passwords by running a program designed to crack poorly contrived passwords. Although Schwartz was at various times authorized to perform such testing, he never obtained written authorization for the specific tests he performed. A system administrator discovered Schwartz's actions and alerted police. Schwartz was eventually charged, tried, and convicted.

The Oregon statute under which Schwartz was convicted provides that "[a]ny person who knowingly and without authorization uses, accesses or attempts to access any computer, computer system, computer network, or any computer software, program, documentation or data contained in such computer, computer system or computer network, commits computer crime." Under this law, an attempt to knowingly access a computer network without authorization constitutes a crime. This broad definition encompasses many typical actions performed by computer attackers.

However, prosecutions under Oregon's law have been rare. And, other jurisdictions may define computer crime more narrowly or entirely lack computer crime statutes. Likewise, U.S. federal law concerning computer crime has not yet matured.

Two conclusions flow from the consideration of U.S. laws concerning computer crime:

- ◆ The actions of computer attackers may or may not be seen as crimes under U.S. state and federal law.

- ◆ System administrators should seek written, specific authorization for any actions that might be misunderstood as attempts to breach system or network security.

Like Oregon law, the laws of some other countries and jurisdictions appear to be more explicit than U.S. federal law. In particular, the U.K. Computer Misuse Act reportedly defines and criminalizes denial-of-service attacks.

Risks of Attack

Now that I have characterized computer attackers, turn your attention to the attacks themselves, first considering the sorts of risks posed by attacks. These generally fall into one or more of the following categories:

- ◆ Loss of data integrity

- ◆ Breach of confidentiality

- ◆ Loss of resource availability

LOSS OF DATA INTEGRITY

A particularly serious sort of risk associated with computer attacks is the loss of data integrity. Data integrity is lost when an attacker succeeds in modifying files, programs, the operating system itself, or other data residing on a compromised system.

Often, such modification is well hidden and not readily discovered by administrators of the compromised system. As noted, attackers often create backdoors whereby they can reenter a compromised system, and the attackers often go to considerable lengths to conceal the modifications that constitute the backdoor. For instance, popular rootkits allow attackers to hide files and processes from administrators' scrutiny. Generally, rootkits install modified versions of system software, popularly called *trojans,* after the Trojan horse of antiquity. Some trojans preserve many of the characteristics of the files they mimic, such as length and checksums. In this way, they can escape detection and, hence, removal. In particular, trojan Linux kernel modules can be very difficult to detect.

At other times, modification is obvious – for instance, in the case of a defaced Web site. A particularly serious loss of data integrity is one affecting records of online financial transactions. Many organizations conduct a significant portion of their business via the Internet. The loss of even one day's receipts could be a major blow to such an organization.

One type of data integrity loss that's particularly important to Internet commerce is repudiation. *Repudiation* occurs when a party to a transaction later disavows participation in the transaction. Various forms of identification and authorization, such as electronic "signatures," are used to protect against repudiation. However, an attacker who compromises the security of a system may be able to successfully repudiate, or enable others to repudiate, transactions, thereby gaining something of value for free.

Organizations generally know that they should maintain backups to protect against the loss of data integrity. Backups are generally effective against loss of data integrity resulting from random and non-malicious causes, such as hardware failure. However, backups are potentially less effective in protecting against loss of data integrity arising from malicious action, especially surreptitious modifications. Unlike hardware failures, malicious actions might not be promptly noticed. By the time they're detected, the most recent unaffected backup may be too old to be useful in achieving recovery. So, backups alone provide little protection against loss of data integrity resulting from computer attacks.

BREACH OF CONFIDENTIALITY

Another potentially serious consequence of a computer attack is *breach of confidentiality,* which entails the revelation, publication, or theft and use of privileged information. Breach of confidentiality may be even more difficult to detect than a surreptitious loss of data integrity.

The breach can be significant for any of several reasons beyond the obvious. The information may decline in value as a result of its having been made known to unauthorized persons. Competitors may derive value from access to trade secrets and other privileged information. Or, the inability of the organization to maintain the confidentiality of its information may reflect negatively on its reputation.

As a hypothetical example, consider an organization whose sales list falls into the hands of a competitor, who successfully steals several key accounts as a result. Or, consider an organization whose new product plans are leaked to competitors, who bring their own version of the product to market before the originator can do so. Examples are by no means only hypothetical. For instance, the European Union accused the U.S. government of using electronic equipment to monitor European trade delegations and disclosing the delegations' plans and activities to U.S. competitors. And, news reports of attackers' obtaining access to confidential credit card data occur regularly. However, many such crimes may never be reported. For instance, suppose that a company uses the services of a blackhat to learn the production costs of a competitor. The company can use such information to advantage without sustaining much risk of discovery.

LOSS OF RESOURCE AVAILABILITY

Another possible consequence of an attack is a loss of computing resource availability. Loss of availability is often the result of a DOS attack, as earlier described. Sometimes, such a loss can pose a mere inconvenience, especially if the loss is merely of short duration. Consequences can be more serious, however. On-line merchants, for instance, may suffer serious financial harm as a result of the inability of their customers to complete transactions. Moreover, the damage to a merchant's reputation may be considerable, as customers forgo on-line purchasing in favor of more reliable, traditional alternatives.

Attack Goals

Another way of characterizing attacks is by the short-term goals of the attacker. These types of attacks are generally one or more of the following:

- ◆ Reconnaissance
- ◆ Denial of service
- ◆ Exploitation and compromise

RECONNAISSANCE

Some attacks are preliminary to planned or possible subsequent attacks; that is, they're a form of reconnaissance. When a host or network is subjected to a reconnaissance attack, the attacker is said to be *scanning,* or *probing,* the host or network.

Reconnaissance attacks are not intended to directly compromise services or deny service. However, an inexpertly conducted reconnaissance attack may overwhelm the victim, resulting in a denial of service. Instead, reconnaissance attacks are intended to disclose the identities of hosts and networks, the services they offer, and the versions of operating systems and server software they use. An attacker can use the information gathered during reconnaissance to more efficiently conduct a more damaging attack at another time.

For instance, a reconnaissance attack may disclose that a particular host provides FTP service and may provide the version of the FTP server. If the particular version of the FTP server has a known vulnerability, the attacker can launch a follow-up attack that has a good prospect of success. Blackhats are more apt than script kiddies to launch reconnaissance attacks. Script kiddies tend to throw the proverbial kitchen sink at target hosts without performing significant reconnaissance beforehand. As a result, alert system administrators are much more likely to detect the activities of script kiddies and therefore have the opportunity to implement countermeasures.

A typical reconnaissance attack takes the form of a *host scan,* which scans a particular host for services it makes available. Alternatively, the attack can take the form of a *network scan,* or *service scan*, which scans an entire network for hosts offering one or more particular services. Some scans, termed *noisy scans,* are more likely to be detected than others. Other scans, known as *stealthy scans,* are less likely to be detected. Script kiddies are more apt than blackhats to use noisy scans because they lack the skill to scan more stealthily.

Scans can also be positive or negative, terms that describe how a scanned host responds to the scan. A *positive scan* elicits information in the form of a response by the target host. For example, sending an SYN packet to a host providing a public TCP server elicits an SYN-ACK packet in response. The SYN-ACK packet discloses the public availability of the service. A *negative scan* elicits information in the form of an absence of response by, or on behalf of, the target host. For example, a host not listening on a particular UDP port may respond to a UDP datagram with an ICMP error message. On the other hand, a host actually listening on the port may not respond at all, unless the client is trusted. The absence of an ICMP error message points indirectly to the availability of the UDP service.

Stealthy scans often involve unusual settings of the TCP flags of packets. For example, an *SYN-FIN scan* involves sending packets having the SYN and FIN flags set. These flags should not normally occur in combination because the SYN flag is used in establishing TCP connections and the FIN flag is used in tearing down TCP connections. Some firewalls are relatively permeable to SYN-FIN scans, which can therefore be an effective attack tool.

The tool named nmap, a popular reconnaissance tool, can be useful for testing the operation of a firewall, as explained in Chapter 12, "Testing and Troubleshooting a Firewall." The nmap tool is part of the Red Hat Linux distribution. You can learn more about nmap from its Web page, at http://www.insecure.org/nmap/.

DENIAL OF SERVICE

As mentioned, some attacks are intended to prevent the use, or impair the performance, of hosts or networks. Such attacks often involve sending the targets large volumes of data. To achieve large data volume, denial-of-service attackers may employ multiple attacking hosts. Sometimes, many attacking hosts are used. Generally, the packets that are sent have been specially crafted to tax the resources of the target. Not all denial-of-service attacks involve sending large volumes of data. Sometimes, specially crafted packets can impair the performance of hosts or networks even when relatively few such packets are sent.

A well-known type of denial-of-service attack is known as a Smurf, after the diminutive blue children's cartoon characters. A *Smurf attack* entails sending ICMP echo request packets having a broadcast address as their destination address. The packets are sent to a third-party network, not to the victim network. Hosts on the third-party network respond to the ICMP echo requests by sending ICMP echo replies to the host indicated by the source address of the ICMP echo requests. However, the attacker *spoofs* the source address; that is, the attacker uses the IP address of the victim host as the source address of the ICMP echo requests. Special packet-construction programs enable nonprogrammers to generate such packets.

A Smurf attack can overwhelm its victim because of a phenomenon known as *multiplication*. Because the echo requests are sent to a broadcast address, each host on the third-party network can potentially respond. Therefore, each echo request can trigger the sending of dozens or even hundreds of echo replies to the victim network, saturating and overwhelming its capacity. Figure 3-1 shows how a Smurf attack works.

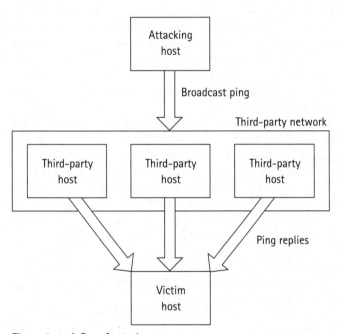

Figure 3-1: A Smurf attack

It's difficult or impossible to avoid being the victim of a Smurf attack. However, network administrators who properly configure their networks can prevent them from being used by Smurf attackers as the means of attacking other networks. A firewall should not permit packets bearing a network's broadcast address to enter from the Internet or other external interface. However, many network administrators have not properly configured their networks. At the time of this writing, the Smurf Amplification Registry Web page, http://www.powertech.no/smurf/, identifies 311 networks that are not properly configured. Since its inception, that site has identified 192,510 misconfigured networks that have subsequently been properly configured. The site includes an easy-to-use feature that lets you test your own network's configuration.

Most denial-of-service attacks are simply that: They aim to deny the use of a network or host. Occasionally, however, a denial-of-service attack is conducted as part of a larger attack aimed at compromising a host or network. A sophisticated attack known as *man in the middle* involves taking a trusted host offline so that a host controlled by the attacker can masquerade as the trusted host and use the fraudulent trust relationship to undermine the security of target hosts.

EXPLOITATION AND COMPROMISE

Having one's network scanned or subjected to a denial-of-service attack can be worrisome. But the type of attack most feared by network administrators is the exploitation-and-compromise attack. This sort of attack more often leads to serious harm than do reconnaissance or denial-of-service attacks. In particular, exploitation-and-compromise attacks often lead to a loss of data integrity or breach of confidentiality, which are generally more serious consequences than a lack of resource availability.

Exploitation-and-compromise attacks are made possible by human error. Often, the error is a defect in a software application or operating system. Network or host misconfiguration is another common cause.

Two popular types of exploitation-and-compromise attacks are buffer overflow attacks and format string overflow attacks. In each case, the attacker manages to supply a program with more data than the programmer anticipated. The result is that the data overwrites areas of program memory designed for other purposes. An attacker who is particularly clever in the choice of data provided may implant machine code instructions and cause the program to execute them. Typically, the implanted instructions perform an operation that confers special privileges on the user running the program (the attacker) or nullifies some security safeguard.

Buffer overflow and format string overflow attacks depend on programming errors. However, programming is a complex activity, and most sophisticated programs contain numerous defects, some of which may be exploitable. Such a defect is known as *vulnerability*. A program or recipe for taking advantage of a known vulnerability is known as an *exploit*. Some exploits, known as *local exploits*, can be run only by users logged in to a host. Other exploits, known as *remote exploits*, can be used even by remote users.

Attackers use many means other than buffer and format string overflow attacks to compromise systems. Taking advantage of absent or poorly contrived passwords is one common means. Another is sample programs, which are often installed with servers such as Microsoft Internet Information Server (IIS) or Macromedia ColdFusion. Often, sample programs lack sufficient security provisions. For example, some sample programs permit a user to view or download any file from the system on which they reside. Removing or securing sample programs is a prudent system administration practice, as is ensuring that all user accounts are properly protected by strong passwords.

Defense Principles

This section surveys some broad principles that should guide the design of defensive countermeasures intended to thwart computer attacks. Many of these principles are familiar slogans. Like most slogans, the principles are not to be applied strictly. In a real-world situation, one must often trade off these principles against one another and against other considerations, such as cost or schedule. Therefore, it's best to view the principles as describing an ideal that we strive to achieve rather than a recipe or roadmap.

However, you can use the principles to provide a quick assessment of the adequacy of the security measures protecting a host or network. For convenience, ten principles are presented here. Scoring the host or network on each principle, award 0, ½, or 1 point for each principle. Add the total, a number from 0 to 10, and use the traditional classroom grading scale:

- ◆ A = 9 points and higher
- ◆ B = 8 to 8½ points
- ◆ C = 7 to 7½ points
- ◆ D = 6 to 6½ points
- ◆ F = 0 to 5½ points

Rather than focus on firewalls, the principles take a general view of network security. You'll find that although the principles mention firewalls from time to time, the emphasis is on the overall design of defensive countermeasures. This emphasis is appropriate because the term *firewall* hasn't yet been defined in this book or the operation of typical firewalls explained.

The definition of *firewalls* and the operation of typical firewalls are covered in Chapter 5, "Firewall Architecture."

Principle 1: Upping the Ante

A strong defense ups the ante on the attacker. That is, it aims at requiring the attacker to spend more time and effort in attacking the network than a rational attacker – one who expends no more effort than might thereby be gained – would choose to spend. As implied earlier in this chapter, upping the ante isn't always sufficient to protect a network because some attackers act irrationally. For example, an irrational attacker may choose to attack a hardened target that has little value, simply for what he or she perceives as the inherent challenge. However, upping the ante is a necessary practice if security is to repel the rational attacker.

A corollary principle is that when defensive resources are limited, they should be allocated to provide greater protection to vulnerable parts of a network and resources that might be valuable to attackers. A defense that provides the same, small degree of protection to each host and service fails to up the ante.

Principle 2: Least Privilege

The bedrock of security is the principle of least privilege: Extend only necessary privileges to each user, host, and network. Behind this principle lies the notion of a security policy, a document reviewed and blessed by management, specifying what privileges will be extended and to whom and under what circumstances.

Management concurrence in a security policy is necessary because users generally find security cumbersome. Users are rewarded for performing their job functions, not for repelling attackers. So, security measures that slightly impede users' performance – even while thwarting a variety of potentially serious attacks – may not be seen by users as warranted or desirable. Some particularly forgetful and grumpy users may go so far as to balk at the simple and ordinary requirement that their user accounts be protected by confidential passwords. Without management concurrence, such users may hold network administrators responsible for what they perceive as unnecessarily onerous security measures.

Another way of looking at the principle of least privilege is to think of it as the principle of least trust. Simply put, computer attacks succeed when trust is abused – that is, when a trusted user or host behaves in an untrustworthy manner. Therefore, an important defensive countermeasure is to extend trust cautiously and sparingly.

Trust is more ubiquitous than may be obvious. One particularly important privilege is the privilege of remotely accessing a service. Services that can be accessed only locally or from trusted hosts are more easily monitored and supervised than services offered to the general public. One key role of a firewall is to exclude non-trusted hosts from accessing protected services.

However, not all services can be restricted to trusted hosts. For instance, an on-line retailer cannot reasonably restrict customers from remotely accessing its Web servers, for obvious reasons. Nevertheless, many services are not intended for, or needed by, the general public, such as those used to remotely administer systems. These should be identified and restricted.

Principle 3: Restrictive versus Permissive Policies

The security principle that is perhaps most often violated is the principle of restrictive versus permissive policies. The principle applies to firewalls and to defensive countermeasures generally. With respect to firewalls, the principle observes that you can configure a firewall in either of two ways:

- ◆ To block known bad traffic
- ◆ To accept only traffic known to be good

The first firewall configuration is termed *permissive*. The second configuration is termed *restrictive*.

At first, the two configurations may seem to be the same. However, they're not because three kinds of traffic exist:

- Traffic known to be good

- Traffic known to be bad

- Indeterminate traffic – that is, traffic that might be good or bad

The two firewall configurations differ in their handling of the third kind of traffic, indeterminate traffic not confidently identified as either good or bad. A permissive firewall accepts indeterminate traffic, whereas a restrictive firewall does not.

From a security standpoint, the restrictive firewall is ideal. If an unanticipated type of traffic is presented to a restrictive firewall, the restrictive firewall blocks it. In contrast, if a permissive firewall is passed unanticipated traffic, the permissive firewall accepts it. The permissive firewall, therefore, is vulnerable to novel attacks that have not been anticipated and specifically blocked.

As explained earlier in this chapter, however, *vulnerability* is not the only term in the security policy equation. Organizations don't invest in computing resources merely to employ network administrators to secure them. Someone has observed that the only secure computer is one that's disconnected from the network, disconnected from its power source, encased in concrete, and buried 50 feet underground. However, a sufficiently motivated attacker could manage to compromise even a computer subjected to these ridiculously stringent security measures.

Instead, organizations expect their computing resources to be useful. In some organizations, such as research laboratories, flexibility is a particularly important parameter. Research scientists, for instance, often feel that they cannot be bothered with consulting network administrators every time they decide to use their computing resources in a new way. Serving such users properly may entail the configuration of a permissive firewall. Management should authorize and approve a security policy that appropriately balances security against flexibility and other business-value concerns, such as productivity. However, strictly from the standpoint of security, the restrictive firewall configuration is the more resistant to attack.

Principle 4: Weakest Link

A proverb has it that a chain is no stronger than its weakest link. This proverb is true of defensive countermeasures as well as of chains. An intelligent attacker strives to find the weakest component of a network or host and attacks that component. Such a strategy is the reason behind reconnaissance attacks.

Therefore, no assets should be left undefended that might fall prey to an attacker who could then use them to attack better-defended hosts. This advice is especially crucial when trust relationships exist between hosts – for example, when users are allowed to log in to a heavily protected host from only one or another of a set of trusted hosts.

Another way of looking at this principle is to see that it implies having a wide rather than a narrow network perimeter. Figure 3-2 illustrates this concept.

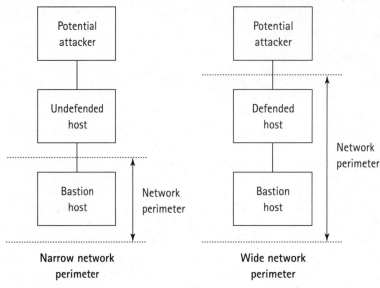

Figure 3-2: Narrow and wide network perimeters

Principle 5: Defense in Depth

The principle of defense in depth holds that a good defense is one that requires an attacker to overcome multiple countermeasures. Defense in depth provides two main benefits. Requiring an attacker to overcome multiple countermeasures ups the ante and may discourage rational attackers. Moreover, defense in depth protects computing resources against possible errors and oversights by defenders. If one countermeasure is improperly configured and therefore ineffective, other counter-measures may nevertheless thwart an attack. Lawyers speak of this principle when they refer to "belt and suspenders"; the point is that a careful man uses both a belt and suspenders to hold his trousers in place.

A corollary principle to defense in depth is that a single firewall is not sufficient in itself to protect the security of a network. Even the best firewall is likely to have weaknesses. Therefore, an effective defense supplements the firewall with additional countermeasures, such as TCP wrappers and host intrusion detection monitoring.

For more information on these and other countermeasures, see Chapter 11, "Bastion Host Implementation," and *Red Hat Linux Security and Optimization,* by Mohammed J. Kabir (Red Hat Press/Wiley, 2002).

Principle 6: Defense in Breadth

The principle of defense in breadth is closely related to the principle of defense in depth. A defense that uses only a single type of countermeasure can be considered deep if it uses multiple instances of the countermeasure. For example, a defense consisting of multiple firewalls could be considered deep. A broad defense, on the other hand, must consist of multiple types of countermeasures.

Breadth is important because hosts and countermeasures of a single type tend to share vulnerabilities. One way to add breadth to a defense is by using multiple platform types; for example, combining a Red Hat Linux–based firewall with commercial firewall such as those offered by CheckPoint or Cisco. These dissimilar platforms are unlikely to suffer from the same design or implementation defect, if any, and are therefore unlikely to share vulnerabilities.

However, as explained in Chapter 5, "Firewall Architecture," all packet-filtering firewalls work in a fundamentally similar fashion: They inspect the headers of incoming packets and accept or reject each packet accordingly. So, even dissimilar firewalls may be vulnerable to a single attack if that attack is not recognizable by the contents of packet headers. Using multiple firewalls is more like using belt and belt than belt and suspenders.

Using dissimilar types of countermeasures provides more breadth and more effective defense than a single type of countermeasure, even if that countermeasure is implemented on dissimilar platforms.

Principle 7: Single Choke Point

Like many principles of defense, the principle of the single choke point can be seen in the design of medieval castles. Figure 3-3 shows a typical castle entry, consisting of inner and outer gates and a narrow passage. Attackers must negotiate the narrow passage, called a *choke point,* before entering the courtyard. Because the passage is small, it accommodates only a few attackers at a time. Consequently, even if the defenders are outnumbered, they may be able to hold the castle against attack.

A well-designed network defense likewise forces traffic through one choke point or, at most, a few choke points. It's more economical to thoroughly protect a few choke points than to protect every host on a network. Of course, the principles of defense in depth and breadth may – and should – lead you to implement defensive countermeasures throughout your network. However, such countermeasures are apt to be supplementary and supportive of primary measures located at a few choke points. Indeed, the primary role of a firewall is to serve as such a choke point. A network that can be entered in many possible ways undermines the effectiveness of the firewall and places stress on the hosts that are protected by secondary countermeasures.

Principle 8: Security through Obscurity

Some open source advocates have given the phrase *security through obscurity* a negative connotation. Their perspective is that software manufacturers often write insecure code that is easily compromised by anyone having the right knowledge. In other words, the manufacturers rely merely on the scarcity of relevant knowledge to protect their inherently insecure products. This irresponsible approach suffers from several difficulties. For instance, as computer literacy increases, formerly scarce knowledge becomes more widely known. The result is that software is less secure.

In contrast to most commercial software, for which the source code is held confidential as proprietary, open source software is by its nature open for inspection. Therefore, some open source advocates maintain, open source software is less reliant on security through obscurity and is therefore more secure.

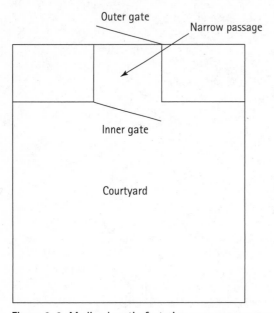

Figure 3-3: Medieval castle featuring a narrow passage

But, such arguments can go too far. Certainly, an intentional reliance on a mere lack of knowledge to protect an otherwise flawed product is unwise. But the actual problem lies with the flaws. For instance, is a well-designed and -constructed combination lock faulty because it relies merely on an attacker's ignorance of its combination? Or, is the concept of login authentication flawed because it relies on the use of confidential passwords? Most people agree that secrecy has its place in security.

The principle of *security through obscurity* holds that concealing information from potential attackers is an important element of defense. To determine whether security through obscurity is being properly employed in defense of a network, ask yourself whether security of the network *depends* on secrecy or whether security of the network is *enhanced* by the concealment of network information. You should up the ante on the attacker by making the attacker work for every bit of information about your networks and hosts. For example, don't make DNS information concerning internal hosts available to external hosts. There's no point in giving attackers a free roadmap of your network. Instead, run separate DNS servers for internal and external use and disable zone transfers except to trusted hosts.

 Red Hat Linux Security and Optimization, by Mohammed J. Kabir (Red Hat Press/Wiley, 2002), presents useful information on securing DNS and other Internet services.

Principle 9: Social Engineering Countermeasures

Hosts and networks are sometimes compromised by computer attacks. But, they often fall victim to much more low-tech forms of aggression. For instance, clever attackers have sometimes obtained high-level passwords by pretending to be busy executives who have forgotten passwords and browbeating help desk personnel to disclose them. "Dumpster diving" for (unwisely) unshredded documents containing confidential information is another well-known technique. Such low-tech approaches are known as *social engineering* because they directly target the human side of the organization rather than the technological. However, they're ultimately no less effective than more high-tech approaches.

A key countermeasure to social engineering is more social engineering, in the form of training and policies. Employees must be alerted to the threat to the organization posed by computer attacks and must be directed to follow policies that restrict them from inappropriately disclosing information or otherwise compromising the security of the organization's systems. Computer security policies must address the protection of noncomputerized data that could lead to the compromise of computer systems. For instance, documents that describe network security measures should be shredded before disposal. Because training consumes organizational resources and requires the cooperation of the trainees and the trainees' superiors, management must authorize training programs and the policies they aim at inculcating.

Principle 10: Simplicity

The final principle, simplicity, is one that must underlie the application of every other principle. The notion of simplicity does not imply that countermeasures should not be elaborate. Instead, it means that they should be no more elaborate than required. As Albert Einstein wrote, "Everything should be made as simple as possible, but not simpler" (*Reader's Digest*, October 1977). Human error is a chief source of security vulnerabilities and, with other things equal, humans are more likely to avoid error in simple rather than complicated contexts.

One helpful technique for achieving simplicity is to draw diagrams and maps. The human mind is adept at grasping concepts from visual patterns. Therefore, by representing countermeasures visually, you may be able to discover alternative countermeasures and configurations of countermeasures that are simpler than those now used or planned.

But, the principle of simplicity is not a mere technique. Instead, it is an attitude or determination. In assessing whether simplicity characterizes a network's defenses, don't focus on diagrams or on the countermeasures themselves. Instead, ask yourself whether the network's administrators seem to understand the virtue of simplicity. If they do, you can be reasonably sure that the network reflects the benefits of simplicity. If, on the other hand, the administrators seem more likely to elaborate than to simplify or seem to be more zealous of the capabilities of their tools than interested in improving their skills, you can be reasonably sure that their networks lack simplicity.

Vigilance

The tenth principle, simplicity, was seen to be as much a characteristic of a network's administrators as of the network. Another criterion of effectiveness, one therefore not given as a principle, is wholly a characteristic of a network's administrators rather than of their network. That characteristic is vigilance.

Effective network administrators are vigilant in the sense of leaving no stone unturned in their efforts to secure their networks. It's relatively easy to discern whether network administrators are vigilant by assessing how they monitor network events. Particularly inattentive administrators may avoid monitoring altogether, postponing action until the advent of a crisis. Somewhat more attentive administrators may give event logs a quick look-see now and then. The vigilant administrator, however, is not content until he or she understands the cause and significance of every log entry. Vigilance is a rare quality because many – perhaps most – network events are *false positives;* that is, they have no special significance. Therefore, as often as not, chasing them down leads to nothing novel. That's why the vigilant network administrator is so valuable to the organization that employs him or her. Only the most stalwart and devoted administrator persists in investigating anomalies, knowing from the beginning that chances are they're unimportant. However, only a vigilant administrator finds the unexpected and thereby buys an organization time to shore up its defenses in the face of what might otherwise have been a lethal attack.

A crucial manifestation of vigilance is the timely updating of software in response to updates and errata issued by software vendors. A great majority of computer attacks are perpetrated by script kiddies using well-known attacks for which software vendors have long since issued updates and errata. Administrators who timely respond to update and errata notices can protect themselves against such attacks. Therefore, timely response to update and errata notices is the single most important means of defending your hosts and networks.

Summary

In this chapter, you've learned about security threats, attackers, and attacks. You've also learned several principles of defense that should guide you in designing defensive countermeasures to protect your networks.

In Chapter 4, you learn about common Internet services. In particular, you learn what ports they use and the structure of their communications dialogs. These ports and dialogs form the basis of firewall rules that you use to accept desired traffic and reject undesired traffic. You also learn about several Red Hat Linux tools important to the operation and monitoring of Internet services.

Chapter 4

Internet Services

THIS CHAPTER DESCRIBES THE CHARACTERISTICS of network traffic that are relevant to the design and operation of packet-filtering firewalls and explains important terms that identify the traffic characteristics. The chapter describes in particular the characteristics of several dozen commonly used TCP/IP application protocols. In addition, it describes several Red Hat Linux tools that are important in administering and troubleshooting services.

Like other chapters in Part I, this chapter's treatment of these topics is not comprehensive. However, it does include all the information about services and datagrams that you're likely to need in constructing Red Hat Linux–based firewalls.

Network Traffic

Red Hat Linux–based firewalls are generally implemented as packet-filtering firewalls. You learn more about packet-filtering firewalls in Chapter 5, "Firewall Architecture." Essentially, a packet-filtering firewall looks at packet headers and accepts or rejects packets according to the header contents.

Chapter 2, "TCP/IP Quick Start," describes the structure of common TCP/IP packet types. Several packet header fields described in Chapter 2 are especially important in firewall design and operation. These fields include the protocol, source and destination port, source and destination IP address, and TCP flags.

Protocol

The protocol field of the IP header identifies the member protocol of the TCP/IP protocol family encapsulated by the IP datagram. The primary protocols of concern in the design and operation of firewalls are shown in this list:

- ◆ TCP

- ◆ UDP

- ◆ ICMP

Source and Destination Port

TCP and UDP datagrams include a source and destination port. Recall from Chapter 2 that ports are numbered ranging from 1 to 65535. Ports 1 to 1023 are known as *system* ports, whereas ports 1024 to 65535 are known as *ephemeral* ports.

The source and destination ports are used to indicate the application layer protocol encapsulated by the TCP or UDP datagram. Recall that application layers protocols specify how data in the body of the datagram is structured. HTTP and FTP are examples of common application layer protocols.

Bear in mind that the association between a port number and the service that uses a particular application layer protocol is an arbitrary one. For instance, running a Web server on port 80 is standard practice; however, a system administrator can choose to run a Web server on port 8080 or some other port. Therefore, the association between a port number and a service is fixed for a given host and time. But, the association can vary across hosts and time.

ICMP Type and Code

ICMP packets are used to communicate information about errors and network status. Unlike TCP and UDP datagrams, ICMP packets have no source or destination port. But, ICMP packets include two fields not found in TCP or UDP datagrams: ICMP type and ICMP code. These fields indicate the nature of the ICMP packet. The ICMP type indicates general information, whereas the ICMP code indicates more detailed information. For instance, the ICMP type value 3 indicates that a packet failed to reach its destination. The ICMP code value indicates the reason for the failure.

Source and Destination IP Addresses

Most computer network traffic consists of two-way communication between hosts. The host that initiates communication is the *client,* and the host that responds is the *server.* The IP datagram includes fields that indicate the IP address of the datagram source and destination hosts. A datagram flowing from the client to the server is a *request datagram,* whereas a datagram flowing from the server to the client is a *reply datagram* or *response datagram.*

For a request datagram, the source IP address is generally the address of the client, and the destination address is generally the address of the server. Conversely, for a reply datagram, the source IP address is generally the address of the server, and the destination address is generally the address of the client. ICMP datagrams don't always follow this principle. In particular, ICMP datagrams indicating an error condition can arise in response to request or reply datagrams. Moreover, ICMP datagrams indicating an error condition can originate in a host other than the client or server, such as a router between the client and server.

Another exception to the principle arises when the source or destination address is a broadcast address. For instance, a request datagram having a broadcast destination address has multiple potential servers. So, in the case of a broadcast address, the principle can be generalized to state that the destination address of a request datagram *includes* the address of the originating server or that the destination address indicates one or more servers.

TCP Flags

The TCP flags in a TCP datagram contain useful information about the status of a TCP connection. TCP flags that are particularly important to the design and operation of firewalls include the SYN and ACK flags. Recall that the SYN flag is used when establishing a TCP connection. The ACK flag is used when establishing a connection and for data transfer across an established connection.

Traffic Flow

Implicit in the source and destination IP addresses of an IP datagram is the characteristic known as *traffic flow* or *direction*. Some IP addresses are considered part of the protected network — the network protected by a firewall — whereas most IP addresses are not. Each datagram is therefore one of the following:

- An *inbound* datagram has a source address outside the network and a destination address inside the network.

- An *outbound* datagram has a source address inside the network and a destination address outside the network.

- An *internal* datagram has source and destination addresses inside the network.

Table 4-1 summarizes the rules for classifying datagrams by traffic flow. Most firewalls focus on inbound traffic. However, as you learn in Chapter 5, addressing outbound traffic is also important. Internal traffic is not generally a primary firewall concern. However, as explained in Chapter 5, large organizations may place firewalls between segments of their networks. In these cases, the firewalls can be said to filter internal traffic. But, another way of looking at these cases is to consider the term *network* as referring to the segments of a large network rather than to the entire network. From that perspective, the rule that firewalls are concerned primarily with inbound and outbound traffic continues to apply.

TABLE 4-1 TRAFFIC FLOW CATEGORIES

Source	Destination	Category
Internal	Internal	Internal
Internal	External	Outbound
External	Internal	Inbound

Firewalls: Actions, Rules, and States

Chapter 5 describes firewalls in detail. However, for purposes of this chapter, a simple characterization of a packet-filtering firewall is needed. Basically, a packet-filtering firewall consists of these components:

- A multi-homed host
- A set of firewall actions
- A set of firewall rules
- A set of firewall states

A firewall host must be multi-homed because it joins two networks – the internal and the external. Packets cannot flow between these networks except by permission of the firewall. Let's look at the sets of actions, rules, and states that make up a typical packet-filtering firewall.

Firewall Actions

A typical packet-filtering firewall examines network traffic and performs one of these actions:

- Accept
- Drop
- Reject

To allow a packet to flow from one network to another, the firewall *accepts* the packet. The firewall protects networks by accepting only authorized packets.

A firewall that detects an unauthorized packet can drop or reject the packet. Dropping or rejecting a packet is known as *blocking* the packet. When a firewall blocks a packet, the packet is not allowed to pass from one network to another.

The two ways of blocking a packet – dropping and rejecting – differ slightly. When a firewall *drops* a packet, the sender of the packet is not notified of the event. Generally, the sender tries again, sending another packet – known as a *retry packet* – and waiting for a response. Eventually, if no response is received, the sender *times out* – that is, it determines that that the destination host or service is down or otherwise unavailable and ceases sending retry packets. Dropping unwanted packets is sometimes referred to as working in *stealth mode,* because an attacker who sends packets to a stealth mode host has no way of telling that the host is listening. In contrast, when a firewall *rejects* a packet, the firewall sends an ICMP error message to the sender. This error message notifies the sender that the destination host or service is unavailable. Therefore, the sender does not send retry packets.

The terms *drop* and *reject* are not universally understood as defined here. The usage given here conforms to that used in the context of Red Hat Linux IPTables firewalls. If you're communicating with someone having a different background, be sure that you're both using consistent definitions of these and other important terms.

Firewalls can generally perform a fourth action: logging. *Logging* a packet writes a record of the packet to a log so that an administrator can review firewall traffic and the operation of the firewall. Logs help verify that a firewall is functioning properly. They can also alert administrators to successful and failed attempts to compromise network security. Logging is not mutually exclusive of the other three actions. That is, you can log packets before accepting, dropping, or rejecting them.

Accepted packets are generally not logged because they're numerous and logs must have a manageable size or else they're too expensive to review. However, logging dropped and rejected packets is generally important because blocking packets disrupts communication. If the communication was authorized and therefore should not have been blocked, the log can help administrators detect and repair the problem. If the communication was unauthorized, the log can alert administrators to the network intrusion. However, as mentioned, logs must be of a manageable size. Therefore, it's common to omit logging of packets routinely blocked in large volume. Selectively logging accepted packets is often helpful, in order to have a record of network activity. So, the principle that accepted packets are not logged whereas dropped and rejects packets are logged is a broad principle with common exceptions.

Firewall Rules

To determine whether to accept or block a packet, a firewall uses a set of rules. The rules associate an action – accepting, dropping, or rejecting a packet – with a set of packet characteristics, such as protocol, port number, IP addresses category, and TCP flag values. Schematically, a firewall rule might resemble the following:

Source Addr.	Dest. Addr.	Protocol	Source Port	Dest. Port	SYN	Action
any	10.0.2.1	TCP	>1023	22	Yes	Accept

This firewall rule specifies that TCP traffic from any source to the host 10.0.2.1 should be accepted, as long as the source port is greater than 1023, the destination port is 22, and the datagram's TCP SYN flag is set. Beginning in the following section, I use a similar schematic form to represent the characteristics of application layer protocols.

Firewall design includes the process of determining the optimum firewall rule set for a given network. Firewall rules are one of two types:

- *Ingress rules* specify actions for inbound packets.

- *Egress rules* specify actions for outbound packets.

Firewall States

Two major types of packet-filtering firewalls exist: *non-stateful packet-filtering firewalls* and *stateful packet-filtering firewalls.* Non-stateful packet-filtering firewalls inspect only datagram headers, as explained previously in this chapter. Stateful packet-filtering firewalls maintain a database, called the *state table,* that tracks datagrams accepted by the firewall. Using the state table, a firewall can determine whether an arriving datagram is part of an existing, authorized communication.

Stateful firewalls have two potential advantages over non-stateful firewalls. A stateful firewall can potentially operate more quickly than a non-stateful firewall. When a datagram is part of an existing communication, the firewall does not need to compare the datagram's characteristics with the firewall rule set, which may entail evaluating dozens or hundreds of rules. Instead, the firewall can simply accept the datagram. Whenever the process of checking the state table can be performed more quickly than evaluating the rule set – which is typically the case – the stateful firewall outperforms the non-stateful firewall.

Moreover, the stateful firewall is potentially more secure. Non-stateful firewalls, which lack a state table, depend on the TCP ACK flag to indicate that a TCP datagram is part of an existing communication. If the sender of a datagram fraudulently sets the ACK flag, a nonstateful firewall may believe that the datagram is part of an existing connection and therefore accept the datagram. As a result, the security of the firewall and the network it protects may be compromised.

The Red Hat Linux IPTables firewall is a stateful firewall. Its state table defines four connection states:

- New
- Established
- Related
- Invalid

In this context, the term *connection* is broader than when used in the context of the TCP protocol. Here, the term refers to an entry in the state table. The entry can pertain to TCP or UDP communication between hosts. Connections are identified by protocol, source and destination IP address, and source and destination port. A new connection is created whenever a client attempts to contact a server. The connection is maintained during this communication. When the communication terminates, the connection is removed. The connection is also removed after a long period of inactivity. Doing so prevents the table from becoming cluttered with unnecessary connections and eventually running out of space for new connections.

The state of a connection is changed from new to established whenever the server responds. The term *established* does not have its usual TCP/IP meaning, which is a TCP connection having a completed three-way handshake as explained in Chapter 2. Instead, the first datagram that establishes two-way communication is deemed to have established the connection.

A related connection is one that has an association with an established connection but involves a different protocol, source or destination IP address, or source or destination port. A simple example of a related connection is the ICMP datagram sent by a router when communication across an established connection is interrupted. The router's IP address is distinct from that of the client and server, so the ICMP error datagram is not part of an established connection. But, the ICMP datagram is clearly related to the established connection. In the section "Active versus Passive Mode FTP," you see further examples of related connections.

The connection state of a datagram has the value `invalid` when an error occurs during the processing of the datagram, the datagram is an ICMP error message not related to an existing connection, or in some other anomalous situation. Generally, for obvious reasons, a firewall blocks invalid datagrams.

Examples of Packet Filtering

To better understand how packet how packet filtering of application layer protocols works, let's examine two common protocols: Secure Shell Protocol (SSH) and File Transfer Protocol (FTP).

Secure Shell Protocol (SSH)

The Secure Shell Protocol (SSH) is commonly used to remotely log in to a server and execute shell commands. SSH options also enable users to copy files to and from remote hosts and create tunnels — or virtual private networks — that enable programs to send and receive encrypted data via the network. The SSH protocol and related programs were carefully designed and implemented to provide secure communications and employ cryptographic technology to protect against eavesdroppers. However, they have not proven completely immune to defects and consequent security vulnerabilities. Hence, SSH has become a favored tool of both system administrators and attackers.

Figure 4-1 shows the operation of the SSH protocol. On the client, an ephemeral (user) port is used; on the server, port 22 is used. Recall that a system administrator can configure the SSH service to run on a port other than port 22, if desired. However, clients cannot contact the service unless they're aware of the port on which it runs.

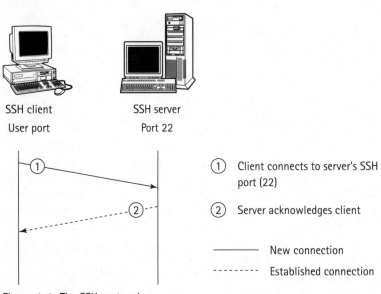

Figure 4-1: The SSH protocol

The client initiates communication by sending a datagram to port 22 of the server. The server replies with a datagram sent to the port used by the client. A stateful firewall considers the first datagram to be part of a new connection. The second and subsequent datagrams are part of an established connection. After the client and server have exchanged datagrams, the exchange of application data commences.

Table 4-2 summarizes the datagram characteristics of the SSH protocol. Notice that

- Datagrams sent by the client have a user (ephemeral) port as the source port and port 22 of the server as the destination port.
- Datagrams sent by the server have port 22 as the source port and the client's user port as the destination port.
- The client's initial datagram has the TCP `SYN` flag set.
- The server's acknowledgement has the TCP `SYN` and `ACK` flags set.
- Subsequent datagrams of the established TCP connection have the TCP `ACK` flag set.

TABLE 4-2 THE SSH PROTOCOL

Conn. State	Source Addr.	Dest. Addr.	Protocol	Source Port	Dest. Port	SYN	Ack	Notes
New	Client	Server	TCP	>1023	22	Yes	No	Client opens SSH connection to server
Est.	Server	Client	TCP	22	>1023	Yes	Yes	Server acknowledges client
Est.	Client	Server	TCP	>1023	22	No	Yes	Established TCP connection, client to server
Est.	Server	Client	TCP	22	>1023	No	Yes	Established TCP connection, server to client

The protocol information presented in the table is all that's required to create firewall rules that control SSH access to hosts protected by a firewall. You learn how to create such rules in Chapter 7, "IPChains Firewalls," and Chapter 8, "The IPTables Facility."

The AUTH Service

Many SSH servers are configured to attempt to verify the identity of clients by using the AUTH protocol – also known as the IDENTD protocol – which is described in the section "AUTH." Generally, servers permit access even if AUTH verification is not possible; however, it may require several seconds for the server's AUTH request to time out.

The proper configuration for a host that supports SSH clients depends on whether the host runs AUTH. If the host runs AUTH, configure the firewall to accept AUTH traffic. If the host does not run AUTH, configure the firewall to reject AUTH traffic. Don't configure the firewall to merely drop AUTH traffic, or else your SSH clients may experience annoying delays. If you're especially security conscious, however, you may prefer that your clients sustain such delays in the interest of further concealing information about your network.

 You can also configure an SSH server for compatibility with the .rhosts and .hosts.equiv authentication methods used by the Berkeley r-commands, described in the section "Remote User Services." When using r-command authentication methods, the client uses ports in the range 513–1023 rather than ports above 1023. However, the authentication methods used by the Berkeley r-commands are less secure than the SSH default method, and therefore they should not generally be used over a public network.

FTP

The datagram characteristics of most TCP application protocols resemble those of SSH, as you see in the next section. The datagrams of UDP application protocols and ICMP datagrams are not very different, as you also will see. However, a few exceptions exist.

One notable exception is File Transfer Protocol (FTP), which is widely used for transferring files across private and public networks. Popular Web browsers provide built-in support for FTP. An FTP server can be set up to allow anonymous access or to allow access to only authenticated users. However, unlike SSH, FTP sends all information across the network in unencrypted form. An eavesdropper can intercept FTP communications and read the client's password and any information exchanged between the client and server.

FTP has two modes of operation:

◆ Passive mode

◆ Active mode

Most Web browsers use passive mode FTP by default. Many FTP clients let the user choose passive or active mode. Most FTP servers support both modes.

However, a few support only one mode or the other. The two modes differ significantly in their datagram characteristics. Therefore, I examine them serially.

PASSIVE MODE FTP

Passive mode FTP uses a pair of TCP connections. One connection is used for commands and replies; the other connection is used for data. Figure 4-2 depicts the operation of passive mode FTP. Using an ephemeral port, the client sends a datagram to port 21 of the server. The server then acknowledges the client by sending a response datagram. The server's response tells the client which server port to use as the data port. Next, the client opens the data connection by using an ephemeral port to send a datagram to the server's data port, which is an ephemeral port. The server acknowledges the client by sending a response packet. Thereafter, the client and server freely exchange commands, command responses, and data.

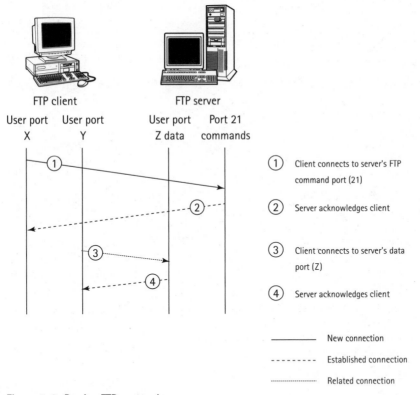

Figure 4-2: Passive FTP protocol

Table 4-3 summarizes the passive mode FTP protocol. Notice the following information about the protocol:

- The client opens two connections to the server – one for commands and one for data.

- Two ports are used on the client, and two ports are used on the server.

- The server command port is port 21.

- The client ports and server data port are ephemeral ports.

- The datagrams used by the client to open the command and data connections and the associated datagrams sent by the server in reply have the TCP SYN flag set.

- The datagrams sent by the server in reply to client requests have the TCP SYN and ACK flags set.

- The datagrams associated with the established command and data connections have the TCP ACK flag set.

TABLE 4-3 PASSIVE FTP PROTOCOL

Conn. State	Source Addr.	Dest. Addr.	Protocol	Source Port	Dest. Port	SYN	ACK	Notes
New	Client	Server	TCP	>1023	21	Yes	No	Client opens FTP command connection to server
Est.	Server	Client	TCP	21	>1023	Yes	Yes	Server acknowledges client
Rel.	Client	Server	TCP	>1023	>1023	Yes	No	Client opens FTP data connection to server
Est.	Server	Client	TCP	>1023	>1023	Yes	Yes	Server acknowledges client
Est.	Client	Server	TCP	>1023	21	No	Yes	Established TCP connection, client to server
Est.	Client	Server	TCP	>1023	>1023	No	Yes	Established TCP connection, client to server

Conn. State	Source Addr.	Dest. Addr.	Protocol	Source Port	Dest. Port	SYN	ACK	Notes
Est.	Server	Client	TCP	21	>1023	No	Yes	Established TCP connection, server to client
Est.	Server	Client	TCP	>1023	>1023	No	Yes	Established TCP connection, server to client

ACTIVE MODE FTP

Active mode FTP is the older of the two FTP modes. Sometimes, it is referred to as normal mode FTP or standard mode FTP. Recall that in passive mode FTP, the client opens two connections to the server, one for commands and one for data. Active mode FTP, like passive mode, uses two connections. However, in active mode FTP, the client opens the command connection, but the server opens the data connection.

Figure 4-3 depicts the operation of active mode FTP. The client uses an ephemeral port to open the command connection to port 21 of the server. The server acknowledges the client's request and informs the client which port the client should make available for the data connection. The server then opens the data connection to the client, and the client responds. Thereafter, the client and server exchange commands and data freely.

Table 4-4 summarizes the characteristics of packets associated with active mode FTP. Notice the following protocol characteristics:

- The client opens the command connection to the server.

- The server opens the data connection to the client.

- Two ports are used on the client, and two ports are used on the server.

- The server command port is port 21.

- The client ports and server data port are ephemeral ports.

- The datagram used by the client to open the command connection and the associated datagram sent by the server in reply have the TCP SYN flag set.

- The datagrams used by the server to open the data connection and the associated datagram sent by the client in reply have the TCP SYN flag set.

- The datagram sent by the server in reply to the client request to open the command connection has the TCP SYN and ACK flags set.

◆ The datagram sent by the client in reply to the server request to open the data connection has the TCP `SYN` and `ACK` flags set.

◆ The datagrams associated with the established command and data connections have the TCP `ACK` flag set.

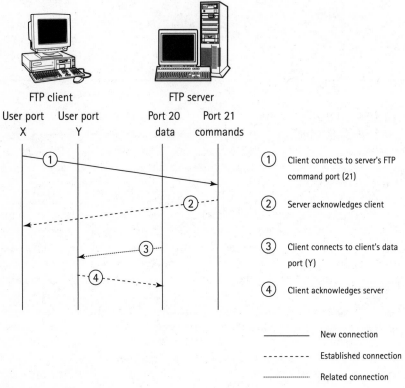

Figure 4-3: Active FTP protocol

TABLE 4-4 ACTIVE FTP PROTOCOL

Conn. State	Source Addr.	Dest. Addr.	Protocol	Source Port	Dest. Port	SYN	ACK	Notes
New	Client	Server	TCP	>1023	21	Yes	No	Client opens FTP command connection to server
Est.	Server	Client	TCP	21	>1023	Yes	Yes	Server acknowledges client

Conn. State	Source Addr.	Dest. Addr.	Protocol	Source Port	Dest. Port	SYN	ACK	Notes
Rel.	Server	Client	TCP	20	>1023	Yes	No	Server opens FTP data connection to client
Est.	Client	Server	TCP	>1023	20	Yes	Yes	Client acknowledges server
Est.	Client	Server	TCP	>1023	20	No	Yes	Established TCP connection, client to server
Est.	Client	Server	TCP	>1023	21	No	Yes	Established TCP connection, client to server
Est.	Server	Client	TCP	20	>1023	No	Yes	Established TCP connection, server to client
Est.	Server	Client	TCP	21	>1023	No	Yes	Established TCP connection, server to client

 Like SSH servers, many FTP servers are configured to attempt using AUTH to verify client identities. When configuring a host to support FTP clients, observe the recommendation given earlier in this chapter in connection with SSH. In particular, if the host does not run AUTH, you should generally reject — not drop — incoming AUTH requests.

ACTIVE VERSUS PASSIVE MODE FTP

Sometimes, you have no choice between active and passive mode FTP. For instance, if you want to access an FTP server that supports only active mode FTP, you must configure your FTP client for active mode. Moreover, firewalls between the client and server must be configured to accept datagrams related to active FTP connections.

However, sometimes you do have a choice. From the standpoint of the client's security, passive mode FTP is preferred because the client need not be configured to accept connections from the server. Essentially, active mode FTP compels the FTP client host to act as a server, opening potential security vulnerabilities. The possibility that these vulnerabilities can be compromised is higher when a non-stateful rather than stateful firewall protects the client host. A stateful firewall is capable of discerning that the server's request to open the data connection is related to an established connection. So, a stateful firewall can accept legitimate requests while blocking fraudulent ones.

A non-stateful firewall cannot inspect the packet state. Therefore, it must accept any request to open a connection to an ephemeral port as long as the source port of the request is port 20. Otherwise, active mode FTP cannot operate. If the request is fraudulent, no process is listening on the ephemeral port, so no TCP connection is established. But, attackers can exploit the inability of the non-stateful firewall to deny such datagrams, causing the firewall to disclose information about its host.

From the standpoint of the server's security, the situation is reversed. To support passive FTP, the server must be willing to accept connections to its ephemeral ports, potentially decreasing security, especially if a non-stateful firewall is used.

Consequently, the client, the server, or both may suffer some reduction in security as a consequence of supporting the FTP protocol. Moreover, FTP transmits commands and data — including user names and passwords — in clear text. Therefore, FTP is a protocol best avoided where security is concerned. But, FTP has become an established standard and remains widely used. Therefore, sometimes administrators must support it, relying on firewalls and other measures to manage the security problems that may arise.

Common TCP Application Protocols

This section describes the characteristics of datagrams of common TCP protocols. It doesn't include a description of every possible TCP protocol because they are too numerous for a book even several times the size of this one. Moreover, many TCP protocols are proprietary or are rarely used.

This section introduces no new important concepts or terms. It is written primarily as a reference to help you design and implement firewalls. Chapters 7, 9, and 10 explain how to use the information contained in this section.

The TCP protocols described in this section are shown in this list:

- ◆ AUTH
- ◆ DNS (Domain Name Service)
- ◆ Mail protocols:
    - ■ IMAP
    - ■ POP
    - ■ SMTP

- ◆ Multimedia protocols:

  - ■ QuickTime

  - ■ RealAudio

  - ■ RealVideo

- ◆ NNTP (Network News Transport Protocol)

- ◆ RSYNC (Remote Synchronization Protocol)

- ◆ Web protocols:

  - ■ HTTP (HyperText Transfer Protocol)

  - ■ HTTPS (HyperText Transfer Protocol over SSL)

  - ■ Web proxy

- ◆ WHOIS

AUTH

The AUTH protocol, also known as IDENTD, is used by some mail, news, FTP, SSH, IRC, and other servers. When requested, a host running an AUTH server responds with the account name of the user who initiated a connection. Servers use AUTH to verify the identity of a user who requests access. However, if the host running the AUTH server has been compromised, the information provided by AUTH is not reliable. Hence, AUTH is of little real value.

However, as explained in a sidebar earlier in this chapter, a client contacting a server configured to use AUTH may experience delays if the client's host fails to respond in a timely manner to an AUTH request from the server. It's sufficient for the host to respond with an ICMP error message. Either an affirmative response or an ICMP error message prevents the server from waiting the duration of its configured time-out period.

Table 4-5 shows the datagram characteristics of the AUTH protocol, which uses server port 113.

TABLE 4-5 **THE AUTH PROTOCOL**

Conn. State	Source Addr.	Dest. Addr.	Protocol	Source Port	Dest. Port	SYN	ACK	Notes
New	Client	Server	TCP	>1023	113	Yes	No	Client opens AUTH connection to server

Continued

TABLE 4-5 THE AUTH PROTOCOL *(Continued)*

Conn. State	Source Addr.	Dest. Addr.	Protocol	Source Port	Dest. Port	SYN	ACK	Notes
Est.	Server	Client	TCP	113	>1023	Yes	Yes	Server acknow-ledges client
Est.	Client	Server	TCP	>1023	113	No	Yes	Established TCP connection, client to server
Est.	Server	Client	TCP	113	>1023	No	Yes	Established TCP connection, server to client

Domain Name Service (DNS)

The Domain Name Service (DNS) is also known as bind or named, after the name of the program that provides it. DNS primarily uses the UDP protocol. However, large data transfers are performed using TCP, to work around restrictions on the maximum size of a UDP datagram. Large data transfers occur primarily in dialogues between hosts that run DNS servers. In particular, DNS zone transfers are sometimes performed using TCP. Hosts that run only a DNS client generally do not need to enable DNS communication via TCP.

For more information on zone transfers and DNS security, see Mohammed J. Kabir's *Red Hat Linux Security and Optimization* (Red Hat Press/Wiley, 2002).

Table 4-6 summarizes the datagram characteristics of the DNS TCP protocol. Just as the DNS UDP protocol uses UDP port 53, the DNS TCP protocol uses TCP port 53. Bear in mind that TCP and UDP ports are wholly separate. Therefore, the two ports used by DNS are unrelated, even through they're similarly numbered for easy recall.

TABLE 4-6 THE DNS TCP PROTOCOL

Conn. State	Source Addr.	Dest. Addr.	Protocol	Source Port	Dest. Port	SYN	ACK	Notes
New	Client	Server	TCP	>1023	53	Yes	No	Client opens DNS TCP connection to server
Est.	Server	Client	TCP	53	>1023	Yes	Yes	Server acknowledges client
Est.	Client	Server	TCP	>1023	53	No	Yes	Established TCP connection, client to server
Est.	Server	Client	TCP	53	>1023	No	Yes	Established TCP connection, server to client

Mail Protocols

This section describes three common e-mail protocols, which are commonly known simply as *mail protocols:*

- ◆ IMAP is used to retrieve mail.

- ◆ POP is used to retrieve mail.

- ◆ SMTP is used to send mail.

IMAP and POP provide similar functions. Many people consider the IMAP protocol, which is more recent than POP, superior because it allows the manipulation of messages and message folders without downloading them. However, POP continues in widespread use.

IMAP

As explained, IMAP is used to retrieve incoming mail. The IMAP service runs by default on server port 143. Table 4-7 summarizes the datagram characteristics of the IMAP protocol.

Table 4-7 THE IMAP PROTOCOL

Conn. State	Source Addr.	Dest. Addr.	Protocol	Source Port	Dest. Port	SYN	ACK	Notes
New	Client	Server	TCP	>1023	143	Yes	No	Client opens IMAP connection to server
Est.	Server	Client	TCP	143	>1023	Yes	Yes	Server acknow-ledges client
Est.	Client	Server	TCP	>1023	143	No	Yes	Established TCP connection, client to server
Est.	Server	Client	TCP	143	>1023	No	Yes	Established TCP connection, server to client

POP

Like IMAP, POP is used to retrieve mail. By default, POP uses server port 110. Table 4-8 summarizes the datagram characteristics of the POP protocol.

Table 4-8 THE POP PROTOCOL

Conn. State	Source Addr.	Dest. Addr.	Protocol	Source Port	Dest. Port	SYN	ACK	Notes
New	Client	Server	TCP	>1023	110	Yes	No	Client opens POP connection to server
Est.	Server	Client	TCP	110	>1023	Yes	Yes	Server acknow-ledges client
Est.	Client	Server	TCP	>1023	110	No	Yes	Established TCP connection, client to server
Est.	Server	Client	TCP	110	>1023	No	Yes	Established TCP connection, server to client

SMTP

SMTP is used to send outgoing mail. The sendmail program is a popular Linux mail server. Many system administrators employ a figure of speech and refer to mail servers generally – if somewhat inaccurately – as sendmail.

Popular mail clients use the SMTP protocol to send mail to a designated mail relay host. Mail servers forward mail to one another and act as mail relays for clients.

By default, SMTP uses server port 25. Table 4-9 summarizes the datagram characteristics of the SMTP protocol.

TABLE 4-9 THE SMTP PROTOCOL

Conn. State	Source Addr.	Dest. Addr.	Protocol	Source Port	Dest. Port	SYN	ACK	Notes
New	Client	Server	TCP	>1023	25	Yes	No	Client opens SMTP connection to server
Est.	Server	Client	TCP	25	>1023	Yes	Yes	Server acknowledges client
Est.	Client	Server	TCP	>1023	25	No	Yes	Established TCP connection, client to server
Est.	Server	Client	TCP	25	>1023	No	Yes	Established TCP connection, server to client

Network News Transfer Protocol (NNTP)

The Network News Transfer Protocol (NNTP) is used to communicate Usenet news postings. The protocol is sometimes referred to as the Usenet or news protocol. The datagram characteristics of NNTP, which uses server port 119, are summarized in Table 4-10.

TABLE 4-10 THE NNTP PROTOCOL

Conn. State	Source Addr.	Dest. Addr.	Protocol	Source Port	Dest. Port	SYN	ACK	Notes
New	Client	Server	TCP	>1023	119	Yes	No	Client opens NNTP connection to server
Est.	Server	Client	TCP	119	>1023	Yes	Yes	Server acknowledges client
Est.	Client	Server	TCP	>1023	119	No	Yes	Established TCP connection, client to server
Est.	Server	Client	TCP	119	>1023	No	Yes	Established TCP connection, server to client

Multimedia Protocols

Multimedia protocols are used to communicate audio and video data via the network. Popular multimedia protocols include RealAudio, used to communicate audio data, and RealVideo and QuickTime, used to communicate video or combined audio-video data. However, many other multimedia protocols are in common use.

Multimedia protocols present special problems. They tend to be proprietary, and vendors tend to revise them with each new release of their clients. Moreover, problems attend the tracking of multimedia connections. A stateful firewall can, in principle, identify traffic associated with an established multimedia connection. However, many firewall implementations, including Red Hat Linux IPChains and IPTables, lack modules that do so.

Fortunately, most multimedia protocols can function using a single TCP connection, and so it's possible to configure a Red Hat Linux firewall that supports them. However, data transfer rates and latencies may not be optimal when multimedia protocols are forced to operate in this fashion. If supporting multimedia protocols is an important firewall function, investigate the protocols of interest and determine how to configure them. The best way to do so is by obtaining and studying documentation provided by the author of the protocol.

Table 4-11 summarizes the datagram characteristics of the three popular multimedia protocols just mentioned. Each of these is based on the standard Real-Time

Streaming Protocol (RTSP), and so they have characteristics in common. The protocols use server port 554 or 7070; some older clients use port 7071. Alternatively, these protocols can use UDP ports 6770–7170, although the table does not show this mode of operation.

Many multimedia protocols, including these three, can also operate on TCP port 80. If your firewall accepts Web traffic, they require no additional configuration.

TABLE 4-11 THE REALAUDIO, REALVIDEO, AND QUICKTIME PROTOCOLS

Conn. State	Source Addr.	Dest. Addr.	Protocol	Source Port	Dest. Port	SYN	ACK	Notes
New	Client	Server	TCP	>1023	554 or 7070	Yes	No	Client opens RealAudio, RealVideo, or QuickTime connection to server
Est.	Server	Client	TCP	554 or 7070	>1023	Yes	Yes	Server acknowledges client
Est.	Client	Server	TCP	>1023	554 or 7070	No	Yes	Established TCP connection, client to server
Est.	Server	Client	TCP	554 or 7070	>1023	No	Yes	Established TCP connection, server to client

Remote File Synchronization Protocol (RSYNC)

The Remote File Synchronization Protocol (RSYNC) is used to efficiently transfer files between hosts. RSYNC has an important feature that facilitates the synchronizing of copies of files that are subject to change. The feature enables the transmission of only the portion of a file that has changed, rather than the entire file. This feature can greatly accelerate transfer and reduce bandwidth consumption.

RSYNC, which uses server port 873 by default, is summarized in Table 4-12.

TABLE 4-12 THE RSYNC PROTOCOL

Conn. State	Source Addr.	Dest. Addr.	Protocol	Source Port	Dest. Port	SYN	ACK	Notes
New	Client	Server	TCP	>1023	873	Yes	No	Client opens RSYNC connection to server
Est.	Server	Client	TCP	873	>1023	Yes	Yes	Server acknow-ledges client
Est.	Client	Server	TCP	>1023	873	No	Yes	Established TCP connection, client to server
Est.	Server	Client	TCP	873	>1023	No	Yes	Established TCP connection, server to client

Web Protocols

This section describes three important Web protocols:

- ◆ HyperText Transfer Protocol (HTTP)
- ◆ HyperText Transfer Protocol over SSL (HTTPS)
- ◆ Web Proxy Protocol

These proxies are used by most Web clients (browsers) and many Web servers.

HYPERTEXT TRANSFER PROTOCOL (HTTP)

Most Web traffic uses the HyperText Transfer Protocol (HTTP). One important use of this protocol that is especially significant to users of Red Hat Linux is the Red Hat Network service, which uses HTTP to exchange information between a subscribed host and the Red Hat Network server.

Table 4-13 summarizes the datagram characteristics of HTTP, which generally uses server port 80. However, system administrators routinely run HTTP servers on a variety of other ports.

TABLE 4-13 THE HTTP PROTOCOL

Conn. State	Source Addr.	Dest. Addr.	Protocol	Source Port	Dest. Port	SYN	ACK	Notes
New	Client	Server	TCP	>1023	80	Yes	No	Client opens HTTP connection to server
Est.	Server	Client	TCP	80	>1023	Yes	Yes	Server acknowledges client
Est.	Client	Server	TCP	>1023	80	No	Yes	Established TCP connection, client to server
Est.	Server	Client	TCP	80	>1023	No	Yes	Established TCP connection, server to client

HYPERTEXT TRANSFER PROTOCOL OVER SSL (HTTPS)

The HyperText Transfer Protocol over SSL (HTTPS) uses the Secure Socket Layer (SSL) and Transport Layer Security (TLS) to provide encrypted communication between Web clients and servers. Like HTTP, HTTPS is used by the Red Hat Network service.

Table 4-14 summarizes the HTTPS protocol, which uses server port 443.

TABLE 4-14 THE HTTPS PROTOCOL

Conn. State	Source Addr.	Dest. Addr.	Protocol	Source Port	Dest. Port	SYN	ACK	Notes
New	Client	Server	TCP	>1023	443	Yes	No	Client opens HTTPS connection to server
Est.	Server	Client	TCP	443	>1023	Yes	Yes	Server acknowledges client

Continued

TABLE 4-14 THE HTTPS PROTOCOL *(Continued)*

Conn. State	Source Addr.	Dest. Addr.	Protocol	Source Port	Dest. Port	SYN	ACK	Notes
Est.	Client	Server	TCP	>1023	443	No	Yes	Established TCP connection, client to server
Est.	Server	Client	TCP	443	>1023	No	Yes	Established TCP connection, server to client

WEB PROXY PROTOCOL

Web proxy servers perform HTTP and HTTPS transfers on behalf of Web clients. They can cache frequently used pages and perform other optimizations that improve performance. Moreover, they can be used to hide the identity of Web clients, making them more resistant to attack.

Table 4-15 summarizes the Web proxy protocol. Web proxy servers are commonly run on any of a variety of ports. The table shows the most popular ports.

TABLE 4-15 THE WEB PROXY PROTOCOL

Conn. State	Source Addr.	Dest. Addr.	Protocol	Source Port	Dest. Port	SYN	ACK	Notes
New	Client	Server	TCP	>1023	3128, 8008, 8080, or other	Yes	No	Client opens web proxy connection to server
Est.	Server	Client	TCP	3128, 8008, 8080, or other	>1023	Yes	Yes	Server acknowledges client
Est.	Client	Server	TCP	>1023	3128, 8008, 8080, or other	No	Yes	Established TCP connection, client to server

Conn. State	Source Addr.	Dest. Addr.	Protocol	Source Port	Dest. Port	SYN	ACK	Notes
Est.	Server	Client	TCP	3128, 8008, 8080, or other	>1023	No	Yes	Established TCP connection, server to client

WHOIS Protocol

The WHOIS protocol provides a facility for accessing the InterNIC Registration Services database. This database contains information about IP addresses, host names, domain names, and registrants. Using the whois command, you can access the database and view information pertaining to an IP address of interest.

Table 4-16 summarizes the datagram characteristics of the WHOIS protocol. The protocol uses TCP port 43. Only registering agencies run WHOIS servers. So, it's likely that your firewall needs to be configured to support only WHOIS clients.

TABLE 4-16 THE WHOIS PROTOCOL

Conn. State	Source Addr.	Dest. Addr.	Protocol	Source Port	Dest. Port	SYN	ACK	Notes
New	Client	Server	TCP	>1023	43	Yes	No	Client opens whois connection to server
Est.	Server	Client	TCP	43	>1023	Yes	Yes	Server acknowledges client
Est.	Client	Server	TCP	>1023	43	No	Yes	Established TCP connection, client to server
Est.	Server	Client	TCP	43	>1023	No	Yes	Established TCP connection, server to client

Common UDP Application Protocols

Many common application protocols are based on UDP rather than on TCP. This section explains several of the most common:

- Dynamic Host Configuration Protocol (DHCP)
- Domain Name Service (DNS)
- Network Time Protocol (NTP)
- Traceroute

UDP datagrams do not include TCP flags. Nevertheless, the tables in this section include columns for the SYN and ACK TCP flags, for consistency with other tables appearing in this chapter.

Dynamic Host Configuration Protocol (DHCP)

The Dynamic Host Configuration Protocol (DHCP) is used to provide clients with configuration data. DHCP is particularly useful for transient and mobile clients, such as dial-up hosts and laptop computers. It provides clients with such information as

- IP address
- Network mask
- Host name
- Gateway IP address
- DNS server IP address

It can also provide a variety of other information.

The DHCP service helps system administrators make efficient use of a limited pool of IP addresses. When a DCHP server provides a client with a configuration, called a *lease,* the server makes note of the client and time. After a configurable interval expires, the server requests that the client renew the lease. If the client does not do so, the server reclaims the IP address for use by other clients. Thus, the IP address pool need be no larger than the number of concurrent clients, even though the number of potential clients may be several times larger.

Table 4-17 summarizes the datagram characteristics of the DHCP protocol, which uses UDP ports 67 and 68. The server listens on port 67, and the client listens for responses on port 68. Unfortunately, DHCP servers and clients sometimes implement the DHCP protocol in idiosyncratic ways. Therefore, in practice, you can expect some variation from the characteristics indicated in Table 4-17. However, by using tcpdump to inspect packets, you can easily discover such variations and accommodate them in your firewall implementation.

TABLE 4-17 THE DHCP PROTOCOL

Conn. State	Source Addr.	Dest. Addr.	Protocol	Source Port	Dest. Port	SYN	ACK	Notes
New	0.0.0.0	255. 255. 255. 255	UDP	68	67	N/A	N/A	Client requests lease
Est.	Server	255. 255. 255. 255	UDP	67	68	N/A	N/A	Server offers lease
Est.	Server	255. 255. 255. 255	UDP	67	68	N/A	N/A	Server declines to offer lease
Est.	Client	255. 255. 255. 255	UDP	68	67	N/A	N/A	Client accepts lease
Est.	Server	Client	UDP	67	68	N/A	N/A	Server acknowledges acceptance by client

Domain Name Service (DNS) Protocol

As explained earlier in this chapter, the Domain Name Service (DNS) protocol uses both TCP and UDP. However, most DNS traffic is sent via UDP.

Table 4-18 summarizes the UDP datagram characteristics of the DNS protocol. Like the TCP datagrams used by DNS, the UDP datagrams specify server port 53.

TABLE 4-18 THE DNS UDP PROTOCOL

Conn. State	Source Addr.	Dest. Addr.	Protocol	Source Port	Dest. Port	SYN	ACK	Notes
New	Client	Server	UDP	>1023	53	N/A	N/A	Client sends DNS query to server
Est.	Server	Client	UDP	53	>1023	N/A	N/A	Server sends DNS reply

Network Time Protocol (NTP)

The Network Time Protocol (NTP) is used to precisely synchronize the clocks of hosts. Synchronization is helpful because computer clocks are not perfectly accurate and therefore tend to drift, eventually accumulating significant error. Several Internet hosts provide publicly accessible time servers that derive their time value from atomic clocks or other ultraprecise means.

If you administer a single host or a small network, you can configure your hosts to synchronize their clocks with an Internet time server. If you administer a larger network, you should configure one or two hosts to synchronize with an Internet time server. Other hosts on your network should synchronize with your server or servers, minimizing the traffic volume that must be handled by Internet time servers.

For more information on NTP, see the NTP HOWTO and FAQ, at `http://www.ntp.org/ntpfaq/NTP-a-faq.htm`.

Table 4-19 shows the datagram characteristics of the NTP protocol, which uses UDP port 123.

TABLE 4-19 THE NTP PROTOCOL

Conn. State	Source Addr.	Dest. Addr.	Protocol	Source Port	Dest. Port	SYN	ACK	Notes
New	Client	Server	UDP	>1023	123	N/A	N/A	Client queries NTP server

Conn. State	Source Addr.	Dest. Addr.	Protocol	Source Port	Dest. Port	SYN	ACK	Notes
Est.	Server	Client	UDP	123	>1023	N/A	N/A	Server sends NTP reply

Traceroute Protocol

The Traceroute protocol enables you to measure the network distance to a host. The distance is measured in units called *hops*. Each router or similar device along the path from the source to the destination is counted as one hop.

Traceroute does not require a server process. Instead, Traceroute depends on the operation of the TCP/IP stack, which decrements the Time To Live (TTL) value of incoming datagrams and discards datagrams with expired TTLs. The standard action when a datagram is discarded is the sending of an ICMP destination unreachable message. However, attackers often use Traceroute to map a target network. So, many administrators configure their systems to suppress such messages in the interest of improved security.

Traceroute can use any UDP port, and some Traceroute clients enable the user to choose the port to be used. Table 4-20, therefore, identifies only the most common ports. Windows hosts perform traceroutes using ICMP datagrams rather than UDP datagrams. The table uses the term *client* to designate the host that sends the traceroute datagrams and the term *server* to designate the host that receives the traceroute datagrams.

TABLE 4-20 THE TRACEROUTE PROTOCOL

Conn. State	Source Addr.	Dest. Addr.	Protocol	Source Port	Dest. Port	SYN	ACK	Notes
New	Client	Server	UDP	32769 to 65535	33434 to 33523	N/A	N/A	Client performs traceroute of server
Est.	Server	Client	UDP	33434 to 33523	32769 to 65535	N/A	N/A	Server responds to traceroute

ICMP Traffic

Chapter 3 briefly describes the ICMP datagram, which is used to inform hosts of error and other network events. The correct operation of a network requires that certain types of ICMP datagrams be allowed to enter the network. Other types of ICMP datagrams are considered potentially harmful and generally should be blocked. Still others can be accepted or blocked, according to local policy. This section explains which types of ICMP datagrams are associated with each category. Table 4-21 summarizes the ICMP message type codes.

TABLE 4–21 ICMP MESSAGES

MessageType	MessageCode	Description
0		echo-reply
3		destination-unreachable
	0	network-unreachable
	1	host-unreachable
	2	protocol-unreachable
	3	port-unreachable
	4	fragmentation-needed
	5	source-route-failed
	6	network-unknown
	7	host-unknown
	8	source-host-isolated
	9	network-prohibited
	10	host-prohibited
	11	TOS-network-unreachable
	12	TOS-host-unreachable
	13	communication-prohibited
	14	host-precedence-violation
	15	precedence-cutoff
4		source-quench
5		redirect

MessageType	MessageCode	Description
	0	network-redirect
	1	host-redirect
	2	TOS-network-redirect
	3	TOS-host-redirect
8		echo-request
9		router-advertisement
10		router-solicitation
11		time-exceeded
	0	ttl-zero-during-transit
	1	ttl-zero-during-reassembly
12		parameter-problem
	0	ip-header-bad
	1	required-option-missing
13		timestamp-request
14		timestamp-reply
17		address-mask-request
18		address-mask-reply

Echo Request and Echo Reply

The echo request ICMP message type is also known as the *ping* type, after the Unix command that sends ICMP echo requests to a designated host. Recall that the default behavior of a host receiving an echo request is to respond with an echo reply. The echo request and echo reply ICMP message types are useful for testing network connectivity. However, they're also useful to attackers interested in mapping a network. You can reasonably accept or block ICMP echo requests and replies, according to your preference. However, here are some recommended policies:

◆ Allow network hosts to ping the default gateway.

◆ Allow hosts in your service provider's network to ping your perimeter hosts, but not your internal hosts.

◆ Allow one or more service hosts used by network administrators to ping external hosts.

Bear in mind that, for ping to operate, the echo request and echo reply must be accepted. Blocking either datagram prevents ping from working properly.

Destination Unreachable

The destination unreachable ICMP message indicates that a host or network could not be contacted. For correct operation of your network, your firewall must accept incoming destination unreachable messages. However, your firewall can block outgoing destination unreachable datagrams except for those bearing code 4, fragmentation needed. Fragmentation-needed datagrams are needed for correct network operation and should be accepted.

 Some operating system use fragmentation-needed datagrams to determine the largest packet size a destination network will accept. Thereafter, they maximize performance by sending datagrams no larger than the determined size.

Redirect

The ICMP redirect message is a control message exchanged by routers. The message instructs its recipient to use a different route to reach the host indicated by the message. Your firewall should generally block incoming and outgoing ICMP redirect datagrams. It should definitely block those that originate from a non-adjacent router.

Source Quench

The ICMP source quench message is used to instruct a host to send more slowly so that it does not overwhelm a slower host. Your firewall should generally accept both incoming and outgoing source quench ICMP datagrams.

Router Advertisement and Solicitation

Like ICMP redirect messages, ICMP router advertisement and solicitation messages are primarily exchanged between routers. Your firewall should block incoming and outgoing ICMP router advertisement and solicitation messages.

Time Exceeded

ICMP time-exceeded messages are used to prevent datagrams from endlessly looping around a network. Your firewall should generally accept both incoming and outgoing ICMP time-exceeded messages.

Parameter Problem

The ICMP parameter problem message indicates an error in a datagram header. Your firewall should generally accept both incoming and outgoing ICMP parameter problem messages, in order to detect such errors.

Other ICMP Messages

ICMP message types 13, 14, 17, and 18 are not normally needed for network operation. Your firewall can accept or block the related ICMP datagrams, according to your preference.

Other TCP/UDP Application Protocols

This section describes the datagram characteristics of additional TCP/UDP application protocols. The services associated with these protocols have one or more of these characteristics:

- ◆ They're seldom used or obsolete.

- ◆ They're only marginally useful.

- ◆ They're not generally considered secure enough to be safely run over the Internet or other public networks.

Several popular and important protocols, such as the Samba SMB protocol, are described in this section, so don't assume that it includes only obscure protocols and skip it.

Also, be attentive to the unexpected presence of these protocols on your network. Often, malicious software operates using seldom-used port numbers such as those discussed in this section.

The protocols are organized into these groups:

- ◆ Database services

- ◆ File- and printer-sharing services

- ◆ Messaging and user information services

- ◆ RPC-based services

- ◆ Remote user services

- ◆ "Small" services

- ◆ System and network administration services

- ◆ X Window services

Database Services

Database services are both important and common. They're included in this section because they're generally vulnerable to attack, and therefore they should not generally be run over a public network, such as the Internet. Instead, the relevant ports should be blocked by a firewall at the network perimeter.

LIGHTWEIGHT DIRECTORY ACCESS PROTOCOL (LDAP)

The Lightweight Directory Access Protocol (LDAP) is used to store directory information, such as user account information, address books, or public key certificates. LDAP is not considered intrinsically insecure; however, the information stored in an LDAP database is often highly sensitive. Consequently, LDAP is generally configured to be accessible only by internal hosts. LDAP can be configured to run using TLS and SSL in much the same way as HTTP, as described earlier in this chapter. When run this way, the protocol is known as LDAPS.

Table 4-22 summarizes the datagram characteristics of the LDAP protocol. Notice that LDAP is commonly run over any of several ports. The standard LDAP port is 389, and the standard LDAPS port is 636. Windows 2000 and later use port 3268 for LDAP and port 3269 for LDAPS.

TABLE 4-22 THE LDAP PROTOCOL

Conn. State	Source Addr.	Dest. Addr.	Protocol	Source Port	Dest. Port	SYN	ACK	Notes
New	Client	Server	TCP	>1023	389, 636, 3268, or 3269	Yes	No	Client opens LDAP connection to server
Est.	Server	Client	TCP	389, 636, 3268, or 3269	>1023	Yes	Yes	Server acknowledges client

Conn. State	Source Addr.	Dest. Addr.	Protocol	Source Port	Dest. Port	SYN	ACK	Notes
Est.	Client	Server	TCP	>1023	389, 636, 3268, or 3269	No	Yes	Established TCP connection, client to server
Est.	Server	Client	TCP	389, 636, 3268, or 3269	>1023	No	Yes	Established TCP connection, server to client

MySQL

MySQL, the most popular open source database management system and is highly regarded for its speedy performance. MySQL version 4, which was in alpha testing at the time of this writing, can run securely over a public network by using TLS and SSL. Table 4-23 summarizes the datagram characteristics of MySQL, which listens on server port 3306.

TABLE 4–23 THE MySQL PROTOCOL

Conn. State	Source Addr.	Dest. Addr.	Protocol	Source Port	Dest. Port	SYN	ACK	Notes
New	Client	Server	TCP	>1023	3306		No	Client opens MySQL connection to server
Est.	Server	Client	TCP	3306	>1023	Yes	Yes	Server acknowledges client
Est.	Client	Server	TCP	>1023	3306	No	Yes	Established TCP connection, client to server
Est.	Server	Client	TCP	3306	>1023	No	Yes	Established TCP connection, server to client

PostgreSQL

Like MySQL, PostgreSQL is a popular open-source database management system. PostgreSQL is known for its support for important relational database features, such as transactions and rollback, which have only recently been added to MySQL. Table 4-24 summarizes the datagram characteristics of PostgreSQL, which uses server port 5432.

TABLE 4-24 THE PostgreSQL PROTOCOL

Conn. State	Source Addr.	Dest. Addr.	Protocol	Source Port	Dest. Port	SYN	ACK	Notes
New	Client	Server	TCP	>1023	5432	No	No	Client opens PostgreSQL connection to server
Est.	Server	Client	TCP	5432	>1023	Yes	Yes	Server acknowledges client
Est.	Client	Server	TCP	>1023	5432	No	Yes	Established TCP connection, client to server
Est.	Server	Client	TCP	5432	>1023	No	Yes	Established TCP connection, server to client

File- and Printer-Sharing Services

File- and printer-sharing services, like database management services, are both important and popular. However, the associated protocols – and their sometimes buggy implementations – are not generally regarded as safe for use over public networks.

LINE PRINTER SERVICE (LPD)

The Unix line printer service (LPD) enables clients to print via a remote printer. However, the service has suffered several vulnerabilities and therefore is not considered safe for use over public networks. Table 4-25 summarizes the datagram characteristics of the LPD protocol, which uses server port 515.

TABLE 4-25 THE LPD PROTOCOL

Conn. State	Source Addr.	Dest. Addr.	Protocol	Source Port	Dest. Port	SYN	ACK	Notes
New	Client	Server	TCP	>1023	515	Yes	No	Client opens LPD connection to server
Est.	Server	Client	TCP	515	>1023	Yes	Yes	Server acknowledges client
Est.	Client	Server	TCP	>1023	515	No	Yes	Established TCP connection, client to server
Est.	Server	Client	TCP	515	>1023	No	Yes	Established TCP connection, server to client

NETWORK FILE SYSTEM (NFS)

The Network File System is widely used for sharing files, primarily among Unix and Unix-like systems, such as Linux. NFS can operate over TCP or UDP; however, some implementations, including the implementation distributed with Red Hat Linux, use only UDP.

NFS, a Remote Procedure Call (RPC) service, requires that these related RPC services be accessible:

◆ portmap
◆ mountd
◆ lockd
◆ statd

These services are described in the section "RPC-Based Services."

NFS implementations vary somewhat. Consequently, achieving interoperability among platforms having different NFS implementations can be challenging.

NFS is sometimes used over the Internet. However, that use is not recommended because most implementations suffer from security vulnerabilities. Table 4-26 summarizes the datagram characteristics of the TCP NFS protocol, and Table 4-27 summarizes the datagram characteristics of the UDP NFS protocol.

TABLE 4-26 THE TCP NFS PROTOCOL

Conn. State	Source Addr.	Dest. Addr.	Protocol	Source Port	Dest. Port	SYN	ACK	Notes
New	Client	Server	TCP	>1023	111	Yes	No	Client opens connection to portmapper
Est.	Server	Client	TCP	111	>1023	Yes	Yes	Portmapper responds
Est.	Client	Server	TCP	>1023	111	No	Yes	Established TCP connection, client to server
Est.	Server	Client	TCP	111	>1023	No	Yes	Established TCP connection, server to client
New	Client	Server	TCP	>1023	2049	Yes	No	Client opens NFS connection to server
Est.	Server	Client	TCP	2049	>1023	Yes	Yes	NFS server responds
Est.	Client	Server	TCP	>1023	2049	No	Yes	Established TCP connection, client to server
Est.	Server	Client	TCP	2049	>1023	No	Yes	Established TCP connection, server to client

TABLE 4-27 THE UDP NFS PROTOCOL

Conn. State	Source Addr.	Dest. Addr.	Protocol	Source Port	Dest. Port	SYN	ACK	Notes
New	Client	Server	UDP	>1023	111	N/A	N/A	Client sends request to portmapper
Est.	Server	Client	UDP	111	>1023	N/A	N/A	Portmapper responds

Conn. State	Source Addr.	Dest. Addr.	Protocol	Source Port	Dest. Port	SYN	ACK	Notes
New or Est.	Client	Server	UDP	>1023	2049	N/A	N/A	Client sends request to NFS server
Est.	Server	Client	UDP	2049	>1023	N/A	N/A	NFS server responds

SAMBA

Samba is a reverse-engineered, open-source implementation of the Microsoft file-and printer-sharing protocol, variously known as Common Internet File System (CIFS) or Server Message Block (SMB), which was jointly developed by IBM, Intel, and Microsoft. Older implementations of SMB run using NetBIOS over TCP/IP (NetBT) as transport; newer implementations, such as Windows 2000, use TCP/IP natively.

Table 4-28 summarizes the datagram characteristics of the NetBT protocol, and Table 4-29 summarizes the datagram characteristics of the SMB protocol. SMB is sometimes configured to run using UDP port 138 rather than TCP port 139 or 445.

TABLE 4–28 THE NetBT PROTOCOL

Conn. State	Source Addr.	Dest. Addr.	Protocol	Source Port	Dest. Port	SYN	ACK	Notes
New	Client	Server	UDP	>1023	138	N/A	N/A	Client sends NetBT name service request
Est.	Server	Client	UDP	138	>1023	N/A	N/A	NetBT name server responds
New	Client	Server	TCP	>1023	139	Yes	No	Client opens connection to NetBT session server
Est.	Server	Client	TCP	139	>1023	Yes	Yes	NetBT session server acknowledges client

Continued

TABLE **4-28 THE NetBT PROTOCOL** *(Continued)*

Conn. State	Source Addr.	Dest. Addr.	Protocol	Source Port	Dest. Port	SYN	ACK	Notes
Est.	Client	Server	TCP	>1023	139	No	Yes	Established TCP connection, client to server
Est.	Server	Client	TCP	139	>1023	No	Yes	Established TCP connection, server to client

TABLE **4-29 THE SMB PROTOCOL**

Conn. State	Source Addr.	Dest. Addr.	Protocol	Source Port	Dest. Port	SYN	ACK	Notes
New	Client	Server	TCP	>1023	139 or 445	Yes	No	Client opens connection to SMB server
Est.	Server	Client	TCP	139 or 445	>1023	Yes	Yes	SMB server acknowledges client
Est.	Client	Server	TCP	>1023	139 or 445	No	Yes	Established TCP connection, client to server
Est.	Server	Client	TCP	139 or 445	>1023	No	Yes	Established TCP connection, server to client

Messaging and User Information Services

Messaging and user information services provide information about users or enable users to communicate in real time.

finger

The finger service provides information about a user account. Using finger, you can determine the name of the user to whom the account is assigned and other information, such as the user's home directory and login activity. Because such information is valuable to an attacker, you should generally block the finger service at your perimeter firewall.

Table 4-30 summarizes the datagram characteristics of the finger protocol. The protocol uses TCP port 79.

TABLE 4-30 THE finger PROTOCOL

Conn. State	Source Addr.	Dest. Addr.	Protocol	Source Port	Dest. Port	SYN	ACK	Notes
New	Client	Server	TCP	>1023	79	Yes	No	Client opens finger connection to server
Est.	Server	Client	TCP	79	>1023	Yes	Yes	Server acknowledges client
Est.	Client	Server	TCP	>1023	79	No	Yes	Established TCP connection, client to server
Est.	Server	Client	TCP	79	>1023	No	Yes	Established TCP connection, server to client

INTERNET RELAY CHAT (IRC)

The Internet Relay Chat (IRC) service lets users exchange text messages and files in real time. The related protocol uses TCP port 667, as shown in Table 4-31.

TABLE 4–31 THE IRC PROTOCOL

Conn. State	Source Addr.	Dest. Addr.	Protocol	Source Port	Dest. Port	SYN	ACK	Notes
New	Client	Server	TCP	>1023	6667	Yes	No	Client opens IRC connection to server
Est.	Server	Client	TCP	6667	>1023	Yes	Yes	Server acknow-ledges client
Est.	Client	Server	TCP	>1023	6667	No	Yes	Established TCP connection, client to server
Est.	Server	Client	TCP	6667	>1023	No	Yes	Established TCP connection, server to client

Many IRC clients provide the facility for direct communication with another client. Supporting this facility requires that arbitrary user ports be open for incoming connections. Opening these ports decreases system security and is not generally recommended. Table 4-32 shows the datagram characteristics of client-to-client IRC communication.

TABLE 4–32 DIRECT CLIENT CONNECTIONS USING THE IRC PROTOCOL

Conn. State	Source Addr.	Dest. Addr.	Protocol	Source Port	Dest. Port	SYN	ACK	Notes
New	Client	Server	TCP	>1023	>1023	Yes	No	Client opens IRC connection to remote client
Est.	Server	Client	TCP	>1023	>1023	Yes	Yes	Remote acknow-ledges client
Est.	Client	Server	TCP	>1023	>1023	No	Yes	Established TCP connection, client to remote client

Conn. State	Source Addr.	Dest. Addr.	Protocol	Source Port	Dest. Port	SYN	ACK	Notes
Est.	Server	Client	TCP	>1023	>1023	No	Yes	Established TCP connection, remote client to client

ntalk AND talk

The ntalk and talk services let users write messages to one another's terminals. These services tend to be more distracting than useful because better ways of communicating now exist. Table 4-33 shows the datagram characteristics of the ntalk protocol, and Table 4-34 shows the datagram characteristics of the talk protocol.

TABLE 4-33 THE ntalk PROTOCOL

Conn. State	Source Addr.	Dest. Addr.	Protocol	Source Port	Dest. Port	SYN	ACK	Notes
New	Client	Server	UDP	>1023	518	N/A	N/A	Client sends ntalk request to server
Est.	Server	Client	UDP	518	>1023	N/A	N/A	Server sends ntalk reply

TABLE 4-34 THE talk PROTOCOL

Conn. State	Source Addr.	Dest. Addr.	Protocol	Source Port	Dest. Port	SYN	ACK	Notes
New	Client	Server	UDP	>1023	517	N/A	N/A	Client sends talk request to server
Est.	Server	Client	UDP	517	>1023	N/A	N/A	Server sends talk reply

Remote User Services

Remote user services include those associated with the Berkeley r-commands and Telnet. The Berkeley r-commands are the ones in this list:

- ◆ rcp copies files.

- ◆ rdist synchronizes files.

- ◆ rdump backs up files.

- ◆ rexec executes commands remotely.

- ◆ rlogin provides a remote login.

- ◆ rrestore restores files.

- ◆ rsh executes commands remotely.

The rexec and rsh commands provide similar functionality. However, the rexec command is less often implemented by operating system designers and therefore is seldom used.

Table 4-35 shows the datagram characteristics of the rlogin protocol associated with the rlogin command, which uses TCP port 513.

TABLE **4-35 THE rlogin PROTOCOL**

Conn. State	Source Addr.	Dest. Addr.	Protocol	Source Port	Dest. Port	SYN	ACK	Notes
New	Client	Server	TCP	<1024	513	Yes	No	Client opens rlogin connection to server
Est.	Server	Client	TCP	513	<1024	Yes	Yes	Server acknowledges client
Est.	Client	Server	TCP	<1024	513	No	Yes	Established TCP connection, client to server
Est.	Server	Client	TCP	513	<1024	No	Yes	Established TCP connection, server to client

Table 4-36 shows the datagram characteristics of the rsh protocol and related protocols. Notice that the client port is a system port. Operating an rsh server entails opening system ports 515–1023 to incoming connections. Therefore, rsh is not recommended for use except on private networks. SSH provides similar functions and greater security in even that context and is therefore the preferred means of providing these functions.

TABLE 4-36 THE rsh AND RELATED PROTOCOLS

Conn. State	Source Addr.	Dest. Addr.	Protocol	Source Port	Dest. Port	SYN	ACK	Notes
New	Client	Server	TCP	515–1023	514	Yes	No	Client opens rcp, rdist, rdump, rrestore, or rsh connection to server
Est.	Server	Client	TCP	514	515–1023	Yes	Yes	Server acknow-ledges client
Est.	Client	Server	TCP	515–1023	514	No	Yes	Established TCP connection, client to server
Est.	Server	Client	TCP	514	515–1023	No	Yes	Established TCP connection, server to client
New	Client	Server	TCP	515–1023	515–1023	Yes	No	Client rsh error channel connection to server
Est.	Server	Client	TCP	515–1023	515–1023	Yes	Yes	Server acknow-ledges client

Continued

TABLE 4-36 THE rsh AND RELATED PROTOCOLS *(Continued)*

Conn. State	Source Addr.	Dest. Addr.	Protocol	Source Port	Dest. Port	SYN	ACK	Notes
Est.	Client	Server	TCP	515–1023	515–1023	No	Yes	Established TCP connection, client to server
Est.	Server	Client	TCP	515–1023	515–1023	No	Yes	Established TCP connection, server to client

Table 4-37 shows the datagram characteristics of the rexec protocol. Like the rsh protocol, the rexec protocol uses system ports on the client side. Therefore, the rexec service is not recommended for general use.

TABLE 4-37 THE rexec PROTOCOL

Conn. State	Source Addr.	Dest. Addr.	Protocol	Source Port	Dest. Port	SYN	ACK	Notes
New	Client	Server	TCP	>1023	512	Yes	No	Client opens rexec connection to server
Est.	Server	Client	TCP	512	>1023	Yes	Yes	Server acknowledges client
Est.	Client	Server	TCP	>1023	512	No	Yes	Established TCP connection, client to server
Est.	Server	Client	TCP	512	>1023	No	Yes	Established TCP connection, server to client

Conn. State	Source Addr.	Dest. Addr.	Protocol	Source Port	Dest. Port	SYN	ACK	Notes
New	Client	Server	TCP	515–1023	515–1023	Yes	No	Client rexec error channel connection to server
Est.	Server	Client	TCP	515–1023	515–1023	Yes	Yes	Server acknow-ledges client
Est.	Client	Server	TCP	515–1023	515–1023	No	Yes	Established TCP connection, client to server
Est.	Server	Client	TCP	515–1023	515–1023	No	Yes	Established TCP connection, server to client

TELNET

The Telnet service, like SSH, provides a remote login. However, unlike SSH, Telnet sends user names and passwords across the network in unencrypted form. Therefore, Telnet is not recommended for general use.

Table 4-38 shows the datagram characteristics of the Telnet protocol, which uses TCP port 23.

TABLE 4-38 THE TELNET PROTOCOL

Conn. State	Source Addr.	Dest. Addr.	Protocol	Source Port	Dest. Port	SYN	ACK	Notes
New	Client	Server	TCP	>1023	23	Yes	No	Client opens Telnet connection to server
Est.	Server	Client	TCP	23	>1023	Yes	Yes	Server acknow-ledges client

Continued

TABLE 4-38 THE TELNET PROTOCOL *(Continued)*

Conn. State	Source Addr.	Dest. Addr.	Protocol	Source Port	Dest. Port	SYN	ACK	Notes
Est.	Client	Server	TCP	>1023	23	No	Yes	Established TCP connection, client to server
Est.	Server	Client	TCP	23	>1023	No	Yes	Established TCP connection, server to client

RPC-Based Services

Remote Procedure Call (RPC) is a general term for facilities that enable a programmer to invoke an operation on a remote host as though calling a procedure on the local host. RPC simplifies the task of the programmer by handling many details that would otherwise complicate accessing an operation remotely.

RPC was designed to be a flexible facility that readily accommodates new services. Registering a port number with the Internet Assigned Number Authority (IANA) is cumbersome. So, rather than require each new RPC service to register its port, RPC provides a directory service, called the *portmapper,* or simply *portmap.* Portmap runs on UDP port 111. When a service starts, it can register its port with portmap by contacting portmap on port 111. Alternatively, the service can request portmap to assign it a port. In either case, portmap is aware of each running RPC service and the port on which each RPC service runs. When a client wants to contact an RPC service, it can query portmap by sending a request to UDP port 111.

On a host running RPC, you can view the portmap directory by issuing the rpcinfo command. Here's some typical output of the command:

```
# rpcinfo -p
   program vers proto   port
    100000    2   tcp    111  portmapper
    100000    2   udp    111  portmapper
    100024    1   udp   1024  status
    100024    1   tcp   1024  status
    100011    1   udp    681  rquotad
    100011    2   udp    681  rquotad
    100011    1   tcp    684  rquotad
    100011    2   tcp    684  rquotad
    100005    1   udp   1027  mountd
    100005    1   tcp   1025  mountd
```

```
100005    2    udp    1027    mountd
100005    2    tcp    1025    mountd
100005    3    udp    1027    mountd
100005    3    tcp    1025    mountd
100003    2    udp    2049    nfs
100003    3    udp    2049    nfs
100021    1    udp    1028    nlockmgr
100021    3    udp    1028    nlockmgr
100021    4    udp    1028    nlockmgr
```

The output shows

- `program`, the program number assigned by portmap to identify the service

- `vers`, the RPC version number used

- `proto`, the protocol (TCP or UDP)

- `port`, the port number

- The service name

Notice that several services have allocated, or have been allocated, both a TCP and UDP port.

Portmap nicely resolves the problem of port registration, but it introduces a new problem: A firewall cannot block or permit access to a service unless the firewall designer knows which port the service uses. But, portmap is capable of assigning ports dynamically. Thus, you can't know in advance what port to filter in order to manage an RPC server. Hence, RPC services are notoriously difficult to manage by using packet-filtering firewalls.

Fortunately, many common RPC services run – or can be configured to run – on a standard port rather than on a dynamically assigned port. When an RPC service runs on a known port, it's possible to implement a firewall to manage it. However, it's best not to run RPC services across the firewall; instead, the firewall should block portmap and other RPC services.

Common RPC-based services include these:

- sgi_fam is a file alteration monitor.

- mountd handles client requests to mount volumes shared via NFS.

- Network File System (NFS) is described earlier in this chapter.

- lockd (nlockmgr) provides file locking for files shared via NFS.

- rquotad is used to set and enforce disk space quotas on volumes shared via NFS.

- rstatd (status) is a reboot notification service used by NFS.

- rusersd provides information about logged-in users.

- rwalld sends a message to logged-in users.

- Network Information Services (NIS) is formerly known as Yellow Pages (yp).

  - ypxfrd transfers NIS maps (tables of user information) from one host to another.

  - yppasswdd enables users to change their password remotely.

In addition, portmap itself runs as an RPC service.

> Consult the man pages of RPC services to learn how to manually specify the port number to which a given RPC service binds. For information on NIS, including how to configure it, see Terry Collings and Kurt Wall's *Red Hat Linux Networking and System Administration* (Red Hat Press/Wiley, 2002).

"Small" Services

Several "small" services date from the early days of the Internet. Today, these services are seldom used and can be safely turned off and blocked at the firewall. To turn off a small service, configure it as disabled in the appropriate /etc/xinetd.d file, and instruct xinetd to reload its configuration files, by issuing the command

```
service xinetd reload
```

Each service can work via TCP or UDP, so be sure to disable both.

chargen

The chargen service generates random characters. A TCP client that connects to a chargen server receives a random stream of characters; a UDP client receives a single UDP packet containing random characters.

Table 4-39 shows the datagram characteristics of the TCP chargen protocol. Table 4-40 shows similar information pertaining to the UDP chargen protocol.

Table 4-39 THE TCP chargen PROTOCOL

Conn. State	Source Addr.	Dest. Addr.	Protocol	Source Port	Dest. Port	SYN	ACK	Notes
New	Client	Server	TCP	>1023	19	Yes	No	Client opens chargen connection to server
Est.	Server	Client	TCP	19	>1023	Yes	Yes	Server acknowledges client
Est.	Client	Server	TCP	>1023	19	No	Yes	Established TCP connection, client to server
Est.	Server	Client	TCP	19	>1023	No	Yes	Established TCP connection, server to client

Table 4-40 THE UDP chargen PROTOCOL

Conn. State	Source Addr.	Dest. Addr.	Protocol	Source Port	Dest. Port	SYN	ACK	Notes
New	Client	Server	UDP	>1023	19	N/A	N/A	Client sends chargen request to server
Est.	Server	Client	UDP	19	>1023	N/A	N/A	Server sends chargen reply

daytime

The daytime service generates an ASCII-format date and timestamp. Table 4-41 shows the TCP datagram characteristics, and Table 4-42 shows the UDP datagram characteristics.

TABLE 4–41 THE TCP daytime PROTOCOL

Conn. State	Source Addr.	Dest. Addr.	Protocol	Source Port	Dest. Port	SYN	ACK	Notes
New	Client	Server	TCP	>1023	13	Yes	No	Client opens daytime connection to server
Est.	Server	Client	TCP	13	>1023	Yes	Yes	Server acknowledges client
Est.	Client	Server	TCP	>1023	13	No	Yes	Established TCP connection, client to server
Est.	Server	Client	TCP	13	>1023	No	Yes	Established TCP connection, server to client

TABLE 4–42 THE UDP daytime PROTOCOL

Conn. State	Source Addr.	Dest. Addr.	Protocol	Source Port	Dest. Port	SYN	ACK	Notes
New	Client	Server	UDP	>1023	13	N/A	N/A	Client sends daytime request to server
Est.	Server	Client	UDP	13	>1023	N/A	N/A	Server sends daytime reply

discard

The discard service has a function resembling that of /dev/null, ignoring data sent to it. However, the discard service operates on network traffic rather than on local data streams. Table 4-43 shows the TCP datagram characteristics, and Table 4-44 shows the UDP datagram characteristics.

TABLE 4-43 THE discard PROTOCOL

Conn. State	Source Addr.	Dest. Addr.	Protocol	Source Port	Dest. Port	SYN	ACK	Notes
New	Client	Server	TCP	>1023	9	Yes	No	Client opens discard connection to server
Est.	Server	Client	TCP	9	>1023	Yes	Yes	Server acknowledges client
Est.	Client	Server	TCP	>1023	9	No	Yes	Established TCP connection, client to server
Est.	Server	Client	TCP	9	>1023	No	Yes	Established TCP connection, server to client

TABLE 4-44 THE discard UDP PROTOCOL

Conn. State	Source Addr.	Dest. Addr.	Protocol	Source Port	Dest. Port	SYN	ACK	Notes
New	Client	Server	UDP	>1023	9	N/A	N/A	Client sends discard request to server
Est.	Server	Client	UDP	9	>1023	N/A	N/A	Server sends discard reply

echo

The echo service echoes data sent to it. It can serve a troubleshooting purpose similar to that of ICMP ping. Table 4-45 summarizes the TCP datagram characteristics. Table 4-46 summarizes the UDP datagram characteristics.

TABLE 4-45 THE echo PROTOCOL

Conn. State	Source Addr.	Dest. Addr.	Protocol	Source Port	Dest. Port	SYN	ACK	Notes
New	Client	Server	TCP	>1023	7	Yes	No	Client opens echo connection to server
Est.	Server	Client	TCP	7	>1023	Yes	Yes	Server acknowledges client
Est.	Client	Server	TCP	>1023	7	No	Yes	Established TCP connection, client to server
Est.	Server	Client	TCP	7	>1023	No	Yes	Established TCP connection, server to client

TABLE 4-46 THE echo UDP PROTOCOL

Conn. State	Source Addr.	Dest. Addr.	Protocol	Source Port	Dest. Port	SYN	ACK	Notes
New	Client	Server	UDP	>1023	7	N/A	N/A	Client sends echo request to server
Est.	Server	Client	UDP	7	>1023	N/A	N/A	Server sends echo reply

quotd

The quote-of-the-day (quotd) service provides a randomly selected quote. This service is not installed by default on Red Hat Linux systems. The fortune program provides a similar function for users of the local host.

Table 4-47 shows the TCP datagram characteristics, and Table 4-48 shows the UDP datagram characteristics.

TABLE 4-47 THE quotd PROTOCOL

Conn. State	Source Addr.	Dest. Addr.	Protocol	Source Port	Dest. Port	SYN	ACK	Notes
New	Client	Server	TCP	>1023	17	Yes	No	Client opens quotd connection to server
Est.	Server	Client	TCP	17	>1023	Yes	Yes	Server acknowledges client
Est.	Client	Server	TCP	>1023	17	No	Yes	Established TCP connection, client to server
Est.	Server	Client	TCP	17	>1023	No	Yes	Established TCP connection, server to client

TABLE 4-48 THE quotd UDP PROTOCOL

Conn. State	Source Addr.	Dest. Addr.	Protocol	Source Port	Dest. Port	SYN	ACK	Notes
New	Client	Server	UDP	>1023	17	N/A	N/A	Client sends quotd request to server
Est.	Server	Client	UDP	17	>1023	N/A	N/A	Server sends quotd reply

time

The time service provides a binary value that represents the elapsed time in UTC (Coordinated Universal Time) seconds since January 1, 1900. The xntp service is much more precise and much more widely used for time synchronization. Table 4-49 shows the datagram characteristics of the TCP time protocol, and Table 4-50 shows the datagram characteristics of the UDP time protocol.

TABLE 4-49 THE time PROTOCOL

Conn. State	Source Addr.	Dest. Addr.	Protocol	Source Port	Dest. Port	SYN	ACK	Notes
New	Client	Server	TCP	>1023	37	Yes	No	Client opens x connection to server
Est.	Server	Client	TCP	37	>1023	Yes	Yes	Server acknowledges client
Est.	Client	Server	TCP	>1023	37	No	Yes	Established TCP connection, client to server
Est.	Server	Client	TCP	37	>1023	No	Yes	Established TCP connection, server to client

TABLE 4-50 THE time UDP PROTOCOL

Conn. State	Source Addr.	Dest. Addr.	Protocol	Source Port	Dest. Port	SYN	ACK	Notes
New	Client	Server	UDP	>1023	37	N/A	N/A	Client sends time request to server
Est.	Server	Client	UDP	37	>1023	N/A	N/A	Server sends time reply

System and Network Administration Services

This section describes the datagram characteristics of several protocols used for system or network administration not described elsewhere in this chapter.

RWHO

The RWHO service supports two commands:

- ◆ `rwho` identifies users running on hosts of the local network.

- ◆ `ruptime` reports the up time, idle time, number of users, and average load of hosts on the local network.

The `rwho` command resembles `who`, and the `ruptime` command resembles `uptime`, except that each one operates on the local network rather than on the local host. Table 4-51 summarizes the RWho protocol, which uses UDP port 513.

TABLE 4-51 THE RWHO PROTOCOL

Conn. State	Source Addr.	Dest. Addr.	Protocol	Source Port	Dest. Port	SYN	ACK	Notes
New	Client	Server	UDP	>1023	513	N/A	N/A	Client sends RWHO query to server
Est.	Server	Client	UDP	513	>1023	N/A	N/A	Server sends RWHO reply

SIMPLE NETWORK MANAGEMENT PROTOCOL (SNMP)

The Simple Network Management Protocol (SNMP) provides a variety of network-management facilities and is widely implemented by network devices, such as switches and routers. However, the SNMP protocol does not provide sufficiently strong security mechanisms and safeguards to enable it to be safely run over a public network. Table 4-52 summarizes the datagram characteristics of SNMP.

TABLE 4-52 THE SNMP PROTOCOL

Conn. State	Source Addr.	Dest. Addr.	Protocol	Source Port	Dest. Port	SYN	ACK	Notes
New	Client	Server	UDP	>1023	161 or 162	N/A	N/A	Client sends SNMP request to server
Est.	Server	Client	UDP	161 or 162	>1023	N/A	N/A	Server acknowledges client

SYSTEM LOG

You can use the system log configuration file, /etc/syslog.conf, to specify that a host logs to a remote logging server. The remote logging protocol uses UDP port 514, as shown in Table 4-53. Notice that a remote logging server does not respond to its clients; the service it provides is write-only.

TABLE 4-53 THE syslog PROTOCOL

Conn. State	Source Addr.	Dest. Addr.	Protocol	Source Port	Dest. Port	SYN	ACK	Notes
New	Client	Server	UDP	>1023	514	N/A	N/A	Client sends SYSLOG entry to server

TRIVIAL FILE TRANSFER PROTOCOL (TFTP)

The Trivial File Transfer Protocol (TFTP) is a simple file transfer protocol for unauthenticated communication. The protocol, primarily useful as a booting protocol, is simple enough to be economically encoded in ROM. TFTP should not be allowed to traverse a firewall. Table 4-54 summarizes the datagram characteristics of the TFTP protocol, which uses UDP port 69.

TABLE 4-54 THE TFTP PROTOCOL

Conn. State	Source Addr.	Dest. Addr.	Protocol	Source Port	Dest. Port	SYN	ACK	Notes
New	Client	Server	UDP	>1023	69	N/A	N/A	Client sends TFTP request to server
Est.	Server	Client	UDP	69	>1023	N/A	N/A	Server responds to client
Est.	Client	Server	UDP	>1023	69	N/A	N/A	Client sends data to server

X Window System

The X Window System, also known simply as X, is the *de facto* standard Unix and Linux graphical user interface. A remarkable feature of X is its ability to communicate over a network. This feature enables a user to graphically launch and use a program running on a remote host. X, however, is not a particularly secure protocol. You should not generally extend X sessions across your firewall. If you choose to do so, you should employ SSL or some other form of cryptography to compensate for the weak intrinsic security of X.

From a firewall standpoint, X includes three primary facilities:

- The X server (X)

- The X Display Manager (XDM)

- The X Font Server (XFS)

X SERVER

In the terminology of X, a *server* is a program or host that presents a graphical user interface. An X *client* is a program that uses an X server. We often think of the host under control of the user as the client host. But, from the perspective of X, the host under control of the user runs an X server.

A single host can have several display adapters and can run multiple X servers. Each one runs on a separate TCP port beginning with port 6000. The number of ports used by X depends on the system configuration. The officially registered range extends from 6000 to 6063. Table 4-55 shows the datagram characteristics of the X protocol.

TABLE 4-55 THE X PROTOCOL

Conn. State	Source Addr.	Dest. Addr.	Protocol	Source Port	Dest. Port	SYN	ACK	Notes
New	Client	Server	TCP	>1023	6000-6063	Yes	No	Client opens X connection to server
Est.	Server	Client	TCP	6000-6063	>1023	Yes	Yes	Server acknowledges client

Continued

TABLE 4-55 THE X PROTOCOL *(Continued)*

Conn. State	Source Addr.	Dest. Addr.	Protocol	Source Port	Dest. Port	SYN	ACK	Notes
Est.	Client	Server	TCP	>1023	6000-6063	No	Yes	Established TCP connection, client to server
Est.	Server	Client	TCP	6000-6063	>1023	No	Yes	Established TCP connection, server to client

X DISPLAY MANAGER (XDM)

The X Display Manager (XDM) provides a means whereby users can graphically log in to and use a remote system. As shown in Table 4-56, XDM uses UDP port 177.

TABLE 4-56 THE XDM PROTOCOL

Conn. State	Source Addr.	Dest. Addr.	Protocol	Source Port	Dest. Port	SYN	ACK	Notes
New	Client	Server	UDP	>1023	177	N/A	N/A	Client sends XDM request to server
Est.	Server	Client	UDP	177	>1023	N/A	N/A	Server sends XDM reply

X FONT SERVER (XFS)

Like any graphical user interface, X requires fonts. Fonts can reside in files on the local host, be retrieved over the network, or both. The X Font Server (XFS) provides local and remote clients with access to fonts stored in files of the system on which the server runs. XFS uses TCP port 7100 by default. However, XFS is often configured to use some other port. Table 4-57 shows the datagram characteristics of the XFS protocol.

TABLE 4-57 THE XFS PROTOCOL

Conn. State	Source Addr.	Dest. Addr.	Protocol	Source Port	Dest. Port	SYN	ACK	Notes
New	Client	Server	TCP	>1023	7100	Yes	No	Client opens XFS connection to server
Est.	Server	Client	TCP	7100	>1023	Yes	Yes	Server acknowledges client
Est.	Client	Server	TCP	>1023	7100	No	Yes	Established TCP connection, client to server
Est.	Server	Client	TCP	7100	>1023	No	Yes	Established TCP connection, server to client

Internet Services Administration and Troubleshooting Tools

This section briefly explains how to use several Red Hat Linux commands that are helpful in administering and troubleshooting Internet services:

- ◆ netstat is part of the net-tools package
- ◆ ps is part of the procps package
- ◆ init is part of the initscripts package
- ◆ service is part of the initscripts package
- ◆ chkconfig is part of the chkconfig package

For more information on these and other commands for working with services, see Terry Collings and Kurt Wall's *Red Hat Linux Networking and System Administration* (Red Hat Press/Wiley, 2002).

netstat

The `netstat` command can show services that are listening for TCP or UDP clients. It can also show established TCP connections. To view information on TCP services, issue the command

```
netstat -tapn
```

To view information on UDP services, issue the command

```
netstat -uapn
```

Typical output of the command resembles the following:

```
Active Internet connections (servers and established)
Proto Recv-Q Send-Q Local Address        Foreign Address        State
PID/Program name
tcp        0      0 0.0.0.0:873          0.0.0.0:*              LISTEN
5215/xinetd
tcp        0      0 127.0.0.1:6010       0.0.0.0:*              LISTEN
16670/sshd
tcp        0      0 0.0.0.0:222          0.0.0.0:*              LISTEN
30591/sshd
tcp        0      0 192.168.1.7:56614    192.168.1.5:222        ESTABLISHED
17444/ssh
tcp        0      0 127.0.0.1:6010       127.0.0.1:56612        CLOSE_WAIT
16670/sshd
tcp        0      0 199.107.97.7:222     68.70.62.77:24658      ESTABLISHED
16670/sshd
tcp        0      0 199.107.97.7:222     68.70.62.77:24498      ESTABLISHED
16500/sshd
tcp        0      0 10.0.0.7:40332       10.0.0.6:873           ESTABLISHED
21470/rsync
```

The fields are shown in this list:

- ◆ `Proto`, the protocol (TCP or UDP)
- ◆ `Recv-Q`, the number of entries in the receive queue (normally zero)
- ◆ `Send-Q`, the number of entries in the send queue (normally zero)
- ◆ `Local Address`, the IP address of the local host
- ◆ `Foreign Address`, the IP address of the remote host
- ◆ `State`, the TCP/IP connection state (LISTEN, ESTABLISHED, and so on)
- ◆ `PID/Program name`, the process ID and program name

ps

The `ps` command discloses what processes exist. You can use it to determine whether a given service is running, as long as you know the name of the program or command associated with the service. To view the list of processes, issue the command

```
ps -A
```

The output resembles the following:

```
# ps -Aw
   PID TTY          TIME CMD
     1 ?        00:00:04 init
     2 ?        00:00:00 keventd
     3 ?        00:00:00 kapm-idled
     4 ?        00:00:05 ksoftirqd_CPU0
     5 ?        00:13:05 kswapd
     6 ?        00:00:00 kreclaimd
     7 ?        00:00:00 bdflush
     8 ?        00:01:41 kupdated
     9 ?        00:00:00 mdrecoveryd
    13 ?        00:00:34 kjournald
    88 ?        00:00:00 khubd
   186 ?        00:00:00 kjournald
   861 ?        00:00:04 crond
   914 ?        00:00:00 xfs
   950 ?        00:00:00 atd
   960 tty4     00:00:00 mingetty
   961 tty5     00:00:00 mingetty
   962 tty6     00:00:00 mingetty
 27927 tty3     00:00:00 mingetty
 27929 tty2     00:00:00 mingetty
  5215 ?        00:01:32 xinetd
 30591 ?        00:01:40 sshd
 30039 ?        00:00:58 arpwatch
 29474 ?        00:00:00 rhnsd
 20119 ?        00:00:00 rsync
 27103 ?        00:00:00 ntpd
 21468 ?        00:00:00 crond
 21470 ?        00:00:00 rsync
 21477 ?        00:00:00 sendmail
 21479 ?        00:00:00 rsync
  6304 tty1     00:00:00 mingetty
```

and so on ...

The output includes

- PID, the process identification number
- TTY, the associated console, if any
- TIME, the accumulated CPU time in hours, minutes, and seconds
- CMD, the command or program name

init

The init command enables you to view and set the run level. Each run level has an associated set of services that are configured to run at that level. The principal run levels are shown in this list:

- 1, single-user mode
- 3, multiuser mode
- 5, multiuser mode with XDM log

To set the current run level, issue the command

```
init n
```

where *n* is the desired run level. To view the current run level, issue the command

```
runlevel
```

The command prints the preceding run level, followed by the current run level.

chkconfig

The chkconfig command enables you to specify which services are enabled at a given run level. To view the current configuration, issue the command

```
chkconfig --list
```

The output resembles the following:

```
keytable       0:off   1:on    2:on    3:on    4:on    5:on    6:off
atd            0:off   1:off   2:off   3:on    4:on    5:on    6:off
kdcrotate      0:off   1:off   2:off   3:off   4:off   5:off   6:off
syslog         0:off   1:off   2:on    3:on    4:on    5:on    6:off
gpm            0:off   1:off   2:off   3:off   4:off   5:off   6:off
```

```
kudzu          0:off   1:off   2:off   3:on    4:on    5:on    6:off
sendmail       0:off   1:off   2:off   3:off   4:off   5:off   6:off
netfs          0:off   1:off   2:off   3:off   4:off   5:off   6:off
network        0:off   1:off   2:on    3:on    4:on    5:on    6:off
random         0:off   1:off   2:on    3:on    4:on    5:on    6:off
rawdevices     0:off   1:off   2:off   3:on    4:on    5:on    6:off
apmd           0:off   1:off   2:off   3:off   4:off   5:off   6:off
ipchains       0:off   1:off   2:off   3:off   4:off   5:off   6:off
iptables       0:off   1:off   2:on    3:on    4:on    5:on    6:off
crond          0:off   1:off   2:on    3:on    4:on    5:on    6:off
anacron        0:off   1:off   2:on    3:on    4:on    5:on    6:off
lpd            0:off   1:off   2:off   3:off   4:off   5:off   6:off
xfs            0:off   1:off   2:on    3:on    4:on    5:on    6:off
ntpd           0:off   1:off   2:on    3:on    4:on    5:on    6:off
portmap        0:off   1:off   2:off   3:off   4:off   5:off   6:off
xinetd         0:off   1:off   2:off   3:on    4:on    5:on    6:off
autofs         0:off   1:off   2:off   3:off   4:off   5:off   6:off
nfs            0:off   1:off   2:off   3:off   4:off   5:off   6:off
nfslock        0:off   1:off   2:off   3:off   4:off   5:off   6:off
nscd           0:off   1:off   2:off   3:off   4:off   5:off   6:off
identd         0:off   1:off   2:off   3:off   4:off   5:off   6:off
radvd          0:off   1:off   2:off   3:off   4:off   5:off   6:off
rwhod          0:off   1:off   2:off   3:off   4:off   5:off   6:off
snmpd          0:off   1:off   2:off   3:off   4:off   5:off   6:off
rhnsd          0:off   1:off   2:on    3:on    4:on    5:on    6:off
ypbind         0:off   1:off   2:off   3:off   4:off   5:off   6:off
isdn           0:off   1:off   2:off   3:off   4:off   5:off   6:off
sshd           0:off   1:off   2:off   3:off   4:off   5:off   6:off
rstatd         0:off   1:off   2:off   3:off   4:off   5:off   6:off
rusersd        0:off   1:off   2:off   3:off   4:off   5:off   6:off
rwalld         0:off   1:off   2:off   3:off   4:off   5:off   6:off
vncserver      0:off   1:off   2:off   3:off   4:off   5:off   6:off
yppasswdd      0:off   1:off   2:off   3:off   4:off   5:off   6:off
ypserv         0:off   1:off   2:off   3:off   4:off   5:off   6:off
ypxfrd         0:off   1:off   2:off   3:off   4:off   5:off   6:off
rarpd          0:off   1:off   2:off   3:off   4:off   5:off   6:off
arpwatch       0:off   1:off   2:on    3:on    4:on    5:on    6:off
xinetd based services:
        chargen-udp:    off
        chargen:        off
        daytime-udp:    off
        daytime:        off
        echo-udp:       off
        echo:   off
        time-udp:       off
```

```
time:    off
time:    off
sgi_fam:        off
finger: off
rexec:  off
rlogin: off
rsh:     off
ntalk:  off
talk:    off
telnet: off
rsync:  on
```

The output consists simply of the name of each service, followed by a list of run levels and states. When the designated run level is entered, the system starts or starts the service as indicated. The services listed at the end of the output are controlled by xinetd. These services have no associated run level and are either on or off. However, xinetd itself can be configured to run only at specified run levels. By default, it runs at run levels 3, 4, and 5.

To configure a service, issue the command

```
service --levels x name state
```

where *x* is the run level or levels for which you want to specify operation, *name* is the name of the service, and *state* is the word *on* or *off*. For example, to configure the httpd service to run at level 5 but not at level 3, you could issue the commands

```
service --levels 3 httpd off
service --levels 5 httpd on
```

As another example, to specify that the apmd service should not run at any level, issue the command

```
service apmd off
```

service

Configuring a service to run or not run at a particular run level does not immediately change the state of the service, which is potentially affected the next time the run level changes. To immediately change the state of a service, issue the command

```
service name action
```

where *name* is the name of the service and *action* is the operation you want to perform. Every service implements the actions *start* and *stop*. Many services implement additional actions, such as these:

- `restart` stops and then starts the service.

- `reload` reloads the service's configuration files.

- `status` shows the current status of the service.

To learn which operations a given service supports, issue the command

`service name`

where `name` is the name of the service.

Summary

This chapter explained the relationship between services and datagrams. It described how packet-filtering firewalls inspect datagrams and take action based on fields in the datagram headers. The chapter described in particular how firewalls accept or block datagrams according to whether datagram headers match firewall rules that implement security policies. The chapter explained in detail two commonly used application protocols, SSH and FTP. The chapter then summarized many other TCP/IP application protocols. Finally, the chapter explained several commands important to working with services. The chapter contains many important details that you'll find important and helpful when implementing your own firewalls.

Part II

Firewall Design and Implementation

Chapter 5

Firewall Architecture

IN THIS CHAPTER

- ◆ Packet-filtering technologies
- ◆ Proxying
- ◆ Network address translation (NAT)
- ◆ Virtual private networks (VPNs)
- ◆ Firewall configurations

THE FIRST PART OF THIS BOOK is concerned with the network context in which firewalls exist. As explained, a solid understanding of TCP/IP services and their protocols is crucial to designing secure firewalls. This, the second part of the book, begins the payoff for the effort you expended in reading the first part. This is the first of a series of chapters dealing with firewall design and implementation.

TCP/IP services and their protocols are explained in Chapter 2.

In this chapter, you learn about the technologies that constitute firewalls, including packet forwarding, packet filtering, and proxying. You also learn about important technologies often used in combination with firewalls, including network address translation (NAT) and virtual private networks (VPNs). After explaining firewall technologies, this chapter describes several common firewall architectures, examining the strengths and weaknesses of each.

Firewall Technologies

Part I explains stateless and stateful packet filtering. Most firewalls employ one or the other of these technologies. Stateful packet filtering was introduced in Red Hat Linux 7.0, so modern firewalls are more likely to use stateful filtering than are older firewalls.

151

In this chapter, I often use the term *packet* rather than *datagram* because most of the material applies to packets generally, not only to TCP/IP datagrams.

However, packet filtering isn't the only firewall technology in widespread use. Packet forwarding, a technology available since the first time two networks were joined, is also used. In this section, we look at packet forwarding and packet filtering and show how a sound firewall design can take advantage of both of them.

Packet Forwarding

The term *routing* refers to the process of moving packets from one network to another – that is, internetworking. Routing is performed by units called *routers*. A router can take any of several forms. For instance, several manufacturers – such as Cisco Systems and 3Com – provide hardware units designed to perform routing tasks. Desktop computers, including PCs, can also be used as routers. In the Linux world, it's not uncommon to see a PC that performs routing and provides Internet services. However, security may be compromised as a consequence of one's having combined routing with other functions. Most vulnerabilities are associated with Internet services rather than with routing facilities. Running a vulnerable Internet service on a host that performs routing may provide an attacker with the opportunity to compromise this type of mixed-function host, whereas a host performing only routing would present no such opportunity.

A basic router consists of a *dual-homed host,* or a host having two network adapters, each attached to a different network. A more elaborate router consists of a *multi-homed host,* or a host having more than two network interfaces. The basic function of a router is *packet forwarding:* moving packets from one network to another.

Figure 5-1 shows dual- and multi-homed hosts. The dual-homed host is capable of forwarding packets from Network A to Network B and from Network B to Network A. The multi-homed host is capable of forwarding packets among networks A, B, and C.

Every router has an associated *router table,* a set of rules that specify which packets should be forwarded and where (to what network) they should be forwarded. Figure 5-2 shows why these rules are necessary. Suppose that Router 1 receives from Network A a packet bound for Network F. Networks A and E are not adjacent, so Router 1 cannot forward the packet directly to Network F. Instead, Router 1 forwards the packet to Network E. Subsequently, Router 4 forwards the packet to its ultimate destination, Network F.

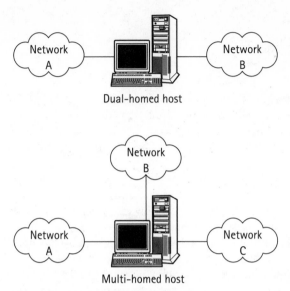

Figure 5-1: Dual- and multi-homed hosts

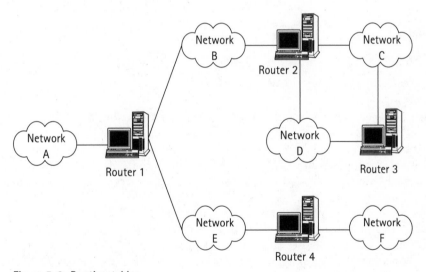

Figure 5-2: Routing tables

A routing table can be thought of as a series of lists, one for each network interface. Each list contains the IP addresses of hosts and networks reachable via the associated network interface. One special list, known as the *default route,* specifies the destination network for hosts and networks that do not explicitly appear in the other lists.

In determining whether and where to forward a packet, a router considers these factors:

- The interface on which the packet arrived

- The source IP address of the packet

- The destination IP address of the packet

More advanced routers may include features other than simple packet forwarding. For instance, they may support Quality of Service functions that prioritize network traffic and limit bandwidth flowing across network segments. On the other hand, some particularly simple routers consider only the destination IP address of packets.

Viewed from this perspective, routers seem to be quite simple devices. Consequently, network administrators sometimes overlook their value and importance to network security. Routers alone can't protect a network because they don't provide the fine level of control necessary to distinguish authorized traffic from unauthorized traffic. In particular, because ordinary routers don't examine the destination port of packets, routers can't determine the Internet service associated with a packet. Thus, routers are not useful for selectively blocking access to services.

However, routers are nevertheless useful as not only a means of joining networks but also a security tool. A router can help manage network security by blocking

- Packets that come from known hostile sources

- Spoofed packets

- Private IP addresses

A well-designed network has a limited number of routers connected to public networks. Such routers are called *border routers*. Programming border routers to block packets from known hostile hosts can be effective. However, doing so entails potentially blocking nonhostile traffic. So, before you make the decision to block a host, consider both the risks and benefits of continuing to accept traffic from the host.

Border routers can also be programmed to block spoofed packets; that is, packets having a fraudulent source address. Attackers often send spoofed packets bearing the source address of the target network against the target network. For instance, suppose that a firewall having an external IP address of 192.0.34.72 protects a network having an IP address of 192.168.0.0/24. An attacker might send spoofed packets having a source IP address of 192.168.0.1, which is within the address block associated with the protected network. If the firewall is not configured to block spoofed packets, it may permit the attacker to access hosts and services the firewall is intended to protect.

Chapter 11, "Bastion Host Implementation," explains how to configure Linux kernel options that block spoofed packets.

Similarly, border routers can — and should generally — be configured to block the private IP addresses identified in Chapter 4. Private IP addresses are intended to be nonroutable — that is, they should never appear on a public network. However, a poorly configured firewall may accept them. Blocking them at the border routers provides a layered defense that protects against a misconfigured firewall. Recall that, as explained in Chapter 3, the point of a layered defense is to prevent a single error or oversight from compromising security.

You should generally program border routers to block inbound packets having hostile, spoofed, or private IP source addresses. You should also generally program border routers to block outbound packets having hostile, spoofed, or private IP destination addresses. Doing so serves the interests of the local network and of the Internet generally. For instance, if every network blocked outgoing spoofed packets, spoofing would not be possible and an entire category of network attacks could be eliminated. Every site that blocks outgoing spoofed packets makes an attacker's task a bit more difficult, thus serving the general interest. Moreover, if your border routers block outbound spoofed traffic, an attacker who compromises one of your hosts cannot use the host in spoofing attacks against other networks. This situation serves the interest of your organization, which then doesn't suffer the loss of resources and reputation that might result from such use.

Packet Filtering

Chapter 4 explains that stateful packet filters look at the state of a connection in determining whether to accept a packet. Table 5-1 summarizes the inspection targets examined by packet forwarding, stateless packet filtering, and stateful packet filtering. You might correctly deduce from the table that stateful packet filtering can perform any task that might be performed by packet forwarding or stateless packet filtering. However, stateful packet filtering does not displace the other technologies. As explained, packet forwarding can be effectively used on border routers that do not support stateful packet filtering. More generally, stateful packet filtering demands greater computational capacity than do stateless packet filtering and packet forwarding.

TABLE 5-1 PACKET-FILTERING TECHNOLOGIES

Technology	Inspection targets
Forwarding	IP address
Stateless filtering	IP address, packet headers
Stateful filtering	IP address, packet headers, connection state

Figure 5-3 illustrates the relationship between the security potentially afforded by a packet-filtering technology and the processing overhead imposed by the technology. An optimal network security architecture is likely to employ all three technologies. For instance, a stateful packet-filtering firewall is likely to include rules that inspect only IP addresses or IP addresses and packet header fields. Not every rule inspects the connection state. The processing overhead imposed by more sophisticated rules generally exceeds that imposed by simpler rules.

I return to this issue in Chapter 10, "Advanced IPTables Firewall Implementation," where we consider firewall performance and optimization.

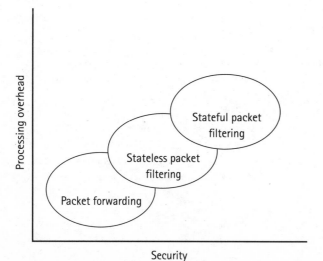

Figure 5-3: Packet-filtering technologies

Proxying

Another important firewall technology is known as *proxying*. The basic idea of proxying is delegation. Rather than allow two hosts to communicate directly, proxying forces them to communicate through an intermediary, known as the *proxy*. Sometimes, a proxy is referred to as a *gateway*. But because that term is also used in the context of routing, I prefer to avoid it and the potential confusion its use entails.

Figure 5-4 illustrates how proxying works. Proxying can be used to protect a client or a server. A proxy that protects a server is sometimes referred to as a *reverse proxy*.

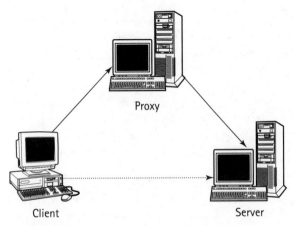

Figure 5-4: Proxying

If you compare proxying and packet forwarding, you find that they share similar characteristics. Both involve an intermediate host – the router or proxy – that enables other hosts to communicate. Various more or less precise definitions of the term *proxy* are intended to clarify this distinction. The most often used definition holds that packet forwarding passes the client's packet to the server whereas proxying entails generating and sending a new packet on behalf of the client. Sometimes, two types of proxies are distinguished:

- ◆ Circuit-level
- ◆ Application-level

Circuit-level proxies, like packet filters, inspect IP addresses and headers. Application-level proxies inspect the data content of packets. Because circuit-level proxies differ little from packet filters, it seems reasonable to refer to them as packet filters and reserve the term *proxy* for what would otherwise be called application-level proxies.

Application-level proxies – or simply proxies, as we call them – are more sophisticated and powerful than packet filters. Because proxies understand the application protocols embedded in the data contents of packets, proxies can analyze the requests issued by a client and accept or block them accordingly. For instance, when a request is spread over multiple packets, a packet filter cannot properly determine whether the request is an authorized one. The packet filter can inspect only the IP addresses and packet headers of each packet, which fail to disclose the state of the application. A proxy can inspect and verify every aspect of the request before determining the fate of a packet.

Moreover, a proxy can protect a client or server by concealing its identity. Because other hosts communicate with the proxy, they must know its IP address. But they don't need to know the IP address of the host the proxy protects, which may even be a nonroutable IP address.

Squid, a popular HTTP proxy that can work on behalf of clients or servers, understands the HTTP protocol and therefore can inspect the URL and other elements of a client's request. Squid can vet packets more comprehensively than a packet filter can, blocking requests or even rewriting URLs to protect a network from attack.

Another example of a popular proxy is the SMTP mail transfer agent sendmail. Mail by nature tends to be relayed from SMTP server to SMTP server, with each intermediate server acting as a proxy that can accept or block messages.

As another example, the IPTables facility included in the Red Hat Linux distribution includes a proxy agent for the FTP protocol, a module named `ip_conntrack_ftp`. This module monitors the traffic between an FTP server and a client. Because the module understands the FTP protocol, it can intercept and analyze the messages that inform an FTP host of the data port it should use. The proxy agent automatically adjusts the firewall's connection table to recognize traffic to and from the data port as related to the connection established via the FTP command port. This ability to analyze FTP messages enables the firewall to open the proper data port, but only to the FTP host that requested it.

Figure 5-5 shows how proxying fits within the firewall technologies scheme presented in Table 5-1 and Figure 5-3. Notice that proxying provides a potentially higher level of security than does packet forwarding or filtering but requires additional resources in order to do so.

Network Address Translation (NAT)

Network address translation (NAT) was originally designed to circumvent the cost and scarcity of routable IP addresses by enabling multiple hosts to share a single IP address. However, NAT has important applications to network security. NAT is a simple packet-filtering operation generally performed by a router or firewall, whereby packets' source or destination IP addresses are modified. In *destination NAT,* the destination IP address is modified. In *source NAT,* the source address is modified.

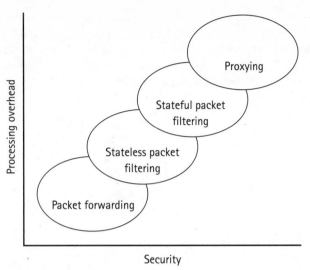

Figure 5-5: Packet filtering and proxying

To see how NAT is used, consider the example of destination NAT given in Figure 5-6. In the figure, a client sends requests to the mail service (port 25) and Web service (port 80) of the host having the IP address 192.0.34.72. This IP address is associated with a NAT-capable router that acts as a proxy. The router relays incoming traffic for destination port 25 to the host 10.0.0.1 and traffic for the destination port 80 to the host 10.0.0.2. Thus, two hosts act as though they share a single IP address. The number of such hosts is not important. It can be one, two, or more. What is important is that the client does not need to know – and moreover cannot discover – the IP address of the server that eventually handles its request. Unless the router is programmed to relay a given request, the request cannot be serviced. So, the router protects its associated servers from unauthorized access. When destination NAT is used this way, it's often referred to as *port forwarding*.

Source NAT works similarly, concealing the IP address of clients rather than servers (see Figure 5-7). When the hosts 10.0.0.1 and 10.0.0.2 send requests to external servers, the router modifies the packets to appear as though they were coming from the IP addresses 192.0.34.73 and 192.0.34.74. A single router can perform both source and destination NAT; however, the network configuration is likely to become complicated and perhaps error-prone.

Source NAT and destination NAT are collectively known as *static NAT*. In each case, the number of hosts associated with the router is fixed, and the associations between the public and concealed IP addresses are preconfigured. Another form of NAT, known as *dynamic NAT,* does not require preconfigured associations. Instead, when a client requests access to an external host, the router allocates a high-numbered port through which it proxies the connection. This type of router may handle thousands or tens of thousands of concurrent connections on behalf of dozens or hundreds of clients. Dynamic NAT is sometimes referred to as *masquerading* because – like source NAT – it conceals the identities of clients.

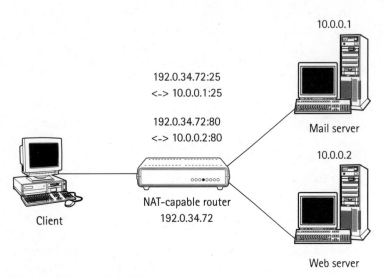

Figure 5-6: Destination NAT

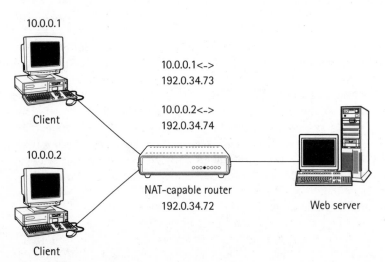

Figure 5-7: Source NAT

Other forms of NAT exist. For instance, NAT can be used to balance the load across multiple servers. It can also be used to improve network reliability by providing access to an alternate server when a primary server fails or becomes overloaded.

However, it's not always possible to use NAT. Some protocols, including such popular videoconferencing protocols as H.323, embed IP addresses in the data portion of packets. Because NAT inspects only packet headers, it does not modify embedded IP addresses. Protocol-specific proxies are required in order to perform network address translation on packets using such protocols.

Virtual Private Networks (VPNs)

Often, it's important to support remote users, such as employees accessing the network from home or the field, who want to be able to access the same services they access from the office and in the same way. Without a special facility to enable this type of access, the organization's firewall would otherwise prevent such users from accessing services remotely.

One popular way of supporting such users is with a virtual private network (VPN). A VPN establishes a connection, called a *tunnel,* between two networks or between a host and a network. The tunnel provides a special route between the two networks or between the host and network. VPNs generally encrypt traffic so that it can travel securely over intermediate networks. Figure 5-8 depicts a typical VPN.

VPNs are sometimes used to replace costly wide-area networks (WANs). Whenever VPN traffic travels across a public network – especially the Internet – the quality of the encryption is especially important. A VPN that uses a weak cryptographic scheme may be vulnerable to being compromised. VPNs tend to be somewhat less reliable than WANs because they involve more components. However, the decreased security and reliability afforded by a VPN may be offset by greater convenience and lower cost. Many routers provide a built-in VPN capability. If your router does not provide a VPN or if you prefer not to use it, you can use stunnel, CIPE, or FreeS/WAN to establish a simple VPN using Red Hat Linux. Because VPNs employ encryption, they tend to consume CPU cycles. You may need to upgrade the memory and speed of routers and hosts that support VPNs.

Appendix F explains how to establish a simple VPN using FreeS/WAN.

An important consideration when incorporating a VPN into a network is that the remote host or network may not be under good administrative control and may be vulnerable to attack. If an attacker compromises the remote network or host, the VPN provides the attacker with a platform from which to attack the local network. If

VPN users are granted special privileges that circumvent normal firewall restrictions, the attacker may quickly compromise vital internal systems. The maxim given in Chapter 3 applies: The security of a network is only as strong as its weakest point.

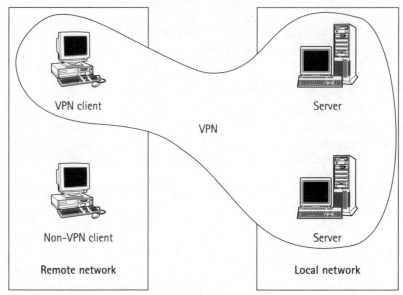

Figure 5–8: A virtual private network (VPN)

Common Firewall Architectures

Firewall design consists of two primary tasks:

◆ Design firewall rule sets.

◆ Specify the placement of the firewall or firewalls.

The placement of firewalls within a network is called the *firewall architecture*. Firewall architecture is tightly coupled with network architecture, and therefore firewall design is tightly coupled with network design. Firewall design is best viewed as a task within the larger task of network design. Considering the firewall without considering the network – or the reverse, considering the network without considering the firewall – is unwise and risky. The firewall and the network it protects must work together smoothly, or else network performance or security will suffer.

This section describes several common firewall architectures. An almost infinite variety of firewall architectures is possible, so the section isn't intended to be comprehensive. Instead, it's intended to introduce you to some common architectures and explain their strengths and weaknesses. Based on the architectures described in the section, you should be able to choose firewall architectures appropriate to your situation.

Router Firewalls

Figure 5-9 shows the first firewall architecture we'll study, an architecture known as the *router firewall*. Arguably, this architecture features no firewall; instead, a mere router joins an external network to an internal network. However, recall that the packet-forwarding operation performed by a router is a simple form of packet filtering that can be used to protect a network. The extent of the protection is small because packet forwarding inspects only the IP addresses of packets. However, this architecture is very common and may be, in fact, the most common. So, it's important to understand it, if for no reason other than to know its weaknesses.

For instance, most cable modem and DSL users employ this architecture. However, home computer users may not be able to offer public services, as shown in the figure, because of contractual or technical constraints imposed by the service provider. However, constraints that are technical in nature indicate the presence of at least a simple firewall within the provider's network. Such a case is an instance of the screened host firewall, described later in this chapter, rather than the router firewall.

The problems with this architecture are replete. Among the most serious are the following:

- The defense is shallow – that is, it lacks depth.
- The defense is inflexible.
- Public and private hosts reside on the same network.

The defense provided by this architecture is shallow because it provides only a single layer of security. If the router is compromised, no network security remains. Moreover, the defense is inflexible. The packet-forwarding router cannot be programmed to block or accept packets based on port numbers. Hence, any service offered on the internal network is also available externally. Therefore, it's not possible to provide private services.

Perhaps the most significant drawback of this architecture is the consequence of compromise of a public server. Because the public servers reside on the private network, each has unrestricted access to hosts of the private network. Moreover, the router can't block access to services that are defined as public. So, public servers are relatively vulnerable, and compromise of a public server is likely to lead to compromise of other hosts.

Despite the weaknesses of the router firewall architecture, you might choose it to minimize costs or maximize performance. Packet forwarding, though it provides poor security at best, is faster than more sophisticated firewall technologies. And, a packet-forwarding router is generally less expensive than a packet-filtering firewall.

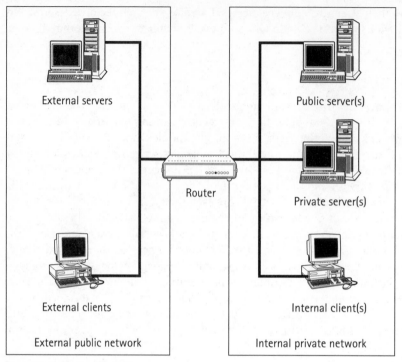

Figure 5-9: Router firewall

If you must use this architecture, note that the use of strong host-based security mechanisms can offset its security weaknesses. For instance, if host-based security mechanisms exist, the defense consists of two layers: the router and the host-based mechanisms. Two layers may not constitute defense in depth, but two layers are better than one. Moreover, host-based mechanisms can prevent external access to private services and can restrict access between local hosts.

Chapter 11, "Bastion Host Implementation," explains important host-based security mechanisms you can use to bolster the router firewall architecture.

Table 5-2 summarizes the pros and cons of the router firewall architecture.

TABLE 5-2 PROS AND CONS OF THE ROUTER FIREWALL ARCHITECTURE

Pros	Cons
Inexpensive	Inflexible
Simple to configure and operate	Leaves public servers and private hosts open to external network
Operates efficiently	Shallow defense depends solely on firewall

Single-Host Firewalls

This section explains several firewall architectures that employ only a single packet-filtering or proxying firewall. Packet-filtering firewalls are more popular than proxying firewalls because packet-filtering firewalls can accommodate a wider variety of protocols. However, bear in mind that proxying firewalls are capable of more sophisticated filtering than are packet-filtering firewalls. Often, both varieties of firewall are used in multi-host firewall architectures, such as those described in the next section.

Having a packet-filtering or proxying firewall rather than merely a packet-forwarding firewall lets you divide the protected network into two subnetworks:

- The internal private network

- The perimeter network, sometimes known as the DMZ (demilitarized zone)

Public servers reside on the perimeter network so that they're isolated from private servers and clients, often referred to as *LAN* (local-area network) *hosts*. Therefore, the compromise of a public server does not place the network in immediate jeopardy.

Figure 5-10 shows a simple single-host firewall architecture known as the *exposed host firewall*. Notice that, as explained, the firewall separates the public servers from the private servers and clients. Therefore, compromise of a public server does not place the internal private network in immediate jeopardy. Consider, too, that the firewall can filter, not merely forward, packets flowing to and from the internal private network. Thus, the firewall rule set can be more sophisticated than that possible with a router firewall. When combined with good host-based security, an exposed host firewall affords reasonable protection of the private internal network.

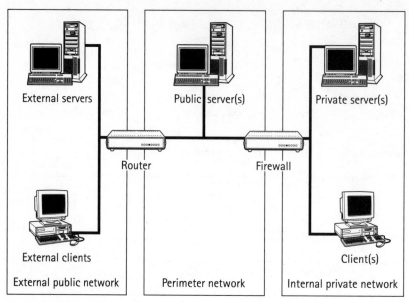

Figure 5-10: Exposed host firewall

The weak point of this architecture is the exposed public hosts. To resist attack, these hosts should be especially hardened – that is, they should be made especially resistant to attack. Consequently, they're sometimes referred to as *bastion hosts,* after the bastions that constitute the strongpoints of a medieval castle. Table 5-3 summarizes the pros and cons of the exposed host firewall architecture.

TABLE 5-3 PROS AND CONS OF THE EXPOSED HOST FIREWALL ARCHITECTURE

Pros	Cons
Only slightly more expensive than router firewall	Public servers vulnerable
More flexible than router firewall	Shallow defense depends solely on firewall
Private hosts screened by firewall	

However, the exposed host architecture places the public servers in a vulnerable position: They're wide open to attack from the external public network. A single-host firewall provides only two networks, and thus public servers can reside in only one of two places: the perimeter network or the internal private network. The exposed host firewall architecture places the public servers on the perimeter net-work. A second single-host firewall architecture, the screened host firewall shown in Figure 5-11, places the public servers on the internal private network.

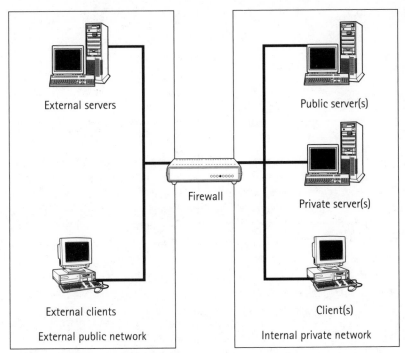

External servers

Public server(s)

Firewall

Private server(s)

External clients

Client(s)

External public network

Internal private network

Figure 5-11: Screened host firewall

The screened host firewall architecture resembles the router firewall architecture. The only distinction is the replacement of the packet-forwarding router with a packet-filtering or proxying firewall. Moving the public servers behind the firewall makes it possible for the firewall to filter traffic directed to and from the servers, thus reducing their vulnerability to attack. However, placing them behind the fire-wall leaves hosts on the internal private network vulnerable when a public server is compromised. On balance, the screened host firewall is generally somewhat more secure than the exposed host firewall because the screened host firewall exposes only the firewall, which is likely to be less vulnerable than a host. Every host is pro-tected from direct access by potential attackers. Table 5-4 summarizes the pros and cons of the screened firewall architecture.

TABLE 5-4 PROS AND CONS OF THE SCREENED HOST FIREWALL ARCHITECTURE

Pros	Cons
Only slightly more expensive than router firewall	LAN hosts vulnerable to compromised public server
More flexible than router firewall	Shallow defense depends solely on firewall
Public servers and private hosts screened by firewall	

Like the router firewall, neither the exposed host nor screened host firewall architecture strongly protects both public servers and private hosts. One or the other is likely to be vulnerable. Either architecture, if used, should be supplemented by strong host-based security mechanisms. On the plus side, these architectures are inexpensive to implement and relatively simple to configure and administer. Therefore, they're appropriate for small networks that do not require elaborate defenses.

Multi-Host Firewalls

Multi-host firewalls can overcome the security limitations of single-host firewalls. Figure 5-12 shows a multi-host firewall architecture known as the *screened* network firewall. The architecture includes two firewalls:

- An exterior firewall, sometimes referred to as the *gateway firewall*
- An interior firewall, sometimes referred to as the *choke firewall*

In comparison to the exposed host firewall, as shown in Figure 5-9, the screened network firewall substitutes a second firewall for the router.

This second firewall can protect the public servers from access by attackers. Every host in a screened network firewall is shielded by a firewall. Consequently, the screened network firewall architecture can provide a high degree of security. Table 5-5 summarizes the pros and cons of the architecture.

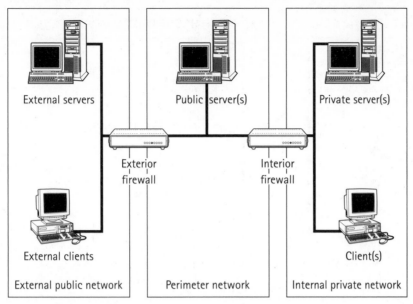

Figure 5-12: Screened network firewall

TABLE 5-5 PROS AND CONS OF THE SCREENED NETWORK FIREWALL
ARCHITECTURE

Pros	Cons
Public servers screened by firewall	More expensive than single-host architectures
Private hosts screened by firewall	
Multi-layered defense	

The security advantages of the screened network firewall in comparison to the single-host firewalls described earlier in this chapter are significant. You can simulate this architecture using a single, multi-homed host. The resulting configuration, shown in Figure 5-13, is known as the *three-way firewall architecture* because the firewall has three network adapters. Like the screened network firewall architecture, the three-way architecture places both public servers and private hosts behind a firewall. Therefore, like the screened network architecture, it can provide a high degree of security. Table 5-6 summarizes the pros and cons of the three-way firewall architecture.

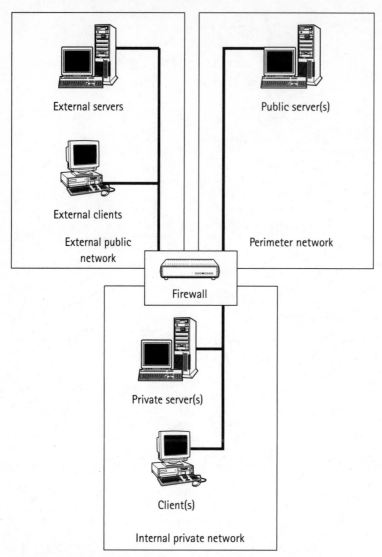

Figure 5-13: Three-way firewall

TABLE 5-6 PROS AND CONS OF THE THREE-WAY FIREWALL ARCHITECTURE

Pros	Cons
Less expensive than screened network architecture	More expensive than single-host architectures

Pros	Cons
Public servers screened by firewall	More complicated to set up and administer than screened network architecture
Private hosts screened by firewall	
Multi-layered defense	

Still more sophisticated architectures are possible. One popular variation, shown in Figure 5-14, is the *split-screened network architecture.* It closely resembles the screened network architecture, substituting dual-homed public servers in place of the screened network architecture's single-homed public servers. Dual-homed servers provide another layer of defense for hosts on the internal private network because traffic cannot flow from the external public network to the internal private network except by passing through a dual-homed host, which forwards traffic from one perimeter network to the other. The public server may provide proxies that thoroughly screen network traffic. Where this is the case, ordinary routers may be used in place of the firewalls shown in the figure.

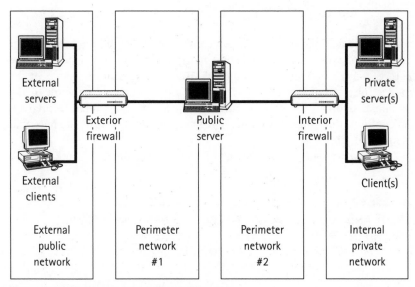

Figure 5-14: Split-screened network firewall

This arrangement also provides a means whereby hosts on the internal private network can communicate securely with the public server. The internal perimeter network, identified as perimeter Network #2 in the figure, is not directly accessible to external hosts. Commonly, this architecture is used as a means of providing administrative access to the public server so that it can be controlled, backed up, and so on. Often, multiple public servers are included, as shown in Figure 5-15.

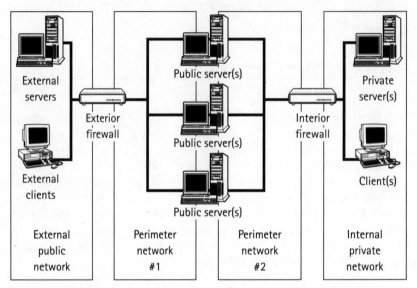

Figure 5-15: Multiple split-screened network firewall

Larger enterprises may require still more sophisticated firewall architectures. For instance, an enterprise that communicates via multiple external networks might use an architecture such as that shown in Figure 5-16. The architecture shown in the figure provides fully redundant routing from the internal private network to the external public networks. So, network access can be made reliable. Moreover, because the configuration is basically a screened network architecture, the potential level of security is high.

Table 5-7 summarizes the pros and cons of the split-screened network firewall architecture.

TABLE 5-7 PROS AND CONS OF THE SPLIT-SCREENED NETWORK FIREWALL
          ARCHITECTURE

Pros	Cons
Less expensive than screened network architecture	More expensive than single-host architectures
Public servers screened by firewall	Slightly more expensive than screened network architecture

Pros

Private hosts screened by firewall

Provides secure access to public servers
for administrative purposes

Multi-layered defense

Cons

Slightly more complicated to set up and
administer than screened network architecture

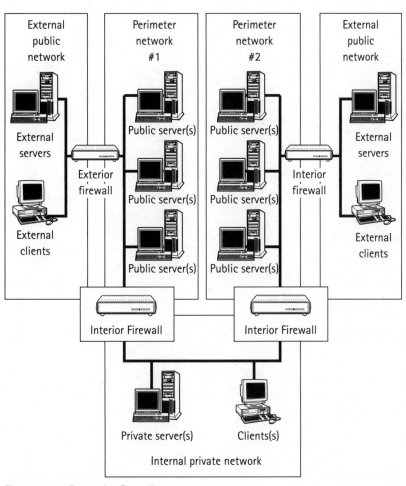

Figure 5-16: Enterprise firewall

Summary

This chapter explained firewall technologies, including packet forwarding, packet filtering, and proxying. It described the advantages of stateful packet filtering in comparison to stateless packet filtering. It explained two facilities often used with firewalls: network address translation (NAT) and virtual private networks (VPNs). Finally, it described several common firewall architectures, pointing out the pros and cons of each. The following chapter continues the discussion of firewall design and implementation by treating the topic of firewall policy design.

Chapter 6

Firewall Design

IN THIS CHAPTER

- ◆ The firewall life cycle
- ◆ Firewall costs and benefits
- ◆ Firewall architectures
- ◆ Firewall products
- ◆ Firewall policies

THIS CHAPTER ADDRESSES the managerial process and decisions related to firewall implementation. The chapter introduces the firewall life cycle and discusses the trade-offs inherent in balancing convenience and security. It explains a cost-benefit approach that can be used to quantify the benefits obtainable via a firewall. The chapter also addresses the choice of architecture and technology and the specification of firewall policies.

The Firewall Life Cycle

The discipline of software engineering has developed a model of software program development activities called the *software life cycle*. Although a firewall isn't a program as the term *program* is commonly understood, the process of creating a firewall closely resembles that of creating a software program. Both processes involve performing similar steps in a similar sequence. Just as the software life cycle is a useful guide to developing a software program, the *firewall life cycle* is a useful guide to developing a firewall.

The firewall life cycle consists of these steps:

- ◆ Requirements specification
- ◆ Justification
- ◆ Architectural design
- ◆ Policy design
- ◆ Implementation

◆ Testing

◆ Administration and maintenance

Figure 6-1 depicts the firewall life cycle.

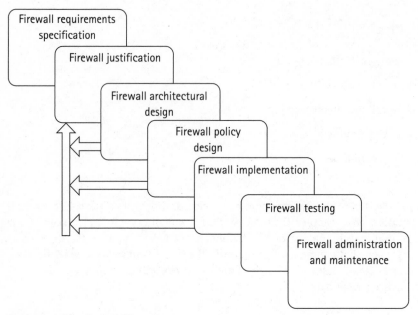

Figure 6-1: The firewall life cycle

Like the software life cycle, the firewall cycle is merely a model. That is, you shouldn't strive to follow it rigidly. For instance, you may sometimes find it convenient to begin one activity before completing the preceding activity. Occasionally, you may prefer to perform the activities in an unusual sequence. Such variations don't necessarily indicate a problem. The primary purpose of the firewall life cycle is to alert you to activities that might otherwise not be performed and to help you see useful relationships between the activities. In other words, the life cycle should *guide* you rather than restrict you.

Firewall Requirements Specification

The firewall requirements specification activity culminates in a document called the *firewall requirements specification*. The requirements specification spells out the function of the firewall. That is, it specifies the threats and risks that the firewall is intended to mitigate. The requirements specification emphasizes *what* the firewall does rather than the details of *how* the firewall works. In other words, the requirements specification is somewhat general.

Think of the requirements specification as defining the goals of the firewall deployment project. That is, the requirements specification provides the criteria by which the finished firewall is evaluated as a success or failure. Some typical criteria include

- Blocking the ingress and egress of spoofed traffic
- Blocking the ingress and egress of traffic bearing private IP addresses
- Blocking access to particular hosts and services
- Performing specified network address translation and masquerading operations

Firewall Justification

Obviously, creating a firewall involves the expenditure of organizational and financial resources. Management, which has the responsibility to scrutinize and authorize proposed expenditures, must be convinced that its losses (the expenditures related to a firewall) will be offset by its gain (the benefits of implementing a firewall). Often, however, the threats and risks associated with computer attacks may not seem significant to members of management, who may therefore be unwilling to fund the project. Conversely, network administrators may lack the business expertise necessary to persuade management that network security is important to the organization and therefore deserving of management's support.

The *justification* part of the firewall life cycle activity involves analyzing the organization's computer network security, assessing the threats and risks, and presenting the resulting conclusions to management in the form of a proposal for action. If the justification activity is omitted or performed in only a casual manner, management may not be convinced. Hence, the justification activity is important and is prerequisite to other firewall life cycle activities.

If management refuses to authorize a firewall, keep a copy of your request and justification. If your network is subsequently attacked and compromised, management may become somewhat more receptive to your proposal. If not, management may at least find it more difficult to blame you for poor network security.

The justification activity is important even to organizations that are already significantly invested in firewalls and network security. Attackers continually seek new ways to penetrate network defenses, compelling network administrators to respond by deploying new and improved countermeasures. If management can't grasp the value of proposed countermeasures and refuses to fund them, network security deteriorates.

Network administrators who lack a background in financial analysis may find that presenting a proposed network security project to management in a compelling manner is difficult. The section "Firewall Costs and Benefits" explains a simple method for assessing the benefits of a proposed firewall deployment. The method can assist the network administrator in translating technical considerations into business terms that managers understand.

Firewall Architectural Design

Chapter 5 describes some common firewall architectures. But, as explained, most firewalls don't precisely follow any of the architectures described in that chapter. Instead, the architecture of most firewalls is determined by local, idiosyncratic circumstances. The *architectural design* of a firewall consists of deciding which basic firewall architecture is most appropriate and then modifying and elaborating on the chosen architecture so that the result optimally meets the specified requirements. The architectural design also involves choosing firewall technologies and products.

Architectural design therefore involves these steps:

1. Identify candidate architectures and technologies.

2. Understand how each candidate architecture and technology would operate in the planned context.

3. Choose the candidate architecture and technology that are best for the organization.

4. Tweak the chosen architecture to improve its performance.

The sections "Firewall Architectural Design" and "Firewall Product Selection," later in this chapter, provide guidelines for performing firewall architectural design. Architectural design, like design generally, involves trade-offs. The most secure architecture is unlikely to be the least expensive. Therefore, the firewall designer must seek to balance a multitude of considerations that can affect the cost and performance of the firewall.

Sometimes, architectural design discloses that the initially estimated costs associated with a proposed project are insufficient. When this situation occurs, the justification activity is revisited. The administrator must prepare revised justification and again seek management approval.

Firewall Policy Design

Policy design entails the design of the firewall policies or rules that govern the operation of the firewall. This relatively straightforward activity involves these tasks:

1. Identify the hosts that will be permitted access to particular services.

2. Identify the datagram characteristics of each service.

3. Prepare a document — the firewall design — that specifies how the firewall handles datagrams, in terms of datagram characteristics.

When designing a relatively small firewall, the designer commonly combines the activities of policy design and implementation. When this part is done, the firewall design takes the form of a finished firewall rather than a document. However, it's generally valuable to create a firewall design for even a small firewall. A firewall design is less bulky and more readable than an implemented firewall. Thus, you can more easily review, and spot deficiencies in, a firewall design than in an implemented firewall. The section "Firewall Policy Design" provides guidelines related to firewall policy design.

Firewall Implementation

Firewall *implementation* involves realizing the firewall policy design in the form of a working firewall. Often, this process involves translating the firewall design into the syntactic form understood by the chosen firewall technology or product. However, some modern firewall products employ graphical user interfaces rather than command languages. In these cases, the firewall implementation consists of configuring the firewall product to perform as specified by the firewall policy design.

The remaining chapters of Part II address the process of firewall implementation.

Firewall Testing

After the firewall has been implemented, determining whether it operates correctly is essential. Firewall *testing* involves creating a dataset that exercises the firewall's features and prescribes how the firewall configuration should respond. By running the dataset against the firewall and comparing the firewall's expected and actual responses, you can determine with high confidence whether the firewall is operating properly. Small firewalls are often subjected merely to cursory testing or are not tested at all. However, you shouldn't rely on a firewall until its operation has been tested and verified. Even the most careful humans are likely to make errors, and a single error can provide an attacker with the opportunity to defeat even a sophisticated firewall.

Chapter 12, "Testing and Troubleshooting a Firewall," describes how to verify the operation of a firewall.

Firewall Administration and Maintenance

Firewalls are not "fire and forget" facilities; they require ongoing *administration and maintenance*. In particular, the firewall log can alert you to attacks, giving you time to bolster your network's defenses against particularly determined attackers.

Chapter 13, "Administering a Firewall," explains the care and maintenance of your implemented firewall.

Firewall Costs and Benefits

Management decisions are often made primarily on the basis of financial considerations. Even in nonprofit organizations, the financial implications of decisions are relevant and must be considered; otherwise, the financial viability of the organization may be compromised. Therefore, in proposing a firewall project to management, you must communicate the costs and benefits of the project in financial terms. This section presents some guidelines to help you in doing so.

One frequent error in assessing the costs associated with a firewall is to consider only the initial costs – that is, the costs of designing and deploying the firewall. Even a simple firewall requires some ongoing administration and maintenance after deployment. Hence, the estimated costs associated with a firewall project should include provision for ongoing expenditures. Generally, these expenditures are reasonably expressed as annualized costs, projected over several years. Most organizations have budgetary guidelines that specify the duration of the relevant period.

With respect to benefits, two distinct approaches are common: quantitative assessment and qualitative assessment. *Quantitative* assessment assigns a financial value to benefits, whereas *qualitative* assessment does not. Each approach has its proponents. Those who favor quantitative assessment often claim that qualitative assessment lacks rigor and is unsuitable as a basis for sound decision-making. Those who favor qualitative assessment often claim that accurately assigning financial value to uncertain and intangible benefits is impossible. Rather than take sides in this dispute, I briefly describe both quantitative and qualitative techniques you can use.

A Quantitative Approach

A popular quantitative approach uses the *annualized loss expectancy (ALE)* value. You can determine the ALE associated with a risk by using this procedure:

1. Determine the *financial value* of the assets or resources at risk.

2. Determine the *exposure factor* – that is, the percentage of the asset value at risk.

3. Compute the *single loss expectancy:*

   Single loss expectancy = Financial value × Exposure factor

4. Determine the *annualized rate of occurrence* – that is, the reciprocal of the average number of years between incidents of the risk.

5. Determine the *annualized loss expectancy* (ALE):

   ALE = Single loss expectancy / Annualized rate of occurrence

Suppose that a threat places at risk an asset worth $100,000. Further, suppose that if the threat is realized, it will reduce the value of the asset to 10% of its value before. The financial value is then $100,000, and the exposure factor is 90 percent. Therefore, the single loss expectancy is $100,000 × 90 percent = $90,000. If the threat is expected to be realized once every 10 years, the annualized rate of occurrence is 1 incident / 10 years = 0.1 incidents per year. The ALE is therefore $90,000 × 0.1 = $9,000.

To use the ALE in firewall decision-making, compute two ALE values – one with the firewall and one without. The difference between the two ALE values is the annualized financial benefit of the firewall. From a financial standpoint, the benefit of the firewall should outweigh its associated costs; otherwise, it would be less expensive to sustain the risk than to deploy the firewall.

Some organizations use more sophisticated financial-analysis techniques, such as discounted cash flow (DCF) or return on investment (ROI). If your organization is among these, you may need the assistance of a financial analyst to properly prepare your firewall proposal for presentation. However, the work of the analyst is facilitated by your determination of the annualized costs and the ALE. So, the technique is valuable even if it fails to meet your organization's financial-analysis standards.

A Qualitative Approach

In contrast to the quantitative approach, the qualitative approach does not involve specific numbers and computation. Instead, the qualitative approach involves identifying situations, or *scenarios,* involving one or more threats. The scenarios are classified according to their likelihood and the magnitude of the potential loss. Then, countermeasures are identified to mitigate the risks presented by each scenario. Ultimately, the scenarios and countermeasures are presented to members of management, who are asked to authorize the expenditures necessary to deploy the countermeasures.

The scenarios *must* be compelling and must be expressed in terms that management can understand. Management's concurrence in projects proposed via the qualitative approach is not rooted in a comparison of costs and benefits. Instead, it's fundamentally rooted in the concept of due care and diligence, the legal obligation of management to safeguard the interests of shareholders and other fiduciaries. Members of management who can be led to understand how computer security threats relate to management's obligation to fiduciaries can be persuaded to support network security projects.

Firewall Architectural Design

Firewall architectural design primarily involves determining the placement of firewalls and the choice of firewall products. This section deals with firewall placement, and the following section deals with firewall product selection.

Firewall architectural design shares many characteristics of other forms of design. Design benefits from iteration. Design also benefits from specific criteria that help the designer compare designs and choose the best. Unfortunately, choosing among firewall designs involves comparing many characteristics and evaluating many trade-offs. Hence, design tends to be learned through experience more than through precept. However, this list shows some clear figures of merit that can help you compare designs:

- The comprehensiveness of the firewall design, as measured by the percentage of hosts screened by at least one firewall

- The depth of the firewall design, as measured by the minimum number of firewalls and hosts that must be compromised in order to place the private network in jeopardy

- The convenience of the firewall design, as measured by the percentage of public hosts that provide private access for administration, backup, and related functions

- The reliability of the firewall design, as measured by the minimum number of firewalls and hosts that must fail in order to shut down an essential function

- The performance of the firewall design, as measured by the maximum sustained bandwidth it can carry

- The economy of the firewall design, as measured by the estimated cost to deploy it and the estimated annualized cost to operate and maintain it

Tips for Performing Architectural Design

Some network administrators design the placement of firewalls by using only a pencil and paper. However, most administrators find that using other forms of media is more convenient. One popular choice is a whiteboard. Its greater visibility is especially useful when multiple people are jointly participating in a firewall's design. If you use a whiteboard, you may find it helpful to obtain rubberized magnets, which you can use to represent firewalls and hosts. The 3" × 5" magnets are ideal in size. If the magnets have an appropriate coating, you can write on them using the same dry erase markers with which you write on the whiteboard and erase them when you're done. Using magnets speeds your work because you can quickly move them from place to place. Erasing and legibly redrawing a host takes only a few seconds, but that short interval adds up when performed dozens or hundreds of times.

Another popular tool is Microsoft Visio, a drawing program that includes common network shapes as well as ordinary geometric figures. Visio automatically aligns shapes and routes connections among them. With Visio, even those who lack artistic talent and training can create drawings that have a professional look. (If you grimace at this recommendation of a non-Linux software product, consider using Dia, which is described at http://www.lysator.liu.se/~alla/dia/. Though Dia doesn't yet include the full range of features available in Visio, it is included in the Red Hat Linux distribution.)

One primary feature of design is iteration. Old designs are repeatedly discarded in favor of new designs — often dozens of times — before an optimal design is discovered. Research has shown that novice designers iterate less than experts do. Novices tend to lock on to first-draft design, whereas experts more diligently probe the boundaries of the problem space. Therefore, tools such as whiteboards and Visio are important to the design process. Without them, the iteration that leads to design quality might be abbreviated because of the effort and tedium iteration entails.

The comparison of firewall architectures described in Chapter 5, "Firewall Architecture," is based on these figures of merit. For instance, the exposed host firewall architecture scores low on comprehensiveness and depth, whereas the screened network configuration scores well on both these figures of merit.

However, for several reasons, you should not simply tally these figures of merit and compare designs based on the resulting score. For instance, the first five figures of merit should be as large as possible, whereas the last figure of merit — economy — should be as small as possible. Moreover, the figures of merit generally have different relevance in different circumstances. In some circumstances, economy is a primary concern; in others, reliability is paramount. Furthermore, the figure of merit for comprehensiveness may be biased by a large number of private hosts so that significantly different designs nevertheless have similar figures of merit. Finally, the list of figures of merit is not comprehensive. You may find that your circumstances are unique in demanding a design characteristic not captured by the given figures of merit. In such a case, you should boldly take due consideration of relevant idiosyncrasies rather than slavishly consider only the given characteristics. If you use the list merely as a guide that helps ensure that you take proper account of commonly important firewall design characteristics, you'll do well.

Firewall Product Selection

The second primary aspect of firewall architectural design is the selection of firewall technology. Bear in mind that, as explained in Chapter 5, firewall technologies can be complementary. A small network may justify the deployment of only a single firewall technology. However, a large network may benefit from a firewall design that incorporates multiple technologies. As a rule of thumb, more sophisticated firewall technologies entail greater expense and processing overhead than simple firewall technologies.

Generally, designers don't choose a firewall technology. Instead, they choose a firewall *product* that implements one or more technologies. The underlying technology is one important reason for choosing among alternative products. Other important characteristics are shown in this list:

- ◆ Cost

- ◆ Features, such as NAT, VPN, logging, and monitoring

- ◆ Quality of support and documentation

- ◆ Ease of use

- ◆ Stability

- ◆ Performance

In this section, I briefly survey several popular firewall products, placing the emphasis on the technologies implemented by the firewall product. I also mention salient features, to communicate a feeling for the sorts of features commonly available. The firewall products surveyed are shown in this list:

- ◆ IPChains

- ◆ IPTables

- ◆ TIS Firewall Toolkit

- ◆ Firewall-1

- ◆ Hardware-based products

New firewall products are released fairly regularly, so this survey doesn't aim at being comprehensive. Instead, it focuses on firewalls that run under Linux. A few minutes spent using a search engine is likely to disclose additional firewall products.

IPChains

Red Hat Linux 6.2 and some earlier releases included support for IPChains. Later releases of Red Hat Linux also include support for IPTables, a newer firewall product described in the following section. Both IPChains and IPTables use Netfilter, a Linux kernel facility that provides hooks for implementing packet filtering. Although Red Hat Linux 8 uses IPTables for default firewalls, older releases used IPChains. So, knowledge of IPChains remains useful to you, the Red Hat Linux network administrator.

IPChains provides stateless packet filtering. Consequently, an IPChains firewall must generally accept incoming connections to registered ports, irrespective of their source or relationship to established connections. Therefore, IPChains firewalls are generally vulnerable to scans that have the TCP ACK flag set. Moreover, IPChains firewalls generally can't prevent users or malicious software, such as Trojan horses, from listening for and accepting incoming connections. Consequently, the potential security afforded by an IPChains firewall is inferior to that afforded by an IPTables firewall, which provides stateful packet filtering.

With respect to features, IPChains supports IP masquerading and port forwarding. *Port forwarding* is a special case of destination NAT in which the port number, but not the destination IP address, is subject to modification. IPChains does not support more general forms of source and destination NAT.

IPChains can log packets using the syslog facility. The standard IPChains user interface consists of a command, ipchains, that provides a variety of flags and arguments to control its operation. However, in releases prior to Red Hat Linux 8, the text-mode tool lokkit and the GUI tool gnomelokkit enable users to construct simple IPChains firewalls without using the command line.

Chapter 7, "IPChains Firewalls," describes the IPChains facility in detail.

Table 6-1 summarizes the characteristics of IPChains.

TABLE 6-1 CHARACTERISTICS OF IPCHAINS

Characteristic	Description
Technology	Stateless packet filtering
Masquerading	Yes

Continued

TABLE **6-1** CHARACTERISTICS OF IPCHAINS *(Continued)*

Characteristic	Description
NAT	Limited
Logging	Syslog
User interface	Command line

IPTables

Red Hat Linux 7.0 and later releases have included the IPTables facility. IPTables provides stateful packet filtering, IP masquerading, and source and destination NAT. Because IPTables performs stateful filtering, it can block incoming packets that are not part of or related to established connections. Consequently, unlike an IPChains firewall, an IPTables firewall can block unwelcome traffic on registered ports. A network protected by an IPTables firewall can be resistant to ACK scans and can restrict the ability of users and malicious software to listen for and accept incoming connections. Firewalls hosted by Red Hat Linux systems should generally be implemented using IPTables.

Like IPChains, IPTables can log accepted and blocked packets via the syslog facility. The IPTables user interface is the iptables command, which provides even more options than the ipchains command. Under Red Hat Linux 8, the tools lokkit and the gnomelokkit enable users to construct simple IPTables firewalls without using the command line.

Chapters 8–10 describe the IPTables facility in detail.

Table 6-2 summarizes the IPTables facility's characteristics.

TABLE **6-2** CHARACTERISTICS OF IPTABLES

Characteristic	Description
Technology	Stateful packet filtering
Masquerading	Yes

Characteristic	Description
NAT	Yes
Logging	Syslog
User interface	Command line

TIS Firewall Toolkit

The TIS Firewall Toolkit was developed in the early 1990s by Trusted Information Systems, Inc., under a grant from the U.S. Defense Advanced Research Projects Agency (DARPA). The Toolkit continues in use and remains somewhat popular. As its name suggests, it is a toolkit for creating firewalls rather than a firewall. Because the Toolkit is a toolkit rather than a ready-to-use firewall, implementing a firewall based on the Toolkit requires considerable tweaking and configuration and may require some programming. It is not, therefore, for the faint of heart.

Unlike IPChains and IPTables, the Toolkit provides a proxy-based firewall, thus affording a potentially high degree of flexibility and security. The Toolkit includes SMTP, HTTP, FTP, and several other proxies and provides templates for writing proxies for still more protocols. You can freely obtain the Toolkit — which is distributed in source form — and information about it at `http://www.fwtk.org/main.html`.

TABLE 6-3 CHARACTERISTICS OF TIS FIREWALL TOOLKIT

Characteristic	Description
Technology	Proxy
Masquerading	Yes
NAT	Yes
Logging	Syslog
User interface	Command line

CheckPoint Firewall-1

Firewall-1, from CheckPoint, is a popular commercial firewall that runs on several platforms, including Red Hat Linux. Some experts consider Firewall-1 the dominant commercial firewall product. Firewall-1 provides stateful packet filtering and NAT. In addition, it provides several important capabilities:

- ◆ High availability

- ◆ GUI-based management console

- ◆ Application-level content filtering

- ◆ Proxying of several protocols, including popular multimedia protocols

A firewall or other device is said to be available at any time it is capable of performing its designated function. A high-availability firewall is one that is designed to operate continuously or nearly continuously. To provide high availability, Firewall-1 can be deployed in multi-host configurations in which a secondary firewall host automatically takes over when a primary host fails. Application-level content filtering enables Firewall-1 to perform such operations as stripping potentially dangerous e-mail attachments. Moreover, Firewall-1 provides application-level proxying of such protocols as RealVideo, Windows Media, and H.323, which is used for Voice Over IP, NetMeeting, and other Internet conferencing applications.

Firewall-1 does not use the standard `syslog` facility; instead, it uses a proprietary log format. In its current release, Firewall-1 is capable of logging only the first packet associated with a connection, falling short of the logging characteristics of even the dated IPChains facility.

For more information on Firewall-1, see the CheckPoint Software Technologies Ltd. Web site, at `http:// www.checkpoint.com/index.html`. Table 6-4 summarizes the characteristics of Firewall-1.

TABLE 6-4 CHARACTERISTICS OF FIREWALL-1

Characteristic	Description
Technology	Stateful packet filtering
Masquerading	Yes
NAT	Yes
Logging	Proprietary log format
User interface	Graphical

Hardware-Based Products

The firewall facilities described so far in this chapter are software-based — that is, they run under Red Hat Linux. An alternative type of firewall facility is one running on a dedicated hardware unit, such as the Cisco PIX family of firewalls. In comparison to a firewall running on a general-purpose PC, PIX and similar units have no moving parts other than fans. Consequently, their reliability — as measured by their mean time between failures (MTBF) — is potentially higher than that of a firewall based on a general-purpose PC.

The PIX employs stateful packet filtering with limited support for special proxies, such as H.323. It is available in several models having bandwidth capacities ranging from about 10 Mbps to 1 Gbps. Because PIX units have no internal disk drive, they must record log entries to a separate logging server. The logging server can be a suitably configured standard `syslog` server or a dedicated hardware unit designed by Cisco to complement the PIX. As with Firewall-1, multiple PIX units can be configured for high availability through automatic failover.

Current versions of PIX provide a GUI for configuration. However, because not all configuration options are available via the GUI, many administrators prefer using the PIX command-line interface. PIX includes an integral DES Virtual Private Network (VPN); a higher-security 3DES VPN is available as an option.

For an overview of VPNs, see Appendix F.

For more information on PIX, see the Cisco Web site, `http://www.cisco.com/`. Table 6-5 summarizes the characteristics of PIX.

TABLE 6-5 CHARACTERISTICS OF PIX

Characteristic	Description
Technology	Stateful packet filtering
Masquerading	Yes
NAT	Yes
Logging	External
User interface	Limited graphical and command line

Firewall Policy Design

Firewall policy design entails the detailed specification of how the firewall responds to packets that have particular characteristics. Perhaps the most important firewall design decision is the choice of a default policy. The *default policy* specifies the handling of packets not matching a firewall rule. A firewall that accepts unmatched packets is a *permissive firewall;* a firewall that blocks unmatched packets is a *restrictive firewall.* A restrictive firewall is potentially more secure than a permissive firewall. However, a restrictive firewall may not provide users with a level of flexibility consistent with organizational culture. For example, research scientists may not be well served by a restrictive firewall because their work habits typically emphasize spontaneity and creativity. The choice between a restrictive and permissive firewall is therefore more of a political than a technical decision, and it should be made with the participation of network administrators, users, and members of management. Generally, the decision is made during the firewall requirements specification rather than during the firewall policy design.

After the default firewall policy has been decided, the firewall rule set can be specified. Doing so entails examining the firewall specifications and creating rules that conform to the specifications. A template, such as the one shown in Table 6-6, can facilitate firewall policy design, especially when the design is implemented as a packet-filtering IPChains or IPTables firewall. The columns of the template are

- ◆ **Act:** The action to be performed. For an IPChains or IPTables firewall, the possible entries are accept, drop, reject, and log.

- ◆ **IF:** The interface on which an incoming packet arrives or to which an outgoing packet is directed.

- ◆ **State:** For an IPTables firewall, the state of the connection, which can be new, established, or related. This column is not used for an IPChains firewall.

- ◆ **TCP Flags:** Flags, such as SYN or ACK, that must be set in a matching packet.

- ◆ **Pro:** The TCP/IP protocol, which can be tcp, udp, or icmp or the value all, which matches any protocol.

- ◆ **SIP:** The source IP address, optionally followed by a slash and the number of one-bits in the network mask. The value 0.0.0.0 matches any IP address.

- ◆ **SPort/ICMP Type:** The source port number (UDP and TCP datagrams) or the ICMP type (ICMP datagrams).

- ◆ **DIP:** The destination IP address, optionally followed by a slash and the number of one-bits in the network mask. The value 0.0.0.0 matches any IP address.

- ◆ **DPort/ICMP Type:** The destination port number (UDP and TCP datagrams) or the ICMP code (ICMP datagrams).

- ◆ **Comments:** Notes that may help you understand or use the template entry.

TIP

You can adapt the template to better suit the implementation vehicle you plan to use for local circumstances. For instance, if your firewall technology or products provide special capabilities, you may choose to add one or more columns to the template, to permit specification of the capabilities.

TABLE 6-6 FIREWALL POLICY DESIGN TEMPLATE

Act	IF	State	TCP Flags	Pro	SIP	SPort/ ICMP Type	DIP	DPort/ ICMP Code	Comments

You complete a design template by analyzing the services identified in the firewall requirements specification to determine their datagram characteristics. The characteristics are then recorded, along with the appropriate action and interface, on the policy design template.

The sample template shown in Table 6-7 shows a set of rules that block incoming spoofed traffic bearing a source IP address within the private 10.0.0.0/8 network and outgoing spoofed traffic bearing a destination address within that network. In addition to dropping the spoofed traffic, the rules specify that the traffic be logged. A completed firewall policy design consists of an ordered series of these types of templates, along with several additional types of templates that specify NAT operations.

TABLE 6-7 FIREWALL POLICY DESIGN EXAMPLE

Act	IF	State	TCP Flags	Pro	SIP	SPort/ ICMP Type	DIP	DPort/ ICMP Code	Comments
log	eth0	Any	Any	Any	10.0. 0.0/8	Any	Any	Any	Log incoming spoofed traffic
drop	eth0	Any	Any	Any	10.0. 0.0/8	Any	Any	Any	Drop incoming spoofed traffic
log	eth0	Any	Any	Any	Any	Any	10.0. 0.0/8	Any	Log outgoing spoofed traffic
drop	eth0	Any	Any	Any	Any	Any	10.0. 0.0/8	Any	Drop outgoing spoofed traffic

The NAT operations destination NAT, source NAT, and IP masquerading can also be specified by using simple templates. Table 6-8 shows a sample template specifying a destination NAT operation that redirects traffic bound for port 80 of the host 192.0.32.74 to port 80 of a host on the private network 10.0.0.1, which runs a Web server.

TABLE 6-8 DESTINATION NAT EXAMPLE

IF	Pro	SIP	SPort/ ICMP Type	DIP	DPort/ ICMP Code	DNAT IP	DNAT DPort	Comments
eth0	Any	Any	Any	192.0. 32.74	80	10.0. 0.1	80	Forward to Web server

Table 6-9 shows a complementary sample template that specifies the source NAT operation that redirects outbound traffic from the private Web server.

TABLE 6-9 SOURCE NAT EXAMPLE

IF	Pro	SIP	SPort/ ICMP Type	DIP	DPort/ ICMP Code	SNAT IP	SNAT DPort	Comments
eth0	Any	10.0.0.1	80	Any	Any	192.0. 32.74	80	Forward to Web client

Similarly, you can use a simple template to specify IP masquerade operations. Table 6-10 shows an example.

TABLE 6-10 MASQUERADE EXAMPLE

IF	Pro	SIP	SPort/ ICMP Type	DIP	DPort/ ICMP Code	MASQ IP	Comments
eth0	any	10.0.0.0/8	any	Any	Any	192.0.32.74	Masquerade clients

Summary

This chapter describes the firewall life cycle and presents several techniques you can use in the early stages of that life cycle, culminating in a firewall policy design. In the next two chapters, you learn how to implement the firewall design as an IPChains or IPTables firewall.

Chapter 7

IPChains Firewalls

IN THIS CHAPTER

- ◆ The IPChains facility
- ◆ The IPChains packet path
- ◆ The ipchains command
- ◆ A simple IPChains firewall
- ◆ IPChains administration
- ◆ The lokkit tool

IPCHAINS IS THE ORIGINAL FIREWALL FACILITY provided in Red Hat Linux. According to Rusty Russell, maintainer of the IPChains HOWTO, "Linux ipchains is a rewrite of the Linux IPv4 firewalling code (which was mainly stolen from BSD) and a rewrite of ipfwadm, which was a rewrite of BSD's ipfw, I believe." You can obtain the IPChains HOWTO at `http://www.tldp.org/HOWTO/IPCHAINS-HOWTO.html`.

Recent versions of Red Hat Linux have also included the newer, more sophisticated IPTables facility. Unlike IPTables firewalls, IPChains firewalls are non-stateful, as explained in the section of Chapter 4 titled "Firewall States." Therefore, IPChains firewalls must generally accept `ACK` datagrams – that is, datagrams having the TCP `ACK` flag set – incoming on the registered ports (1024 and higher) because such datagrams might be return traffic from a remote server. By inspecting the `ACK` flag rather than a connection table, IPChains firewalls rely on the packet itself to determine whether the packet is part of an established connection. Consequently, IPChains firewalls are potentially less secure than IPTables firewalls and may require more effort in implementation. Moreover, IPChains provides only limited support for network address translation.

Nevertheless, learning about IPChains is useful. Red Hat Linux releases 7.0 to 7.3 constructed firewalls using IPChains rather than IPTables. Because IPChains firewalls are potentially less secure than IPTables firewalls, you may not want to deploy an IPChains firewall as your frontline defense. However, if you run IPTables or another stateful firewall at your network's perimeter, you may choose to implement firewalls on network hosts to provide a second layer of defense.

This chapter explains how to use `lokkit` to create a simple firewall. Under Red Hat Linux 7.0 to 7.3, `lokkit` builds an IPChains firewall. Under subsequent releases, `lokkit` builds an IPTables firewall. The chapter also explains the operation of the IPChains facility at a level adequate to equip you to customize the firewalls created by `lokkit` or `gnome-lokkit` or to manually create simple IPChains firewalls. However, the chapter doesn't cover IPChains comprehensively because IPTables — not IPChains — should be the focus of your attention.

The IPChains Facility

The IPChains facility consists of these components:

- ◆ The `ipchains` command
- ◆ The /etc/init.d/ipchains script
- ◆ The scripts `/sbin/ipchains-save` and `/sbin/ipchains-restore`
- ◆ The documentation in `/usr/share/docs/ipchains-*`

In addition, IPChains includes a script used to make IPChains operate like an even older Linux firewall technology, `ipfwadm`. This script makes IPChains easy to use for those familiar with `ipfwadm`.

To implement an IPChains firewall, use the `ipchains` command. To start, stop, and otherwise control the firewall, use the `/etc/init.d/ipchains` script. When you specify the relevant argument to this script, it invokes `/sbin/ipchains-save` or `/sbin/ipchains-restore`, which store firewall status information in `/etc/sysconfig/ipchains`. Thus, you don't need to invoke those scripts directly. The remainder of this chapter explains the `ipchains` command and the `/etc/init.d/ipchains` script. The chapter doesn't explain the script used to make IPChains operate like `ipfwadm` because `ipfwadm` is obsolete. For more information on `ipfwadm`, see the FAQ at `http://www.dreamwvr.com/ipfwadm/ipfwadm-faq.html`.

The IPChains Packet Path

The name of the IPChains facility is descriptive of the facility's operation. IPChains establishes a chain consisting of a series of processing steps that an incoming or outgoing packet must traverse. Several steps apply filters that can result in the packet's being blocked. If none of the filters blocks the packet, IPChains sends it to its destination, which can be a local process or a network interface. Figure 7-1 illustrates the IPChains packet path.

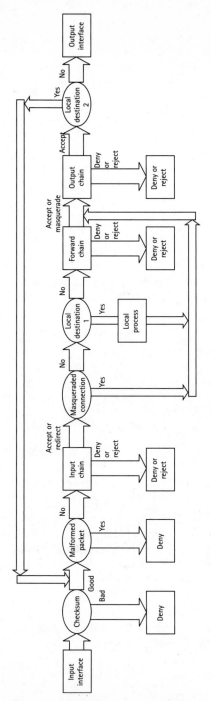

Figure 7-1: The IPChains packet path

The steps on the packet path are

- ◆ Input interface
- ◆ Checksum
- ◆ Malformed packet
- ◆ Input chain
- ◆ Masqueraded connection
- ◆ Local destination 1
- ◆ Local process
- ◆ Forward chain
- ◆ Output chain
- ◆ Local destination 2
- ◆ Output interface

Packets enter the path in either of these ways:

- ◆ An incoming packet arrives at a network interface.
- ◆ A local process generates a packet.

Incoming packets can be delivered to a local process or, if IP forwarding is enabled, sent to an output interface. The following subsections describe the steps of the packet path in detail.

Input Interface

The *input* interface is the interface at which an incoming packet arrives. The interface is associated with a network adapter rather than with the loopback device, which is used when a local process sends a packet to another process on the local host. Packets sent via the loopback device enter the packet path elsewhere. A firewall host may have multiple input interfaces.

Checksum

The checksum step verifies the checksum of the incoming packet. If the checksum is not valid, IPChains writes a system log entry and drops the packet.

Malformed Packet

The malformed packet step performs further checks on data in the packet headers. This step is also performed at other points in the packet path, although these are not shown in Figure 7-1. Like packets having bad checksums, malformed packets are logged and dropped.

Input Chain

The input chain is the first of three processing steps that are specified by the user. The `ipchains` command lets you specify tests that the IPChains facility applies to packets traversing the input chain and actions that the IPChains facility performs when the tests are satisfied. Because all incoming packets traverse the input chain, this processing step is the primary means of restricting traffic flowing into or through the firewall.

Masqueraded Connection

The masquerade connection step checks whether an incoming packet is associated with a masqueraded connection. A *masqueraded* connection is one using the restricted form of network address translation supported by IPChains. Such packets bear the IP address of the firewall host as their destination address but are intended for another host. IPChains modifies their destination address to indicate the actual destination host and sends them to the output chain.

Local Destination 1

The local destination 1 step checks to see whether the destination IP address of an incoming packet is that of the firewall host. If so, the packet is forwarded to the proper local process. Otherwise, the packet is sent to the forward chain.

Local Process

The local process step represents a process on the firewall host. A local process can receive packets, send packets, or receive and send packets. Packets sent by local processes enter the packet path at this step.

Forward Chain

The forward chain is the second of three user-specified chains. Nonmasqueraded packets arriving at an input interface and having a destination address other than that of the local host traverse the forward chain. Thus, you can use the forward chain to specify whether packets are authorized to flow between networks.

Output Chain

The output chain is the third of three user-specified chains. Packets sent by a local process or arriving at an input interface but not intended for the local host must traverse the output chain. You can use the output chain to specify whether packets are authorized to exit the firewall.

Local Destination 2

The local destination 2 step performs the same operation as the local destination 1 step, checking a packet's destination IP address. If the packet's destination is the local host, the step sends the packet back to an earlier point in the path via the loopback device. Otherwise, the packet is sent to the proper output interface.

Output Interface

Like the input interface, the output interface is an actual interface device rather than the loopback device. A firewall host may have several output interfaces. Packets exiting the firewall do so via an output interface.

The ipchains Command

The `ipchains` command is your means for specifying the firewall rules contents associated with the three chains that control the flow of packets: input, forward, and output. In addition, the `ipchains` command lets you perform several administrative functions, such as listing the rules associated with a specified chain. If you prefer to use a text-based or graphical user interface, you can build a firewall using the `lokkit` or `gnome-lokkit` programs, which are explained in the section of this chapter titled "Using the `lokkit` Tool." However, like other non-command-based interfaces, `lokkit` and `gnome-lokkit` present a simplified view of the IPChains facility and do not enable you to express rules as detailed as those expressible via the `ipchains` command.

IPChains Operations

The `ipchains` command provides three types of operation:

- ◆ Operations on rules
- ◆ Operations on chains
- ◆ Operations related to the masqueraded feature

With regard to rules, the basic operations add rules to or delete them from a specified chain. Before explaining how to perform these operations, let me first explain the structure of IPChains rules.

Structure of an IPChains Rule

An IPChains rule specifies packet characteristics. When a packet is tested against a rule, the packet's characteristics either match or don't match those of the rule. If the characteristics match, the action associated with the rule is performed. The packet characteristics that can be inspected are shown in this list:

- The associated network interface or interfaces
- The source IP address
- The destination IP address
- The protocol
- The source and destination ports, if the packet is a TCP or UDP datagram
- The ICMP type and code, if the packet is an ICMP message
- The IP flags and, if the packet is a TCP datagram, the TCP flags

An ipchains rule consists of these parts:

- Command name
- Rule operation
- Packet characteristics
- Rule action

Figure 7-2 shows a typical ipchains rule. The rule specifies that packets incoming on the interface eth0 and having a source address within the Class A address block 10.0.0.0/8 should be dropped. The following subsections explain how packet characteristics and rule actions are specified. The immediately following section explains the possible rule operations and how they're specified. The information is slightly abridged because a comprehensive treatment would require many pages and would include many operations of limited value. For instance, many ipchains flags can be specified in several forms, but generally this chapter gives only the most common form. For more information on the ipchains command, see the command's man page or the IPChains HOWTO, available at http://netfilter. samba.org/ipchains/.

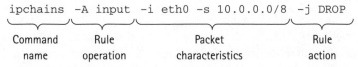

```
ipchains  -A input  -i eth0 -s 10.0.0.0/8  -j DROP
```

| Command name | Rule operation | Packet characteristics | Rule action |

Figure 7-2: A typical IPChains rule

INTERFACE
Packets on the input chain are associated with the interface on which they arrived. Packets on the forward and output chains are associated with the interface to which

they will be sent. The name of an interface is the name reported by the `ifconfig` command. For example, the name of the network interface on a host having a single network interface is typically `eth0`. The name of the loopback interface is `lo`.

To specify the interface associated with a packet, follow the flag `-i` with the name of the interface. For example, the following partial command specifies `eth1` as the interface that a packet must match in order for the action associated with the rule to be performed:

```
-i eth1
```

To see how the interface is specified in an actual command, refer to Figure 7-2.

SOURCE IP ADDRESS

The source IP address of a packet identifies the host that sent the packet. To specify a source address, follow the `-s` flag with the host or network IP address. You can use CIDR notation—explained in Chapter 2, "TCP/IP Quick Start"—to specify the netmask associated with a network IP address. For example, to specify that a packet must have the source IP address 192.0.34.72, use this partial command:

```
-s 192.0.34.72
```

To specify any host within the 192.0.34.0/24 network, use this partial command:

```
-s 192.0.34.0/24
```

To see how the `-s` flag is used in an `ipchains` command, refer to Figure 7-2.
The following partial command matches any source IP address:

```
-s 0.0.0.0/0
```

You may sometimes see it—or the equivalent abbreviated form `0/0`—used to explicitly indicate that the source address doesn't matter. Omitting the `-s` flag and the associated IP address would more concisely achieve the same result.

To specify that a packet must not have a specified source IP address, precede the IP address with an exclamation mark, as in this example:

```
-s ! 192.0.34.0/24
```

The example specifies that the source IP address must not be within the 192.0.34.0/24 network.

DESTINATION IP ADDRESS

The destination IP address can be specified in the same manner as the source IP address. However, the `-d` flag is used rather than `-s`. For example, to specify that a destination address must lie within the 10.0.0.0/8 network, use this partial command:

```
-d 10.0.0.0/8
```

As with the source IP address, you can negate the destination IP address by preceding it with an exclamation mark.

PROTOCOL
To specify the protocol associated with a packet, follow the `-p` flag with a specifier identifying the protocol. The specifier can take any of these forms:

- ◆ The protocol name `tcp`, `udp`, or `icmp`

- ◆ A protocol number

- ◆ A protocol name, as given in `/etc/protocols`

- ◆ The word `all`, designating that any protocol matches

As with the source and destination IP addresses, you can negate the protocol by preceding it with an exclamation mark. For example, to specify that the protocol must not be TCP, use this partial command:

```
-p ! tcp
```

PORTS
For TCP and UDP datagrams, you can specify a source or destination port or both. The source port is specified via the `--sport` flag, and the destination port is specified via the `--dport` flag. Ports can be specified as a number or a range. To specify a range, separate the lower and upper limits by a colon. For example, to specify that a packet must have a source port in the reserved range and a destination port of 80, use this partial command:

```
--sport 1024:65535 --dport 80
```

You can negate a port number or range by preceding it with an exclamation mark and a space in the same manner used to negate a protocol.

ICMP TYPE AND CODE
For ICMP messages, you can specify the ICMP type and code. To do so, follow the flag `--icmp-type` with one of the type names given in Table 7-1. For example, to specify an ICMP host-unreachable message, use this partial command:

```
--icmp-type host-unreachable
```

You can negate the ICMP type by preceding it with an exclamation mark.

TABLE 7-1 IPCHAINS ICMP TYPE NAMES

Type	Code	Type Name
0	0	echo-reply
3		destination-unreachable
	0	network-unreachable
	1	host-unreachable
	2	protocol-unreachable
	3	port-unreachable
	4	fragmentation-needed
	5	source-route-failed
	6	network-unknown
	7	host-unknown
	9	network-prohibited
	10	host-prohibited
	11	TOS-network-unreachable
	12	TOS-host-unreachable
	13	communication-prohibited
	14	host-precedence-violation
	15	precedence-cutoff
4	0	source-quench
5		redirect
	0	network-redirect
	1	host-redirect
	2	TOS-network-redirect
	3	TOS-host-redirect
8	0	echo-request
9	0	router-advertisement
10	0	router-solicitation
11		time-exceeded

Type	Code	Type Name
	0	ttl-zero-during-transit
	1	ttl-zero-during-reassembly
12		parameter-problem
	0	ip-header-bad
	1	required-option-missing
13	0	timestamp-request
14	0	timestamp-reply
17	0	address-mask-request
18	0	address-mask-reply

IP AND TCP FLAGS

By including the -f flag, you can specify that the packet's IP fragment flag must be set. You can negate this specification by preceding it with an exclamation mark and a space: ! -f.

By including the flag --syn, you can specify that the SYN flag of a TCP datagram must be set. You can negate this specification by preceding it with an exclamation mark in the usual way: ! --syn.

TARGET

The action associated with an IPChains rule is referred to as the *target*. IPChains provides these target specifiers:

◆ ACCEPT passes the packet to the next processing step.

◆ REJECT blocks the packet and sends an ICMP error message to the sender.

◆ DENY silently blocks the packet.

◆ RETURN exits a user-defined chain and returns to the chain that invoked it.

In addition, IPChains provides two specifiers that perform network address translation: REDIRECT and MASQ. For information on these specifiers and the RETURN specifier, see the ipchains man page or the IPChains HOWTO.

To specify a target, use the -j flag. For example, to specify that a packet should be denied, use this partial rule:

```
-j DENY
```

Logging

The IPChains facility can also log packets. If you include the -l flag in an ipchains rule, packets matching the rule specification are sent to the syslog facility for logging. The log entry appears as specified in the /etc/syslog.conf file. For example, to log packets having a source IP address in the 192.168.0.0/24 network, use this partial command:

```
-s 192.168.0.0/24 -l
```

Rule Operations

Now that you can specify packet characteristics and IPChains actions, you're ready to learn how to add rules to the firewall rule set. This section explains how to do so and also how to delete existing rules.

APPENDING A RULE TO A CHAIN

Firewall rules can be added to any of the three user-specified chains: input, output, and forward. The rules of a chain are evaluated in sequence; therefore, rules must be added in the proper order or else they don't operate properly. You can add a rule at the beginning or end of a chain. Adding a rule at the beginning of a chain is termed *inserting* the rule. Adding a rule at the end of a chain is termed *appending* the rule. Rules are more commonly appended than inserted because rules appended to a chain are executed in the order in which they were appended.

To append a rule to a chain, issue a command having this form:

```
ipchains -A chain specs -j target
```

where chain is the name of the chain, specs represents one or more flags and values specifying packet characteristics, and target is the action to be performed if a packet matches the specified packet characteristics. For example, to append a rule to the input chain, specifying that TCP packets bound for port 25 of the host 10.0.0.25 should be accepted, issue this command:

```
ipchains -A input -p tcp -d 10.0.0.25 --dport 25 -j ACCEPT
```

The new rule is executed after existing rules on the chain.

INSERTING A RULE INTO A CHAIN

To insert a rule so that it is executed before existing rules on its chain, specify the -I flag rather than the -A flag. For example, to insert a rule into the output chain, specifying that ICMP messages having type echo-reply should be denied, issue this command:

```
ipchains -I -p icmp --icmp-type echo-reply -j DENY
```

The new rule is executed before existing rules on the chain.

DELETING A RULE

To delete an existing rule, specify the `-D` flag. The rule specifications must match those of the rule you want to delete. Suppose that you want to delete the rule created by the command

```
ipchains -I -p icmp --icmp-type echo-reply -j DENY
```

To do so, issue this command:

```
ipchains -D -p icmp --icmp-type echo-reply -j DENY
```

Notice that the two rules are identical except that the `-D` flag replaces the `-I` flag used in the command that created the rule. If more than one rule matches the included specifications, only the first such rule is deleted.

The `ipchains` command provides other flags that enable you to replace rules and delete rules based on a rule number. See the `ipchains` man page or HOWTO for further information.

Chain Operations

In addition to enabling you to perform rule operations, the `ipchains` command enables you to perform several chain operations, including:

- ◆ Set the default policy of a chain.
- ◆ List the rules in a chain.
- ◆ Flush a chain.

In addition, the `ipchains` command provides operations that let you create and delete user chains and zero packet counters associated with a chain. However, these operations are not explained in this book. For more information about them, see the `ipchains` man page or the IPChains HOWTO.

SETTING THE DEFAULT POLICY OF A CHAIN

A packet that reaches the end of a chain is automatically accepted, denied, or rejected. The action that is performed is determined by the default policy of the chain. You can specify the default policy of a chain by using the `-P` flag of the `ipchains` command. For example, to set the default policy of the input chain to DENY, issue the command

```
ipchains -P input DENY
```

If you set the default policies of the firewall's chains to ACCEPT, you generally have a permissive firewall. A firewall having default policies of DENY or REJECT is generally a restrictive firewall, which is potentially more secure than a permissive firewall. However, you can arrange other firewall rules in such a way that packets seldom or never reach the end of a chain. In such a case, the type of firewall may not be obvious merely from an inspection of the default policies.

LISTING THE RULES IN A CHAIN

You can list the rules in a firewall chain by using the -L flag of the ipchains command. For example, to list the rules in the input chain of a firewall, issue the command

```
ipchains -L input
```

The command output resembles the following:

```
[root@patrick root]# ipchains -L input
Chain input (policy ACCEPT):
target      prot opt      source          destination     ports
ACCEPT      all  ------   anywhere        anywhere        n/a
REJECT      tcp  -y----   anywhere        anywhere        any ->    0:1023
REJECT      tcp  -y----   anywhere        anywhere        any ->    nfs
REJECT      udp  ------   anywhere        anywhere        any ->    0:1023
REJECT      udp  ------   anywhere        anywhere        any ->    nfs
REJECT      tcp  -y----   anywhere        anywhere        any ->    x11:6009
REJECT      tcp  -y----   anywhere        anywhere        any ->    xfs
```

You can modify this basic command in several ways:

- ◆ To obtain more detailed output, specify the -v flag.

- ◆ To show protocol numbers rather than port names and host IP addresses rather than host names, specify the -n flag.

- ◆ To list all chains, omit the chain name. For example, the following command lists all chains, showing detailed information and IP addresses:

```
ipchains -n -v -L
```

The output of this command resembles the following:

```
[root@patrick root]# ipchains -n -v -L
Chain input (policy ACCEPT: 3613 packets, 227887 bytes):
 pkts bytes target      prot opt   tosa tosx ifname     mark      outsize ⤶
 source        destination   ports
```

```
    0     0 ACCEPT     all  ------ 0xFF 0x00  lo  ⟳
0.0.0.0/0          0.0.0.0/0   n/a
    0     0 REJECT     tcp  -y---- 0xFF 0x00  *  ⟳
0.0.0.0/0          0.0.0.0/0   * ->   0:1023
    0     0 REJECT     tcp  -y---- 0xFF 0x00  *  ⟳
0.0.0.0/0          0.0.0.0/0   * ->   2049
    3   234 REJECT     udp  ------ 0xFF 0x00  *  ⟳
0.0.0.0/0    0.0.0.0/0         * ->   0:1023
    0     0 REJECT     udp  ------ 0xFF 0x00  *  ⟳
0.0.0.0/0    0.0.0.0/0         * ->   2049
    0     0 REJECT     tcp  -y---- 0xFF 0x00  *  ⟳
0.0.0.0/0    0.0.0.0/0         * ->   6000:6009
    0     0 REJECT     tcp  -y---- 0xFF 0x00  *  ⟳
0.0.0.0/0    0.0.0.0/0         * ->   7100
Chain forward (policy ACCEPT: 0 packets, 0 bytes):
Chain output (policy ACCEPT: 431 packets, 39816 bytes):
```

FLUSHING A CHAIN

Removing all rules from a chain is termed *flushing* the chain. To flush a chain, specify the -F flag and the name of the chain. For example, to flush the input chain, issue the command

```
ipchains -F input
```

 Flushing a chain removes all rules from the chain. If the default policy associated with the chain is ACCEPT, the absence of rules may place your system or network at risk. Consequently, you should not generally flush a chain of a firewall that's exposed to threats. Instead, remove the system from the network before performing firewall maintenance.

Other Operations

The ipchains command provides several other operations, among them specifying masquerading and setting time-outs for various operations. For information about other IPChains operations, see the ipchains man page or the IPChains HOWTO. Table 7-2 summarizes the flags associated with the ipchains command.

TABLE 7-2 FLAGS ASSOCIATED WITH THE ipchains COMMAND

Flag	Meaning
-A	Append a rule to a chain
-D	Delete a rule from a chain
-d	Destination IP address
--dport	Destination port
-F	Flush a chain
-f	Fragment flag set
-I	Insert a rule into a chain
-i	Interface name
--icmp-type	ICMP type name
-j	Jump to specified target
-L	List rules
-l	Log the packet
-n	List port numbers and IP addresses rather than names
-P	Set the default chain policy
-p	Protocol
-s	Source IP address
--sport	Source port
--syn	SYN flag set
-v	Include details in rule list

A Simple Firewall

By inserting rules into chains, you build a complete firewall. Here's a quite simple but complete firewall:

```
ipchains -P input ACCEPT
ipchains -P forward ACCEPT
ipchains -P output ACCEPT
ipchains -A input -s 0/0 -d 0/0 -i lo -j ACCEPT
```

```
ipchains -A input -p tcp -s 0/0 -d 0/0 0:1023 -y -j REJECT
ipchains -A input -p tcp -s 0/0 -d 0/0 2049 -y -j REJECT
ipchains -A input -p udp -s 0/0 -d 0/0 0:1023 -j REJECT
ipchains -A input -p udp -s 0/0 -d 0/0 2049 -j REJECT
ipchains -A input -p tcp -s 0/0 -d 0/0 6000:6009 -y -j REJECT
ipchains -A input -p tcp -s 0/0 -d 0/0 7100 -y -j REJECT
```

The resulting firewall resembles the medium-security firewall built by the lokkit tool; it rejects incoming connections to privileged ports but generally accepts connections to other ports. As the chain policies indicate, it is a permissive firewall and therefore not highly secure. Moreover, it incorporates ingress filtering only; no egress filtering is performed.

This list summarizes the firewall policies implemented by the firewall:

◆ Accept packets arriving from the loopback device.

◆ Reject incoming TCP SYN packets destined for privileged ports (0–1023).

◆ Reject incoming TCP SYN packets destined for port 2049, which is associated with the Network File System.

◆ Reject incoming UDP packets destined for privileged ports (0–1023).

◆ Reject incoming UDP packets destined for port 2049.

◆ Reject incoming TCP SYN packets destined for ports 6000–6009, associated with the X Window System.

◆ Reject incoming TCP SYN packets destined for port 7100, associated with the X Font Server.

◆ Accept all other packets.

Administering IPChains

Several commands and scripts are involved in administering IPChains:

◆ sysctl

◆ /etc/init.d/ipchains

◆ chkconfig

The following subsections explain how these commands and scripts are used in connection with IPChains.

sysctl

The `sysctl` command enables you to specify kernel options, such as one that enables the forwarding of IP packets from one interface to another. When a host boots, it consults the `/etc/sysconfig.ctl` file and issues `sysctl` commands as directed by the contents of that file. If your host has multiple network interfaces, you're likely to want to enable packet forwarding. To do so, include the following line in the `/etc/sysconfig.ctl` file:

```
net.ipv4.ip_forward = 1
```

If a similar line assigns another value to this variable, delete the line or place a hash mark (#) in its first column. For more information on the `sysctl` command, see Chapter 11, "Bastion Host Implementation." For information on other potentially useful kernel options, see the file `/usr/src/linux-2.4/Documentation/Configure.help`.

/etc/init.d/ipchains

The `/etc/init.d/ipchains` script controls the operation of the IPChains facility. The script can be invoked directly, but it is generally invoked via the `service` command, which avoids the need to specify the path, in this fashion:

```
service ipchains argument
```

where *argument* indicates the operation to be performed. Several arguments are supported. You can obtain a list of arguments by issuing the command

```
service ipchains
```

The following subsections explain the related operations.

TIP

If you execute the command

```
su
```

the value of the `PATH` environment variable may not include `/sbin`, the directory in which the `service` command resides. Instead, issue the command

```
su -
```

which causes the new shell's environment to be set up as if you'd logged in as the `root` user. This ensures that the `PATH` variable has an appropriate value.

SERVICE ipchains STATUS

The `status` argument indicates that the script should report the status of the IPChains facility. The script does so by using the `ipchains -L` command to list the contents of the chains. You generally should issue the `ipchains -L` command manually because you can specify flags that better control the extent and type of output.

SERVICE ipchains START

The `start` argument starts the IPChains facility. Starting IPChains entails loading the chains by consulting the file `/etc/sysconfig/ipchains`, which contains saved IPChains rules. The format of this file resembles the one used by the `ipchains` command. However, this format omits the command name and presents some information in a form that differs from that used in the `ipchains` command. For example, this file specifies the firewall given in the preceding section:

```
:input ACCEPT
:forward ACCEPT
:output ACCEPT
-A input -s 0.0.0.0/0.0.0.0 -d 0.0.0.0/0.0.0.0 -i lo -j ACCEPT
-A input -s 0.0.0.0/0.0.0.0 -d 0.0.0.0/0.0.0.0 0:1023 -p 6 -j REJECT -y
-A input -s 0.0.0.0/0.0.0.0 -d 0.0.0.0/0.0.0.0 2049:2049 -p 6 -j REJECT -y
-A input -s 0.0.0.0/0.0.0.0 -d 0.0.0.0/0.0.0.0 0:1023 -p 17 -j REJECT
-A input -s 0.0.0.0/0.0.0.0 -d 0.0.0.0/0.0.0.0 2049:2049 -p 17 -j REJECT
-A input -s 0.0.0.0/0.0.0.0 -d 0.0.0.0/0.0.0.0 6000:6009 -p 6 -j REJECT -y
-A input -s 0.0.0.0/0.0.0.0 -d 0.0.0.0/0.0.0.0 7100:7100 -p 6 -j REJECT -y
```

STOP SERVICE ipchains

The `stop` argument flushes all chains and sets the default policy of each chain to `ACCEPT`. In effect, it turns off the firewall. Be careful in using this command because your firewall and network may be vulnerable to attack when the firewall is disabled.

SERVICE ipchains RESTART

The `restart` argument has the same effect as serially issuing the command

```
service ipchains start
```

In effect, this argument resets the firewall state to that specified in the `/etc/sysconfig/ipchains` file. Because the command flushes firewall chains, your firewall host and network may be vulnerable to attack during its execution. Therefore, you should disconnect the firewall from the public network before issuing this command.

SERVICE ipchains SAVE

The `save` argument causes the current firewall state to be saved in the file `/etc/sysconfig/ipchains`. The next time the firewall is started or restarted, it assumes the current state rather than the one previously stored in the file.

SERVICE ipchains RESTORE AND SERVICE iPCHAINS PANIC

The `restore` argument (Red Hat Linux 7.0 to 7.2) or the `panic` argument (Red Hat Linux 7.3) causes the firewall to assume the state previously saved in the `/etc/sysconfig/ipchains` file. During the transition, the firewall host and network may be vulnerable to attack. Therefore, you should disconnect the firewall from the public network before issuing this command.

chkconfig

The `ckconfig` command specifies whether a given service is started at a given system-run level. In particular, the `chkconfig` command can be used to specify that the IPChains facility starts – or does not start – whenever the system enters run level 3 or 5. To specify that the IPChains facility should be automatically started, issue the command

```
chkconfig --level 345 ipchains on
```

To specify that the IPChains facility should not be automatically started, issue the command

```
chkconfig ipchains off
```

The `chkconfig` command does not start or stop the IPChains facility; its effect occurs the next time the specified run level is entered. To immediately start or stop the IPChains facility, use the `/etc/init.d/ipchains` script, described earlier in this section.

Using the lokkit Tool

The `lokkit` tool, written by Red Hat, provides an easy way to create simple IPChains firewalls. As explained earlier in this chapter, if the user requests during system installation that a firewall be installed, the Red Hat Linux installation program uses `lokkit` to create it.

`lokkit` can be used from a text-mode terminal or an X session and requires the use of only the keyboard and console. The related `gnome-lokkit` tool provides a graphical user interface that enables the use of the mouse. Because many system administrators choose not to install X on servers, this section addresses the `lokkit` tool rather than `gnome-lokkit`. However, the interface presented by `gnome-lokkit` is straightforward. Anyone familiar with X is unlikely to experience difficulty in figuring out the gnome-lokkit user interface.

You can launch the lokkit tool by issuing this command:

lokkit

Upon launch, the lokkit main screen, as shown in Figure 7-3, appears. As explained on the last line of the screen, you operate the lokkit user interface by pressing these keys:

◆ Tab is used to move forward from field to field.

◆ Alt+Tab is used to move backward from field to field.

◆ Space is used to select a choice or click a button.

Figure 7-3: The lokkit main screen

The main screen lets you choose from three security levels:

◆ High blocks all incoming connections.

◆ Medium blocks incoming connections to privileged ports (0–1023) and a few nonprivileged ports that present special vulnerabilities.

◆ No firewall accepts all incoming packets.

Listing 7-1 shows the IPChains rules equivalent to the medium-security firewall generated by lokkit, and Listing 7-2 shows the IPChains rules equivalent to the high-security firewall.

The lokkit user interface is simple. Press Tab to move to the desired security level and press the spacebar to choose it. You can then press Tab to move to the OK button and press the spacebar to exit lokkit. Alternatively, you can press Tab to move to the Customize button and press the spacebar to customize the firewall. If you use Tab to move to the Cancel button and press the spacebar, lokkit exits without changing the firewall configuration.

Listing 7-1: The medium-security firewall

```
ipchains -P input ACCEPT
ipchains -P forward ACCEPT
ipchains -P output ACCEPT
ipchains -A input -s 0/0 -d 0/0 -i lo -j ACCEPT
ipchains -A input -p tcp -s 0/0 -d 0/0 0:1023 -y -j REJECT
ipchains -A input -p tcp -s 0/0 -d 0/0 2049 -y -j REJECT
ipchains -A input -p udp -s 0/0 -d 0/0 0:1023 -j REJECT
ipchains -A input -p udp -s 0/0 -d 0/0 2049 -j REJECT
ipchains -A input -p tcp -s 0/0 -d 0/0 6000:6009 -y -j REJECT
ipchains -A input -p tcp -s 0/0 -d 0/0 7100 -y -j REJECT
```

Listing 7-2: The high-security firewall

```
ipchains -P input ACCEPT
ipchains -P forward ACCEPT
ipchains -P output ACCEPT
ipchains -A input -s 0/0 -d 0/0 -i lo -j ACCEPT
ipchains -A input -s 199.184.237.168 53 -d 0/0 -p udp -j ACCEPT
ipchains -A input -s 0/0 -d 0/0 -p tcp -y -j REJECT
ipchains -A input -s 0/0 -d 0/0 -p udp -j REJECT
```

When you exit `lokkit` by using the OK button, `lokkit` saves the configured firewall to the `/etc/sysconfig/ipchains` file. When you next start IPChains, the firewall is loaded. If you use the Customize button, the `lokkit` Customize screen, as shown in Figure 7-4, appears. This screen lets you specify that a network interface is *trusted,* which means that traffic from the interface should be authorized to freely access services residing on the firewall host. If you have multiple network interfaces, each one should be listed.

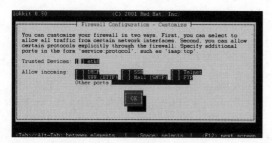

Figure 7-4: The lokkit customization screen

The Customize screen also lets you specify services running on the firewall host that external hosts should be authorized to access. The screen includes check boxes for these services:

◆ DHCP, the Dynamic Host Configuration Protocol, running on UDP ports
   67–68

◆ SSH, the Secure Shell service, running on port 22

◆ Telnet, the remote login service, running on port 23

◆ WWW (HTTP), the Web service, running on port 80

◆ Mail (SMTP), the mail delivery service, running on port 25

◆ FTP, the File Transfer Protocol, running on port 21

You can open the ports associated with services other than those listed. To do so,
specify the name of the protocol, as listed in the /etc/services file. Follow the
name of the protocol with a colon (:) and the name of the related protocol, tcp or
udp. For example, to open TCP port 110 – associated with version 3 of the Postoffice
Protocol (POP) – specify pop3:tcp. Listing 7-3 shows the IPChains rules equivalent
to a medium-security firewall customized to trust the eth1 interface and accept
incoming SSH connections. Listing 7-4 shows the IPChains rules equivalent to a
high-security firewall including the same customizations.

Listing 7-3: A medium-security firewall customized with trusted interface and incoming SSH

```
ipchains -P input ACCEPT
ipchains -P forward ACCEPT
ipchains -P output ACCEPT
ipchains -A input -s 0/0 -d 0/0 22 -p tcp -y -j ACCEPT
ipchains -A input -s 0/0 -d 0/0 -i lo -j ACCEPT
ipchains -A input -s 0/0 -d 0/0 -i eth1 -j ACCEPT
ipchains -A input -p tcp -s 0/0 -d 0/0 0:1023 -y -j REJECT
ipchains -A input -p tcp -s 0/0 -d 0/0 2049 -y -j REJECT
ipchains -A input -p udp -s 0/0 -d 0/0 0:1023 -j REJECT
ipchains -A input -p udp -s 0/0 -d 0/0 2049 -j REJECT
ipchains -A input -p tcp -s 0/0 -d 0/0 6000:6009 -y -j REJECT
ipchains -A input -p tcp -s 0/0 -d 0/0 7100 -y -j REJECT
```

Listing 7-4: A high-security firewall customized with trusted interface and incoming SSH

```
ipchains -P input ACCEPT
ipchains -P forward ACCEPT
ipchains -P output ACCEPT
ipchains -A input -s 0/0 -d 0/0 22 -p tcp -y -j ACCEPT
ipchains -A input -s 0/0 -d 0/0 -i lo -j ACCEPT
ipchains -A input -s 0/0 -d 0/0 -i eth1 -j ACCEPT
ipchains -A input -s 0/0 -d 0/0 -p tcp -y -j REJECT
ipchains -A input -s 0/0 -d 0/0 -p udp -j REJECT
```

Depending on when `lokkit` is run, the firewall may include a rule – not shown in the listings – necessary to permit incoming traffic to UDP port 53. This rule is necessary for the correct operation of the resolver, which translates between host names and IP addresses. When networking is started, the script `/etc/sysconfig/network-scripts/ifup-post` adds the necessary rule to the firewall. The rule has this form (Red Hat Linux 7.0 to 7.2):

```
ipchains -A input -s host 53 -d 0/0 -p udp -j ACCEPT
```

or the similar form (Red Hat Linux 7.3):

```
ipchains -A input -s host/32 53 -d 0/0 1025:65535 -p udp -j ACCEPT
```

where *host* is the IP address of the name server configured in the `/etc/resolv.conf` file.

A Complete IPChains Firewall

Red Hat provides, on its Web site, a complete sample IPChains firewall suitable for a home user or small business. The firewall includes support for IP masquerading and contains comments explaining its use in a DHCP configuration. You can learn a great deal about IPChains by reading the firewall code and perusing the relevant man pages and HOWTO. The firewall code is shown in Listing 7-5.

Listing 7-5: An example of a firewall

```
Example Firewall Script
Example Firewall Service Script
This script is intended for the home user or small business to set up IP-
Masquerading and basic protection for a gateway system using Red Hat Linux.


NO WARRANTY

This script is distributed in the hope that it will be useful, but WITHOUT ANY
WARRANTY, without even the implied warranty of MERCHANTABILITY or FITNESS FOR A
PARTICULAR PURPOSE. See the GNU General Public License for more details.

#!/bin/sh
#
# chkconfig: 2345 11 89
# description: sets up a basic firewall ruleset
#
# This script is setup to use IPCHAINS to protect a small network.   It is
# considered to be 'medium-light' secure.
#
```

```
# This script should be saved as /etc/rc.d/init.d/firewallss
#
# to enable the system to run this script at system start and stop, issue
# the command
#      chkconfig --add firewallss --level 2345
# Make sure the script's executable bits are set.  This can be done with
#      chmod u+x firewallss
#
# Thanks go to various people around the office as well as the Trinity OS
# author, David A. Ranch.  To see a more comprehensive firewall example as
# well as other security related topics, please see David's TrinityOS
# document at:
#       http://www.ecst.csuchico.edu/~dranch/LINUX/index-linux.html
#
# There are three user-configurable sections.  The first is for the network
# values for the firewall.  The second is for CIPE configuration.  The third
# consists of the ipchains commands themselves.  The only thing that should
# need to be changed for the third section is uncommenting the cipe rulesets
# if needed (they are deactivated by default).
#
# Things to watch out for when using this script:
#   a. When starting it by hand it tends to like the network already up.
#      This includes both interfaces.  (When started automatically by
#      init it is started pretty early, there is minimal time for the
#      window to be open. This is medium security, afterall.
#   b. pump, which controls dhcp under Red Hat, isn't very good at picking
#      up a change in address for the interface.  So if the IP addy of the
#      interface changes, the script might need to be start/stopped by hand.
#      You'll loose connectivity and a lot of messages about UDP errors will
#      be logged to /var/log/messages when this happens.
#   c. This script is an example.  It is targeted for a small LAN (a single
#      subnet) and would require work for a more complex network.  It is
#      also not guaranteed to be secure, though it is reasonable.
#
#   NO WARRANTY
# This script is distributed in the hope that it will be useful, but
# WITHOUT ANY WARRANTY, without even the implied warranty of MERCHANTABILITY
# or FITNESS FOR A PARTICULAR PURPOSE.  See the GNU General Public License
# (http://www.gnu.org/copyleft/gpl.html) for more details.
#
#
###### SCRIPT START ########
# ---- these are for the function calls so the script will run as a service
#      only change this if the location on your system is different.  It
#      shouldn't be.
```

```
# Source function library.
. /etc/rc.d/init.d/functions

# Source networking configuration.
#       only change this if the location on your system is different.  It
#       shouldn't be.
. /etc/sysconfig/network
. /etc/sysconfig/cipe


# ---- Basic sanity check.  This makes sure that networking is up.  If it
#       isn't, why continue?
# Check that networking is up.
[ ${NETWORKING} = "no" ] && exit 0



##### USER CONFIGURATION START #######################################
# ---- The device name for the external network interface (in this case "eth1"
#       Change this to match the interface that is your external (WAN) inter-
#       face.  (PPP users would use ppp0, for example).
EXTDEV=eth1
# ---- Don't change the code below.  It uses the ifconfig command and
#       cuts the relevant information out of the display (the IP address) and
#       configures it.  Replacing the code segment with the IP address would
#       result in the same information anyway.  The advantage of using the
#       code below is for DHCP or other dynamic networks.
EXTERNALIP=`ifconfig $EXTDEV | grep "inet addr:" | \
    awk -F: {'print $2'} | cut -d\  -f 1`
if [ -z "${EXTERNALIP}" ]; then
    exit 1
fi

# ---- The device name for the internal network interface (in this case "eth0"
#       See comments above.
INTDEV=eth0
#       See comments above.
INTERNALIP=`ifconfig $INTDEV | grep "inet addr:" | \
    awk -F: {'print $2'} | cut -d\  -f 1`
if [ -z "${INTERNALIP}" ]; then
    exit 1
fi

# ---- The network value for the internal network, in this case it is the
#       reserved block of 192.168.20.xxx  Chance it to match the internal net-
#       work you are using.
INTNET="192.168.20.0"
```

```
# ===== End of the first configuration section

# CIPE Configuration section.
# ---- If running CIPE, uncomment these lines.  If you are not running CIPE
#      DON'T mess with any of these.
#CIPEDEV=cipcb0
#CIPE_INET=`ifconfig $CIPEDEV | grep "inet addr:" | \
#    awk -F: {'print $2'} | cut -d\  -f 1`
#if [ -z "${INTERNALIP}" ]; then
#    exit 1
#fi
#
#CIPE_PTP=`ifconfig $CIPEDEV | grep "P-t-P:" | \
#    awk -F: {'print $3'} | cut -d\  -f 1`
#if [ -z "${INTERNALIP}" ]; then
#    exit 1
# fi
#
# # The internal IPs used for the destination network.
# CIPEINTNET="xxx.xxx.xxx.xxx"
# The real IP network used for Red Hat
# CIPEREALNET="xxx.xxx.xxx.xxx"
# The IP Tunnel Box's IP Addy
# TUNNEL="xxx.xxx.xxx.xxx"
# IMPORTANT NOTE: If using CIPE then the sections below with the same
#                 variables will need to be uncommented.  If you don't
#                 know what CIPE is or don't know how to configure it,
#                 leave it alone.  Variable list: TUNNEL, CIPEREALNET,
#                 CIPEINTNET
# ===== End of CIPE configuration section

echo "EXTDEV: ${EXTDEV} on ${EXTERNALIP}"
echo "INTDEV: ${INTDEV} on ${INTERNALIP}"

# See how we were called.
case "$1" in
  start)
    # Start firewall.
    echo -n "Starting firewall: "

    modprobe ip_masq_ftp
    modprobe ip_masq_irc
    modprobe ip_masq_raudio
```

```
# ---- Begin of firewall/ipchain rules.
#  NOTE:  If you have your own firewall script you would rather use, you
#  can replace the below section with it. Replace everything until the ***
#     Don't mess with these unless you know what you are doing.
   # MASQ timeouts.  Change these only if the timeouts are causing
   #                 problems.
   #   2 hrs timeout for TCP session timeouts (7200 seconds)
   #  10 sec timeout for traffic after the TCP/IP "FIN" packet is
   #   received
   #  60 sec timeout for UDP traffic (MASQ'ed ICQ users must enable
   #   a 30sec firewall
   #
   echo "Setting masq timeouts"
   ipchains -M -S 7200 10 60


   ####################################################################
   # Forwarding, flush and set default policy of deny. Actually the
   # default policy is irrelevant because there is a catch all rule
   # with deny and log.

   echo "Setting new forward rules"
   echo -n "forward..."

   # This makes sure that IP forwarding is turned on for networking.
   echo 1 > /proc/sys/net/ipv4/ip_forward

   # This does the flush
   ipchains -F forward
   # This sets the default to DENY
   ipchains -P forward DENY


   # Masquerade from local net on local interface to anywhere.  The
   # 255.255.255.0 netmasks out to the last section.  Using the above
   # internal network example, it makes it everything in the
   # 192.168.20.xxx range to be legal on this interface.
   ipchains -A forward -s $INTNET/255.255.255.0 -j MASQ
   # Masquerade from local net on local interface to anywhere.  Like the
   # above rule, this one says that anything that has the source of the
   # internal network should be forwarded to the external device and
   # all these packets are to be masquared.  The -d 0.0.0.0/0 indicates
   # that the destination of the traffic can be to anywhere.
   ipchains -A forward -i $EXTDEV -s $INTNET/24 -d 0.0.0.0/0 -j MASQ


   # Backup Rule.  Try this out if forwarding doesn't seem to work with
   # the above rule (make sure to comment out the above).  It says that
```

```
# any packets are to be masq'd and forwarded to the external device.
# ipchains -A forward -i $EXTDEV -j MASQ

# CIPE Forwarding.  Ignore this unless you need it.
# ipchains -A forward -d $CIPEINTNET/255.255.255.0
# ipchains -A forward -d $CIPEREALNET/255.255.254.0

# catch all rule, all other forwarding is denied and logged. pity
# there is no log option on the policy but this does the job instead.
ipchains -A forward -s 0.0.0.0/0 -d 0.0.0.0/0 -l -j DENY

# These are variations of the uncommented rule above.
#ipchains -A forward -j DENY -l
#ipchains -A forward -j DENY


### Port Forwarding Operations ###############################
#   Uncomment these commands only if port forwarding is needed.
#   this one
#   echo "Enabling IPPORTFW Redirection on the external LAN..."
#   this one
#   /usr/sbin/ipmasqadm portfw -f
#
# You probably don't have the ipmasqadm package installed.  If
# not, go to http://juanjox.kernelnotes.org/ for the binaries.
# before trying to run these commands.  "rpm -q ipmasqadm" can
# be used to check for the package.
#
#### ---- These Are Examples of Port Forwards
## This one forwards the httpd port from the firewall and
## points it to another machine on the LAN with the IP address of
## 192.168.100.100
# /usr/sbin/ipmasqadm portfw -a -P tcp -L $EXTERNALIP 80 \
#    -R 192.168.100.100 80

## This one forwards a specilized port from the firewall and
## points it at a machine on the LAN with the IP address of
## 192.168.100.100 at port 7000.
# /usr/sbin/ipmasqadm portfw -a -P tcp -L $EXTERNALIP 7000 \
# -R 192.168.100.100 7000


##############################################################
# Incoming, flush and set default policy of deny. Actually the
# default policy is irrelevant because there is a catch all rule
# with deny and log.
```

```
echo -n "input..."
echo "Setting new input rules"
# Incoming, flush and set default policy of deny.
ipchains -F input
ipchains -P input DENY

# local interface, local machines, going anywhere is valid
ipchains -A input -i $INTDEV -s $INTNET/24 -d 0.0.0.0/0 -j ACCEPT

# multicasting is valid (xntpd)
ipchains -A input -i $EXTDEV -s $EXTERNALIP/32 -d 224.0.0.0/8 -j ACCEPT

# remote interface, claiming to be local machines, IP spoofing,
# the rule tells to get lost
ipchains -A input -i $EXTDEV -s $INTNET/24 -d 0.0.0.0/0 -j DENY

# loopback interface is valid.
ipchains -A input -i lo -s 0.0.0.0/0 -d 0.0.0.0/0 -j ACCEPT

# The following are ports that could not be configured to only
# listen on the internal network, thus we firewall the external side.

# Deny access to the backup software port
# These lines are read as "Add to Input, Protocol "tcp", source "all"
# with the destentation
ipchains -A input -p tcp -s 0.0.0.0/0 -d $EXTERNALIP 617 -j DENY

# Deny access to the firewall auth port
ipchains -A input -p tcp -s 0.0.0.0/0 -d $EXTERNALIP 7777 -j DENY

# Deny access to the echo port (used by squid/junkbuster)
ipchains -A input -p udp -s 0.0.0.0/0 -d $EXTERNALIP 7 -j DENY

# Deny access to syslog
ipchains -A input -p udp -s 0.0.0.0/0 -d $EXTERNALIP 514 -j DENY

# remote interface, any source, going to external address is valid
ipchains -A input -i $EXTDEV -s 0.0.0.0/0 -d $EXTERNALIP/32 -j ACCEPT

# IP-IP tunnel.  Use these only if you need them.
# FIXME: limit this to a device (EXTDEV OR CIPEDEV)
# ipchains -A input -p udp -s $TUNNEL $PORT -j ACCEPT
# ipchains -A input -i $CIPEDEV -j ACCEPT

# catch all rule, all other incoming is denied.
```

```
# ipchains -A input -j DENY -l
# ipchains -A input -j DENY
ipchains -A input -s 0.0.0.0/0 -d 0.0.0.0/0 -l -j DENY


####################################################################
# Outgoing, flush and set default policy of reject. Actually the
# default policy is irrelevant because there is a catch all rule
# with deny and log.

echo "Setting new output rules"
echo -n "output..."

# Outgoing, flush and set default policy of deny.
ipchains -F output
ipchains -P output DENY

# local interface, any source going to local net is valid
#ipchains -A output -i $INTDEV -s 0.0.0.0/0 -d $INTNET/24 -j ACCEPT
ipchains -A output -i $INTDEV -s 0.0.0.0/0 -d $INTNET/24 -j ACCEPT

# loopback interface is valid.
# ipchains -A output -i lo -s 0.0.0.0/0 -d 0.0.0.0/0 -j ACCEPT
ipchains -A output -i lo -s 0.0.0.0/0 -d 0.0.0.0/0 -j ACCEPT

# outgoing to local net on remote interface: stuffed routing, deny
ipchains -A output -i $EXTDEV -s 0.0.0.0/0 -d $INTNET/24 -j DENY

# outgoing from local net on remote interface: stuffed masq, deny
ipchains -A output -i $EXTDEV -s $INTNET/24 -d 0.0.0.0/0 -j DENY

# anything else outgoing on remote interface is valid
#ipchains -A output -i $EXTDEV -d 0.0.0.0/0 -j ACCEPT
ipchains -A output -i $EXTDEV -s $EXTERNALIP/32 -d 0.0.0.0/0 -j ACCEPT

# outgoing to IP-IP tunnel for CIPE server is valid.  Use these
# Only if you need them.
# ipchains -A output -i $CIPEDEV -s $CIPE_INET -d $CIPE_PTP/32 -j ACCEPT
# ipchains -A output -i $CIPEDEV -s $CIPE_INET -d $CIPEREALNET/23 \
#    -j ACCEPT
# ipchains -A output -i $CIPEDEV -s $EXTERNALIP -d $CIPEREALNET/23 \
#    -j ACCEPT
# ipchains -A output -i $CIPEDEV -s $CIPE_INET -d 0.0.0.0/0 -j ACCEPT

# catch all rule, all other outgoing is denied.
# ipchains -A output -j DENY -l
```

```
# ipchains -A output -j DENY
ipchains -A output -s 0.0.0.0/0 -d 0.0.0.0/0 -l -j DENY


echo "Done with the firewall rulesets"
echo -n "acct..."

# Accounting, flush all entries
ipchains -N acctin
ipchains -N acctout
ipchains -N acctio
# Track traffic just to network, not individual hosts
ipchains -I input -j acctio
ipchains -I input -j acctin
ipchains -I output -j acctio
ipchains -I output -j acctout
ipchains -I forward -j acctout

echo "done"
touch /var/lock/subsys/firewall
;;

stop)
  # Stop firewall.
  echo -n "Shutting down firewall: "
  ipchains -F input
  ipchains -A input -j ACCEPT
  ipchains -F output
  ipchains -A output -j ACCEPT
  ipchains -F forward
  ipchains -A forward -j ACCEPT
  ipchains -X acctio
  ipchains -X acctin
  ipchains -X acctout

  rmmod ip_masq_raudio
  rmmod ip_masq_irc
  rmmod ip_masq_ftp

  echo "done"
  rm -f /var/lock/subsys/firewall
  ;;

restart)
  $0 stop
```

```
    $0 start
    ;;

  status)
    status firewall
    ;;

  *)
    echo "Usage: firewall {start|stop|restart|status}"
    exit 1
esac

exit 0
```

Summary

In this chapter, you learned about the IPChains facility and how to use the `ipchains` command or `lokkit` to create simple, stateless packet-filtering firewalls. Because IPChains firewalls are stateless, they're potentially less secure than IPTables firewalls. Therefore, IPChains firewalls are useful primarily as host firewalls that provide a second line of defense behind a more secure IPTables firewall.

Chapter 8

The IPTables Facility

THIS CHAPTER EXPLAINS THE IPTABLES FACILITY, the more modern and sophisticated of the two firewall facilities that have been included in recent Red Hat Linux distributions. IPTables provides a stateful, packet-filtering firewall with powerful inspection capabilities and quite flexible logging capabilities. This chapter assumes you are already familiar with the IPChains facility, which is discussed in Chapter 7.

The chapter focuses on IPTables features and the `iptables` command rather than on IPTables firewalls. Chapter 9 addresses IPTables firewall implementation and basic administration. As explained in Chapter 6, IPTables is the user interface to Netfilter, the Linux kernel facility that enables packet filtering.

How IPTables Operates

Three main chains make up the IPChains facility explained in Chapter 7: `FORWARD`, `INPUT`, and `OUTPUT`. The IPTables facility has six main chains, which are grouped into three *tables:*

◆ `filter`

◆ `nat`

◆ `mangle`

The next several subsections describe these tables and the related chains.

The Filter Table

The `filter` table performs operations similar to those performed by the three main chains of IPChains; that is, it tests the contents of packets and blocks or accepts packets accordingly. The `filter` table has three chains that roughly correspond to the three main chains of IPChains:

- FORWARD
- INPUT
- OUTPUT

Like the IPChains `FORWARD` chain, the IPTables `FORWARD` chain exists to test packets being forwarded from one network interface to another. However, the functions of the IPTables `INPUT` and `OUTPUT` chains differ slightly from those of their IPChains counterparts. In IPChains, packets being forwarded from one interface to another traverse all three main chains. However, in IPTables, such packets traverse only the `FORWARD` chain. The IPTables `INPUT` chain is used only for packets sent to the firewall host. Similarly, the IPTables `OUPUT` chain is used only for packets sent by the firewall host.

Rules in the chains of the IPTables filter table can inspect many packet characteristics cannot be tested by IPChains rules. In particular, IPTables rules are stateful — that is, they can test whether a packet is associated with or related to an established connection. The capability of testing connection status enables IPTables firewalls to be potentially more efficient, more secure, and more simple than similar IPChains firewalls. The section "IPTables Rules," later in this chapter, explains the tests supported by IPTables and how you can specify them.

The nat Table

The `nat` table performs network address translation (NAT) operations, including destination NAT, source NAT, and masquerading. The `nat` table consists of two chains:

- PREROUTING
- POSTROUTING

The `PREROUTING` chain performs destination NAT operations, and the `POST-ROUTING` chain performs source NAT and masquerade operations.

Chapter 10, "Advanced IPTables Firewall Implementation," explains the NAT operations supported by IPTables.

The mangle Table

The mangle table enables you to modify either or both of two packet header fields: Type of Service and Time to Live. In addition, it enables you to mark packets so that they can be recognized by subsequent firewall rules, Linux kernel modules, and subsequent firewalls. The mangle table includes only the PREROUTING chain.

 Most firewall designs don't require use of the mangle table. It is primarily useful when multiple firewalls are associated in a load-balancing or failover configuration. There, the mangle table can be used to prevent the redundant processing of a packet by multiple firewalls.

User Chains

In addition to the chains associated with its three tables, IPTables supports user-defined chains, often simply called *user chains*. Each user chain must be associated with one of the three tables. A packet can be diverted to a user chain by means of a special target. Packets reaching the end of a user chain are diverted again to the rule following the rule that sent them to the user chain. User chains are explained more fully in the section "IPTables Targets," later in this chapter.

The IPTables Packet Path

Figure 8-1 shows the IPTables packet path. Depending on its origin and destination, a packet follows one of three subpaths. A packet being forwarded from one network to another traverses the following chains, in this order:

◆ mangle PREROUTING

◆ nat PREROUTING

◆ filter FORWARD

◆ nat POSTROUTING

Notice that the filter FORWARD chain is traversed after the nat PREROUTING chain and the nat POSTROUTING chain. That is, packets traverse the tables in an interleaved fashion rather than traverse all the chains of one table before moving on to the next table.

Packets sent to the firewall host traverse the following chains, in this order:

◆ mangle PREROUTING

- ◆ nat PREROUTING

- ◆ filter INPUT

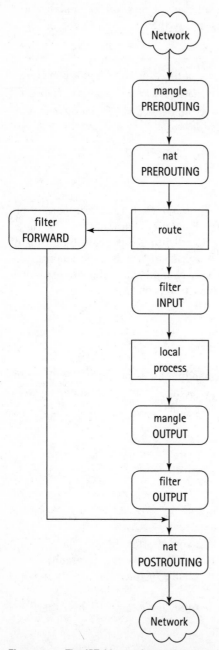

Figure 8-1: The IPTables packet path

Finally, packets sent by the firewall host traverse the following chains, in this order:

- mangle OUTPUT
- filter OUTPUT
- nat POSTROUTING

 The nat PREROUTING chain is traversed by all packets arriving at the firewall host, whether they're bound for the firewall host itself or for a host on a connected network. Similarly, the nat POSTROUTING chain is traversed by all packets leaving the firewall host, whether they originated from the firewall host or from a host on a connected network. You may be tempted to use these chains to filter packets in a manner analogous to the INPUT and OUTPUT chains of the IPChains facility. However, as explained later in this chapter, the proper function of these chains is related to network address translation. Packet filtering should be performed in the INPUT, OUTPUT, and FORWARD IPTables chains.

The following subsections describe the steps of the packet path in more detail.

mangle PREROUTING

Packets entering the firewall first traverse the mangle PREROUTING chain. As explained, this chain seldom includes any rules. Therefore, packets generally flow immediately into the following chain.

nat PREROUTING

The nat PREROUTING chain performs destination network address translation. That is, the chain can contain rules that modify the destination IP address or destination port of packets that traverse it. Packets that are part of established connections skip the nat PREROUTING chain. Consequently, the chain should not be used for packet filtering. Because the mangle PREROUTING chain is seldom used, the nat PREROUTING chain is often referred to simply as the PREROUTING chain.

route

The route step classifies packets according to destination. Packets bearing a destination IP address that matches the IP address of a network interface of the firewall host are sent to the filter INPUT chain for delivery to the firewall host. Other packets are sent to the filter FORWARD chain.

filter FORWARD

The `filter FORWARD` chain processes packets being forwarded from one network to another. Like other chains on the `filter` table, its primary function is *packet filtering,* or determining based on packet characteristics whether a packet should be blocked or accepted. Because no table other than `nat` has a FORWARD chain, the `filter FORWARD` chain is often referred to simply as the FORWARD chain.

nat POSTROUTING

The `nat POSTROUTING` chain performs source network address translation and masquerading. That is, the chain can contain rules that modify the source IP address or source port of packets that traverse it. Like the `nat PREROUTING` chain, packets sometimes skip this chain. Therefore, you should not use this chain for packet filtering. Because no table other than `nat` has a POSTROUTING chain, the `nat POSTROUTING` chain is often referred to simply as the POSTROUTING chain.

filter INPUT

The `filter INPUT` chain processes packets bound for the firewall host itself. It is a packet-filtering chain containing rules that determine whether a packet should be accepted or blocked. Because no table other than `filter` has an INPUT chain, the `filter INPUT` chain is often referred to simply as the INPUT chain.

local process

The `local process` step represents a process running on the firewall host. The process can be the source or destination of packets.

mangle OUTPUT

The `mangle OUTPUT` chain's function resembles that of the `mangle PREROUTING` chain; however, only packets generated by the firewall host traverse the `mangle OUTPUT` chain. Like the `mangle PREROUTING` chain, the `mangle OUTPUT` chain is seldom used.

filter OUTPUT

The `filter OUTPUT` chain processes packets sent by the firewall host. Like other chains of the `filter` table, it is a packet-filtering chain containing rules that determine whether a packet should be blocked or accepted. Because the `mangle OUTPUT` chain is seldom used, the `filter OUTPUT` chain is often referred to simply as the OUTPUT chain.

IPTables Commands

Like the `ipchains` command, which provides the user interface to the IPChains facility, the `iptables` command provides the user interface to the IPTables facility. Like its counterpart, the `iptables` command provides operations on chains and rules. The operations resemble those provided by IPChains.

Operations on rules include these:

◆ Adding a rule at the head of a chain.

◆ Adding a rule at the tail of a chain.

◆ Deleting a rule.

◆ Replacing a rule.

Operations on chains include these:

◆ Listing the rules associated with the chain.

◆ Flushing a chain (i.e., delete its rules).

◆ Zeroing the counters associated with a chain.

◆ Creating a user chain.

◆ Deleting a user chain.

◆ Setting the default policy associated with a chain.

◆ Renaming a user chain.

The following sections explain how IPTables rules are formed, how rule operations are performed, and how chain operations are performed.

IPTables Rules

As shown in Figure 8-2, IPTables rules have the same general form as IPChains rules. Of course, the command name differs. The names of chains and the forms taken by packet characteristics and rule actions also differ somewhat. This section explains how packet characteristics are specified in IPTables. The following section explains the specification of rule actions.

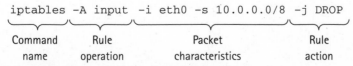

Figure 8-2: The structure of an IPTables rule

IPTables lets you specify the following packet characteristics related to the IP packet header:

- ◆ Protocol
- ◆ Source IP address
- ◆ Destination IP address
- ◆ Input interface
- ◆ Output interface
- ◆ Fragment flag

In addition, you can specify the following header characteristics of the indicated packet types:

- ◆ TCP datagrams
  - ■ Source port
  - ■ Destination port
  - ■ SYN and other TCP flags
  - ■ TCP options
- ◆ UDP datagrams
  - ■ Source port
  - ■ Destination port
- ◆ ICMP messages
  - ■ ICMP type and code

Moreover, IPTables lets you specify a variety of other packet and packet flow characteristics. The following subsections explain how to specify packet characteristics.

The iptables command supports abbreviations for several packet characteristics and provides tests for a few packet characteristics not explained in this chapter. For complete information on the command, see the related man page.

Protocol

To specify the protocol associated with a packet, use the `-p` flag followed by a protocol specifier. The protocol specifier can take any of these forms:

- The protocol name `tcp`, `udp`, or `icmp`

- The name of a protocol listed in `/etc/protocols`

- The number assigned to a protocol

- The number zero or the word `all`, either of which matches all protocols

You can specify a series of protocols by separating each one from the next with a comma. For example, the following specifier indicates that a packet can have either the TCP or UDP protocol:

```
-p tcp,udp
```

Like IPChains, IPTables supports the negation of packet characteristics, specified by using an exclamation mark. For example, the following specifier indicates that a packet has a protocol other than TCP:

```
-p ! tcp
```

Such a packet might have the UDP or ICMP protocol or some other non-IP protocol.

Source IP Address

To specify the source IP address, use the `-s` flag followed by the IP address. If the address is that of a network rather than that of a single host, you can specify the network mask, in either of two ways. The first way is by following the IP address with a slash and the actual network mask. For example:

```
-s 192.168.0.1/255.255.255.0
```

The other is by using CIDR notation (explained in Chapter 2) to specify the number of one-bits in the network mask:

```
-s 192.168.0/24
```

The source IP address can be negated by means of an exclamation mark. For example, to specify any source address other than one in the Class A block 10.0.0.0/8, use this specifier:

```
-s ! 10.0.0.0/8
```

Destination IP Address

The destination IP address is specified much like the source IP address. To specify the destination IP address, use the -d flag followed by the IP address. If the address is that of a network rather than of a single host, you can specify the network mask. You can do this in either of two ways. The first way is by following the IP address with a slash and the actual network mask. For example:

```
-d 192.168.0.1/255.255.255.0
```

The other is by using CIDR notation to specify the number of one-bits in the network mask:

```
-d 192.168.0/24
```

The destination IP address can be negated by means of an exclamation mark. For example, to specify any destination address other than one in the Class A block 10.0.0.0/8, use this specifier:

```
-d ! 10.0.0.0/8
```

Input Interface

To specify the input interface on which a packet arrived, use the -i flag followed by the name of the device. For example, to specify that a packet arrived on the interface eth0, use the following specifier:

```
-i eth0
```

Don't confuse the different usage of the -i flag in IPTables and IPChains. The IPTables -i flag is followed by the name of the input interface, whereas the IPChains -i flag is followed by the name of the input interface (input chain) or output interface (forward or output chain).

You can negate the device by prefixing it with an exclamation mark, For example, the following specifier specifies all devices except eth0:

```
-i ! eth0
```

You can refer to sets of devices by using a special notation. Specifying a partial device name followed by a plus sign matches any device whose name matches the partial device name. For example, the following specifier matches packets arriving on any Ethernet device because the names of such devices always begin with *eth:*

```
-i eth+
```

You can use the input interface specifier in only three chains:

- ◆ INPUT
- ◆ FORWARD
- ◆ PREROUTING

Using the specifier elsewhere causes the `iptables` command to fail.

Output Interface

The output interface is specified much like the input interface. To specify the output interface on which a packet is to be sent, use the `-o` flag followed by the name of the device. For example, to specify that a packet will be sent on the interface eth0, use this specifier:

```
-o eth0
```

You can negate the device by prefixing it with an exclamation mark, For example, this specifier specifies all devices except eth0:

```
-o ! eth0
```

You can refer to sets of devices by using the same special notation used for input interfaces. Specifying a partial device name followed by a plus sign matches any device whose name matches the partial device name. For example, the following specifier matches packets to be sent on any Ethernet device because the names of such devices always begin with *eth:*

```
-o eth+
```

You can use the output interface specifier in only three chains:

- ◆ OUTPUT
- ◆ FORWARD
- ◆ POSTROUTING

Using the specifier elsewhere causes the `iptables` command to fail.

Fragment Flag

To specify that the fragment flag in the IP header is set, use the `-f` flag. Recall that, when a packet is fragmented, datagrams other than the first one carry the fragment flag. You can negate the specifier by using an exclamation mark. For example, the following specifier matches a nonfragmented packet or the first datagram of a fragmented packet:

```
! -f
```

When the `ip_conntrack` module is loaded, IPTables performs fragment reassembly — that is, it automatically reassembles fragments before passing the related packet through IPTables. If fragment reassembly is active, the `-f` flag does not match any packets.

Source Port

TCP and UDP datagrams have an associated source port. To specify the source port of a packet, use the `--sport` specifier. For example, to specify that the source port of a packet is UDP 53 – the source port commonly used by name servers – use these specifiers:

```
-p udp --sport 53
```

The `--sport` specifier is not recognized unless it is combined with a protocol specifier that specifies the TCP or UDP protocol.

If you prefer, you can specify the name of a service, as listed in `/etc/services`. Another option is to specify a range of ports, which can be accomplished by specifying the starting port, a colon, and the ending port. For example, the following specifier matches TCP and UDP source ports 0–1023:

```
-p tcp,udp --sport 0:1023
```

You can omit the starting port number when it has the value 0. The following specifier is equivalent to the one given earlier:

```
-p tcp,udp --sport :1023
```

Similarly, omitting the ending port number is the same as specifying its value as 65535. The following specifier refers to all registered ports, numbered 1024–65535:

```
-p tcp,udp --sport 1024:
```

Destination Port

The destination port is specified much like the destination port. To specify the destination port of a packet, use the `--dport` specifier. For example, to specify that the destination port of a packet is UDP 53 – the destination port commonly used by name servers – use these specifiers:

```
-p udp --dport 53
```

The `--dport` specifier is not recognized unless it is combined with a protocol specifier that specifies the TCP or UDP protocol.

If you prefer, you can specify the name of a service, as listed in `/etc/services`. Another option is to specify a range of ports, which can be accomplished by specifying the starting port, a colon, and the ending port. For example, the following specifier matches TCP and UDP destination ports 0–1023:

```
-p tcp,udp --dport 0:1023
```

You can omit the starting port number when it has the value 0. The following specifier is equivalent to the one given earlier:

```
-p tcp,udp --dport :1023
```

Similarly, omitting the ending port number is the same as specifying its value as 65535. The following specifier refers to all registered ports, numbered 1024–65535:

```
-p tcp,udp --dport 1024:
```

SYN

To specify that the `SYN` flag of a TCP datagram is set, use the `--syn` specifier. The specifier tests not only the `SYN` flag – which must be set – but also the `ACK` and `FIN` flags, which must not be set. For example, the following combination of specifiers matches TCP `SYN` packets:

```
-p tcp --syn
```

You can test for non-`SYN` packets by prefixing the specifier with an exclamation mark. For example, the following specifier matches TCP packets that do not have the `SYN` flag set (or that have the `ACK` or `FIN` flag set along with the `SYN` flag):

```
-p tcp ! --syn
```

Recall that the SYN flag is set — and the ACK and FIN flags are clear — for the first packet of a new TCP connection. Subsequent packets lack the SYN flag or include the ACK or FIN flag. Therefore, the --syn flag can be used to test whether a packet is part of an established connection. The state-matching specifier given in the section "Connection State" later in this chapter determines whether a packet is part of an established connection by inspecting the connection table rather than the TCP flags. The state-matching specifier cannot be spoofed by crafted packets and is therefore a more reliable means of determining packet status.

TCP Flags

You can test TCP flags by using the --tcp-flags flag. This flag is unusual in taking two arguments rather than one. The first argument specifies the TCP flags to be tested. The second argument specifies the TCP flags that must be set. For example, the following combination of specifiers is equivalent to the --syn flag:

```
-p tcp --tcp-flags SYN,ACK,FIN SYN
```

That is, the specifier tests the SYN, ACK, and FIN flags and requires that, of these, only the SYN flag be set.

Notice that each flag within an argument is separated from the next by a comma and that no spaces appear within an argument list. The possible flag values are shown in this list:

- ACK
- FIN
- RST
- PSH
- SYN
- URG

In addition, the value ALL refers to all six flags. The value NONE can be used in the second argument to specify that none of the flags in the first argument should be set.

For a quick refresher on TCP flags, see Table 2-6.

You can use an exclamation mark to negate the meaning of the --tcp-flags specifier. However, the result is often confusing. Because it's always possible to specify a TCP flags combination without using negation, you generally should avoid negation.

TCP Options

Table 2-6 summarizes the TCP flags that appear in TCP headers. IPTables programmers often refer to TCP flags as *TCP options,* to avoid conflicting uses of the word *flags.* IPTables rules can specify TCP options that must be matched. The related flag is --tcp-option, which is followed by a number indicating the TCP option to be tested. The Internet Engineering Task Force (IETF) approves the codes used for TCP options. However, the codes are scattered through multiple Requests for Comments (RFCs) and can be difficult to locate. However, it's seldom necessary to test TCP options and generally, when someone does need to do so, that person has studied the operation of the option and knows its number by heart. Table 8-1 lists several of the most common options.

As an example, to specify that a TCP datagram include the selective acknowledgment option (SACK), use this combination of specifiers:

```
-p tcp --tcp-option 4
```

TABLE 8-1 COMMON TCP OPTIONS

Number	Description
0	End of options list
1	No operation (used to align options)

(Continued)

TABLE 8-1 COMMON TCP OPTIONS *(Continued)*

Number	Description
2	Maximum segment size (MSS)
3	Window scale
4	Selective acknowledgment
8	Timestamp

ICMP Type and Code

To specify the type, or type and code, of an ICMP message, use the `--icmp-type` flag, followed by the name corresponding to the ICMP type or type and code. For example, to specify an ICMP echo request, use the specifier

```
-p icmp --icmp-type echo-request
```

You can negate the ICMP type specifier by including an exclamation mark. For example, the following specifier matches all ICMP messages except the source quench message:

```
-p icmp --icmp-type ! source-quench
```

 Appendix D gives the ICMP names used with the `--icmp-type` flag.

Testing Other Packet Characteristics

In addition to packet characteristics specified by specific `iptables` flags, the `iptables` command can test about one dozen packet characteristics that use a special flag, the `-m` flag, which can also be given as `--match`. The `-m` flag is associated with tests that are implemented as loadable modules and therefore are not available unless the flag is specified.

Don't think that these tests are less important than other tests. Testing the connection state — one of the most important IPTables capabilities — is performed using the `-m` flag.

CONNECTION STATE

You can test whether a packet is associated with a connection having a particular state by using the `-m state --state` specifier. The possible arguments of the specifier are shown in this list:

- ◆ `NEW` indicates that the packet is associated with a connection that has not yet seen a two-way exchange of packets.

- ◆ `ESTABLISHED` indicates that the packet is associated with a connection that has seen a two-way exchange of packets.

- ◆ `RELATED` indicates that the packet is associated with a new connection that is related to an established connection.

- ◆ `INVALID` indicates that the packet is associated with a connection that has a problem, such as a malformed packet or packet header.

You can specify multiple states by separating each one from the next with a comma. For example, to specify that a packet is part of an established or related connection, use the specifier

```
-m state --state ESTABLISHED,RELATED
```

RATE LIMITS

You can specify limits on the number of times a rule is matched in a given period. Doing so is useful in identifying and blocking packets that constitute a denial-of-service attack. Limits are specified using the `-m limit` extension. Two related flags are supported: `--limit` and `--limit-burst`.

The `--limit` flag specifies the maximum permissible average rate. If the flag is omitted, a default rate of three packets per hour is assumed. To use the flag, specify an integer, followed by a slash and a time interval. Permissible time intervals are shown in this list:

- ◆ `second`

- ◆ `minute`

- ◆ `hour`

- ◆ `day`

For example, to specify that a rule matches packets up to an average rate of five packets per second, use the specifier

```
-m limit --limit 5/second
```

Up to the specified rate limit, the associated rule matches packets normally. However, after the rate is exceeded, the rule ceases to match packets until enough time elapses to return the average rate to a value below the specified limit.

The `--limit-burst` flag allows a burst of packets to be matched before the rate limiting specified by `--limit` is applied. If the `--limit-burst` flag is not specified, a default value of five is assumed. For example, the following specifier allows ten packets to be matched; thereafter, packets are limited to an average rate of 5 per minute:

```
-m limit --limit-burst 10 --limit 5/minute
```

If the burst limit is exceeded and the rate limit is applied, the burst limit begins to recharge when the packet rate drops below the rate limit. Specifically, the burst value is increased by one during each time interval in which the packet rate is below the specified limit.

MAC SOURCE ADDRESS

IPTables can test the MAC (media access control) source address of packets on an Ethernet network. To test the MAC source address of a packet, use the `-m mac --mac-source` specifier, followed by the MAC address. The MAC address must take the form of twelve hexadecimal digits, each pair of digits separated from the next by a colon. For example, the following specifier matches only a specific MAC source address:

```
-m mac --mac-source 00:05:69:00:04:BA
```

You can negate the specifier by including an exclamation mark. For example, the following specifier matches any MAC source address other than the one specified:

```
-m mac --mac-source ! 00:05:69:00:04:BA
```

You can use the `-m mac --mac-source` specifier in these chains only:

- ◆ `mangle PREROUTING`
- ◆ `nat PREROUTING`
- ◆ `FORWARD`
- ◆ `INPUT`

MULTIPLE PORTS

You can specify a list, rather than a range, of source or destination ports by using the `-m multiport` flag. This flag is used with either the `--source-port` or `--destination-port` flags or with both these flags. The ports are specified as a comma-separated list of values of the same sort used with the `--sport` and `--dport` flags.

For example, to specify that a packet has a TCP source port of 21, 22, 25, or 80, use this specifier:

```
-p tcp -m multiport --source-port 21,22,25,80
```

 TIP Only TCP and UDP packets have associated source and destination ports. So, the `-m multiport` flag should be used in rules that match only TCP and UDP packets.

DETECTING MARKED PACKETS

The MARK target, described in the following section, can mark packets by setting a special integer valued field. You can identify marked packets by using the `-m mark --mark` specifier, which takes as its argument an integer having a value from 0 to 65535.

For example, to match a packet marked with the value 256, use this specifier:

```
-m mark --mark 256
```

You can also specify a mask value that is logically ANDed with the mark before the comparison is made. To do so, follow the mark value with a slash and the mask value. For example, to test whether bit 2 (having the decimal value 4) of the mark is set, use the following specifier:

```
-m mark --mark 4/4
```

This comparison ignores all bits other than bit 2 because the mask clears them before the comparison is made.

TYPE OF SERVICE

IPTables can match packets based on the type of service code. Several codes have been defined, as summarized in Table 8-2. For example, service type code 8 denotes traffic that should be handled expeditiously. However, most routers cannot — or have not been programmed to — handle traffic according to the type of service codes.

TABLE 8-2 SERVICE CODES

Numerical Value	Type of Service
0	Normal-Service
2	Minimize-Cost

(Continued)

TABLE **8-2** SERVICE CODES *(Continued)*

Numerical Value	Type of Service
4	Maximize-Reliability
8	Maximize-Throughput
16	Minimize-Delay

To match the type of service associated with a packet, use the `-m tos --tos` specifier, followed by the numerical value associated with the type of service. Alternatively, you can specify the type of service as a hexadecimal number or using one of the types of service names shown in Table 8-2. As usual, you can negate the test by including an exclamation mark. For example, the following specifier matches packets not flagged for maximum throughput:

```
-m tos --tos ! 8
```

TIME TO LIVE

IPTables can match packets based on their time to live (TTL) value. To achieve this, use the `-m tos --ttl` specifier, followed by the TTL value, an integer from 0 to 255. For example, the following specifier matches packets having a TTL value of 1:

```
-m ttl --ttl 1
```

This capability is seldom used, in part because it's possible to match only a specific TTL value rather than a range.

PROCESS OWNERSHIP

Although the capability is seldom used, IPTables can match outgoing packets — that is, packets sent by the local host — based on

◆ The user ID of the process that created the packet

◆ The group ID of the process that created the packet

◆ The process ID of the process that created the packet

◆ The session ID of the process that created the packet

These operations are specified by the `-m owner` flag and the related flags `--uid-owner`, `--gid-owner`, `--pid-owner`, and `--sid-owner`, respectively. For more information on using these flags, see the iptables man page.

IPTables Targets

IPTables rules can invoke any of a much richer variety of actions than IPChains rules. Like IPChains targets, IPTables targets are invoked via the -j flag. For instance, the ACCEPT target is invoked this way:

```
-j ACCEPT
```

IPTables targets, as IPTables firewall actions are called, include

- ACCEPT
- DROP
- REJECT
- LOG
- RETURN

The name of a user-defined chain can also be used as a target.

In addition, IPTables provides targets that support network address translation (NAT):

- DNAT
- MASQ
- REDIRECT
- SNAT

IPTables also includes several targets that are not commonly used:

- MARK
- MIRROR
- QUEUE
- TOS
- TTL
- ULOG

The following subsections explain these targets. Targets related to NAT are explained only briefly because they're a main topic of Chapter 10, "Advanced IPTables Firewall Implementation." Likewise, the six targets not commonly used are explained only briefly. For more information on these targets, see the iptables man page.

ACCEPT

The `ACCEPT` target causes a packet to pass to the next chain in the packet path. The target does not denote acceptance of the packet because a rule in a subsequent chain may block the packet.

DROP

The `DROP` target causes a packet to be blocked. The packet does not traverse any subsequent chains of the packet path. No error packet is sent to the sender of the dropped packet. The `REJECT` target, which sends an error packet to the sender, is a more courteous way of blocking packets because the error packet prevents the sender from retrying the connection by sending additional messages or waiting until a time-out occurs. However, you may prefer to configure sensitive hosts in so-called *stealth* mode – that is, so that they do not respond to unwelcome packets. The `DROP` target is appropriate for such cases. Sensitive hosts are those performing important private functions that can operate without being visible to public hosts. Often, the compromise of a sensitive host can jeopardize the security of a network. Hence, sensitive hosts should be specially protected.

REJECT

The `REJECT` target causes a packet to be blocked and an error packet to be sent to the host that sent the rejected packet. The `REJECT` target is valid in only the following built-in chains:

- ◆ `INPUT`
- ◆ `FORWARD`
- ◆ `OUTPUT`

However, the `REJECT` target can also be used in user-defined chains invoked from one of these chains. For example, to block a packet and send a default error message, use the following target:

```
-j REJECT
```

By default, the error packet is an ICMP port unreachable message. However, you can specify the desired response by using the `--reject-with` flag, followed by a specifier for the response you desire. These specifiers are supported:

- ◆ `icmp-net-unreachable`
- ◆ `icmp-host-unreachable`
- ◆ `icmp-port-unreachable`

- ◆ `icmp-proto-unreachable`

- ◆ `icmp-net-prohibited`

- ◆ `icmp-host-prohibited`

- ◆ `tcp-reset`

All but the last specifier cause IPTables to send an ICMP error message of the specified type. The last specifier causes IPTables to send a TCP `RST` datagram that tears down a TCP connection, as explained in Chapter 2. This response is the same one sent automatically by a TCP stack that receives a TCP `SYN` packet addressed to a port that has no listening server. For example, the following specifier causes a packet matching the associated rule to be blocked and a TCP `SYN` datagram to be sent:

```
-j REJECT --reject-with tcp-reset
```

LOG

The `LOG` target causes the packet to be logged via the Syslog facility. Several options enable you to specify the log entry:

- ◆ `--log-ip-options`

- ◆ `--log-level`

- ◆ `--log-prefix`

- ◆ `--log-tcp-options`

- ◆ `--log-tcp-sequence`

You should generally specify `--log-prefix`, which enables you to include a descriptive comment in the log entry. The comment is specified within quotes, following the option. Although you can use single or double quotes, the beginning and ending quote character must be the same. The comment must not be longer than 29 characters. For example, the following specifier includes a comment identifying the reason that the associated packet was dropped:

```
-j LOG --log-prefix "IPT Invalid IP address: "
```

TIP Each log entry should include the name of the facility that generated it. However, the IPTables limit on the length of the comment included in a log entry is quickly reached. You may prefer tagging IPTables log entries with the designation `IPT` rather than `IPTABLES`, thereby saving five characters that can be used for some more descriptive purpose.

User Chains and the RETURN Target

User chains can make a firewall more modular and readable. They provide no special functions and are merely a device for structuring your firewall source code. You can send a packet to a user chain by referencing the user chain with a -j flag. For example, to send a packet to a user chain named test, use this specifier:

```
-j test
```

The user chain must be associated with the same table as the chain containing the rule that jumps to it. When the packet reaches the end of the user chain, it returns to the chain from which it was sent to the user chain. To immediately send a packet back to the invoking chain, use the RETURN target:

```
-j RETURN
```

If a packet is sent from a main chain — INPUT, OUTPUT, or FORWARD — to the RETURN target, the packet is handled according to the default policy of the chain. That is, if the default policy is ACCEPT, the packet continues to the next chain in the packet path. Otherwise, the packet is denied or rejected.

Network Address Translation Targets

As explained, network address translation is covered in Chapter 10, "Advanced IPTables Firewall Implementation." Therefore, only brief descriptions of the related targets appear in this chapter.

DNAT TARGET
The DNAT target specifies destination network address translation. It is used with the --to-destination flag, which specifies the destination IP address to be substituted into the packet.

MASQUERADE TARGET
The MASQUERADE target specifies masquerading, a special form of source network address translation. It is often used with the --to-ports flag, which specifies the source port to be substituted into the packet.

REDIRECT TARGET
The REDIRECT target specifies a special form of destination network address translation that redirects packets to the firewall host. It is often used with the --to-ports flag, which specifies the destination port to be substituted into the packet.

SNAT TARGET
The SNAT target specifies source network address translation. It is used with the --to-source flag, which specifies the source IP address to be substituted into the packet.

Seldom Used Targets

IPTables includes several targets that are seldom used. They're briefly described here. For further details, see the iptables man page.

MARK TARGET

The MARK target enables you to mark packets with an integer value from 0 to 65535. The value can be tested via the -m mark specifier. The target is used with the --set-mark specifier, which specifies the value of the mark with which the packet is tagged. The target may be used only in chains of the mangle table.

MIRROR TARGET

The MIRROR target is labeled as experimental because it can cause serious network havoc if misused. The target causes the exchange of the source and destination IP addresses and, for TCP and UDP datagrams, the source and destination ports. The modified packet is then retransmitted, which returns it to its source. The use of the MIRROR target is not recommended.

QUEUE TARGET

The QUEUE target is used to pass packets to user-written programs, using a standard interface. For more information on this target, see the Netfilter Hacking HOWTO, available at http://netfilter.samba.org/documentation/HOWTO/netfilter-hacking-HOWTO.html.

TOS TARGET

The TOS target is used to modify the Type of Service field of a packet. The target is used with the --set-tos flag, which specifies the desired value, and is valid only in the mangle table.

TTL TARGET

The TTL target is used to modify the Time to Live (TTL) field of a packet. The target is used with one of these flags:

- ◆ --ttl-set sets the TTL field to a specified value.

- ◆ --ttl-dec decrements the TTL field.

- ◆ --ttl-inc increments the TTL field.

Bear in mind that the firewall host automatically decrements the TTL value by one. The target is valid only in chains of the mangle table.

ULOG TARGET

The ULOG target sends a packet through a socket. The destination socket can be associated with a database or user application. You can learn more about this target at the home page of the related project, http://www.advogato.org/proj/ulogd/.

Performing Rule Operations

IPTables supports rule operations that enable you to add, delete, and replace rules. The related `iptables` syntax is described in the following subsections.

Adding a Rule at the Head of a Chain

To add a rule at the head of a chain of the `filter` table, specify the `-I` flag. To add a rule at the head of a chain in a table other than the `filter` table, specify the `-I` flag and the `-t` flag specifying the table. For example, to add a rule to the head of the `INPUT` chain, use a command of this form:

```
iptables -I INPUT specifiers
```

where `specifiers` are the rule specifiers and target. To add a rule to the head of the `PREROUTING` chain of the `nat` table, use a command of this form:

```
iptables -t nat -I PREROUTING specifiers
```

Rules added at the head of a chain — that is, *inserted* rules — are executed before existing rules.

Adding a Rule at the Tail of a Chain

To add a rule at the tail of a chain of the `filter` table, specify the flag `-A`. To add a rule at the tail of a chain in a table other than the `filter` table, specify the `-A` flag and the `-t` flag specifying the table. For example, to add a rule to the tail of the `INPUT` chain, use a command of this form:

```
iptables -A INPUT specifiers
```

where `specifiers` are the rule specifiers and target. To add a rule to the tail of the `PREROUTING` chain of the `nat` table, use a command of this form:

```
iptables -t nat -A PREROUTING specifiers
```

Rules added at the tail of a chain — that is, *appended* rules — are executed after existing rules.

Deleting a Rule

You can specify a rule to be deleted in either of two ways. You can specify the rule content, in which case the matching rule is deleted. Or, you can specify a line number, in which case the rule bearing the specified line number is deleted. To use the first method, issue a command of this form:

```
iptables -D chain specifiers
```

where *chain* is the name of the chain and *specifiers* are the rule specifiers and target. If the chain is part of a table other than `filter`, you must also specify the name of the table:

```
iptables -t table -D chain specifiers
```

To use the second method of deleting a rule, issue a command of this form:

```
iptables -D chain line
```

where *chain* is the name of the chain and *line* is the number of the line to be deleted. If the chain is not part of the `filter` chain, you must also specify the table name:

```
iptables -t table -D chain line
```

You can obtain the line number by listing the rule set using the `--line-numbers` option.

Replacing a Rule

To replace a rule, issue a command of this form:

```
iptables -t table -R chain line specifiers
```

where *table* is the name of the table, *chain* is the name of the chain, *line* is the line number of the rule to be replaced, and *specifiers* give the new rule content. If the rule resides on a chain of the `filter` table, the `-t table` specifier can be omitted.

Performing Chain Operations

IPTables provides these chain operations:

- ◆ List a chain.
- ◆ Flush a chain.
- ◆ Set the default policy of a chain.
- ◆ Zero a chain's counters.
- ◆ Create a user chain.

- ◆ Delete a user chain.

- ◆ Rename a user chain.

The following subsections explain how to perform these operations.

Listing a Chain

To list a chain, issue a command of this form:

```
iptables -t table -L chain
```

where *table* is the name of the table containing the chain and *chain* is the name of the chain. If the chain is part of the `filter` table, you can omit the table name:

```
iptables -L chain
```

To list all chains, omit the chain name:

```
iptables -L
```

To show IP addresses and port numbers rather than host and port names, specify the -n flag. The flag also causes TCP flag values to be printed in hexadecimal. An IPTables chain listing using the -n flag resembles the following:

```
Chain INPUT (policy ACCEPT)
target     prot opt source          destination
ACCEPT     all  --  0.0.0.0/0       0.0.0.0/0
ACCEPT     udp  --  192.0.34.72     0.0.0.0/0     udp spt:53
REJECT     tcp  --  0.0.0.0/0       0.0.0.0/0     tcp flags:0x16+0x02
_ reject-with icmp-port-unreachable
REJECT     udp  --  0.0.0.0/0       0.0.0.0/0
_ reject-with icmp-port-unreachable

Chain FORWARD (policy ACCEPT)
target     prot opt source          destination

Chain OUTPUT (policy ACCEPT)
target     prot opt source          destination
```

The iptables -L command supports several other options. These include

- ◆ -v, which causes detailed (verbose) output

- ◆ --line-numbers, which causes the listing to include line numbers

Flushing a Chain

To *flush* a chain – that is, to delete all its associated rules – issue a command of this form:

```
iptables -t table -F chain
```

where `table` is the name of the table containing the chain and `chain` is the name of the chain. If the chain is part of the `filter` table, you can omit the table name:

```
iptables -F chain
```

To flush all chains, omit the chain name:

```
iptables -F
```

 Flushing a chain removes all rules from the chain. If the default policy associated with the chain is `ACCEPT`, the absence of rules may place your system or network at risk. Consequently, you should not generally flush a chain of a firewall that's exposed to threats. Instead, remove the system from the network before performing firewall maintenance.

Setting the Default Policy of a Chain

To set the default policy of a chain, issue a command of this form:

```
iptables -P chain policy
```

where `chain` is the name of the chain and `policy` is the desired policy: `DROP`, `ACCEPT`, or `REJECT`. Only chains of the `filter` table can have an associated default policy.

Zeroing a Chain's Counters

Each rule includes counters that show the number of packets and bytes processed by the rule. To zero the counters of the rules associated with a chain, issue a command of this form:

```
iptables -t table -Z chain
```

where `table` is the name of the table containing the chain and `chain` is the name of the chain. If the chain is part of the `filter` table, you can omit the table name:

```
iptables -Z chain
```

To zero all chains, omit the chain name:

```
iptables -Z
```

Creating a User Chain

To create a user chain, issue a command of this form:

```
iptables -t table -N chain
```

where *table* is the name of the table containing the chain and *chain* is the name of the chain. If the chain will be part of the filter table, you can omit the table name:

```
iptables -N chain
```

Deleting a User Chain

To delete a user chain, issue a command of this form:

```
iptables -t table -X chain
```

where *table* is the name of the table containing the chain and *chain* is the name of the chain. If the chain is part of the filter table, you can omit the table name:

```
iptables -X chain
```

The command

```
iptables -X
```

deletes all user chains.

Renaming a User Chain

To rename a user chain, issue a command of this form:

```
iptables -t table -E old new
```

where *table* is the name of the table containing the chain, *old* is the existing name of the chain, and *new* is the new name. If the chain is part of the filter table, you can omit the table name:

```
iptables -t table -E old new
```

A Simple IPTables Firewall

Following is a simple but complete IPTables firewall:

```
# Replace xxx.xxx.xxx.xxx with IP address of name server
iptables -F
iptables -X
iptables -P INPUT   ACCEPT
iptables -P OUTPUT  ACCEPT
iptables -P FORWARD ACCEPT
iptables -A INPUT -i lo -j ACCEPT
iptables -A INPUT -p udp -s xxx.xxx.xxx.xxx --sport 53 -j ACCEPT
iptables -A INPUT -p tcp --syn -j REJECT
iptables -A INPUT -p udp -j REJECT
```

The operation of the firewall resembles that of the high-security IPChains firewall built by lokkit. It blocks all incoming TCP SYN packets and all UDP packets except those coming from UDP port 53, which are likely to be replies to name service queries. The firewall performs no logging and has other manifest deficiencies; for instance, it blocks all incoming TCP requests and therefore can't be used on a firewall or host that provides TCP services. Therefore, it is not recommended for actual use because constructing more effective firewalls is simple. Chapter 9 shows you how to do so.

Migrating from IPChains to IPTables

As mentioned, the IPTables firewall facility resembles the IPChains firewall in several respects. The two facilities are so similar that it may seem trivial to convert IPChains firewall code to run under IPTables. Such a conversion is not difficult, but you should be mindful of the following salient differences between the two facilities:

- ◆ The names of the IPTables built-in chains must appear in uppercase.

- ◆ The IPTables target for dropping a packet is DENY, not DROP.

- ◆ An IPTables output interface must be specified using the -o flag rather than the -i flag, which IPTables uses for the input interface.

- ◆ The IPTables INPUT and OUPUT chains see only packets sent to or from the firewall host; they do not see forwarded packets.

- ◆ As explained in Chapter 10, IPTables network address translation uses different syntax from IPChains'.

Summary

This chapter explained the basic operation of the IPTables facility and described how to use the `iptables` command to create IPTables rules. The next chapter explains how to create IPTables firewalls.

Chapter 9

IPTables Firewall Implementation

IN THIS CHAPTER

- ◆ Firewall policies
- ◆ IPTables firewall organization
- ◆ Filtering inbound packets
- ◆ Filtering outbound packets
- ◆ Filtering ICMP messages
- ◆ Blocking bad packets
- ◆ Protecting against floods
- ◆ Logging interesting packets
- ◆ Setting up the chains
- ◆ Installing and operating the firewall
- ◆ The complete host firewall

CHAPTER 8 EXPLAINED THE OPERATION OF IPTABLES and the use of the IPTables user interface, the `iptables` command. This chapter explains how to use IPTables to implement a simple firewall of the sort suitable for protecting a host. The model firewall includes features lacking in several leading firewall products. In particular, it includes protection against two kinds of denial-of-service attacks, protection against certain TCP scans, and sophisticated logging. A host firewall based on the model firewall of this chapter can effectively supplement the protection provided by a gateway or choke firewall of the sort explained in Chapter 10, "Advanced IPTables Firewall Implementation," providing multiple layers of defense.

Model Firewall Policies

The model firewall described in this chapter is a relatively simple IPTables firewall. Nevertheless, it implements security policies consistent with a high degree of protection. Table 9-1 summarizes the policies implemented by the model firewall.

TABLE 9-1 MODEL FIREWALL POLICIES

Policy	Description
Egress filtering	Restrictive: Only explicitly authorized packets may exit the protected host.
Hostile hosts	Hostile hosts may be shunned — that is, all related inbound and outbound traffic can be blocked.
Inbound ICMP	Only the following messages are authorized: destination unreachable, parameter problem, source quench, and time exceeded.
Inbound services	Remote clients can access SSH and Web (HTTP) services provided by the protected host. Remote clients are blocked from accessing other services.
Ingress filtering	Restrictive: Only explicitly authorized packets may enter the protected host.
Logging	All blocked packets are logged via the Syslog facility.
Outbound ICMP	Only the following messages are authorized: destination unreachable, fragmentation needed, parameter problem, and source quench.
Outbound services	Local clients can access remote DNS, FTP, HTTP, HTTPS, RSYNC, SMTP, SSH, and WHOIS servers. Local clients are blocked from accessing other remote services.
Ping	Only specified hosts can ping, or be pinged by, the protected host.
Special IPs	Traffic from special IPs, such as RFC 1918 addresses, can be blocked.
SYN Flood	The firewall can block SYNs when their rate of arrival exceeds a specified threshold, blunting the effects of SYN flood attacks.
TCP flags	TCP flags are validated, blocking certain types of TCP scans.

Notice that both ingress and egress filtering are *restrictive* — that is, only authorized packets may enter or exit the protected host. Many administrators prefer to relax egress filtering, configuring it as permissive so that only unauthorized packets are blocked. You can easily change the model firewall to implement permissive egress filtering. Indeed, you can easily change the model firewall to implement permissive ingress filtering. However, it's not generally recommended that you configure a firewall for permissive ingress filtering.

Model Firewall Organization

Because the firewall is designed to protect a single-homed host, the IPTables FOR-WARD chain is not used. Apart from the IPTables built-in chains INPUT and OUTPUT, the model firewall contains 13 user chains. Table 9-2 summarizes the user chains.

TABLE 9-2 USER CHAINS OF THE MODEL FIREWALL

Chain	Description
BADIP	Checks for unwanted source and destination IP addresses
FLAGS	Checks for unwanted TCP flag combinations
FLOOD	Checks for excessive rate of arrival of SYN packets
In	Checks for inbound TCP/UDP datagrams
IN_ICMP	Checks for inbound ICMP messages
LBADIP	Logs and drops packets having unwanted source or destination IP addresses
LDROP	Logs and drops packets
LFLAGS	Logs and drops packets having unwanted TCP flag combinations
LFLOOD	Logs and drops SYN packets
LSHUN	Logs and drops packets from shunned hosts
OUT	Checks for outbound TCP/UDP datagrams
OUT_ICMP	Checks for outbound ICMP messages
SHUN	Checks for hostile source and destination IP addresses

As the table shows, the firewall includes separate chains for handling inbound TCP/UDP datagrams (IN) and inbound ICMP messages (IN_ICMP). Similarly, it includes separate chains for handling outbound TCP/UDP datagrams (OUT) and outbound ICMP messages (OUT_ICMP). The firewall includes several chains used to log and drop unwanted packets (LBADIP, LDROP, LFLAGS, and LSHUN). And, it includes several chains that filter packets based on specific characteristics (BADIP, FLAGS, FLOOD, and SHUN). The following sections explain the operation of each chain in detail.

The INPUT Chain: Filtering Inbound Packets

Figure 9-1 shows the structure of the INPUT chain, which processes all inbound packets. The INPUT chain

1. Accepts packets arriving via the loopback interface because they originate from processes local to the host itself.

2. Uses the BADIP chain to check packets for bad source and destination IP addresses, such as RFC 1918 addresses. Bad packets are logged and dropped. Other packets return to the INPUT chain for further processing.

3. Uses the SHUN chain to check packets against a list of hostile IP addresses. Packets originating from a hostile host are logged and dropped. Other packets return to the INPUT chain for further processing.

4. Uses the IN chain to perform further tests on TCP/UDP datagrams and uses the IN_ICMP chain to perform further tests on ICMP messages. As usual, bad packets are logged and dropped. In addition, these chains accept authorized packets.

5. Logs and drops any remaining packets not accepted by IN or IN_ICMP as authorized.

Listing 9-1 shows the iptables commands that make up the INPUT chain. Compare the listing with Figure 9-1 and the list of processing steps until you're comfortable that you understand how the chain operates.

Listing 9-1: The INPUT chain

```
$IPT -A INPUT -i lo        -j ACCEPT
$IPT -A INPUT              -j BADIP
$IPT -A INPUT              -j SHUN
$IPT -A INPUT -p ! icmp   -j IN
$IPT -A INPUT -p   icmp   -j IN_ICMP
$IPT -A INPUT              -j LDROP
```

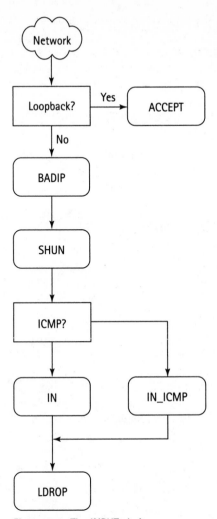

Figure 9-1: The INPUT chain

 In Listing 9-1, the token $IPT is an environment variable giving the location of the iptables binary. The variable is initialized near the beginning of the firewall script, as shown in Listing 9-13.

The OUTPUT Chain: Filtering Outbound Packets

Figure 9-2 shows the OUTPUT chain, which processes all outbound packets. Its processing steps closely resemble those performed by the INPUT chain. The OUTPUT chain

1. Accepts packets destined for the loopback interface because such packets have been sent by processes local to the protected host itself.

2. Uses the BADIP chain to check packets for bad source and destination IP addresses, such as RFC 1918 addresses. Bad packets are logged and dropped. Other packets return to the OUTPUT chain for further processing.

3. Uses the SHUN chain to check packets against a list of hostile IP addresses. Packets destined for a hostile host are logged and dropped. Other packets return to the OUTPUT chain for further processing.

4. Uses the OUT chain to perform further tests on TCP/UDP datagrams; uses the OUT_ICMP chain to perform further tests on ICMP messages. As usual, bad packets are logged and dropped. In addition, these chains accept authorized packets.

5. Logs and drops any remaining (unauthorized) packets not accepted by OUT or OUT_ICMP.

Listing 9-2 shows the iptables commands that make up the OUTPUT chain. As you did with the INPUT chain, compare the listing with the figure and the list of processing steps until you're comfortable that you understand how the chain operates.

Listing 9-2: The OUTPUT chain

```
$IPT -A OUTPUT -o lo      -j ACCEPT
$IPT -A OUTPUT            -j BADIP
$IPT -A OUTPUT            -j SHUN
$IPT -A OUTPUT -p ! icmp -j OUT
$IPT -A OUTPUT -p   icmp -j OUT_ICMP
$IPT -A OUTPUT            -j LDROP
```

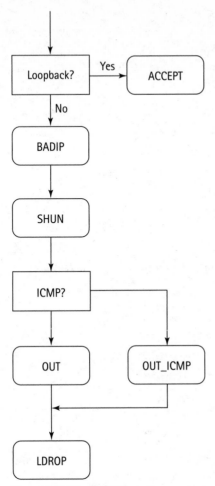

Figure 9-2: The OUTPUT chain

The IN Chain: Filtering Inbound TCP/UDP Datagrams

The IN chain, represented in Figure 9-3, checks inbound TCP and UDP datagram. The IN chain

1. Logs and drops datagrams that have an invalid connection state, by sending them to the LDROP chain. Generally, these consist of malformed packets.

2. Uses the FLOOD chain to check whether TCP SYN datagrams are arriving at an excessive rate and logs and drops unwanted datagrams. Other datagrams return to the IN chain for further processing.

3. Uses the FLAGS chain to check whether TCP datagrams have an unauthorized combination of TCP flags and logs and drops those that do. Other datagrams return to the IN chain for further processing.

4. Accepts datagrams associated with established or related connections.

5. Drops datagrams having the local host's IP address as their source address; these are spoofed datagrams originating elsewhere.

6. Accepts datagrams associated with an authorized service.

7. Rejects datagrams bound for the AUTH service, which is explained in Chapter 4. Doing so prevents the sending host from retrying the connection until the host times out.

8. Returns other datagrams to the INPUT chain, which contains rules that log and drop them.

Listing 9-3 shows the iptables commands that make up the IN chain. The chain is configured to accept SSH (port 22) and WWW (port 80) connections from remote clients on specified hosts. The chain uses the $IP variable to refer to the firewall's external IP address. This variable is initialized near the beginning of the firewall source code, as shown in Listing 9-3.

Rather than a series of rules to specify the authorized connections, a shell loop is used. The shell variables $SSH and $WWW each contain zero or more IP addresses of hosts or networks that may access the protected host.

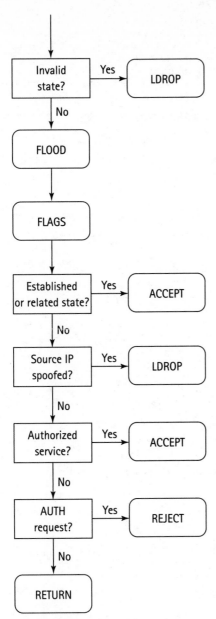

Figure 9-3: The IN chain

Listing 9-3: The IN chain

```
$IPT -N IN
$IPT -A IN -m state --state INVALID -j LDROP
$IPT -A IN -p tcp --syn -j FLOOD
$IPT -A IN -p tcp         -j FLAGS
$IPT -A IN -m state --state ESTABLISHED,RELATED -j ACCEPT
$IPT -A IN -s $IP -j LDROP

# Accept new inbound connections.

for sip in $SSH; do
  $IPT -A IN -p tcp -s $sip --dport 22 -m state --state NEW \
    -j ACCEPT
done

for sip in $WWW; do
  $IPT -A IN -p tcp -s $sip --dport 80 -m state --state NEW \
    -j ACCEPT
done

# Reject AUTH requests

$IPT -A IN -p tcp --dport 113 -j REJECT --reject-with tcp-reset

# Add additional rules accepting authorized traffic here.
# Traffic not explicitly accepted will be logged and dropped.
```

For example, the $SSH variable might have been assigned a value in the following way:

```
SSH="192.0.34.12 192.0.34.13"
```

This would cause the shell loop to execute the following iptables commands:

```
$IPT -A IN -p tcp -s 192.0.34.12 --dport 22 -m state --state NEW \
  -j ACCEPT
$IPT -A IN -p tcp -s 192.0.34.13 --dport 22 -m state --state NEW \
  -j ACCEPT
```

Notice that each successive value in the shell variable substitutes for the loop variable $sip, resulting in two rules' being added to the IPTables rule set.

To specify that any host on the Class C network 192.0.3.0 is authorized to access the SSH server, assign the following value to the $SSH shell variable:

```
SSH="192.0.3.0/24"
```

To specify that any host can access the local SSH server, assign the following value to the $SSH shell variable:

```
SSH="0.0.0.0/0"
```

To specify that no host can access the local SSH server, assign the following value to the $SSH shell variable:

```
SSH=""
```

You can assign values to the $WWW shell variable in the same fashion. The complete firewall source code listing, which appears in Listing 9-13, shows how to do so. Note that the shell variable must be assigned a value before the commands that build the IN chain are executed.

 TIP Many administrators find shell loops convenient because the firewall is shorter and easier to maintain than one that includes multiple commands rather than shell loops. However, if you don't like shell loops, you can code iptables commands individually. After the firewall is configured, it runs the same regardless of whether its rules were specified individually or under the control of a loop.

You can easily modify the model firewall to accept connections to additional or other services. Simply create a shell variable to hold the list of authorized hosts and properly initialize its value. Then, create a shell loop using this pattern:

```
for sip in $service; do
  $IPT -A IN -p proto -s $sip --dport port -m state --state NEW \
    -j ACCEPT
done
```

where *service* is the name of the shell variable, *proto* is either tcp or udp, and *port* is the port on which the server listens.

Most common services can be authorized by coding a single rule accepting new connections to the port on which the server listens. However, complicated protocols may require that you specify multiple rules. A few protocols — such as H.323 — cannot be supported by a nonproxying firewall. Consult Chapter 4, "Internet Services," to learn more about protocols you want to authorize.

The OUT Chain: Filtering Outbound TCP/UDP Datagrams

The OUT chain, as depicted in Figure 9-4, processes outbound TCP and UDP datagrams. The OUT chain

1. Uses the FLAGS chain to check whether TCP datagrams have invalid TCP flag combinations and logs and drops unwanted datagrams. Other datagrams return to the OUT chain for further processing.

2. Logs and drops datagrams not having the local host's IP address as their source address; these are spoofed datagrams that may trouble some other network administrator. The LDROP chain logs and drops packets sent to it.

3. Accepts datagrams associated with established or related connections.

4. Accepts datagrams associated with an authorized service.

5. Returns other datagrams to the OUTPUT chain, which logs and drops them.

The model firewall is not appropriate for all situations. For instance, the model firewall enables you to specify only a single external IP address for the firewall host. If the firewall host has multiple external IP addresses, the model firewall code must be modified.

Listing 9-4 shows the commands that make up the OUT chain. The OUT chain does not restrict local clients from accessing remote services host by host. If a service is authorized, a local client can connect to any server offering the service. However, it would be simple to add the -d flag used to restrict the destination address of packets.

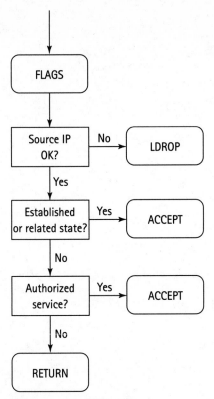

Figure 9-4: The OUT chain

Listing 9-4: The OUT chain

```
$IPT -N OUT
$IPT -A OUT -p tcp -j FLAGS
$IPT -A OUT -s ! $IP -j LDROP
$IPT -A OUT -m state --state ESTABLISHED,RELATED -j ACCEPT
#
# This firewall is configured to block outbound connections by
# default. To allow any output not explicitly blocked, uncomment the
# following line. Place blocking rules here.
#$IPT -A OUT -m state --state NEW -j ACCEPT

# Accept new outbound connections.
```

Continued

Listing 9-4 *(Continued)*

```
$IPT -A OUT -m state --state NEW -p tcp --dport  21 -j ACCEPT # ftp
$IPT -A OUT -m state --state NEW -p tcp --dport  22 -j ACCEPT # ssh
$IPT -A OUT -m state --state NEW -p tcp --dport  25 -j ACCEPT # smtp
$IPT -A OUT -m state --state NEW -p tcp --dport  43 -j ACCEPT # whois
$IPT -A OUT -m state --state NEW -p tcp --dport  53 -j ACCEPT # domain
$IPT -A OUT -m state --state NEW -p tcp --dport  80 -j ACCEPT # http
$IPT -A OUT -m state --state NEW -p tcp --dport 443 -j ACCEPT # https
$IPT -A OUT -m state --state NEW -p tcp --dport 873 -j ACCEPT # rsync

$IPT -A OUT -m state --state NEW -p udp --dport  53 -j ACCEPT # domain


# Add additional rules accepting authorized traffic here.
# Traffic not explicitly accepted will be logged and dropped.
```

As configured, the model firewall permits local clients to connect to these services:

- FTP (TCP port 21)
- SSH (TCP port 22)
- SMTP (TCP port 25)
- WHOIS (TCP port 43)
- DNS (TCP port 53 and UDP port 53)
- HTTP (TCP port 80)
- HTTPS (TCP port 443)
- RSYNC (TCP port 873)

You can easily modify the rules to accept outbound connections to other or additional services. Consult Chapter 4, "Internet Services," for the port or ports associated with services you want to authorize.

If you prefer a firewall that has permissive outbound filtering, uncomment the line that unconditionally accepts new outbound connections. To prohibit a service, precede the uncommented line with a rule that logs and rejects the related datagrams. For example, to prohibit outbound FTP but authorize all other TCP and UDP services, your firewall should include these two rules:

```
$IPT -A OUT -p tcp --dport 21 -j LDROP
$IPT -A OUT -m state --state NEW -j ACCEPT
```

The LDROP chain, which is explained in the section "The Logging Chains," logs and drops packets sent to it. Consequently, the two rules accept all new connections except those bound for port 21, the FTP command port.

Recall that, as explained in Chapter 8, packets reaching the end of an IPTables user chain such as the OUT chain return to the calling chain.

The IN_ICMP Chain: Filtering Inbound ICMP Messages

Figure 9-5 shows the IN_ICMP chain, which handles inbound ICMP messages. The IN_ICMP chain:

1. If the message is an echo request or reply from an authorized host, accepts the message.

2. If the message is a destination unreachable message, accepts the message.

3. If the message is a source quench message, accepts the message.

4. If the message is a time-exceeded message, accepts the message.

5. If the message is a parameter problem message, accepts the message.

6. Otherwise, returns the packet to the INPUT chain, which logs and drops it.

Listing 9-5 shows the commands that make up the IN_ICMP chain. Notice that the firewall code includes a loop that executes commands accepting ping (echo request) messages based on the IP addresses contained in the shell variable $PING. The value of this variable must be set before the commands are executed. The value of the variable takes the same form as that of the $SSH shell variable, described earlier in this chapter.

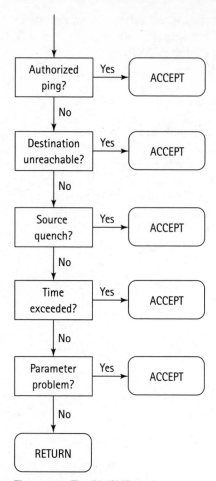

Figure 9-5: The IN_ICMP chain

Listing 9-5: The IN_ICMP chain

```
$IPT -N IN_ICMP
for sip in $PING; do
  $IPT -A IN_ICMP  -p icmp --icmp-type echo-request -s $sip  \
    -d $IP -j ACCEPT
  $IPT -A IN_ICMP  -p icmp --icmp-type echo-reply    -s $sip  \
    -d $IP -j ACCEPT
done
$IPT -A IN_ICMP  -p icmp --icmp-type destination-unreachable \
  -j ACCEPT
$IPT -A IN_ICMP  -p icmp --icmp-type source-quench          \
  -j ACCEPT
```

```
$IPT -A IN_ICMP  -p icmp --icmp-type time-exceeded         \
  -j ACCEPT
$IPT -A IN_ICMP  -p icmp --icmp-type parameter-problem      \
  -j ACCEPT
```

If you prefer a different policy for handling inbound ICMP messages, you can delete one or more of the given commands, thereby dropping the related message type or types. Or, you can add one or more commands that accept other message types. However, your firewall should generally accept the message types accepted by the model firewall, with the exception of echo requests; otherwise, the firewall host doesn't comply with TCP/IP standards. If you prefer that your firewall not respond to echo requests, simply set the $PING shell variable to an empty value:

```
PING=""
```

The OUT_ICMP Chain: Filtering Outbound ICMP Messages

Figure 9-6 depicts the OUT_ICMP chain, which handles outbound ICMP messages. The structure of this chain closely resembles that of the IN_ICMP chain. The OUT_ICMP chain

1. If the message is an echo request or a reply to an authorized host, accepts the message.

2. If the message is a destination unreachable message, accepts the message.

3. If the message is a fragmentation needed message, accepts the message.

4. If the message is a source quench message, accepts the message.

5. If the message is a parameter problem message, accepts the message.

6. Otherwise, returns the packet to the OUTPUT chain, which logs and drops it.

Listing 9-6 shows the firewall code associated with the OUT_ICMP chain. The code follows the same general pattern as the IN_ICMP chain, except that it accepts fragmentation unreachable messages and does not accept time-exceeded messages.

TIP   You can make your firewall somewhat more secure by deleting the rules accepting destination unreachable and parameter problem messages. However, doing so is discourteous to other hosts, which may resend packets until they time out unless an ICMP message informs them of an error condition.

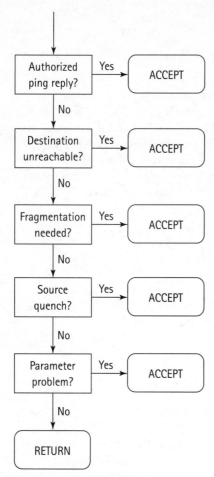

Figure 9-6: The OUT_ICMP chain

Listing 9-6: The OUT_ICMP chain

```
$IPT -N OUT_ICMP
for dip in $PING; do
  $IPT -A OUT_ICMP -p icmp --icmp-type echo-request -d $dip  \
    -j ACCEPT
  $IPT -A OUT_ICMP -p icmp --icmp-type echo-reply    -d $dip  \
    -j ACCEPT
done
$IPT -A OUT_ICMP -p icmp --icmp-type destination-unreachable \
  -j ACCEPT
```

```
$IPT -A OUT_ICMP -p icmp --icmp-type fragmentation-needed    \
  -j ACCEPT
$IPT -A OUT_ICMP -p icmp --icmp-type source-quench           \
  -j ACCEPT
$IPT -A OUT_ICMP -p icmp --icmp-type parameter-problem       \
  -j ACCEPT
```

The BADIP, FLAGS, and SHUN Chains: Blocking Bad Packets

The model firewall blocks three types of unwanted packets:

◆ Packets associated with bad IP addresses, such as those of private and reserved networks

◆ Packets having an invalid combination of TCP flags

◆ Packets associated with known hostile hosts

In addition, Linux kernel facilities can be configured to block these types of unwanted packets:

◆ Source routed packets

◆ Fragmented packets

◆ Malformed packets

The section "Installing and Operating the Firewall," later in this chapter, explains how to configure these facilities. The following subsections explain how the firewall blocks each of the three types of unwanted packets.

Bad IP Addresses

Packets bearing certain IP addresses are generally unwanted, particularly if they're associated with an interface configured for a public rather than a private network. For instance, you probably don't want your hosts responding to broadcast messages sent via the Internet. Likewise, packets claiming to come from the loopback IP address or from private networks designated by RFC 1918 should not arrive via the Internet. Finally, the Internet Assigned Number Authority (IANA) has reserved certain address blocks. Inbound traffic should not have originated from, and outbound traffic should not be destined for, reserved networks.

TIP The IANA has begun assigning addresses that were previously reserved. If you choose to block reserved networks, monitor your firewall logs and be prepared to unblock reserved networks that have been assigned.

Figure 9-7 represents the BADIP chain, which checks source and destination IP addresses and blocks packets that fail its tests. This chain is invoked by both the INPUT and OUTPUT chains. The BADIP chain

1. Checks for a bad source address and drops and logs any packet having a bad source address by sending it to the LBADIP chain.

2. Checks for a bad destination address and drops and logs any packet having a bad destination address.

3. Returns any remaining packets to the calling chain for further processing.

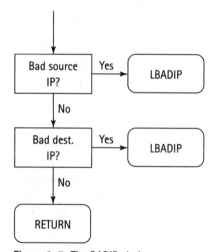

Figure 9-7: The BADIP chain

Listing 9-7 shows the code associated with the BADIP chain. The chain uses a shell variable, $BADIP, to specify network addresses that are considered bad. The following network addresses are included:

◆ Broadcast addresses

  ■ 0.0.0.0/8

  ■ 255.255.255.255

- ◆ The loopback address
  - ▪ 127.0.0.0/8
- ◆ Multicast addresses
  - ▪ 224.0.0.0/4
  - ▪ 240.0.0.0/5
- ◆ Reserved addresses
  - ▪ 169.254.0.0/16
  - ▪ 192.0.0.0/24
  - ▪ 192.0.34.0/24
- ◆ RFC 1918 addresses
  - ▪ 10.0.0.0/8
  - ▪ 172.16.0.0/12
  - ▪ 192.168.0.0/16

You can tailor this list according to your own preferences. In particular, if the protected host resides on a network using an RFC 1918 address, you need to remove that address from the list of bad IP addresses.

Listing 9-7: The BADIP chain

```
BADIP="0.0.0.0/8 10.0.0.0/8 127.0.0.0/8 169.254.0.0/16 \
   172.16.0.0/12 192.0.0.0/24 192.168.0.0/16 192.0.34.0/24 \
   224.0.0.0/4 240.0.0.0/5 255.255.255.255"

$IPT -N BADIP
for ip in $BADIP; do
  $IPT -A BADIP -s $ip -j LBADIP
  $IPT -A BADIP -d $ip -j LBADIP
done
```

TCP Flags

Some combinations of TCP flags do not occur in normal TCP datagrams. Scanners and other hostile programs use these flag combinations to determine the operating system being run by a target host, to probe a target host's firewall, and to perform other unwanted reconnaissance. The FLAGS chain, as depicted in Figure 9-8, drops datagrams with invalid combinations of TCP flags. The chain tests for specific flag combinations and sends any matching datagrams to the LFLAGS chain, which logs and drops them.

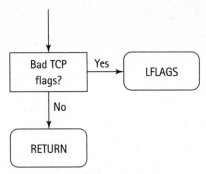

Figure 9–8: The FLAGS chain

Listing 9-8 shows the firewall code associated with the FLAGS chain. Notice that only TCP datagrams are tested. You can generally use this chain without modification. However, it's easily modified to implement a different policy, if required.

Listing 9–8: The FLAGS chain

```
$IPT -N FLAGS
$IPT -A FLAGS -p tcp --tcp-flags ACK,FIN FIN              -j LFLAGS
$IPT -A FLAGS -p tcp --tcp-flags ACK,PSH PSH              -j LFLAGS
$IPT -A FLAGS -p tcp --tcp-flags ACK,URG URG             -j LFLAGS
$IPT -A FLAGS -p tcp --tcp-flags FIN,RST FIN,RST         -j LFLAGS
$IPT -A FLAGS -p tcp --tcp-flags SYN,FIN SYN,FIN         -j LFLAGS
$IPT -A FLAGS -p tcp --tcp-flags SYN,RST SYN,RST         -j LFLAGS
$IPT -A FLAGS -p tcp --tcp-flags ALL ALL                -j LFLAGS
$IPT -A FLAGS -p tcp --tcp-flags ALL NONE               -j LFLAGS
$IPT -A FLAGS -p tcp --tcp-flags ALL FIN,PSH,URG        -j LFLAGS
$IPT -A FLAGS -p tcp --tcp-flags ALL SYN,FIN,PSH,URG    -j LFLAGS
$IPT -A FLAGS -p tcp --tcp-flags ALL SYN,RST,ACK,FIN,URG    -j LFLAGS

# Remaining flag combinations considered valid.
```

Hostile Hosts

Sometimes, network monitoring discloses hostile activity associated with a particular host. In these situations, it's useful to be able to quickly and easily block all traffic to and from such a host. The SHUN chain, as shown in Figure 9-9, provides this capability. The chain's structure closely resembles that of the BADIP chain, as does its function. The distinction is that hosts are added to and removed from the SHUN chain during firewall operation. Hosts are added to the BADIP chain when the chain is created and are not removed unless the firewall is redesigned.

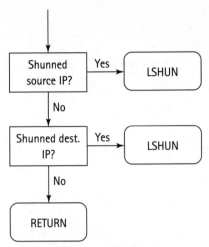

Figure 9-9: The SHUN chain

Listing 9-9 shows the code associated with the SHUN chain. The code uses a shell variable to hold the IP addresses of hosts that are blocked. Normally, this variable is initialized to an empty value. To add a host to the SHUN chain, execute a command having the following form:

```
iptables -A SHUN -s address -j LSHUN
```

where *address* is the IP address of the host or network to be shunned. To remove a host from the SHUN list, execute a command having this form:

```
iptables -D SHUN -s address -j LSHUN
```

To hold a general amnesty, removing all hosts from the SHUN list, execute this command:

```
iptables -F SHUN
```

Listing 9-9: The SHUN chain

```
$IPT -N SHUN
for ip in $SHUNIP; do
  $IPT -A SHUN -s $ip -j LSHUN
  $IPT -A SHUN -d $ip -j LSHUN
done
```

The site www.dshield.org maintains a list of hosts that are actively probing and attacking other hosts. Rather than wait for such a host to appear on your network monitoring reports, you may prefer to proactively block it using the SHUN chain.

The FLOOD Chain: Protecting Against SYN Floods

The FLOOD chain, as shown in Figure 9-10, protects the host against SYN flood attacks. The chain contains a rule that fires — that is, that matches packets — at only a limited rate. If packets arrive at a rate that exceeds the specified threshold, they are logged and dropped.

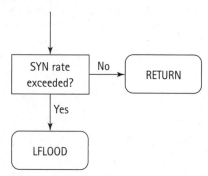

Figure 9-10: The FLOOD chain

Listing 9-10 shows the commands that make up the chain. The threshold is set to allow the acceptance of as many as ten SYN datagrams. Thereafter, until the rule recharges, no more than five SYN datagrams per second are accepted. Excess datagrams are passed to the LFLOOD chain, which logs and drops them.

Listing 9-10: The FLOOD chain

```
SYNOPT="-m limit --limit 5/second --limit-burst 10"

$IPT -N FLOOD

# Following rule accepting datagram fires at limited rate.
```

```
$IPT -A FLOOD $SYNOPT -j RETURN
$IPT -A FLOOD         -j LFLOOD
```

 TIP Because the rate at which a host can accept SYN datagrams depends on the performance of the host, the burst limit and threshold rate set in the model firewall may not be ideal for a given host. The best way to set these values is by experimentation. However, many administrators are reluctant to expose hosts to a SYN flood, even one generated for beneficial purposes. In such a case, the given values, which are somewhat conservative, will probably suffice. Simply monitor the firewall log to ensure that datagrams are not being inappropriately dropped. If you find that they are, increase the burst limit, the threshold rate, or both until no datagrams are inappropriately dropped.

The Logging Chains

The model firewall includes four chains that log and drop specific types of packets sent to them. In addition, it includes the LDROP chain, which logs and drops packets culled for a variety of reasons. Listing 9-11 shows the code associated with the logging chain. Notice that each chain includes a rule that limits the logging rate to one packet per second, after an initial burst of ten packets. These rules help prevent the firewall host from being the victim of a denial-of-service attack aimed at filling up the host's logging space.

Listing 9-11: The logging chains

```
LOGOPT="--log-level=3 -m limit --limit 1/second --limit-burst 10"

$IPT -N LDROP
$IPT -A LDROP   -j LOG --log-prefix "IPT Drop:   " $LOGOPT
$IPT -A LDROP   -j DROP

$IPT -N LBADIP
$IPT -A LBADIP    -p tcp --dport 137:139 -j DROP
$IPT -A LBADIP    -p udp --dport 137:139 -j DROP
$IPT -A LBADIP    -j LOG --log-prefix "IPT BAD:   " $LOGOPT
$IPT -A LBADIP    -j DROP
```

Continued

Listing 9-11 *(Continued)*

```
$IPT -N LSHUN
$IPT -A LSHUN    -j LOG --log-prefix "IPT Shun:    " $LOGOPT
$IPT -A LSHUN    -j DROP

$IPT -N LFLOOD
$IPT -A LFLOOD   -j LOG --log-prefix "IPT Flood:   " $LOGOPT
$IPT -A LFLOOD   -j DROP

$IPT -N LFLAGS
$IPT -A LFLAGS   -j LOG --log-prefix "IPT Flags:   " $LOGOPT
$IPT -A LFLAGS   -j DROP
```

Notice that the LBADIP chain includes two rules that drop datagrams destined for ports 137–39 without logging:

```
$IPT -A LBADIP   -p tcp --dport 137:139 -j DROP
$IPT -A LBADIP   -p udp --dport 137:139 -j DROP
```

Such packets are generally broadcast packets sent at regular intervals by Microsoft hosts on the local network. Rather than clog the log with entries pertaining to these routine packets, the packets are silently dropped. If you prefer to log such packets, you can remove the rules. If you want to silently drop other types of packets, you can add new rules following the pattern implicit in these rules.

Setting Up the Chains

Several commands must be issued to set up the firewall chains before the firewall can commence operation. Listing 9-12 shows these commands, which

1. Ensure that the iptables command is available for execution. Otherwise, fail with a descriptive error message.

2. Set the default policy of each built-in chain to DROP.

3. Flush and delete all built-in chains.

4. Delete all user chains and reset all counters.

Listing 9-12: Firewall initialization commands

```
if [ ! -x $IPT ]
then
  echo "firewall: can't execute \$IPTABLES"
  exit 1
```

```
fi

$IPT -P INPUT   DROP # Set default policy to DROP
$IPT -P OUTPUT  DROP # Set default policy to DROP
$IPT -P FORWARD DROP # Set default policy to DROP
$IPT -F  # Flush all chains
$IPT -X  # Delete all user chains

for table in filter nat mangle
do
  $IPT -t $table -F  # Delete the table's rules
  $IPT -t $table -X  # Delete the table's chains
  $IPT -t $table -Z  # Zero the table's counters
done
```

Installing and Operating the Firewall

To install and operate the host firewall, several steps are required:

- Set the kernel configuration options.
- Configure the IPTables service to run.
- Start the IPTables service.

The following subsections explain these steps.

Setting Kernel Configuration Options

The Linux kernel provides several options that are useful when implementing a firewall. For a single-homed host, the important options are shown in this list:

- net.ipv4.conf.default.rp_filter controls the blocking of packets with source addressing errors.

- net.ipv4.conf.eth0.accept_source_routing controls the blocking of source routed packets.

The best way to set these options is by including the following lines in the /etc/sysctl.conf file:

```
net.ipv4.conf.default.rp_filter = 1
net.ipv4.conf.eth0.accept_source_routing = 0
```

However, the /etc/sysctl.conf file – like the /etc/rc.local file – is executed only when the system boots. Unless you want to reboot your system before starting your firewall for the first time, you need to set these kernel options manually. To do so, issue these commands:

```
sysctl -w net.ipv4.conf.default.rp_filter = 1
sysctl -w net.ipv4.conf.eth0.accept_source_routing = 0
```

You may find it convenient to first update the /etc/sysctl.conf file andthen set the options by issuing the command

```
sysctl -p
```

Configuring the IPTables Service to Run

To configure the IPTables service to run when the system enters run levels 2, 3, or 5, issue this command:

```
chkconfig iptables on
```

Note that this command does not actually start the IPTables service, which starts the next time a run level from 2–5 is entered.

To disable the IPTables service from automatically running, issue this command:

```
chkconfig iptables off
```

Note that this command does not stop the IPTables service. You can stop the service by using the command given in the following section.

Starting and Stopping the IPTables Service

To start the IPTables service, issue this command:

```
service iptables start
```

This command initializes the IPTables service using the last saved configuration. You can overwrite the current configuration by running the firewall code. After you've done so, save the new configuration by issuing the command

```
service iptables save
```

Thereafter, the revised configuration in /etc/sysconfig/iptables is loaded whenever the IPTables service starts.

To stop the IPTables service, issue this command:

```
service iptables stop
```

You can stop the IPTables service and restart it — effectively resetting the service — by issuing this command:

```
service iptables restart
```

 When you stop the IPTables facility, the firewall is disabled and accepts all inbound and outbound packets. When your host is in this state, it may be vulnerable to attack. You should remove the host from the network — or otherwise protect it from attack — before performing firewall maintenance.

The Complete Host Firewall

Listing 9-13 gives the complete host firewall. Notice the order in which the various firewall code elements appear:

1. Assignments of shell variables

2. Firewall initialization code

3. User chains

4. Built-in chains

In particular, notice that each user chain is defined before it is referenced. This order is necessary to the correct functioning of the firewall, although it does make the firewall code somewhat difficult to read because relatively unimportant code sometimes precedes more important code. The order of the code is designed to create each user chain before the chain is referenced, avoiding IPTables errors. The order is also designed to minimize the duration of the interval during which the host is unprotected during firewall maintenance. Nevertheless, you generally should not perform firewall maintenance on a host that's attached to a potentially hostile network.

To use the firewall, you must provide the IP address of the firewall host, which is assigned to the shell variable $IP. However, you're likely to need to perform many other customizations and tweaks. For instance, you'll probably want to provide values for the shell variables that determine which hosts can access services running on the protected host. In most cases, you want to modify the list of authorized inbound and outbound services. To do so, you need to add, change, or delete firewall rules as appropriate to your situation. The material in Chapters 4, 6, and 8 should help you plan and make the proper changes.

Just as programmers regularly update programs, network administrators regularly update firewalls. If you update your firewall often, be sure to keep a record of the changes made. Many firewall problems arise because of incorrect changes. Being able to identify recent changes can accelerate troubleshooting. A good way to keep a record of firewall changes is by using the RCS (Revision Control System) facility. Another is to simply mail yourself a backup copy of the firewall whenever you change it. But, if you choose to mail yourself the firewall, be sure that your e-mail account and the path traveled by e-mail messages are secure from intruders. An intruder would find it much easier to crack your firewall if he had a copy of its rule set.

Listing 9-13: The Complete host firewall

```
#!/bin/sh


##############################################################################
#  Host firewall 1.0                                                         #
#                                                                            #
# Firewall for single-homed host, featuring restrictive (blocked by         #
# default) input and output rule sets and restrictive ICMP rule set.        #
# Includes TCP flag validation and SYN rate limiting.                       #
#                                                                            #
# Copyright (C) 2002 Bill McCarty                                           #
#                                                                            #
# This program is free software; you can redistribute it and/or modify      #
# it under the terms of the GNU General Public License as published by      #
# the Free Software Foundation, version 2 or later.                         #
#                                                                            #
#                                                                            #
# This program is distributed in the hope that it will be useful, but       #
# WITHOUT ANY WARRANTY, not even implied warranties such as                 #
# MERCHANTABILITY or FITNESS FOR A PARTICULAR PURPOSE. See the GNU          #
# General Public License for details.                                       #
#                                                                            #
# You should have received a copy of the GNU General Public License         #
# with this program or have been able to obtain it from the program's       #
# download site. If not, you can obtain it from the Free Software           #
# Foundation's web site, www.gnu.org.                                       #
##############################################################################
```

```
##########################################################################
# Assignments
##########################################################################

# Firewall host IP address
IP="xxx.xxx.xxx.xxx"

# Host lists for inbound services
PING=""
SSH="0.0.0.0/0"
WWW="0.0.0.0/0"

# Rate limits
SYNOPT="-m limit --limit 5/second --limit-burst 10"
LOGOPT="--log-level=3 -m limit --limit 1/second --limit-burst 10"

# The following assignments should not generally need to be changed
BADIP="0.0.0.0/8 10.0.0.0/8 127.0.0.0/8 169.254.0.0/16 172.16.0.0/12 192.0.0/24
192.168.0.0/16 192.0.34.0/24 224.0.0.0/4 240.0.0.0/5 255.255.255.255"
SHUNIP=""
LO="127.0.0.1"
SSH="$SSH $LO"
WWW="$WWW $LO"
IPT=/sbin/iptables


##########################################################################
# Clear the existing firewall rules
##########################################################################

if [ ! -x $IPT ]
then
  echo "firewall: can't execute \$IPTABLES"
  exit 1
fi

$IPT -P INPUT   DROP     # Set default policy to DROP
$IPT -P OUTPUT  DROP     # Set default policy to DROP
$IPT -P FORWARD DROP     # Set default policy to DROP
$IPT -F                  # Flush all chains
$IPT -X                  # Delete all userchains
```

Continued

Listing 9-13 *(Continued)*

```
 for table in filter nat mangle
do
  $IPT -t $table -F      # Delete the table's rules
  $IPT -t $table -X      # Delete the table's chains
  $IPT -t $table -Z      # Zero the table's counters
done


#############################################################################
# Logging chain
#############################################################################

$IPT -N LDROP
$IPT -A LDROP   -j LOG --log-prefix "IPT Drop:   " $LOGOPT
$IPT -A LDROP   -j DROP


$IPT -N LBADIP
$IPT -A LBADIP   -p tcp --dport 137:139 -j DROP
$IPT -A LBADIP   -p udp --dport 137:139 -j DROP
$IPT -A LBADIP   -j LOG --log-prefix "IPT BAD:   " $LOGOPT
$IPT -A LBADIP   -j DROP


$IPT -N LSHUN
$IPT -A LSHUN   -j LOG --log-prefix "IPT Shun:   " $LOGOPT
$IPT -A LSHUN   -j DROP


$IPT -N LFLOOD
$IPT -A LFLOOD  -j LOG --log-prefix "IPT Flood:  " $LOGOPT
$IPT -A LFLOOD  -j DROP


$IPT -N LFLAGS
$IPT -A LFLAGS  -j LOG --log-prefix "IPT Flags:  " $LOGOPT
$IPT -A LFLAGS  -j DROP


#############################################################################
# Bad IPs
#############################################################################

$IPT -N BADIP
for ip in $BADIP; do
  $IPT -A BADIP -s $ip -j LBADIP
  $IPT -A BADIP -d $ip -j LBADIP
done
```

```
##############################################################################
# Shunned Hosts
##############################################################################

$IPT -N SHUN
for ip in $SHUNIP; do
  $IPT -A SHUN -s $ip -j LSHUN
  $IPT -A SHUN -d $ip -j LSHUN
done


##############################################################################
# SYN Flood Protection (TCP SYN datagrams)
##############################################################################

$IPT -N FLOOD

# Following rule accepting datagram fires at limited rate.

$IPT -A FLOOD $SYNOPT -j RETURN
$IPT -A FLOOD          -j LFLOOD


##############################################################################
# TCP Flag Validation (TCP datagrams)
##############################################################################

$IPT -N FLAGS
$IPT -A FLAGS -p tcp --tcp-flags ACK,FIN FIN                 -j LFLAGS
$IPT -A FLAGS -p tcp --tcp-flags ACK,PSH PSH                 -j LFLAGS
$IPT -A FLAGS -p tcp --tcp-flags ACK,URG URG                 -j LFLAGS
$IPT -A FLAGS -p tcp --tcp-flags FIN,RST FIN,RST             -j LFLAGS
$IPT -A FLAGS -p tcp --tcp-flags SYN,FIN SYN,FIN             -j LFLAGS
$IPT -A FLAGS -p tcp --tcp-flags SYN,RST SYN,RST             -j LFLAGS
$IPT -A FLAGS -p tcp --tcp-flags ALL ALL                     -j LFLAGS
$IPT -A FLAGS -p tcp --tcp-flags ALL NONE                    -j LFLAGS
$IPT -A FLAGS -p tcp --tcp-flags ALL FIN,PSH,URG             -j LFLAGS
$IPT -A FLAGS -p tcp --tcp-flags ALL SYN,FIN,PSH,URG         -j LFLAGS
$IPT -A FLAGS -p tcp --tcp-flags ALL SYN,RST,ACK,FIN,URG     -j LFLAGS

# Remaining flag combinations considered valid.


##############################################################################
# Input TCP/UDP datagrams
##############################################################################
```

Continued

Listing 9-13 *(Continued)*

```
$IPT -N IN
$IPT -A IN -m state --state INVALID -j LDROP
$IPT -A IN -p tcp --syn -j FLOOD
$IPT -A IN -p tcp        -j FLAGS
$IPT -A IN -m state --state ESTABLISHED,RELATED -j ACCEPT
$IPT -A IN -s $IP -j LDROP

# Accept new inbound connections.

for sip in $SSH; do
  $IPT -A IN -p tcp -s $sip --dport 22 -m state --state NEW -j ACCEPT
done

for sip in $WWW; do
  $IPT -A IN -p tcp -s $sip --dport 80 -m state --state NEW -j ACCEPT
done

# Reject AUTH requests

$IPT -A IN -p tcp --dport 113 -j REJECT --reject-with tcp-reset

# Add additional rules accepting authorized traffic here.
# Traffic not explicitly accepted will be logged and dropped.


##############################################################################
# Output TCP/UDP datagrams
##############################################################################

$IPT -N OUT
$IPT -A OUT -p tcp -j FLAGS
$IPT -A OUT -s ! $IP -j LDROP
$IPT -A OUT -m state --state ESTABLISHED,RELATED -j ACCEPT
#
# This firewall is configured to block outbound connections by default.
# To allow any output not explicitly blocked, uncomment the following
# line. Place blocking rules here.
#$IPT -A OUT -m state --state NEW               -j ACCEPT

# Accept new outbound connections.

$IPT -A OUT -m state --state NEW -p tcp --dport  21 -j ACCEPT   # ftp
$IPT -A OUT -m state --state NEW -p tcp --dport  22 -j ACCEPT   # ssh
$IPT -A OUT -m state --state NEW -p tcp --dport  25 -j ACCEPT   # smtp
```

```
$IPT -A OUT -m state --state NEW -p tcp --dport  43 -j ACCEPT     # whois
$IPT -A OUT -m state --state NEW -p tcp --dport  53 -j ACCEPT     # domain
$IPT -A OUT -m state --state NEW -p tcp --dport  80 -j ACCEPT     # http
$IPT -A OUT -m state --state NEW -p tcp --dport 443 -j ACCEPT     # https
$IPT -A OUT -m state --state NEW -p tcp --dport 873 -j ACCEPT     # rsync


$IPT -A OUT -m state --state NEW -p udp --dport  53 -j ACCEPT     # domain

# Add additional rules accepting authorized traffic here.
# Traffic not explicitly accepted will be logged and dropped.


#############################################################################
# Inbound ICMP messages
#############################################################################

$IPT -N IN_ICMP
for sip in $PING; do
  $IPT -A IN_ICMP  -p icmp --icmp-type echo-request -s $sip -d $IP \
                                                          -j ACCEPT
  $IPT -A IN_ICMP  -p icmp --icmp-type echo-reply   -s $sip -d $IP \
                                                          -j ACCEPT
done
$IPT -A IN_ICMP  -p icmp --icmp-type destination-unreachable  -j ACCEPT
$IPT -A IN_ICMP  -p icmp --icmp-type source-quench            -j ACCEPT
$IPT -A IN_ICMP  -p icmp --icmp-type time-exceeded            -j ACCEPT
$IPT -A IN_ICMP  -p icmp --icmp-type parameter-problem        -j ACCEPT


#############################################################################
# Outbound ICMP messages
#############################################################################

$IPT -N OUT_ICMP
for dip in $PING; do
  $IPT -A OUT_ICMP -p icmp --icmp-type echo-reply   -d $dip     -j ACCEPT
  $IPT -A OUT_ICMP -p icmp --icmp-type echo-request -d $dip     -j ACCEPT
done
$IPT -A OUT_ICMP -p icmp --icmp-type destination-unreachable  -j ACCEPT
$IPT -A OUT_ICMP -p icmp --icmp-type fragmentation-needed     -j ACCEPT
$IPT -A OUT_ICMP -p icmp --icmp-type source-quench            -j ACCEPT
$IPT -A OUT_ICMP -p icmp --icmp-type parameter-problem        -j ACCEPT


#############################################################################
# Rules for built-in chains
#############################################################################
```

Continued

Listing 9-13 *(Continued)*

```
$IPT -A INPUT -i lo      -j ACCEPT
$IPT -A INPUT            -j BADIP
$IPT -A INPUT            -j SHUN
$IPT -A INPUT -p ! icmp  -j IN
$IPT -A INPUT -p   icmp  -j IN_ICMP
$IPT -A INPUT            -j LDROP

$IPT -A OUTPUT -o lo      -j ACCEPT
$IPT -A OUTPUT            -j BADIP
$IPT -A OUTPUT            -j SHUN
$IPT -A OUTPUT -p ! icmp -j OUT
$IPT -A OUTPUT -p   icmp -j OUT_ICMP
$IPT -A OUTPUT            -j LDROP
```

Summary

This chapter explained the operation and structure of a simple but potentially effective firewall to protect a single host. The firewall makes extensive use of the IPTables user chain facility to organize its rules into a cohesive system. The next chapter explains how to implement more complex firewalls that deal with packet forwarding and network address translation.

Chapter 10

Advanced IPTables Firewall Implementation

IN THIS CHAPTER

- ◆ Packet forwarding
- ◆ Network Address Translation (NAT)
- ◆ Firewall performance optimization
- ◆ Modifying the firewall
- ◆ Sysctl options
- ◆ Kernel options
- ◆ Bridging firewalls

THIS CHAPTER EXPLAINS several advanced IPTables facilities. Foremost among these facilities are packet forwarding and Network Address Translation (NAT), which enables you to modify the source or destination IP address of packets. The chapter also provides guidance on optimizing the performance of an IPTables firewall. Next, the chapter explains Sysctl and kernel options important to using firewalls. Finally, the chapter describes bridging firewalls, a special type of firewall supported by version 2.4.18 and later of the Linux kernel.

Packet Forwarding

The simple firewall presented in Chapter 9 was designed for a host having only a single network interface. The firewall protected its host from a variety of potential attacks. Firewalls are more useful and important for hosts having multiple network interfaces. By implementing a firewall on a multi-homed host, you can filter packets that traverse from one network to another via the host. Thereby, you can protect entire networks rather than merely a single host.

Recall that the Linux kernel facility that enables packets to move from one network to another via a multi-homed host is called *packet forwarding,* or simply *forwarding.* Sometimes, the host that performs the forwarding is called a *routing host,* or *router.* Figure 10-1 shows a router that connects the 192.0.34.0/24 and

192.168.1.0/24 networks. Interface `eth0` of the router is associated with the 192.0.34.0/24 network, and interface `eth1` is associated with the 192.168.1.0/24 network.

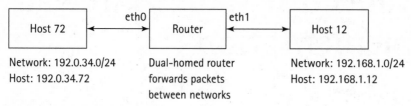

Figure 10-1: Forwarding packets

If the router runs IPTables, forwarded packets traverse the IPTables `FORWARD` chain, which is associated with the `filter` table. By adding rules to the `FORWARD` chain, you can control the flow of traffic between two networks. For example, the following commands would permit traffic to flow between the networks depicted in the figure:

```
iptables -P FORWARD DROP
iptables -A FORWARD -i eth0 -o eth1 -j ACCEPT
iptables -A FORWARD -i eth1 -o eth0 -j ACCEPT
```

Note that two rules are used, establishing a two-way flow of traffic between the hosts and any associated networks. You can include additional specifiers that restrict the operation of such rules. Suppose that the router is intended to route packets only between host 72 and host 12. The following rules accomplish this result:

```
iptables -P FORWARD DROP
iptables -A FORWARD -i eth0 -o eth1 -s 192.0.34.72 -d 192.168.1.12 -j ACCEPT
iptables -A FORWARD -i eth1 -o eth0 -s 192.168.1.12 -d 192.0.34.72 -j ACCEPT
iptables -A FORWARD -j LOG --log-prefix "IPT FWD Drop "
```

The last rule logs traffic that is not authorized to be forwarded. In practice, you might find that this rule generates an overly large volume of log traffic. In that case, you might choose to restrict or remove the rule.

Similarly, suppose that traffic should be forwarded in both directions, but only hosts on the 192.168.1.0/24 network should be allowed to initiate connections. The following code achieves this result:

```
iptables -P FORWARD DROP
iptables -A FORWARD -i eth1 -o eth0 -j ACCEPT
```

```
iptables -A FORWARD -i eth0 -o eth1 -m state --state ESTABLISHED,RELATED -j
ACCEPT
iptables -A FORWARD -j LOG --log-prefix "IPT FWD Drop "
```

Forwarding is a relatively simple concept, and the IPTables facility for working with forwarded packets is easy to use. However, forwarding can become quite complicated if a router has many interfaces, especially if the policies that determine which packets may be forwarded are themselves complicated. In such cases, consider each pair of interfaces a unit and keep the related rules together. By attacking the problem one piece at a time in this fashion, you can make your task easier and minimize errors.

A host forwards packets only if the kernel option `ip_forward` is set. See the "Sysctl Options" section, later in this chapter, to learn how to set this option.

Network Address Translation (NAT)

One of the most useful IPTables facilities is Network Address Translation (NAT). NAT enables the firewall to modify the source or destination IP address of packets. Recall that modifying the source IP address of a packet is termed source network address translation (SNAT) and modifying the destination address of a packet is termed destination network address translation (DNAT). Figure 10-2 shows a simplified version of the IPTables packet path, highlighting two steps important to NAT.

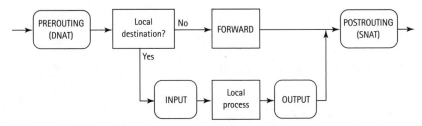

Figure 10-2: NAT packet path

As the figure shows, DNAT is performed in the `PREROUTING` chain of the `nat` table and SNAT is performed in the `POSTROUTING` chain of the `nat` table. If a packet's destination address is modified, the `FORWARD` and `INPUT` chains see the modified address. However, if a packet's source address is modified, the `FORWARD`, `INPUT`, and `OUTPUT` chains see the original, unmodified source address.

The following sections describe ways in which NAT can be used.

Destination Network Address Translation (DNAT)

DNAT can be used to accomplish any of three objectives:

- ◆ Transparent proxying
- ◆ Port forwarding
- ◆ Load balancing

Transparent Proxying

Transparent proxying enables clients to request services using a surrogate IP address. For instance, a client can use a routable IP address to access a server residing on a private network and having a nonroutable, RFC 1918 IP address. Figure 10-3 shows such a configuration. In the figure, the server has the nonroutable IP address 192.168.1.72. The client accesses the server as though the server had the IP address 192.0.34.72, which is routable. The firewall performs DNAT on the client's requests. That is, it replaces the destination address 192.0.34.72 with 192.168.1.72. The firewall also modifies the source IP address of the replies sent by the server, so that the client believes that the replies actually came from 192.0.34.72.

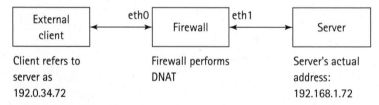

Figure 10-3: DNAT used to accomplish transparent proxying

The transparent proxying shown in the figure could be implemented by using a single IPTables rule:

```
iptables -t nat -A PREROUTING -i eth0 -o eth1 -d 192.0.34.72 \
  -j DNAT --to-destination 192.168.1.72
```

This rule maps the IP addresses in both the requests sent to the server and the server's replies. You can easily build more sophisticated rules that include additional specifiers, such as -s or --dport. Notice that the rule includes specifiers for the input and output interfaces. Including these specifiers isn't strictly necessary. But, particularly if the router has more than two interfaces, it is a good way to avoid confusion that can lead to an incorrect rule.

Port Forwarding

Basic DNAT alters the destination IP address of a packet. Port forwarding, which entails the modification of the destination port, enables clients to access a service via a destination port other than that on which the service listens. For instance, using port forwarding, a Web server running on port 8080 can be reached via destination port 80. Here's a simple example:

```
iptables -t nat -A PREROUTING -i eth0 -o eth1 -p tcp -d 192.0.34.72 --dport 80 \
  -j DNAT --to-destination 192.168.1.72:8080
```

The example maps port 80 of IP address 192.0.34.72 to port 8080 of the host having the IP address 192.168.1.72. As is true of transparent proxying via DNAT, IPTables automatically modifies reply packets so that two-way communication is possible.

Bear in mind that only TCP and UDP datagrams have source and destination ports. ICMP messages do not. Therefore, IPTables rules that include specifiers referring to ports must also include the -p flag and either the tcp or udp specifier. Otherwise, the IPTables facility rejects the rule as syntactically invalid.

Load Balancing

IPTables allows you to specify multiple IP addresses in a DNAT rule. When a packet traverses such a rule, IPTables chooses one of the indicated destinations. If you have a server farm (a group of servers combined to increase their collective power), you can specify its IP address range in a DNAT rule. Each host in the farm receives a fractional share of the traffic, balancing the load across the farm.

Assume that a server farm resides on 192.168.1.2-4 and that clients query the routable IP address 192.0.34.72. The following IPTables rule balances the incoming traffic across the three hosts of the farm:

```
iptables -t nat -A PREROUTING -i eth0 -o eth1 -d 192.0.34.72 \
  -j DNAT --to-destination 192.168.1.2-192.168.1.4
```

The General Case

IPTables permits rules that include both port forwarding and load balancing. The general form of a DNAT rule is

```
iptables -t nat -A PREROUTING -i if specifiers -j DNAT \
  --to-destination ip[-ip][:port[-port]]
```

where *ip* or *ip-ip* gives the destination IP address and *port* or *port-port* gives the destination port.

Redirect NAT

Redirect is a special form of NAT in which requests sent to a host are handled by the firewall host itself. Figure 10-4 shows a typical application of redirect. A firewall is configured to route for the network 1.2.3.0/24, which may or may not include actual hosts. When an external client initiates a connection to the host 1.2.3.4, the firewall intercepts the packets and DNATs them to contain its own address. A service running on the firewall host receives the packets and responds to the client.

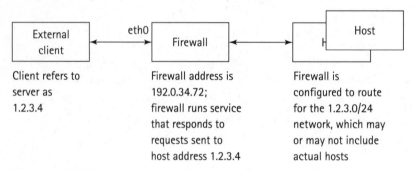

External client	eth0	Firewall		Host

Client refs to server as 1.2.3.4

Firewall address is 192.0.34.72; firewall runs service that responds to requests sent to host address 1.2.3.4

Firewall is configured to route for the 1.2.3.0/24 network, which may or may not include actual hosts

Figure 10–4: Redirect

The configuration shown in the figure can be implemented using the following IPTables rule:

```
iptables -t nat -A PREROUTING -i eth0 -d 1.2.3.4 -j REDIRECT
```

As usual, the rule could include additional specifiers, such as -s or --dport, that limit the application of the redirect.

 TIP   Bear in mind that running one or more public services on your firewall host may expose vulnerabilities that lead to its compromise. Be prudent and use the redirect facility only for access by trusted or local hosts.

Redirect NAT with Port Forwarding

You can perform port forwarding in a redirect rule, enabling you to map requests to an unusual or nonstandard port. For instance, the following rule maps requests to port 80 of host 1.2.3.4 to port 8080 of the firewall host:

```
iptables -t nat -A PREROUTING -i eth0 -d 1.2.3.4 -j REDIRECT --to-ports 8080
```

If the firewall host is running the same service on multiple ports, you can balance the load among them by specifying a port range:

```
iptables -t nat -A PREROUTING -i eth0 -d 1.2.3.4 -j REDIRECT --to-ports
8080-8089
```

However, this feature is seldom used because most servers are capable of spawning multiple threads or processes and balancing the load among them.

Source Network Address Translation (SNAT)

SNAT is the mirror image of DNAT. That is, SNAT modifies the source IP address of packets, whereas DNAT modifies the destination address. SNAT can be used for any of several purposes:

- ◆ To enable hosts having nonroutable addresses to communicate with Internet hosts

- ◆ To enable multiple client hosts to share a single IP address

- ◆ To hide the true IP address of a host

- ◆ To resolve certain problems when using DNAT, as explained in the section titled "Accessing a DNAT Host from the Local Network"

Figure 10-5 shows a typical application of SNAT, in which a client host having a nonroutable IP address is enabled to contact a remote server via the Internet. In the figure, the IP address 192.0.34.72 could be the IP address of the firewall host. Alternatively, it could be an address within a network for which the firewall host acts as a router.

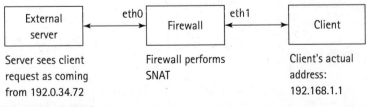

Figure 10–5: SNAT

You implement SNAT in much the same way as you implement DNAT. However, SNAT is implemented in the POSTROUTING chain of the nat table rather than in the PREROUTING chain. The following IPTables rule implements the SNAT configuration shown in the figure:

```
iptables -t nat -A POSTROUTING -o eth0 -s 192.168.1.1 \
   -j SNAT --to-source 192.0.34.72
```

Because of the -s flag, the rule applies only to outbound traffic from the designated client. A rule such as the following provides SNAT for the entire private LAN:

```
iptables -t nat -A POSTROUTING -o eth0 -s 192.168.1.0/24 \
   -j SNAT --to-source 192.0.34.72
```

Notice that each client on the LAN shares the specified IP address. IPTables assigns source ports and uses the source port fields of reply packets to match replies with the proper LAN host.

If outbound traffic from the LAN is heavy, available ports might be exhausted. To avoid this problem, you can assign multiple SNAT addresses:

```
iptables -t nat -A POSTROUTING -o eth0 -s 192.168.1.1 \
   -j SNAT --to-source 192.0.34.72-192.0.34.81
```

IPTables chooses an IP address within the specified range and inserts it as the source address of an outgoing packet to which the rule applies. You can explicitly specify the pool of source ports used by SNAT. To do so, use a rule such as the following:

```
iptables -t nat -A POSTROUTING -o eth0 -s 192.168.1.1 \
   -j SNAT --to-source 192.0.34.72:32768-65535
```

This rule specifies that ports 32768 to 65535 may be assigned as source ports of SNATed packets.

As with DNAT, IPTables automatically de-NATs reply packets associated with a connection established via SNAT. That is, IPTables replaces the original source address in reply packets and forwards them to the proper client.

Masquerading

IP masquerading, often call simply *masquerading,* is a simplified form of SNAT in which packets receive the IP address of the output interface as their source address. IP masquerading is useful when the IP address of the output interface is not fixed and therefore can't be embedded in firewall rules. It's commonly used with interfaces configured via DHCP (Dynamic Host Control Protocol), especially those associated with dial-up connections. Masquerading is the mirror image of redirect, which affects packets' destination addresses. Figure 10-6 shows a typical application of masquerading. Note that the only distinction between masquerading and SNAT is that in masquerading, the substituted source address is that of the firewall host.

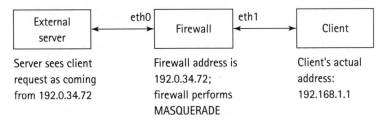

Figure 10-6: Masquerading

To implement masquerading, use an IPTables rule such as the following:

```
iptables -t nat -A POSTROUTING -o eth0 -s 192.168.0.1 \
  -j MASQUERADE
```

If you want, you can explicitly specify the range of source ports used. To do so, use a rule such as the following:

```
iptables -t nat -A POSTROUTING -o eth0 -s 192.168.0.1 \
  -j MASQUERADE --to-ports 32768-65535
```

This rule instructs IPTables to choose a source port in the inclusive range 32768 to 65535.

Accessing a DNAT Host from the Local Network

When you provide external access to a server on the LAN via DNAT, you may complicate local access to the server. For instance, consider the situation shown in Figure 10-7. External clients use the routable IP address 192.0.34.72 to access the server 192.168.1.72 residing on the LAN. If a client on the LAN attempts to access the server using the IP address 192.0.34.72, the firewall performs DNAT, modifying the destination address to 192.168.1.72 and passing the request on to the server. However, the firewall does not automatically adjust the source address of the packets, which is an address on the LAN. Therefore, the server replies directly to the client rather than send replies via the firewall.

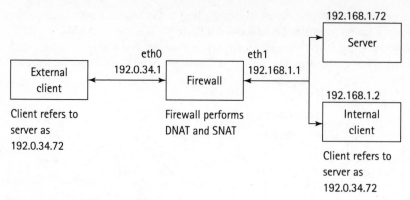

Figure 10-7: DNAT on the LAN

Replying directly to the client presents a problem because the reply packets bear a source address of 192.168.1.72, whereas the client's requests were directed to 192.0.34.72. Consequently, the client doesn't properly associate the replies with its request, and the connection does not succeed.

You can resolve this problem in either of two ways. One way is to configure DNS so that LAN client requests are sent to 192.168.1.72 rather than to 192.0.34.72. You can do so by running two DNS servers, one responding to external hosts and another responding to internal hosts. The DNS server responding to external hosts associates the IP address 192.0.34.72 with the host name of the server. The DNS server responding to internal hosts associates the IP address 192.168.1.72 with the host name of the server. Such a configuration is called a *split-horizon DNS*.

Another way to resolve the problem is by combining DNAT and SNAT. The trick is to substitute the IP address of the firewall host as the source IP address of packets sent to the server. Then, the server sends replies to the firewall host rather than directly to the client. When the firewall host receives a reply from the server, the firewall host reverses the DNAT and SNAT and forwards the reply to the client, where the addresses in the reply properly match those in the original request.

The following two IPTables rules configure DNAT and SNAT for the situation described:

```
iptables -t nat -A PREROUTING -i eth0 -o eth1 -d 192.0.34.72 \
  -j DNAT --to-destination 192.168.1.72
iptables -t nat -A POSTROUTING -s 192.168.1.0/24 -d 192.168.1.72 \
  -j SNAT --to-source 192.168.1.1
```

Firewall Performance Optimization

After a firewall has been designed and implemented, you can tune it to improve its performance. Generally, the most important performance characteristic of a firewall is the time taken by packets traversing the packet path, which adds to latency, the round-trip time required for a packet transmitted to the firewall or a host on a network protected by the firewall. In some cases, the traversal time can be large enough that it restricts the volume of traffic the firewall can handle. The firewall then becomes a network performance bottleneck.

You can address such bottlenecks in either – or both – of two ways:

- Use a firewall host with more RAM and a faster CPU.

- Tune the firewall rule set.

Tuning the firewall rule set involves minimizing the traversal time of packets. If less time is required to process a packet, the firewall will be capable of handling a larger volume of packets. The traversal time taken by a packet is determined primarily by these factors:

- The number of rules executed

- The number of specifiers executed

- The type of specifiers executed

However, taking account of the number and type of specifiers is complex. For most purposes, you can successfully optimize a firewall by considering only the number of rules executed as a packet traverses the firewall. That is, given two firewalls, the one that requires fewer rules to handle a given packet generally outperforms the other in their handling of the packet.

If all packet characteristics – source and destination IP addresses and ports, for instance – were equally likely, tuning a firewall would be simple. However, packet characteristics typically take on some values more often than others. For example, a Web server farm is likely to see lots of inbound traffic having destination port 80 and outbound traffic having source port 80. If such packets are handled early in each chain, they traverse the firewall more quickly.

For example, Listings 10-1 and 10-2 show two excerpts from some hypothetical firewall code. The code in Listing 10-1 is organized lexically – that is, in sequence by port number and protocol. This organization makes the listing easy to read and, in particular, makes it easy to find the rule associated with a given service.

Listing 10-1: Lexically organized code

```
iptables -A FORWARD -i eth0 -o eth1 -p tcp --dport 22 -j SSH
iptables -A FORWARD -i eth0 -o eth1 -p tcp --dport 25 -j SMTP
iptables -A FORWARD -i eth0 -o eth1 -p tcp --dport 53 -j DNSTCP
iptables -A FORWARD -i eth0 -o eth1 -p tcp --dport 80 -j HTTP
iptables -A FORWARD -i eth0 -o eth1 -p udp --dport 53 -j DNSUDP
```

Listing 10–2: Code optimized for performance

```
iptables -A FORWARD -i eth0 -o eth1 -p tcp --dport 80 -j HTTP
iptables -A FORWARD -i eth0 -o eth1 -p tcp --dport 25 -j SMTP
iptables -A FORWARD -i eth0 -o eth1 -p tcp --dport 22 -j SSH
iptables -A FORWARD -i eth0 -o eth1 -p udp --dport 53 -j DNSUDP
iptables -A FORWARD -i eth0 -o eth1 -p tcp --dport 53 -j DNSTCP
```

The code in Listing 10-2, however, is organized so that the rules most likely to apply appear first. For instance, the first rule handles traffic inbound to port 80. If 99 percent of inbound traffic is directed to port 80, the firewall associated with Listing 10-2 performs much better than the one associated with Listing 10-1, which executes five rules rather than one in handling HTTP traffic.

The basic goal of firewall optimization, therefore, is to *minimize the average path length*. However, it may not be clear how to determine this firewall character-istic. The `iptables -L` command provides a surrogate for this characteristic. Consider the following sample output:

```
iptables -n -v --line-number -L FORWARD
Chain FORWARD (policy ACCEPT 78032 packets, 34M bytes)
num pkts bytes target    prot opt in    out   source     destination
1   457K   58M PROTOCOL all  --  *     *     0.0.0.0/0  0.0.0.0/0
2   379K   24M DROP      udp  --  *     *     0.0.0.0/0  0.0.0.0/0
3   5645  427K UDPTRACE  udp  --  *     *     0.0.0.0/0  0.0.0.0/0
4   358 20928 SYNTRACE   tcp  --  *     *     0.0.0.0/0  0.0.0.0/0
5   219 13140 THROTTLE   tcp  --  *     *     0.0.0.0/0  0.0.0.0/0
6     0     0 LOG        all  --  eth0 eth1 0.0.0.0/0  0.0.0.0/0
7     0     0 DROP       all  --  eth0 eth1 0.0.0.0/0  0.0.0.0/0
8     0     0 LOG        all  --  eth1 eth0 0.0.0.0/0  0.0.0.0/0
9     0     0 DROP       all  --  eth1 eth0 0.0.0.0/0  0.0.0.0/0
```

By including the `-v` flag, we cause the command to list the number of packets that have traversed each rule and the number of bytes contained in those packets. Notice that the rules having the largest associated traffic volume appear near the beginning of the chain and thus are executed first. Thus, common packets have short paths, leading to low average path length and high firewall performance.

Of course, modifying the sequence of rules on a chain may modify the firewall policies. So, it's not possible to blindly rearrange firewall rules to place the most commonly used rules at the head of the chain. To correctly implement firewall pol-icy, you must sometimes place a seldom-used rule before an often-used rule. However, it's sometimes possible to modify rule specifiers in a way that permits rules to be moved without affecting the firewall policies.

As a rule of thumb, most firewall traffic is TCP rather than UDP or ICMP. Therefore, your firewall should generally handle packets in the following sequence: first, TCP datagrams; second, UDP datagrams; and, finally, ICMP messages. If your firewall rules follow this sequence, they are generally nearly optimal even before you begin tuning them.

A Sample Screened Network Firewall

Listing 10-3 shows a simple screened network firewall. You should use the firewall as an example that helps you build your own firewall rather than simply install it on a host. The firewall policies it implements are unlikely to suit your needs. However, rather than build a firewall from scratch, you may choose to make suitable modifications to the sample firewall.

Listing 10-3: A screened network firewall

```
#!/bin/sh
#
# requirements:
# - sysctls in /etc/sysctl.conf
# - modprobes in /etc/rc./rc.local


#-------------------------------------------------------------------------------
#  Screened network firewall
#
#  Copyright (C) 2002 Bill McCarty
#
# This program is free software; you can redistribute it and/or modify
# it under the terms of the GNU General Public License as published by
# the Free Software Foundation, version 2 or later.
#
# This program is distributed in the hope that it may be useful, but
# WITHOUT ANY WARRANTY, not even implied warranties such as
# MERCHANTABILITY or FITNESS FOR A PARTICULAR PURPOSE. See the GNU
# General Public License for details.
#
# You should have received a copy of the GNU General Public License
# with this program or have been able to obtain it from the program's
```

Continued

Listing 10-3 *(Continued)*

```
 # download site. If not, you can obtain it from the Free Software
 # Foundation's web site, www.gnu.org.
 #------------------------------------------------------------------------


 #------------------------------------------------------------------------
 # Assignments
 #------------------------------------------------------------------------


 # Change these assignments to conform to your network architecture
 # Weed unneeded variables

 EXTDEV=eth0
 EXTIP="192.0.34.72"
 EXTBASE="192.0.34.0"
 EXTBCAST="192.0.34.255"
 EXTGATE="192.0.34.254"


 INTDEV=eth1
 INTIP="10.0.0.1"
 INTBASE="10.0.0.0"
 INTBCAST="10.0.0.255"
 INTNET="10.0.0.0/8"


 # IP addresses of hosts and networks authorized to ping firewall
 PING="192.0.34.2 $INTNET"

 # IP addresses of hosts and networks allowed to SSH into firewall
 SSH="192.0.34.2"

 # IP address of each public server on internal network
 SMTPIP="10.0.0.2"
 DNSIP="10.0.0.2"
 HTTPIP="10.0.0.2"
 POPIP="10.0.0.2"
 AUTHIP="10.0.0.2"
 IMAPIP="10.0.0.2"


 # IP addresses of hosts and networks not to be communicated with.
 SHUN=""


 # The following assignments should not generally need to be changed
```

```
BADIP="$EXTBASE $EXTBCAST $INTBASE $INTBCAST 0.0.0.0/8 10.0.0.0/8 127.0.0.0/8
169.254.0.0/16 172.16.0.0/12 192.0.2.0/24 224.0.0.0/4 240.0.0.0/5
255.255.255.255"

IPT=/sbin/iptables
LOGOPT="--log-level=3 -m limit --limit 3/minute --limit-burst 3"
SYNOPT="-m limit --limit 5/second --limit-burst 10"


#-----------------------------------------------------------------------------
# Clear the existing firewall rules
#-----------------------------------------------------------------------------


if [ ! -x $IPTABLES ]
then
  die "firewall: can't execute $IPTABLES"
fi

$IPT -P INPUT   DROP # Set default policy to DROP
$IPT -P OUTPUT  DROP # Set default policy to DROP
$IPT -P FORWARD DROP # Set default policy to DROP
$IPT -F   # Flush all chains
$IPT -X   # Delete all chains

for table in filter nat mangle
do
  $IPT -t $table -F  # Delete the table's rules
  $IPT -t $table -X  # Delete the table's chains
  $IPT -t $table -Z  # Zero the table's counters
done


#-----------------------------------------------------------------------------
# Bad TCP Flags
#-----------------------------------------------------------------------------


$IPT -N BADFLAGS
$IPT -A BADFLAGS -j LOG --log-prefix "IPT BADFLAGS: " $LOGOPT
$IPT -A BADFLAGS -j DROP


#-----------------------------------------------------------------------------
# TCP Flag Validation
#-----------------------------------------------------------------------------


$IPT -N TCP_FLAGS
$IPT -A TCP_FLAGS -p tcp --tcp-flags ACK,FIN FIN               -j BADFLAGS
```

Continued

Listing 10-3 *(Continued)*

```
$IPT -A TCP_FLAGS -p tcp --tcp-flags ACK,PSH PSH              -j BADFLAGS
$IPT -A TCP_FLAGS -p tcp --tcp-flags ACK,URG URG             -j BADFLAGS
$IPT -A TCP_FLAGS -p tcp --tcp-flags FIN,RST FIN,RST         -j BADFLAGS
$IPT -A TCP_FLAGS -p tcp --tcp-flags SYN,FIN SYN,FIN         -j BADFLAGS
$IPT -A TCP_FLAGS -p tcp --tcp-flags SYN,RST SYN,RST         -j BADFLAGS
$IPT -A TCP_FLAGS -p tcp --tcp-flags ALL ALL                 -j BADFLAGS
$IPT -A TCP_FLAGS -p tcp --tcp-flags ALL NONE                -j BADFLAGS
$IPT -A TCP_FLAGS -p tcp --tcp-flags ALL FIN,PSH,URG         -j BADFLAGS
$IPT -A TCP_FLAGS -p tcp --tcp-flags ALL SYN,FIN,PSH,URG     -j BADFLAGS
$IPT -A TCP_FLAGS -p tcp --tcp-flags ALL SYN,RST,ACK,FIN,URG -j BADFLAGS


#-----------------------------------------------------------------------------
# SYN Flood Protection
#-----------------------------------------------------------------------------


$IPT -N SYN_FLOOD
$IPT -A SYN_FLOOD -p   tcp   --syn $SYNOPT -j RETURN
$IPT -A SYN_FLOOD -p ! tcp                 -j RETURN
$IPT -A SYN_FLOOD -p   tcp ! --syn         -j RETURN
$IPT -A SYN_FLOOD -j LOG --log-prefix "IPT SYN_FLOOD: " $LOGOPT
$IPT -A SYN_FLOOD -j DROP


#-----------------------------------------------------------------------------
# Bad IP Chain
#-----------------------------------------------------------------------------


$IPT -N BAD_IP
$IPT -A BAD_IP -j LOG --log-prefix "IPT BAD_IP: " $LOGOPT
$IPT -A BAD_IP -j DROP


#-----------------------------------------------------------------------------
# Shunned Hosts
#-----------------------------------------------------------------------------


$IPT -N SHUN
for ip in $SHUN; do
  $IPT -A SHUN -s $ip -j BAD_IP
  $IPT -A SHUN -d $ip -j BAD_IP
done


#-----------------------------------------------------------------------------
# Inbound IP Checks
#-----------------------------------------------------------------------------
```

```
$IPT -N IN_IP_CHECK
for sip in $BADSIP
do
  $IPT -A IN_IP_CHECK -s $sip -j BAD_IP
done
$IPT -A IN_IP_CHECK -i $EXTDEV -s $EXTIP  -j BAD_IP
$IPT -A IN_IP_CHECK -i $EXTDEV -s $INTNET -j BAD_IP
$IPT -A IN_IP_CHECK -i $INTDEV -s $EXTIP  -j BAD_IP


#-----------------------------------------------------------------------
# Outbound IP Checks
#-----------------------------------------------------------------------


$IPT -N OUT_IP_CHECK
for dip in $BADIP
do
  $IPT -A OUT_IP_CHECK -d $dip -j BAD_IP
done
$IPT -A OUT_IP_CHECK -o $EXTDEV -s $EXTIP  -j RETURN
$IPT -A OUT_IP_CHECK -o $INTDEV -s $INTIP  -j RETURN
$IPT -A OUT_IP_CHECK -j BAD_IP


#-----------------------------------------------------------------------
# Inbound ICMP
#-----------------------------------------------------------------------


$IPT -N IN_ICMP
for sip in $PING; do
  $IPT -A IN_ICMP  -p icmp --icmp-type echo-request -s $sip   -j ACCEPT
  $IPT -A IN_ICMP  -p icmp --icmp-type echo-reply   -s $sip   -j ACCEPT
done
$IPT -A IN_ICMP  -p icmp --icmp-type destination-unreachable  -j ACCEPT
$IPT -A IN_ICMP  -p icmp --icmp-type source-quench            -j ACCEPT
$IPT -A IN_ICMP  -p icmp --icmp-type time-exceeded            -j ACCEPT
$IPT -A IN_ICMP  -p icmp --icmp-type parameter-problem        -j ACCEPT
$IPT -A IN_ICMP -j LOG --log-prefix "IPT In ICMP: " $LOGOPT
$IPT -A IN_ICMP -j DROP


#-----------------------------------------------------------------------
# Outbound ICMP
#-----------------------------------------------------------------------


$IPT -N OUT_ICMP
for dip in $PING; do
```

Continued

Listing 10-3 *(Continued)*

```
   $IPT -A OUT_ICMP -p icmp --icmp-type echo-request -d $dip     -j ACCEPT
   $IPT -A OUT_ICMP -p icmp --icmp-type echo-reply    -d $dip     -j ACCEPT
done
#
# For a less courteous -- but potentially more secure -- firewall,
# replace destination-unreachable by fragmentation-needed in the
# following rule.
#
$IPT -A OUT_ICMP -p icmp --icmp-type destination-unreachable  -j ACCEPT
$IPT -A OUT_ICMP -p icmp --icmp-type source-quench            -j ACCEPT
#
# For a less courteous -- but potentially more secure -- firewall,
# delete the following parameter-problem rule.
#
$IPT -A OUT_ICMP -p icmp --icmp-type parameter-problem        -j ACCEPT
$IPT -A OUT_ICMP -j LOG --log-prefix "IPT Out ICMP: " $LOGOPT
$IPT -A OUT_ICMP -j DROP


#---------------------------------------------------------------------------
# Destination NAT
#---------------------------------------------------------------------------

if [ "$SMTPIP" != "" ]
then
  $IPT -t nat -A PREROUTING -i $EXTDEV -p tcp -d $EXTIP --dport 25 \
    -j DNAT --to-destination $HTTPIP
fi

if [ "$DNSIP" != "" ]
then
  $IPT -t nat -A PREROUTING -i $EXTDEV -p udp -d $EXTIP --dport 53 \
    -j DNAT --to-destination $HTTPIP
fi

if [ "$HTTPIP" != "" ]
then
  $IPT -t nat -A PREROUTING -i $EXTDEV -p tcp -d $EXTIP --dport 80 \
    -j DNAT --to-destination $HTTPIP
fi

if [ "$POPIP" != "" ]
then
  $IPT -t nat -A PREROUTING -i $EXTDEV -p tcp -d $EXTIP --dport 110 \
    -j DNAT --to-destination $POPIP
```

```
fi

if [ "$AUTHIP" != "" ]
then
  $IPT -t nat -A PREROUTING -i $EXTDEV -p tcp -d $EXTIP --dport 113 \
    -j DNAT --to-destination $HTTPIP
fi

if [ "$IMAPIP" != "" ]
then
  $IPT -t nat -A PREROUTING -i $EXTDEV -p tcp -d $EXTIP --dport 143 \
    -j DNAT --to-destination $IMAPIP
fi

#---------------------------------------------------------------------------
# Source NAT
#---------------------------------------------------------------------------

$IPT -t nat -A POSTROUTING -o $EXTDEV          -j SNAT --to-source $EXTIP

#---------------------------------------------------------------------------
# Inbound traffic to protected network
#---------------------------------------------------------------------------

$IPT -N IN_NETWORK
$IPT -A IN_NETWORK -p icmp                              -j IN_ICMP
$IPT -A IN_NETWORK -p tcp                               -j TCP_FLAGS
$IPT -A IN_NETWORK -p tcp --syn                         -j SYN_FLOOD
$IPT -A IN_NETWORK -p tcp -m state --state ESTABLISHED,RELATED -j ACCEPT
$IPT -A IN_NETWORK -p udp -m state --state ESTABLISHED,RELATED -j ACCEPT

if [ "$SMTPIP" != "" ]
then
  $IPT -A IN_NETWORK -p tcp --syn -d $SMTPIP --dport 25      -j ACCEPT
fi

if [ "$DNSIP" != "" ]
then
  $IPT -A IN_NETWORK -p udp       -d $DNSIP  --dport 53      -j ACCEPT
fi

if [ "$HTTPIP" != "" ]
then
  $IPT -A IN_NETWORK -p tcp --syn -d $HTTPIP --dport 80      -j ACCEPT
```

Continued

Listing 10-3 *(Continued)*

```
fi

if [ "$POPIP" != "" ]
then
   $IPT -A IN_NETWORK -p tcp --syn -d $POPIP  --dport 110        -j ACCEPT
fi
#
# If the AUTH service is not running -- which it generally should
# not be -- the TCP/IP stack will respond to clients with a TCP
# RST packet, effectively rejecting the connection. So, it's
# reasonable to open this port even if no service is running.
#
if [ "$AUTHIP" != "" ]
then
   $IPT -A IN_NETWORK -p tcp --syn -d $AUTHIP --dport 113        -j ACCEPT
fi

if [ "$IMAPIP" != "" ]
then
   $IPT -A IN_NETWORK -p tcp --syn -d $IMAPIP --dport 143        -j ACCEPT
fi


#-------------------------------------------------------------------------
# Outbound traffic from protected network
#-------------------------------------------------------------------------


$IPT -N OUT_NETWORK
$IPT -A OUT_NETWORK -p icmp -j OUT_ICMP
$IPT -A OUT_NETWORK -p tcp  -j TCP_FLAGS
$IPT -A OUT_NETWORK -m state --state ESTABLISHED,RELATED -j ACCEPT
#
# The following six rules enable clients running on the protected network
# to connect to remote servers. Add and delete rules to customize the
# authorized services.
#
$IPT -A OUT_NETWORK -m state --state NEW -p tcp --dport  21 -j ACCEPT  # ftp
$IPT -A OUT_NETWORK -m state --state NEW -p tcp --dport  22 -j ACCEPT  # ssh
$IPT -A OUT_NETWORK -m state --state NEW -p tcp --dport  25 -j ACCEPT  # smtp
$IPT -A OUT_NETWORK -m state --state NEW -p tcp --dport  80 -j ACCEPT  # http
$IPT -A OUT_NETWORK -m state --state NEW -p tcp --dport 443 -j ACCEPT  # https

$IPT -A OUT_NETWORK -m state --state NEW -p udp --dport  53 -j ACCEPT  # domain


#-------------------------------------------------------------------------
```

```
# Inbound traffic to firewall host
#---------------------------------------------------------------------------------

$IPT -N IN_FIREWALL
$IPT -A IN_FIREWALL -p icmp                                    -j IN_ICMP
$IPT -A IN_FIREWALL -p tcp                                     -j TCP_FLAGS
$IPT -A IN_FIREWALL -p tcp --syn                              -j SYN_FLOOD
$IPT -A IN_FIREWALL                                           -j IN_IP_CHECK
$IPT -A IN_FIREWALL -m state --state ESTABLISHED,RELATED -j ACCEPT
$IPT -A IN_FIREWALL -m state --state ESTABLISHED,RELATED -j ACCEPT
for sip in $SSH
do
   $IPT -A IN_FIREWALL -p tcp -s $sip --dport 22 -m state --state NEW -j ACCEPT
done
#
# Add additional rules authorizing traffic inbound to firewall
# host here.
#
$IPT -A IN_FIREWALL -j LOG --log-prefix "IPT IN_FIREWALL: " $LOGOPT
$IPT -A IN_FIREWALL -j DROP


#---------------------------------------------------------------------------------
# Outbound traffic from firewall host
#---------------------------------------------------------------------------------

$IPT -N OUT_FIREWALL
$IPT -A OUT_FIREWALL -p icmp                                   -j OUT_ICMP
$IPT -A OUT_FIREWALL -p tcp                                    -j TCP_FLAGS
$IPT -A OUT_FIREWALL -m state --state ESTABLISHED,RELATED    -j ACCEPT
$IPT -A OUT_FIREWALL                                          -j OUT_IP_CHECK
#
# The following six rules enable clients running on the firewall host to
# connect to remote servers. Add and delete rules to customize the
# authorized services.
#
$IPT -A OUT_FIREWALL -m state --state NEW -p tcp --dport  21 -j ACCEPT  # ftp
$IPT -A OUT_FIREWALL -m state --state NEW -p tcp --dport  22 -j ACCEPT  # ssh
$IPT -A OUT_FIREWALL -m state --state NEW -p tcp --dport  25 -j ACCEPT  # smtp
$IPT -A OUT_FIREWALL -m state --state NEW -p tcp --dport  80 -j ACCEPT  # http
$IPT -A OUT_FIREWALL -m state --state NEW -p tcp --dport 443 -j ACCEPT  # https

$IPT -A OUT_FIREWALL -m state --state NEW -p udp --dport  53 -j ACCEPT  # domain

$IPT -A OUT_FIREWALL -j LOG --log-prefix "IPT OUT_FIREWALL: " $LOGOPT
```

Continued

Listing 10-3 *(Continued)*

```
$IPT -A OUT_FIREWALL -j DROP

#--------------------------------------------------------------------------
# Main Firewall Rules
#--------------------------------------------------------------------------

$IPT -A FORWARD              -j SHUN
$IPT -A FORWARD -i $EXTDEV -j IN_NETWORK
$IPT -A FORWARD -i $INTDEV -j OUT_NETWORK
$IPT -A FORWARD              -j LOG --log-prefix "IPT FORWARD: " $LOGOPT
$IPT -A FORWARD              -j DROP

$IPT -A INPUT               -j SHUN
$IPT -A INPUT    -i lo      -j ACCEPT
$IPT -A INPUT               -j IN_FIREWALL
$IPT -A INPUT               -j LOG --log-prefix "IPT INPUT: "   $LOGOPT
$IPT -A INPUT               -j DROP

$IPT -A OUTPUT              -j SHUN
$IPT -A OUTPUT -o lo        -j ACCEPT
$IPT -A OUTPUT              -j OUT_FIREWALL
$IPT -A OUTPUT              -j LOG --log-prefix "IPT OUTPUT: "  $LOGOPT
$IPT -A OUTPUT              -j DROP
```

The firewall protects a private network having the network address 10.0.0.0/8. The firewall's public network interface has the address 192.0.34.72, and its private network interface has the address 10.0.0.1. The firewall restricts hosts allowed to remotely log in via SSH or to ping its interfaces to trusted hosts. It supports screened servers for these services:

- ◆ SMTP
- ◆ DNS
- ◆ HTTP and HTTPS
- ◆ POP
- ◆ AUTH
- ◆ IMAP

The firewall code checks for bad IP addresses, bad TCP flags, access by shunned hosts, and SYN floods. It also restricts the types of ICMP messages that flow between the public and private networks and to and from its own interfaces. The firewall restricts both inbound and outbound connections. Only the following remote services can be contacted:

- ◆ FTP

- ◆ SSH

- ◆ SMTP

- ◆ HTTP and HTTPS

- ◆ DNS

Comments within the code suggest likely changes, such as changing the outbound policy from restrictive to permissive, and explain how to implement the changes.

Modifying a Firewall

When modifying a firewall, you should address three concerns:

- ◆ Keeping a record of changes made

- ◆ Keeping a backup copy of the firewall

- ◆ Recovering from a possible error in a firewall script

The following subsections explain these concerns and describe ways of addressing them.

Configuration Control

Keeping a record of changes made to a firewall or another software unit is called *configuration control*. Configuration control is an important means of troubleshooting because recent problems often arise from recent changes.

A simple way to control the configuration of a firewall is by using the Revision Control System (RCS), which is a part of the basic Red Hat Linux installation. Issuing the command

```
ci -l /etc/rc.d/rc.iptables
```

creates a configuration snapshot of the firewall code in the file /etc/rc.d/rc.iptables. The snapshot is stored as a file named rc.iptables,v in the /etc/rc.d directory or, if it exists, the /etc/rc.d/RCS directory. Before storing the snapshot, the command lets you enter text describing the snapshot. Terminate the text by typing a single period on a line by itself. For example:

```
#ci -l rc.iptables
RCS/rc.iptables,v  <--  rc.iptables
new revision: 1.3; previous revision: 1.2
```

```
enter log message, terminated with single '.' or end of file:
>> Enabled remote SSH access to host 12.
>> .
done
```

When a configuration snapshot exists, you can compare the current version of the firewall code with a previous version by issuing this command:

```
rcsdiff /etc/rc.d/rc.iptables
```

For example, the command might produce output such as the following:

```
rcsdiff rc.iptables
=====================================================================
RCS file: RCS/rc.iptables,v
retrieving revision 1.2
diff -r1.2 rc.iptables
356,360c356
< $IPT -A INPUT -p ALL -d $ADMIN_IP -m state \
<    --state ESTABLISHED,RELATED -j ACCEPT
< $IPT -A INPUT -p ALL -d $DTC_IP -m state \
<    --state ESTABLISHED,RELATED -j ACCEPT
< $IPT -A INPUT -p ALL -d $LOOP_IP -m state \
---
> $IPT -A INPUT -p ALL -m state \
```

The first several lines indicate that the current version of the firewall is 1.2. That is, three versions exist: 1.0, 1.1, and 1.2. One block of changes has been made. The changes occurred in lines 356–60 of version 1.1, which became line 356 of version 1.2. The remaining lines show the changes. The output lines beginning with < are associated with the preceding version of the firewall. Those beginning with > are associated with the current version. The commands associated with the RCS provide many other capabilities. For more information, see the rcs man page.

TIP You can use CVS (Concurrent Versions System) instead of RCS to control your firewall configuration. Though CVS is more sophisticated and therefore entails a longer learning curve, it stores files in a central database. Having files in a central database makes it easier to back them up. It can also avoid potential problems with scripts that attempt to iterate over the contents of a directory that unexpectedly contains an RCS subdirectory.

Firewall Backup

A simple way of maintaining a backup copy of a firewall is including in the firewall script a command that mails a copy of the firewall to a designated user. For instance, you might use a command such as the following:

```
mail -s "Firewall backup" user@host < /etc/rc.d/rc.iptables
```

where *user@host* is the e-mail address of the user who is to receive the backup copy. Of course, you should use this method only if you have reasonable grounds for believing that no would-be attacker is likely to compromise the security of your e-mail system. Generally, you should not send a backup copy of a firewall across the Internet. Instead, you should send it to a secure host on your private network. Alternatively, you can use a program such as GnuPG to encrypt the backup copy before sending it, making it difficult for anyone other than the intended recipient to read the message.

Error Recovery

As explained in Chapter 9, you should not generally modify a firewall that is in service; doing so may compromise the security of the hosts or networks it protects.

However, this guideline primarily applies to a central firewall protecting an entire network. Applying the principle of layered defense may lead you to implement firewalls on individual hosts, supplementing the protection afforded by the central firewall. In this case, you may consider it prudent to modify the firewalls installed on hosts residing on the network. Depending on your firewall design, the momentary unavailability of a host firewall may not jeopardize the security of the host.

If you're modifying the firewall remotely, you run the risk that a coding error will break your connection with the host. Depending on the nature of the error, you may be unable to reestablish contact with the host and may therefore be forced to travel to the location of the host to resolve the problem.

You can avoid this situation by adding a dead-man switch to your firewall script. The dead-man switch automatically rolls back the firewall to its preceding state unless you instruct it otherwise. If your connection is broken and you're unable to disable the dead-man switch, it trips and restores the firewall to a state that allows you to connect and fix the error.

You can append the following commands to the end of a host firewall script. The commands provide a dead-man switch, configuration control, saving of the revised firewall, and a backup of the firewall code:

```
# Revert to old firewall if new firewall not approved within
# 30 seconds.
( sleep 30; service iptables restart; ) &
```

```
echo "Do you want to activate emergency firewall restart?"
read line
case $line in
y*|Y*)    ;;
*) kill $! ;;
esac

# Keep RCS log of firewall changes.
echo "Do you want to annotate this firewall version?"
read line
case $line in
y*|Y*) ci -l /etc/rc.d/rc.iptables ;;
*)     ;;
esac

# Save current firewall configuration for next IPTables start.
echo "Do you want to make the new firewall the default?"
read line
case $line in
y*|Y*) service iptables save ;;
*)     ;;
esac

mail -s "Firewall updated" user@host.domain \
  </etc/rc.d/rc.iptables
```

To use the code, change the e-mail address in the final command to the e-mail address of the user who should receive the backup copy of the firewall. When the firewall script runs, you're prompted with a series of questions, to which you can answer *y* or *n*.

Another way to implement a dead-man switch is by using the Cron facility. Merely configure Cron to launch a job running the command service iptables restore a minute or so in the future. Then, run the firewall script. If the firewall script completes successfully, you can delete the job before it runs.

Sysctl Options

Many kernel options related to networking and firewalls can be manipulated via the Sysctl facility. These options are described in the file /usr/src/linux-2.4/ Documentation/networking/ip-sysctl.txt associated with the kernel-source package. Table 10-1 summarizes the most important kernel options you can configure via Sysctl. Note that, in the table, slashes in option names have been replaced by periods, consistent with the form of option names used by Sysctl. The leading /proc/sys has also been stripped from the name of each option for consistency with the forms used by Sysctl.

TABLE 10-1 IMPORTANT KERNEL OPTIONS CONFIGURABLE VIA SYSCTL

Option	Description
net.ipv4.conf.*interface*.accept_redirects	0: ignore redirects
	1: accept redirects
net.ipv4.conf.*interface*.accept_source_route	0: ignore source-routed packets
	1: accept source-routed packets
net.ipv4.conf.*interface*.log_martians	0: disable logging of packets with impossible addresses
	1: enable logging of packets with impossible addresses
net.ipv4.conf.*interface*.rp_filter	0: disable source address validation
	1: enable source address validation
net.ipv4.conf.*interface*.send_redirects	0: disable sending redirects
	1: enable sending redirects
net.ipv4.icmp_echo_ignore_broadcasts	0: enable response to broadcast echo requests
	1: disable response to broadcast echo requests
net.ipv4.ip_forward	0: disable packet forwarding
	1: enable packet forwarding
net.ipv4.ip_no_pmtu_disc	0: enable MTU discovery
	1: disable MTU discovery
net.ipv4.ipfrag_time	Time in seconds to retain an IP fragment in memory

Some options exist for each interface. For instance, the net.ipv4.conf.*inter face*.accept_redirects option can be separately enabled or disabled for each interface by substituting the name of the interface for *interface*. You can set the value for all interfaces by specifying all as the name of the interface. For example, the command

```
sysctl -w net.ipv4.conf.all.accept_redirects=1
```

enables the acceptance of redirects on every interface. You can set the values of Sysctl options by using the sysctl command or via the /etc/sysctl.conf file, which is processed at boot time. Generally, the default values are appropriate. However, I recommend that you consider setting nondefault values for the following options:

- accept_redirects sets all interfaces of all hosts except the external gateway to ignore redirects

- accept_source_route sets all interfaces to ignore source-routed packets

- log_martians sets all interfaces to log martians

- rp_filter sets all interfaces to enable source address validation

- ip_forward sets all interfaces except router interfaces to disable forwarding

You may choose to retain default values for these options or set nondefault values for other options, according to local needs.

Kernel Options

The Linux kernel installed by the Red Hat Linux installation program, and updated kernels installed via RPM, are configured to include the kernel options generally required for IPTables firewalls. However, you may find it necessary to compile your own kernel. This section identifies the kernel options you should select in order to be able to use the new kernel on an IPTables firewall host.

Two kernel options are required:

- CONFIG_PACKET

- CONFIG_NETFILTER

In addition, a number of kernel options are recommended but not required. These include the following:

- CONFIG_PROC_FS

- CONFIG_INET_ECN

- CONFIG_IP_ADVANCED_ROUTER

- ◆ CONFIG_IP_ROUTE_VERBOSE

- ◆ CONFIG_IP_ROUTE_LARGE_TABLES

- ◆ CONFIG_IP_NF_NAT_NEEDED

Unless you have a specific reason for doing otherwise, you should enable the recommended options.

Many other kernel options related to firewalls can be configured as loadable modules. That way, they're loaded only if needed. You should generally enable module support for the following options:

- ◆ CONFIG_IP_NF_COMPAT_IPCHAINS

- ◆ CONFIG_IP_NF_COMPAT_IPFWADM

- ◆ CONFIG_IP_NF_CONNTRACK

- ◆ CONFIG_IP_NF_FILTER

- ◆ CONFIG_IP_NF_FTP

- ◆ CONFIG_IP_NF_IPTABLES

- ◆ CONFIG_IP_NF_MANGLE

- ◆ CONFIG_IP_NF_MATCH_LIMIT

- ◆ CONFIG_IP_NF_MATCH_MAC

- ◆ CONFIG_IP_NF_MATCH_MARK

- ◆ CONFIG_IP_NF_MATCH_MULTIPORT

- ◆ CONFIG_IP_NF_MATCH_OWNER

- ◆ CONFIG_IP_NF_MATCH_STATE

- ◆ CONFIG_IP_NF_MATCH_TCPMSS

- ◆ CONFIG_IP_NF_MATCH_TOS

- ◆ CONFIG_IP_NF_MATCH_UNCLEAN

- ◆ CONFIG_IP_NF_NAT

- ◆ CONFIG_IP_NF_NAT_FTP

- ◆ CONFIG_IP_NF_QUEUE

- ◆ CONFIG_IP_NF_TARGET_LOG

- ◆ CONFIG_IP_NF_TARGET_MARK

- ◆ CONFIG_IP_NF_TARGET_MASQUERADE

- ◆ CONFIG_IP_NF_TARGET_MIRROR

- ◆ CONFIG_IP_NF_TARGET_REDIRECT

- ◆ CONFIG_IP_NF_TARGET_REJECT

- ◆ CONFIG_IP_NF_TARGET_TCPMSS

- ◆ CONFIG_IP_NF_TARGET_TOS

For more information on kernel options related to firewalls, see the file /usr/ src/linux-2.4/Documentation/Configure.help associated with the kernel-source package.

Bridging Firewalls

A *bridging* firewall is a firewall that operates at TCP/IP Layer 2 rather than at Layer 3. Because the network interfaces of a bridging firewall have no associated IP addresses, a bridging firewall is potentially more resistant to attack than an ordinary firewall. Moreover, you can add a bridging firewall to your network without changing the network configuration.

Like an ordinary firewall, a bridging firewall can filter packets. However, a bridging firewall does not route packets between networks. Instead, a bridge directly joins two parts of a single network. That is, the IP addresses of hosts on each side of the bridge should be part of a single network.

Linux kernel 2.4.18 and later kernels distributed with Red Hat Linux include bridging firewall code. These kernels are part of Red Hat Linux 7.3 and subsequent releases. However, the developers of the bridging firewall code have provided a Red Hat Linux 7.2 kernel RPM containing a patched kernel, making it convenient to implement a bridging for Red Hat Linux 7.2. You can obtain the kernel RPM at http://bridge.sourceforge.net/download.html.

 Running a non–Red Hat kernel poses several potential disadvantages. For instance, you won't be able to apply kernel errata released by Red Hat without breaking the functionality of your firewall. Therefore, it's generally better to upgrade to a newer release than use the non–Red Hat packages.

You also need a set of utilities known as the bridge-utils. These are distributed as part of Red Hat Linux 7.3 and subsequent releases; however, they're not installed by default. You can obtain an RPM package for installing the utilities under an older version of Red Hat Linux at the Web location just mentioned.

If you choose to set up a bridging firewall, you may find it convenient to use a host having three network interfaces. Two of the interfaces can be joined to form the bridge. These have no associated IP addresses. You can assign an IP address to the third interface, preferably an IP address on a private network reserved for administrative access, and use it to access the firewall host remotely. To set up the bridging firewall, issue the following commands from the local console rather than remotely:

```
# Change the assignments as needed
$PUBLIC_IFACE=eth0
$PRIVATE_IFACE=eth1
$BRIDGE_IFACE=br0

ifdown $PUBLIC_IFACE
ifdown $PRIVATE_IFACE

ifconfig $PUBLIC_IFACE 0.0.0.0
ifconfig $PRIVATE_IFACE 0.0.0.0

brctl addbr $BRIDGE_IFACE

brctl addif $BRIDGE_IFACE $PUBLIC_IFACE
brctl addif $BRIDGE_IFACE $PRIVATE_IFACE

ifconfig $BRIDGE_IFACE 0.0.0.0
```

At this point, the bridge should be able to pass packets between the public and private interfaces. If it cannot do so, check to see whether IPTables rules are interfering with the bridge. When you're satisfied that the bridge is working, add to the /etc/rc.local file the commands to set it up so that the bridge is established each time the system is booted. You can then configure IPTables to implement the desired firewall policies.

Summary

This chapter explained advanced IPTables firewall facilities, including packet forwarding and network address translation, and presented a sample firewall implementing the screened network architecture. The chapter also explained how to optimize firewall performance by minimizing the average path length of packets. The chapter gave suggestions for modifying firewalls, including maintaining configuration control by using RCS, and keeping a backup copy of every firewall. The chapter summarized important kernel compile-time and Sysctl options related to firewalls. Finally, the chapter explained why and how to implement a bridging firewall.

The next chapter begins Part III of this book, which focuses on firewall maintenance. Chapter 11 begins Part III by giving suggestions for hardening hosts used as firewalls or servers.

Part III

Firewall Operation

Chapter 11

Bastion Host Implementation

IN THIS CHAPTER

- ◆ Choosing the bastion host and its placement
- ◆ Hardening the bastion host
- ◆ Establishing change control and backup procedures

THE TERM *bastion host* can be used in several ways. Here, it means a host that is accessible via the public network. Hence, a bastion host is open to external attack and therefore requires special protection. Some people use the term *hardened host* to refer to this type of host.

This chapter presents some tips and guidelines for hardening (i.e., protecting) your bastion hosts. The chapter isn't comprehensive. Entire books have been written on hardening hosts. But, the chapter does present several of the most salient ways in which you can protect bastion hosts. The overwhelming majority of attacks can be thwarted by using the countermeasures described in this chapter. For a more thorough presentation of how to harden a host, see Mohammed J. Kabir's *Red Hat Linux Security and Optimization* (Red Hat Press/Wiley, 2002).

Choosing a Location

Before I explain specific means of hardening hosts, consider the issue of bastion host placement. As explained in Chapter 5, a host can reside in any of three basic locations:

- ◆ The private network
- ◆ A DMZ
- ◆ The external network

Only two of these options are viable locations for a bastion host. Placing a bastion host on the external network removes it from the protection provided by the network and complicates the process of communicating with the host in a secure manner.

Of the two remaining options, placing the bastion host in a DMZ is preferred. Because a bastion host accepts connections from external hosts, it is open to compromise. If you place a bastion host on the private network and the host is compromised, the security of the private network is jeopardized. On a nonswitched private network, the compromised bastion host can eavesdrop by sniffing traffic on the private network and freely attack hosts on the private network. Even on a switched private network, the compromised bastion host can employ ARP spoofing to eavesdrop on hosts of the private network. Therefore, placing a bastion host on the private network is inconsistent with the principle of layered defense. When the bastion host fails, the remainder of the network is likely to fail soon thereafter.

Placing a bastion host on the DMZ separates it from the private network because a router or firewall stands between the bastion host and hosts on the private network. An attacker must compromise both the bastion host and the router or firewall in order to have a free hand in attacking hosts on the private network. Placing bastion hosts on the DMZ provides an extra layer of defense that buys time in which to detect the compromise of a bastion host and isolate it so that it cannot attack other hosts.

Hardening the Host

The process for hardening a bastion host consists of these steps:

- ◆ Set up the hardware.
- ◆ Install Red Hat Linux.
- ◆ Configure system and kernel options.
- ◆ Configure user accounts.
- ◆ Configure services.
- ◆ Configure logging.
- ◆ Configure time synchronization.
- ◆ Protect services.
- ◆ Update the system.
- ◆ Establish a file integrity baseline.
- ◆ Establish change control and backup.

The following sections describe the steps in detail.

Set Up the Hardware

When setting up the hardware on which a bastion host will run, consider the physical security of the host and the quality of the environmental controls in its location. Most security measures can be circumvented by someone who has sufficient skill and access to the hardware. For example, BIOS passwords can often be defeated by opening a computer's case and shorting two jumper pins that reset the computer's NVRAM. Depending on the nature of your organization, you may deem it necessary to place the bastion host in a locked cage or room so that only authorized staff members can have access to it.

Because the operation of an entire network often depends on the availability of key bastion hosts, evaluate the quality of electrical power, temperature regulation, and humidity control. Uninterruptible power supplies (UPS) can provide protection against power anomalies and outages. In the event of a power outage, a more expensive UPS is likely to provide longer uptime than a less expensive UPS. But, even a relatively inexpensive UPS can provide substantial protection against spikes, surges, and power line noise.

Ideally, bastion hosts should operate in an environment that provides a stable temperature in the range of 66–70 degrees Fahrenheit (19–21 degrees Celsius). However, most modern PCs tolerate somewhat higher temperatures. Some facilities managers set thermostats to provide a comfortable temperature during the workday but allow temperatures to soar overnight or on weekends and holidays. Be sure that thermostats are set to provide proper computer operating temperatures around the clock. You may benefit by installing monitoring equipment that notifies you by pager or phone of an unexpected variation in power or temperature.

Conditions of high humidity can cause condensation within computing equipment, particularly if the equipment is powered down. On the other hand, some air conditioning equipment dries air excessively. Conditions of low humidity can lead to electrostatic discharges that damage computing equipment. Be sure that your bastion hosts are not exposed to extremes of humidity. If necessary, install a humidifier to avoid conditions of low humidity. To help avoid damage from condensation, keep equipment powered on even when it's not in use.

If you're concerned that someone may tamper with your bastion hosts but you cannot secure them in a locked cage or room, purchase computers with lockable cases or purchase add-on locks that make opening the cases difficult for unauthorized persons. Install BIOS and bootloader passwords so that only authorized administrators can configure the BIOS and bootloader. In addition, you may want to disable recognition of the keystroke Ctrl+Atl+Del, used to reboot a PC-based bastion host. Other measures to consider are disabling or removing the floppy drive and disabling the ability to boot from a CD-ROM. An intruder can use the floppy, bootable USB token, or CD-ROM as a means of thwarting your other security measures.

Install Red Hat Linux

Before installing Red Hat Linux, remove the host from the network or ensure that it is protected by a firewall. Otherwise, an attacker may find a way to compromise the host before you put defensive countermeasures in place.

Don't install packages you don't need, particularly packages that have associated services. An attacker can't successfully exploit a vulnerability in a service you've not installed. So, if all other things are equal, the fewer services a bastion host runs, the more secure it is.

You should generally install the `tripwire` package, which provides host-based intrusion detection. The section "How to Establish a File Integrity Baseline" explains how to configure Tripwire. Use the Select Additional Packages check box to inform the installation program that you want to install Tripwire and other packages not part of a standard component.

Consider installing these utilities:

◆ arpwatch detects new MAC addresses and changes in MAC addresses.

◆ iptraf monitors TCP/IP traffic volumes.

◆ nmap scans for open ports.

◆ tcpdump sniffs and interprets network traffic.

You can determine whether a package is already installed by issuing the command

```
rpm -q package
```

where *package* is the name of the package.

Normally, network interfaces operate in nonpromiscuous mode, listening only for packets related to an associated MAC address. A network interface operating in promiscuous mode listens for any network traffic, regardless of the associated MAC addresses. Attackers often set network interfaces to operate in promiscuous mode in order to sniff network traffic. Therefore, a network interface that is unexpectedly operating in promiscuous mode may indicate that a system has been compromised. When arpwatch operates, it sets network interfaces to promiscuous mode. Therefore, arpwatch may inhibit your ability to detect the compromise of a host. However, tripwire provides a more reliable means of detecting a host compromise than does the state of a network interface. Consequently, if you install Tripwire as recommended, the use of arpwatch is reasonable.

Configure System and Kernel Options

Most system administrators have preferred system and kernel options that they like to set to values other than the default Red Hat Linux values. These preferences are somewhat idiosyncratic. However, I'll share my personal favorites and explain why I prefer them.

In `/etc/syctl.conf`, I set the following two nonstandard option values:

```
kernel.sysrq = 1
net.ipv4.conf.all.accept_source_route = 0
```

The `kernel.sysrq` option enables a special menu you can access by pressing Alt+Print Scrn. The menu enables you to halt or reboot the system or perform a variety of other operations. Because the menu is a kernel feature, it is sometimes accessible when the system is otherwise locked up. Pressing *h* in response to the menu causes the system to display a help screen that describes the supported operations. This option is also useful when the host has a remote serial console. You can `cat` the file `/proc/sys/kernel/sysrq` to determine whether the option is enabled. The value 1 indicates the enabled state.

The `net.ipv4.conf.all.accept_source_route` option disables the acceptance of source-routed packets. These are seldom used for legitimate purposes but can provide ways of successfully attacking hosts behind a firewall. So, you should disable their use.

In the `/etc/sysconfig/init` file, I set this nonstandard option value:

```
BOOTUP=verbose
```

This option provides detailed information during system booting. Without it, significant error messages may not be displayed to the console.

In addition, I configure `/etc/modules.conf` to include specifications that set the mode and speed of network interfaces. The manner of doing so varies depending on the make and model of the network interface. For example, to specify that an Intel EEPro 100 interface should operate at 100 Mbps, full-duplex mode, I use

```
options eepro100 options=48
```

To learn how to set other options for the EEPro 100 or to set options for other network adapters, see the documentation for the associated driver. If the documentation is not handy, you can install the kernel-sources package and examine the C source files in `/usr/src/linux/drivers/net`. If you can locate the proper source file, you may be able to determine how to set driver options by reading the source and comments.

Configure User Accounts

Ideally, ordinary users would not have accounts on a bastion host. It's much harder to monitor and control the behavior of a host that has multiple users than that of a host used only by administrators. So, you should limit the number of user accounts available on bastion hosts.

You should also ensure that every user account has a strong password – that is, one that includes a least eight characters of several types and that is not a dictionary word or a simple variation on a dictionary word.

> **TIP** Using the `mkpasswd` command is a handy way to generate strong passwords. Read its man page for further information.

Consider altering the standard `umask` value associated with the root user. To alter the value, add the command

```
umask 007
```

to the script `/root/bash_profile`. This setting prevents files created by `root` from being accessed by other users unless chmod is used to explicitly permit such access. Therefore, the setting is particularly valuable when non-administrative users have accounts on the host.

> **NOTE** Some programs and packages include scripts which assume that files created by the root user are publicly accessible. Setting the `umask` option may break these scripts. However, getting them to work is generally a simple matter of using chmod to provide access to selected files or directories. Often, the permission to access can be provided temporarily and can be withdrawn when installation is complete. The enhanced security provided by the `umask` option may be worth the inconvenience it sometimes entails.

Configure Services

A host is generally compromised by an attack on a vulnerable service. Therefore, one of the most important means of hardening a host is disabling unneeded services.

Ideally, a bastion host should not support Telnet or authenticated FTP because these services send user and password information over the network in clear text. If remote login must be supported, use SSH rather than Telnet because SSH traffic is encrypted.

To further secure a host for which remote logins are enabled, you can configure SSH to prohibit remote logins by the root user. To do so, specify

```
PermitRootLogin no
```

in the `/etc/ssh/sshd_config` file. To administer the host, you then log in remotely as a non-root user and issue the `su` command to become `root` or use the `sudo` command to execute individual commands as `root`.

Another security measure to consider is running the SSH service on a nonstandard port. To do so, specify

```
Port n
```

in the `/etc/ssh/sshd` file, where *n* is the port number on which the service should run. To connect to an SSH server running on a nonstandard port, issue a command of the form

```
ssh -p n host
```

where *host* is the host name or IP address of the host running the SSH service and *n* is the port on which the server listens.

 You should not generally run SSH on a nonprivileged (1024-65535) port. An attacker who managed to obtain non-root access to your host might somehow terminate the SSH service and plant a trojan service on the nonprivileged port. Running SSH on a privileged port prevents a non-root user from using the port.

You generally should not run NIS, NFS, or RPC services on a bastion host. Therefore, you can generally disable these services:

- autofs
- netfs
- nfs
- nfslock
- nscd
- portmap
- ypbind

- ◆ yppasswdd

- ◆ ypserv

- ◆ ypxfrd

To disable a service, issue these commands:

```
chkconfig name off
service name stop
```

where *name* is the name of the service. You may find it convenient to disable multiple services by using a shell loop. For example:

```
for i in autofs netfs nfs nfslock nscd portmap ypfind ; do
  chkconfig $i off
  service $i stop
done
```

Once a service is disabled in this manner, it will not automatically start when the system is booted.

Several other services are likely candidates for being disabled, including

- ◆ anacron is needed only if the host is not powered up and running 24×7.

- ◆ identd is needed only if you prefer not rejecting IDENT requests by FTP, mail, SSH, and other servers.

- ◆ ipchains is needed only if you prefer to run an IPChains firewall rather than an IPTables firewall.

- ◆ radvd is needed only if the host must support IPv6.

- ◆ kdcrotate is needed only if the host must support Kerberos authentication.

- ◆ rstatd leaks information of potential value to attackers.

- ◆ rusersd leaks information of potential value to attackers.

- ◆ rwalld leaks information of potential value to attackers.

- ◆ rwhod leaks information of potential value to attackers.

- ◆ sendmail is needed only if the host is a mail relay or host.

These services should generally be enabled if needed:

- ◆ apmd

- ◆ atd

- ◆ crond

- gpm
- iptables
- keytable
- kudzu
- network
- random
- rawdevices
- rhnsd
- sshd
- syslog

TIP Unless you crave the use of the mouse, it's best to disable gpm, which has been the source of some nonremote vulnerabilities. Similarly, kudzu is needed only if you've added new hardware. You may prefer to disable it under normal circumstances and enable it only when you've changed the hardware configuration.

Depending on the choices that were made during system installation, your system may support services not mentioned in this section, such as http, ldap, lpd, smb, snmpd, squid, tux, xfs, and xinetd. Investigate any such services and disable them unless you're convinced that they're needed.

TIP Using either unnecessary services or unnecessary packages can lead to vulnerabilities. On a bastion host, you should install only packages that are actually needed. For example, you probably don't need packages related to X or games. Moreover, you generally should install only packages made by Red Hat, because third-party packages may present unanticipated vulnerabilities. If you do install third-party packages, you may prefer to compile and install them from sources, so that you can audit their contents before installation.

Configure Logging

Configuring system logging and regularly monitoring system logs are the most important ways to harden a host against attack. Relatively few attacks succeed without leaving evidence in system logs. If logs are regularly monitored, few successful attacks go unnoticed. If your defense includes multiple layers, you can detect that a host has been compromised before its failure leads to the overall failure of network security.

Chapter 13, "Administering a Firewall," explains how to configure and monitor system logs. You should generally follow the suggestions given in that chapter. In particular, you generally should configure a bastion host to send log entries to a remote syslog server. Doing so protects against the possibility that an attacker will erase system log entries on a compromised bastion host and thereby escape detection. If a compromised bastion host's log entries also reside on a central logging server, the attacker must also compromise the logging server in order to conceal the intrusion.

Configure Time Synchronization

To accurately correlate network events, all network hosts must be time synchronized. Without some explicit synchronization measure, the clocks of most hosts drift, sometimes by as much as seconds per day. Over time, the clocks fall into significant disagreement.

Maintaining accurate system time is somewhat complicated. The NTP (Network Time Protocol) is the primary means of doing so. You can learn more about NTP from *The NTP FAQ and HOWTO,* available at `http://www.eecis.udel.edu/~ntp/ntpfaq/NTP-a-faq.htm`.

However, for purposes of event correlation, system clocks don't have to be accurate to the millisecond. They can just be in agreement, even if the agreed time is off by several tens of milliseconds or perhaps more.

You can achieve time synchronization by installing the NTP service on each network host. Choose a host with a reasonably accurate internal clock and synchronize the other hosts to it. To specify the synchronization options, edit the `/etc/ntp.conf` file to specify the IP address of the designated time server. The following excerpt from an `/etc/ntp.conf` file shows how:

```
server    192.0.3.72        # my time server
#server   132.239.254.49    # NTP.UCSD.EDU
#server   192.6.38.127      # NTP-CUP.EXTERNAL.HP.COM
server    127.127.1.0       # local clock
fudge     127.127.1.0 stratum 10
```

Notice that the two lines referring to external time servers have been commented out.

To configure the ntpd service to run, issue these commands:

```
chkconfig --level 235 ntpd on
service ntpd start
```

When the ntpd service is not running on the local host, you can set the time of the local host to that of another host on which the ntpd service is running. To do so, issue the command

```
ntpdate -buv server
```

where *server* is the host name or IP address of the host running ntpd. The options have the following meaning:

- ◆ -b means that the time is adjusted immediately rather than gradually
- ◆ -u means that the client will listen for a response on a nonprivileged port
- ◆ -v means that output will be verbose

To compare the local host's clock with that of another host running ntpd, issue the command

```
ntpdate -d server
```

where *server* is the host name or IP address of the host running ntpd. You can view the status of the ntpd service when it is running by issuing the command

```
ntpq -p
```

Protect Services

The next step in hardening a bastion host is to protect the services it runs from unauthorized access. You can accomplish this task in two main ways:

- ◆ A firewall
- ◆ TCP wrappers

Because this book as a whole deals with firewalls, this section is concerned with the second alternative, TCP wrappers. TCP wrappers can be used with a firewall, providing an additional layer of security that may protect the host if the firewall fails.

You can protect almost any service by using a firewall. However, TCP wrappers are effective only for services compiled to use them. Services that use TCP wrappers include essentially all services that run under the control of the xinetd service. In addition, Red Hat Linux SSH is compiled with support for TCP wrappers.

To configure TCP wrappers, edit the files /etc/hosts.allow and /etc/hosts. deny. Together, the two files determine which service requests are allowed. If the /etc/hosts.allow file contains a line matching a service request, the request is allowed. Otherwise, the /etc/hosts.deny file is consulted. If a matching line is found, the request is denied; otherwise, it is allowed.

The format of the `/etc/hosts.allow` and `/etc/hosts.deny` files is the same. Each file contains one line per configured service. The lines have this form:

```
service: host host host ...
```

where `service` designates the service and `host` designates a host authorized to access the service. The service designation corresponds to the name of the process corresponding to the service. For instance, the SSH service is known as `sshd`, and the FTP service is known as `in.ftpd`. The word `ALL` can be used to refer to all services.

The host designation consists of a host name or IP address. Alternatively, the host designation can consist of an IP address and netmask, separated by a slash (/). The word `ALL` can be used to refer to all hosts, and the word `LOCAL` can be used to refer to the local host.

Here's a sample `/etc/hosts.allow` file that allows hosts on a specified network and the local host to access the SSH service:

```
sshd: 192.0.3.0/255.255.255.0 127.0.0.1
```

To limit access to only these hosts, the `/etc/hosts.deny` file contains this directive:

```
ALL: ALL
```

The TCP wrappers facility supports a variety of other options. For example, you can substitute a specified service in place of the requested one. For more information on TCP wrappers, see the man page `/etc/hosts.allow`.

Update the System

After configuring and reviewing system logs and disabling unneeded services, keeping a system updated is the most important defensive countermeasure you can undertake. Red Hat regularly releases errata that repair vulnerabilities discovered in Red Hat Linux. If your host is up to date, few attackers possess exploits capable of compromising your system.

You can subscribe to `redhat-watch-list`, an e-mail list that notifies you whenever Red Hat releases updated packages. When you learn that a package you're using has been updated, you can download the package via anonymous FTP from `updates.redhat.com` and use the `rpm -F` command to update your host. Or, you can visit `http://rhn.redhat.com/errata/` for lists of errata that currently apply to your release. However, you're likely to find it much more convenient to use Red Hat Network, a fee-based service that provides convenient access to updates.

TIP   To subscribe to `redhat-watch-list`, visit the Web page at `http://www` `.redhat.com/mailing-lists/redhat-watch-list/index.html`.

Before using Red Hat Network, you should install the Red Hat GnuPG key, which enables you to verify that downloaded packages have not been tampered with. To do so, issue this command:

```
/usr/bin/gpg --import /usr/share/rhn/RPM-GPG-KEY
```

Beginning with the Red Hat Linux 8 release, you must import the GnuPG key into RPM rather than GPG. To do so, issue this command:

```
rpm --import /usr/share/doc/rpm-version/RPM-GPG-KEY
```

where *version* is the version of RPM.

GnuPG may request that you execute the command a second time. If so, do as directed.

If you're working with a host that does not include the `RPM-GPG-KEY` file, you can download the key from `http://www.redhat.com/about/contact.html`. Simply copy the text beginning with the line

```
-----BEGIN PGP PUBLIC KEY BLOCK-----
```

and ending with the line

```
-----END PGP PUBLIC KEY BLOCK-----
```

Include both indicated lines in the copy block. Then, save the copied text in a file named `redhat.asc`. Then, issue the following command to import the key and make it available for verification:

```
gpg --import redhat.asc
```

After you've imported the key, verify that the correct key was imported. To do so, issue the command

```
gpg --list-keys --fingerprint
```

The result should resemble the following:

```
pub  1024D/DB42A60E 1999-09-23 Red Hat, Inc <security@redhat.com>
     Key fingerprint = CA20 8686 2BD6 9DFC 65F6  ECC4 2191 80CD DB42 A60E
```

If you see a different key fingerprint, you can conclude that someone has tampered with the key. In that case, you should suspect that your host — or the Red Hat Web site from which you obtained the key — has been compromised.

 To learn more about GnuPG, see the user's guide at `http://www.gnupg .org/gph/en/manual.html`.

After you've installed the GnuPG key, you're ready to register the system with Red Hat Network. Terry Collings and Kurt Wall's book *Red Hat Linux Networking and System Administration* (Red Hat Press/Wiley, 2002) describes how to do so using the X interface to Red Hat Network. Because many system administrators omit X from servers, this section describes the command-line interface to Red Hat Network.

First, you should sign up for Red Hat Network. If you purchased an official copy of Red Hat Linux, you may be entitled to a free subscription to Red Hat Network. Otherwise, you should have your credit card handy. Sign up by visiting `https://rhn.redhat.com/` and following the sign-up instructions.

After you're signed up, you're ready to register your host. To do so, issue the command

```
rhn_register --nox
```

A series of dialog boxes prompt you to enter information about yourself and your host. Documentation describing the use of these dialog boxes is available on the Red Hat Network site.

After you've registered the host, again visit the Red Hat Network site and specify that the host is entitled to Red Hat Network services. When you've done so, you're ready to update the host, which can be accomplished by issuing this command:

```
up2date -u --nox
```

This command form does not automatically install any updates to the kernel or other critical packages. To override this safety feature and install all updates, issue the command

```
up2date -u --nox --force
```

Red Hat Network provides priority access to downloads. So, depending on the speed of your Internet connection, you may require only a few minutes to update your host.

You can configure Red Hat Network to automatically "push" updates to your system as they're released. Or, you can manually execute the `up2date` command whenever you learn of new updates, perhaps from the e-mail list. By visiting the Red Hat Network site, you can view a personalized page that summarizes the status of all your subscribed hosts, showing any out-of-date packages. Whichever way you choose to apply updates, you should regularly ensure that all applicable updates have been downloaded and installed.

Establish a File Integrity Baseline

Defensive measures are of two main types: One type is intended to prevent a host from being compromised; the other type is intended to detect that a host has been compromised and to alert administrators.

Tripwire is a security measure of the second type, a host-based intrusion-detection system that operates by detecting changes to sensitive files and directories. The RPM facility is also capable of detecting changes. But, it is not suitable as a host intrusion-detection facility.

Both RPM and Tripwire detect changes to files and directories by developing checksums and comparing them with a baseline. When the checksum associated with a file or directory fails to match its baseline, the file has evidently been changed.

To configure Tripwire, modify the `/etc/twcfg.txt` file to include these directives:

```
LOOSEDIRECTORYCHECKING=true
SYSLOGREPORTING=true
REPORTLEVEL=1
```

Strictly speaking, you don't have to make these modifications. However, they reduce the number of false alerts generated by Tripwire. If you're especially paranoid, you may prefer to forgo making these modifications.

Next, initialize the Tripwire policy file by issuing the command

```
/etc/tripwire/twinstall.sh
```

Then, initialize Tripwire by issuing this command:

```
tripwire --init
```

Tripwire prompts you for two passwords that it assigns and uses to protect its configuration. One password is designed to be common to all hosts of a site. The other is designed to be specific to the local host. Be sure to take note of the passwords; without them, you cannot modify the Tripwire configuration. Also, be sure to assign strong passwords. Otherwise, an attacker may be able to break in to Tripwire and conceal modifications made to sensitive files.

Tripwire creates a database file and informs you of its location. You should move or copy the file to the directory /var/lib/tripwire. You should also back up the database to offline media.

After Tripwire is initialized, you can check whether files or directories have been modified by issuing the command

```
tripwire --check
```

The tripwire package installs a Cron task that daily executes this command and mails the result to the root user.

To update the baseline to reflect authorized changes to file and directories, issue the command

```
tripwire --update -r /var/lib/tripwire/report/file
```

where *file* is the name of a report file created when the system status was checked. The names of report files include the name of the host, the date the report was run, and the time at which the report was run. Generally, you should choose the latest such file in the indicated directory. The update facility uses the default text editor — usually vi — to edit a specification file. Using the editor, you can specify which files or directories are updated. Those designated with an adjacent *x* are updated, whereas others are not. By default, all files and directories are initially flagged with an *x*. When you exit the editor, you're prompted for the host password you entered when you configured Tripwire. If you supply the correct password, the baseline configuration is updated; otherwise, the configuration is not changed.

Tripwire has a tendency to produce many false positives, particularly in the aftermath of installing new packages or software. You can tune the Tripwire operation to minimize such false positives. To learn how to do so, see Mohammed J. Kabir's *Red Hat Linux Security and Optimization* (Red Hat Press/Wiley, 2002).

After you've completed the hardening of your system, you must check it before placing it in service. The procedure for doing so is in Chapter 12, "Testing and Troubleshooting a Firewall." Be sure to correct any problems before putting the system online.

Establish Change Control and Backup Procedures

The final step in hardening a system is to put in place change control and backup procedures that protect against a loss of system integrity. Chapter 10 explained how to use RCS to maintain change control of firewall code. You can use RCS to maintain change control of most Red Hat Linux configuration files. Before making configuration changes, simply execute the command

```
ci -l file
```

where *file* is the name of the configuration.

TIP   You may find it helpful to create an automated script that runs as a Cron task, identifying the RCS files created by this command and sending them to a central repository for backup.

Establish a means and procedure for regularly backing up your host. You can use any of a variety of programs and methods, which are too numerous to be surveyed here. For some suggested backup methods, see Terry Collings and Kurt Wall's *Red Hat Linux Networking and System Administration* (Red Hat Press/Wiley, 2002).

Summary

This chapter described a multistep process for hardening a bastion host. However, you can use the same process to harden hosts other than bastion hosts. The three primary hardening measures are establishing and monitoring system logs, eliminating unnecessary services, and keeping necessary services up to date. If you employ these measures and the other measures described in this chapter, your systems will be much more resistant to attack than most.

Chapter 12

Testing and Troubleshooting a Firewall

IN THIS CHAPTER

- ◆ Firewall testing tools
- ◆ Testing ports
- ◆ Regression testing
- ◆ Troubleshooting

AFTER IMPLEMENTING A FIREWALL, you must test the firewall to verify that it correctly implements the associated security policies. This chapter describes tools and techniques that can help you do so. Testing is intended to determine whether a firewall functions properly. A related process, *troubleshooting,* is intended to pinpoint the source or cause of a problem so that the problem can be resolved. This chapter also provides some guidance that can help you efficiently troubleshoot known firewall problems.

Firewall Testing Tools

You can test a firewall by using paired clients and servers for each authorized service. For example, you can test whether a firewall properly handles HTTP traffic by using a Web browser and server. However, unless the number of authorized services is small, using actual clients and servers becomes cumbersome.

Instead, testing a firewall by using specialized tools is generally more convenient. The following subsections describe three tools that are useful for this purpose and provide strategies for using these tools to test and troubleshoot firewalls:

- ◆ Nmap
- ◆ Firewall Tester
- ◆ Nessus

If you read the IPTables documentation, you may discover the -C flag, which is intended to facilitate the testing of firewalls. Unfortunately, the -C flag is unimplemented. So, don't waste time trying to figure out how to use it.

Nmap

Nmap is perhaps the most popular and commonly used network security tool. It is fundamentally a *scanner* – that is, a program that determines which ports of a target host have associated listening services. Nmap, which is included in Red Hat Linux and requires no configuration, can be used immediately after installation. To check whether Nmap is installed, issue the command

```
rpm -q nmap
```

If you find that Nmap is missing, you can install it from Red Hat Linux distribution media.

A simple way to use Nmap is to specify only a host name or IP address:

```
nmap 192.0.3.74
```

Nmap may take several minutes to complete its analysis. Eventually, a report such as the following should appear:

```
Starting nmap V. 2.54BETA22 ( www.insecure.org/nmap/ )
Interesting ports on example.com (192.0.3.74):
(The 1532 ports scanned but not shown below are in state: closed)
Port       State       Service
21/tcp     open        ftp
22/tcp     open        ssh
23/tcp     open        telnet
37/tcp     open        time
53/tcp     open        domain
79/tcp     open        finger
80/tcp     open        http
199/tcp    open        smux
3389/tcp   open        msrdp
6667/tcp   open        irc
```

Nmap output identifies ports as one of the following:

◆ Open

◆ Closed

◆ Filtered

A *filtered* port is one that may accept or block traffic depending on packet characteristics. For instance, a port configured to accept incoming connections from only trusted hosts may be listed as filtered.

By default, Nmap scans TCP ports 1–1024 and any TCP ports identified in /usr/ share/nmap/nmap-services. However, by including the -p option, you can specify the ports to be scanned:

```
nmap -p 21-25,53,80 192.0.3.74
```

This command scans TCP ports 21–25 (inclusive), TCP port 53, and TCP port 80.

Nmap is also capable of scanning UDP ports. To scan UDP ports, specify the -sU option:

```
nmap -sU -p 53 192.0.3.74
```

This command scans UDP port 53 and reports its status.

Nmap can scan multiple hosts. You can specify in a variety of ways the hosts to be scanned. One simple and convenient way is to specify a range of IP addresses:

```
nmap 192.0.3-4.1-255
```

This command scans all hosts having IP addresses in the inclusive range 192.0.3.1 to 192.0.4.255.

Before commencing a scan, Nmap pings each target host. If the target host does not respond, Nmap does not scan it. If you know or suspect that the target host is up but has been configured not to respond to pings, you may want Nmap to scan it even though it doesn't respond to pings. To instruct Nmap to scan unconditionally, specify the -P0 option:

```
nmap -P0 192.0.3.1-255
```

Nmap includes many other useful features and options. To learn more about them, see the Nmap man page.

Don't run Nmap against systems other than those whose administrators have given you permission to do so. Ideally, your permission should be written rather than merely oral. If you run Nmap against a host without first obtaining permission, you may lead system administrators to believe that their host is under attack. In some jurisdictions, running an unwelcome Nmap port scan may be illegal.

Firewall Tester

Firewall Tester, designed specifically for testing firewalls, consists of a client and a server, both written in Perl. You run the client on an external host and the server on an internal host. The client sends specified packets to the server. Some of these packets are likely to be accepted by the firewall, and some are likely to be blocked. The server simply logs the packets it receives. After the client has sent all the specified packets, you can compare the list of packets sent with the server's log. You can then identify the packets blocked by the firewall and thereby determine whether the firewall is functioning properly.

Firewall Tester is not included in the Red Hat Linux distribution. Instead, you can obtain it from its Web page, `http://ftester.sourceforge.net/`. Firewall Tester is somewhat inconvenient to install under Red Hat Linux because it is distributed as a .tar file and requires several components not included in the base Red Hat Linux distribution.

INSTALLING FIREWALL TESTER

To install Firewall Tester, obtain these components:

- The `ftester` .tar file, available from the Firewall Tester Web page
- `libpcap` RPM, from the Red Hat Linux distribution or contributed library
- The following Perl modules, available from `www.cpan.org`:
  - NetPacket
  - Net-Pcap
  - Net-PcapUtils
  - Net-RawIP

Then, follow these steps on both the host to be used as a client and the host to be used as a server:

1. Install the `libpcap` RPM:

   ```
   rpm -Uvh libpcap-*.rpm
   ```

2. Move to the directory containing the .tar file for the NetPacket Perl module and install the module:

   ```
   tar zxf NetPacket-0.03.tar.gz
   cd NetPacket-0.03
   perl Makefile.PL
   make
   make install
   ```

3. Move to the directory containing the .tar file for the Net-Pcap Perl module and install the module:

```
tar zxf Net-Pcap-0.04.tar.gz
cd Net-Pcap-0.04
perl Makefile.PL
make
make install
```

TIP If the compilation fails because of a missing header file, edit Makefile, replacing the line

```
CCFLAGS = -fno-strict-aliasing -I/usr/local/include
```

with the line

```
CCFLAGS = -fno-strict-aliasing -I/usr/local/include -I/
usr/include/pcap
```

Then, reissue the make command and issue the make install command.

4. Move to the directory containing the .tar file for the Net-PcapUtils Perl module and install the module:

```
tar zxf Net-PcapUtils-0.01.tar.gz
cd Net-PcapUtils-0.01
perl Makefile.PL
make
make install
```

5. Move to the directory containing the .tar file for the Net-RawIP Perl module and install the module:

```
tar zxf Net-RawIP-0.09d.tar.gz
cd Net-RawIP-0.09d
perl Makefile.PL
make
make install
```

TIP If compilation fails because of a missing header file, edit Makefile, replacing the line

```
CCFLAGS = -fno-strict-aliasing -I/usr/local/include
```

with the line

```
CCFLAGS = -fno-strict-aliasing -I/usr/local/include -I/usr/include/pcap
```

Then, reissue the make command and issue the make install command.

5. Move to the directory containing the Firewall Tester .tar file and unpack it:

```
tar zxf ftester-0.7.tar.gz
```

CONFIGURING FIREWALL TESTER

You're now ready to configure and use Firewall Tester. To configure Firewall Tester, move to the directory into which the program's .tar file was unpacked. First, copy the Firewall Tester man page to the proper directory:

```
cp ftester.8 /usr/share/man/man8
```

You can now read the Firewall Tester documentation by issuing the command

```
man ftester
```

The documentation explains that the file ftest.conf specifies the test packets to be sent. Modify the instance of the file residing on the host outside the firewall to include the desired test packets. Lines in the file consist of a series of fields, with each field separated from the next by a colon. The fields used to specify a TCP or UDP datagram are shown in this list:

- Source IP address
- Source port
- Destination IP address
- Destination port
- TCP flags, which can be any of the following:
  - A (ACK)
  - F (FIN)
  - P (PSH)

- R (RST)

- S (SYN)

- U (URG)

- ◆ Protocol (TCP or UDP)

- ◆ Type of service (generally 0)

For example, here's the specification for a TCP SYN-ACK datagram:

```
199.199.199.199:1024:192.0.3.74:22:SA:TCP:0
```

Notice that multiple TCP flags can be specified. The source IP address is spoofed by Firewall Tester as the specified value. The destination IP address must be the address of the host on which the Firewall Tester server listens. For information on specifying ICMP messages, see the Firewall Tester man page.

You must also include a special stop rule in the ftest.conf file. The rule specifies a datagram which informs the server that the test run is complete. To specify the rule, prepend the text stop_signal= to a packet rule. For instance, here's a typical stop rule:

```
stop_signal=199.199.199.199:22:192.0.3.74:22:SA:TCP:0
```

Note that the stop rule must specify a packet that successfully traverses the firewall; otherwise, the server does not receive the stop signal.

RUNNING FIREWALL TESTER

To run Firewall Tester, log in to the host inside the firewall, move to the directory containing the Firewall Tester scripts, and issue a command of this form:

```
./ftestd -i ethn
```

where ethn is the interface on which the server should listen.

Then, log in to the host outside the firewall, move to the directory containing the Firewall Tester scripts, and issue the command

```
./ftest
```

The client should send the specified packet, including the stop signal that causes the server to terminate. Then, the client should terminate.

ANALYZING FIREWALL TESTER'S RESULTS

To analyze the results of a Firewall Tester run, copy the logs created on the client and server to the directory containing the Firewall Tester scripts on either the client or server, whichever is more convenient. The client's log file is named `ftest.log`, and the server's log file is named `ftestd.log`. Then, issue the command

```
./freport ftest.log ftestd.log
```

The output should resemble the following:

```
Authorized packets:
--------------------


Modified packets (probably NAT):
--------------------------------

2 - 192.0.4.2:1024 > 192.0.3.74:22 S TCP 0
3 - 192.0.4.3:1024 > 192.0.3.74:22 S TCP 0
4 - 192.0.4.2:22 > 192.0.3.74:22 S TCP 0
                >>>>>>>>
2 - 192.0.4.2:1024 > 10.0.0.6:22 S TCP 0
3 - 192.0.4.3:1024 > 10.0.0.6:22 S TCP 0
4 - 192.0.4.2:22 > 10.0.0.6:22 S TCP 0

Filtered or dropped packets:
----------------------------

1 - 199.199.199.199:1024 > 192.0.3.74:22 S TCP 0
```

By examining the report, you can determine whether the firewall is correctly handling the test packets.

Firewall Tester has many other features, including the ability to test network intrusion-detection systems. Of importance to testing IPTables and other stateful firewalls, Firewall Tester can simulate TCP connections between its client and server rather than merely isolated packets. However, doing so requires some fiddling with TTL values. See the man page for details.

Nessus

Nessus is a general-purpose security scanner. Like Nmap, Nessus can identify open and filtered ports associated with a target system. However, Nessus goes further than Nmap by attempting to assess whether running services are vulnerable to known attacks. Because Nessus is frequently updated, periodically running it is a good way to verify that your network defenses are in order. If new vulnerabilities have been published since the last time you ran Nessus, a newer version of Nessus is likely to check for them and report any that affect your network.

Nessus includes two components:

- ◆ A server, which performs the scans

- ◆ A client, which enables you to specify and control scans

The client is GUI-based and available in two versions. One runs under Linux, and the other runs under Microsoft Windows. You can run the server and the Linux version of the client on a single host. However, to do so, the host must have X installed and configured. Many Nessus users find it convenient to install the server under Linux and install the client on a Windows laptop.

Like other security tools, Nessus is not perfect. It generates both *false positives* and *false negatives*. A false positive is an indication that a vulnerability is present when it actually is not. A false negative is an indication that a vulnerability is not present when it actually is.

When used against hosts running Red Hat Linux, Nessus is particularly prone to false positives. Among other means of identifying vulnerabilities, Nessus relies on the version banners presented by services when a client establishes a connection. Red Hat regularly backports security fixes to released versions of software packages. Therefore, a package released by Red Hat may be more secure than a like-numbered version of the package released by a source other than Red Hat. Nevertheless, the version number that appears in a banner may lead Nessus to erroneously conclude that the Red Hat Linux service is vulnerable.

You should always treat the results presented by a security tool with skepticism. Verify results before relying on them.

SETTING UP THE NESSUS SERVER

You can download Nessus, which is not part of the Red Hat Linux distribution, via its Web page, at http://www.nessus.org/. To install Nessus, download the Nessus installer script, nessus-installer.sh. Then, execute the script by issuing this command:

```
sh nessus-installer.sh
```

The installer script downloads and installs the necessary components.
Before using Nessus for the first time, you must perform two operations:

- ◆ Generate a security certificate identifying the server.

- ◆ Create a Nessus user account.

To create the security certificate, issue the command

```
/usr/local/bin/nessus-mkcert
```

To create a Nessus user account, issue the command

```
/usr/local/bin/nessus-adduser
```

The program asks whether you want to authenticate users by password or certificate. Authentication by certificate requires more effort to set up. So, initially, you should specify password authentication. The program then prompts for a user name and password. You need not specify a user name that has a corresponding Linux user account. The password you enter is echoed in clear text, so be sure that no unauthorized person is shoulder surfing as you type it.

Finally, the program asks you to specify rules that restrict the hosts the user can scan. You can use these rules to, for example, enable the administrator of a system to scan only that system. Initially, it's convenient to work without restrictions, which can be accomplished by pressing Ctrl+D. Here is a sample user creation dialogue:

```
#/usr/local/bin/nessus-adduser
Using /var/tmp as a temporary file holder

Add a new nessusd user
----------------------



Login : nessus-root
Authentication (pass/cert) [pass] :
Login password : secret

User rules
----------
nessusd has a rules system which allows you to restrict the hosts
that root has the right to test. For instance, you may want
him to be able to scan his own host only.

Please see the nessus-adduser(8) man page for the rules syntax

Enter the rules for this user, and hit ctrl-D once you are done :
(the user can have an empty rules set)
```

```
Login          : root
Password       : XXXXXXXX
DN             :
Rules          :


Is that ok ? (y/n) [y] y
user added.
```

SETTING UP THE NESSUS CLIENT

After setting up the Nessus server, install and set up the Nessus client. This section shows how to set up the Microsoft Windows client. The procedure for setting up the Linux client is similar.

1. After downloading and installing the Nessus client, fill in the host, user login, and password fields of the Nessus Setup dialog box, shown in Figure 12-1. Unless the Nessus server is running on a nonstandard port, you can accept the default port number of 1241.

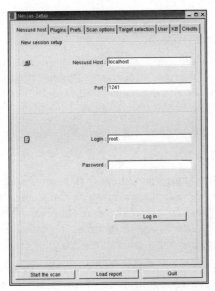

Figure 12-1: The Nessus Setup dialog box

2. Next, click the Plugins tab. The Plugins list, as shown in Figure 12-2, appears.

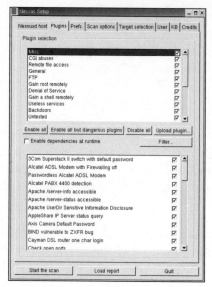

Figure 12-2: The Plugins list

3. Use the Plugins List to select the types of scans that Nessus performs. To quickly make a choice, choose Enable All or Enable All But Dangerous Plugins. The Enable All But Dangerous Plugins button enables all scans other than those likely to cause a denial of service. After choosing either default option, you can scroll through the listed plugins and individually enable or disable them according to your preferences.

4. When you've enabled the desired plugins, click Prefs. The Prefs tab, as shown in Figure 12-3, appears.

   The Prefs tab lets you configure options pertaining to individual scans. Several such options are available. Initially, you may choose to use the default options and thereby avoid being overwhelmed. However, after you gain experience with Nessus, you may want to return to this tab and change the default settings to values more consistent with your preferences.

5. When you've selected the desired preferences, click the Scan Options tab. The appearance of the dialog box changes to that shown in Figure 12-4.

   Use the Scan Options tab to specify the ports to be scanned and set other options. The default choices are generally satisfactory.

6. Finally, click the Target Selection tab. The appearance of the dialog box changes to that shown in Figure 12-5.

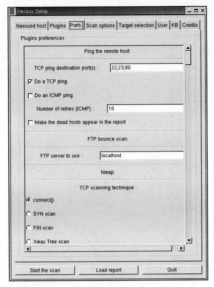

Figure 12-3: The Prefs tab

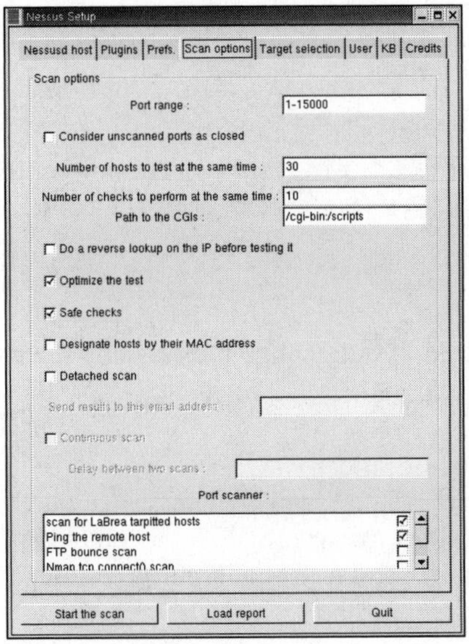

Figure 12-4: The Scan Options tab

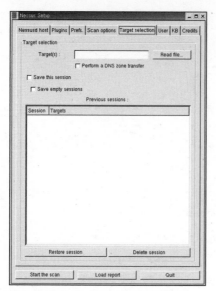

Figure 12-5: The Target Selection tab

Use the Targets Tab to specify the host names or IP addresses of the hosts to be scanned.

PERFORMING A SCAN

To perform a scan, ensure that /usr/local/bin/nessusd is running on the server and listening on port 1241. To verify that this is the case, issue the command

```
netstat -tapn
```

You should see the Nessus server listed. If not, launch it by issuing the command

```
/usr/local/bin/nessusd &
```

On the Nessus client, click on the User tab and then click the button labeled Start the scan. The scan may take several minutes to execute. When it completes, you can view the results, which identify open ports and potential security vulnerabilities. A typical report follows:

```
o 192.0.3.27 : port http (80/tcp) was found to be open

o 192.0.3.27 : port https (443/tcp) was found to be open

o 192.0.3.27 : Security hole found on port general/tcp :

Nmap did not do a UDP scan, I guess.
```

o 192.0.3.27 : port http (80/tcp) was found to be open

o 192.0.3.27 : port https (443/tcp) was found to be open

o 192.0.3.27 : Security hole found on port http (80/tcp) :
a web server is running on this port

o 192.0.3.27 : Security hole found on port https (443/tcp) :
A TLSv1 server answered on this port

o 192.0.3.27 : Security hole found on port http (80/tcp) :
The remote web server type is :

Apache/1.3.20 (Unix) (Red-Hat/Linux) mod_ssl/2.8.4 OpenSSL/0.9.6b
DAV/1.0.2 PHP/4.0.6 mod_perl/1.24_01

We recommend that you configure your web server to return
bogus versions in order to not leak information

o 192.0.3.27 : Security hole found on port https (443/tcp) :
The remote web server type is :

Apache/1.3.20 (Unix) (Red-Hat/Linux) mod_ssl/2.8.4 OpenSSL/0.9.6b
DAV/1.0.2 PHP/4.0.6 mod_perl/1.24_01

We recommend that you configure your web server to return
bogus versions in order to not leak information

o 192.0.3.27 : Security hole found on port general/tcp :
QueSO has found out that the remote host OS is
* Standard: Solaris 2.x, Linux 2.1.???, Linux 2.2, MacOS

CVE : CAN-1999-0454

o 192.0.3.27 : Security hole found on port general/icmp :

The remote host answers to an ICMP timestamp

request. This allows an attacker to know the
date which is set on your machine.

This may help him to defeat all your
time based authentication protocols.

Solution : filter out the ICMP timestamp
requests (13), and the outgoing ICMP
timestamp replies (14).

Risk factor : Low
CVE : CAN-1999-0524

o 192.0.3.27 : Security hole found on port http (80/tcp) :

The remote host is using a version of mod_ssl which is
older than 2.8.10.

This version is vulnerable to an off by one buffer overflow
which may allow a user with write access to .htaccess files
to execute abritrary code on the system with permissions
of the web server.

Solution : Upgrade to version 2.8.10 or newer
Risk factor : High

o 192.0.3.27 : Security hole found on port http (80/tcp) :

The remote host is using a version of mod_ssl which is
older than 2.8.7.

This version is vulnerable to a buffer overflow which,
albeit difficult to exploit, may allow an attacker
to obtain a shell on this host.

*** Some vendors patched older versions of mod_ssl, so this
*** might be a false positive. Check with your vendor to determine
*** if you have a version of mod_ssl that is patched for this
*** vulnerability

Solution : Upgrade to version 2.8.7 or newer
Risk factor : High
CVE : CAN-2002-0082

o 192.0.3.27 : Security hole found on port https (443/tcp) :

The remote host is using a version of mod_ssl which is
older than 2.8.7.

This version is vulnerable to a buffer overflow which,
albeit difficult to exploit, may allow an attacker
to obtain a shell on this host.

*** Some vendors patched older versions of mod_ssl, so this
*** might be a false positive. Check with your vendor to determine
*** if you have a version of mod_ssl that is patched for this
*** vulnerability

Solution : Upgrade to version 2.8.7 or newer
Risk factor : High
CVE : CAN-2002-0082

o 192.0.3.27 : Security hole found on port general/udp :
For your information, here is the traceroute to 192.0.3.27 :
192.0.3.27

o 192.0.3.27 : Security hole found on port https (443/tcp) :
Here is the SSLv2 server certificate:
Certificate:
    Data:
        Version: 3 (0x2)
        Serial Number: 0 (0x0)
        Signature Algorithm: md5WithRSAEncryption
        Issuer: C=--, ST=SomeState, L=SomeCity, O=SomeOrganization,
OU=SomeOrganizationalUnit,
CN=localhost.localdomain/Email=root@localhost.localdomain
        Validity
            Not Before: Jul 22 13:43:48 2002 GMT
            Not After : Jul 22 13:43:48 2003 GMT
        Subject: C=--, ST=SomeState, L=SomeCity, O=SomeOrganization,
OU=SomeOrganizationalUnit,
CN=localhost.localdomain/Email=root@localhost.localdomain
        Subject Public Key Info:
            Public Key Algorithm: rsaEncryption

```
              RSA Public Key: (1024 bit)
                  Modulus (1024 bit):
                      00:be:3f:12:6d:a8:c0:31:5d:18:0a:cb:54:df:69:
                      d5:85:50:97:be:2f:71:e1:80:08:f9:94:5f:a4:c9:
                      c8:45:c9:ce:6e:f0:6d:bc:04:41:b2:74:54:8e:e1:
                      52:3c:9e:3e:33:bd:26:00:fc:af:44:86:fe:28:df:
                      2a:98:13:2c:d7:08:da:ef:e9:c3:39:c7:7b:fb:4c:
                      a5:8e:79:04:33:12:47:98:80:2b:c4:df:ff:11:f8:
                      c2:89:2a:ae:90:42:a3:65:99:41:33:80:aa:65:09:
                      f3:9a:56:a1:43:d4:fe:66:f2:d1:f2:b5:ef:70:e1:
                      7e:6e:91:17:50:5f:30:6a:35
                  Exponent: 65537 (0x10001)
          X509v3 extensions:
              X509v3 Subject Key Identifier:

26:F8:DA:EB:FC:7C:78:AD:79:2B:53:D0:85:4A:ED:A4:3C:C1:14:99
              X509v3 Authority Key Identifier:

keyid:26:F8:DA:EB:FC:7C:78:AD:79:2B:53:D0:85:4A:ED:A4:3C:C1:14:99
                  DirName:/C=--
/ST=SomeState/L=SomeCity/O=SomeOrganization/OU=SomeOrganizationalUni
t/CN=localhost.localdomain/Email=root@localhost.localdomain
                  serial:00

              X509v3 Basic Constraints:
                  CA:TRUE
          Signature Algorithm: md5WithRSAEncryption
              11:71:5d:ef:93:6d:47:46:1c:73:68:64:75:88:de:ac:e1:51:
              fa:30:6f:b7:7d:8b:cf:29:23:e6:d1:e0:aa:71:fa:33:77:38:
              b1:59:54:76:b4:b5:7e:dd:df:99:d5:40:1b:35:46:30:05:4e:
              ab:64:1e:b0:93:5d:dc:0a:4e:2a:a9:a9:ba:bd:08:b7:67:63:
              1c:46:23:f0:da:8a:1b:44:5b:ae:55:73:61:bb:fa:20:2e:64:
              33:75:41:fc:e5:06:b1:58:4a:1b:48:13:04:cc:88:96:69:8b:
              d9:cb:d5:2c:ff:1b:95:61:f3:f6:2a:f4:be:9b:ed:d8:4f:b0:
              74:ee


o 192.0.3.27 : Security hole found on port https (443/tcp) :
Here is the list of available SSLv2 ciphers:
DES-CBC3-MD5            SSLv2 Kx=RSA       Au=RSA   Enc=3DES(168)
Mac=MD5
RC2-CBC-MD5            SSLv2 Kx=RSA       Au=RSA   Enc=RC2(128)
Mac=MD5
RC4-MD5               SSLv2 Kx=RSA       Au=RSA   Enc=RC4(128)
Mac=MD5
```

```
RC4-64-MD5                SSLv2 Kx=RSA      Au=RSA  Enc=RC4(64)
Mac=MD5
DES-CBC-MD5               SSLv2 Kx=RSA      Au=RSA  Enc=DES(56)
Mac=MD5
EXP-RC2-CBC-MD5           SSLv2 Kx=RSA(512) Au=RSA  Enc=RC2(40)
Mac=MD5  export
EXP-RC4-MD5              SSLv2 Kx=RSA(512) Au=RSA  Enc=RC4(40)
Mac=MD5  export
```

o 192.0.3.27 : Security hole found on port https (443/tcp) :
The SSLv2 server offers 3 strong ciphers, but also
2 medium strength and 2 weak "export class" ciphers.
The weak/medium ciphers may be chosen by an export-grade
or badly configured client software. They only offer a
limited protection against a brute force attack

Solution: disable those ciphers and upgrade your client
software if necessary

o 192.0.3.27 : Security hole found on port https (443/tcp) :
Here is the list of available SSLv3 ciphers:
```
EDH-RSA-DES-CBC3-SHA    SSLv3 Kx=DH       Au=RSA  Enc=3DES(168)
Mac=SHA1
EDH-DSS-DES-CBC3-SHA    SSLv3 Kx=DH       Au=DSS  Enc=3DES(168)
Mac=SHA1
DES-CBC3-SHA           SSLv3 Kx=RSA      Au=RSA  Enc=3DES(168)
Mac=SHA1
DHE-DSS-RC4-SHA        SSLv3 Kx=DH       Au=DSS  Enc=RC4(128)
Mac=SHA1
RC4-SHA               SSLv3 Kx=RSA      Au=RSA  Enc=RC4(128)
Mac=SHA1
RC4-MD5              SSLv3 Kx=RSA      Au=RSA  Enc=RC4(128)
Mac=MD5
EXP1024-DHE-DSS-RC4-SHA SSLv3 Kx=DH(1024) Au=DSS  Enc=RC4(56)
Mac=SHA1 export
EXP1024-RC4-SHA         SSLv3 Kx=RSA(1024) Au=RSA  Enc=RC4(56)
Mac=SHA1 export
EXP1024-DHE-DSS-DES-CBC-SHA SSLv3 Kx=DH(1024) Au=DSS  Enc=DES(56)
Mac=SHA1 export
EXP1024-DES-CBC-SHA     SSLv3 Kx=RSA(1024) Au=RSA  Enc=DES(56)
Mac=SHA1 export
EXP1024-RC2-CBC-MD5    SSLv3 Kx=RSA(1024) Au=RSA  Enc=RC2(56)
Mac=MD5  export
EXP1024-RC4-MD5       SSLv3 Kx=RSA(1024) Au=RSA  Enc=RC4(56)
```

```
Mac=MD5  export
EDH-RSA-DES-CBC-SHA      SSLv3 Kx=DH       Au=RSA  Enc=DES(56)
Mac=SHA1
EDH-DSS-DES-CBC-SHA      SSLv3 Kx=DH       Au=DSS  Enc=DES(56)
Mac=SHA1
DES-CBC-SHA             SSLv3 Kx=RSA      Au=RSA  Enc=DES(56)
Mac=SHA1
EXP-EDH-RSA-DES-CBC-SHA SSLv3 Kx=DH(512)  Au=RSA  Enc=DES(40)
Mac=SHA1 export
EXP-EDH-DSS-DES-CBC-SHA SSLv3 Kx=DH(512)  Au=DSS  Enc=DES(40)
Mac=SHA1 export
EXP-DES-CBC-SHA         SSLv3 Kx=RSA(512) Au=RSA  Enc=DES(40)
Mac=SHA1 export
EXP-RC2-CBC-MD5         SSLv3 Kx=RSA(512) Au=RSA  Enc=RC2(40)
Mac=MD5  export
EXP-RC4-MD5             SSLv3 Kx=RSA(512) Au=RSA  Enc=RC4(40)
Mac=MD5  export


o 192.0.3.27 : Security hole found on port http (80/tcp) :
The following directories were discovered:
/cgi-bin
/icons


o 192.0.3.27 : Security hole found on port http (80/tcp) :

The remote host appears to be vulnerable to the Apache
Web Server Chunk Handling Vulnerability.

If Safe Checks are enabled, this may be a false positive
since it is based on the version of Apache.  Although
unpatched Apache versions 1.2.2 and above, 1.3 through
1.3.24 and 2.0 through 2.0.36, the remote server may
be running a patched version of Apache

*** Note : as safe checks are enabled, Nessus solely relied on the
banner to issue this  alert


Solution : Upgrade to version 1.3.26 or 2.0.39 or newer
See also :
http://httpd.apache.org/info/security_bulletin_20020617.txt
    http://httpd.apache.org/info/security_bulletin_20020620.txt
Risk factor : High
CVE : CAN-2002-0392
```

```
o 192.0.3.27 : Security hole found on port http (80/tcp) :

The remote host is running a version of PHP earlier
than 4.1.2.

There are several flaws in how PHP handles
multipart/form-data POST requests, any one of which can
allow an attacker to gain remote access to the system.

Solution : Upgrade to PHP 4.1.2
Risk factor : High
CVE : CVE-2002-0081
```

Many reported potential vulnerabilities may not correspond to actual vulnerabilities. Some analysis of the report is necessary in order to interpret it properly. To help you perform this type of analysis, the report includes CVE (Common Vulnerability and Exposure) numbers that uniquely identify each reported potential vulnerability. You can learn about the referenced vulnerabilities by studying the information available at http://cve.mitre.org/.

 Red Hat security errata issued since 2000 have included CVE names. To determine whether a given CVE has been incorporated in an erratum, enter the CVE name into the search box on www.redhat.com. You can also study the errata themselves, which are available at http://rhn.redhat.com/errata.

Port Testing

To test a firewall, you can use tools such as those described in the preceding section. However, the tool you choose matters less than the approach you take. Every time you revise your firewall, you would, ideally, test every port of every host on your network and note whether any ports that should be closed are open or filtered and whether any ports that should be filtered are open. However, if you have many hosts, this type of scan can be prohibitively time consuming. Here are some ways to improve the efficiency of your scanning:

- ◆ Scan only restricted ports and ports on which listeners are known to exist, based on the results of the netstat command.

- ◆ Because UDP scans are more time consuming than TCP scans, scan only UDP ports known to be in use.

- ◆ Inspect your firewall code and scan only ports mentioned in the firewall code, plus a few randomly selected ports for which accesses are logged.

Bear in mind that each such workaround entails risk that you'll fail to notice a quirk that presents an attacker with an opportunity to breach your network security. Even if you can't fully scan every host every time you tweak your firewall, you should fully scan every host regularly. Chances are, if you're not doing so, a would-be attacker is.

Regression Testing

Regression testing is commonly performed in connection with software application maintenance. Whenever an application program is modified, a test suite is run to verify that

- ◆ The change was implemented correctly

- ◆ Previously working code has not been broken by the change

The term *regression testing* reflects the concern to ensure that the program has not regressed – that is, that all functionality existing before maintenance continues to operate properly.

If the integrity of your firewall is important, you should perform regression testing whenever the firewall code is modified, however slightly. However, regression testing is quite time consuming if it's performed manually.

An alternative to the manual regression testing of a firewall is the use of Firewall Tester – or a similar tool – to submit selected test data to the firewall and record the results. The results obtained via Firewall Tester can be compared with an *oracle,* a file that specifies the expected test results. If the firewall is operating properly, a diff between the Firewall Tester results and the oracle should be empty. It's not difficult to write one or more scripts that automate the firewall testing process and then compare the test results with an oracle.

Troubleshooting

Firewall testing aims at determining whether a firewall is operating properly. If you determine that a firewall is not operating properly, troubleshooting aims at determining the cause of improper operation.

A firewall can fail

- ◆ As the firewall script is being executed

- ◆ During operation of the firewall

Generally, it's simpler to deal with a failure of the firewall script than with a failed firewall operation.

Script problems are generally the result of syntax problems with IPTables commands or other commands included in the firewall script. Unfortunately, IPTables error messages are often unhelpful in identifying the erroneous line or lines. To troubleshoot script problems, insert this command before the likely point of error:

```
set -x
```

This command causes the script to print each command as it's being executed. You can pipe the output of the script into the `more` command to determine the specific command or commands responsible for the error:

```
/etc/rc.d/rc.iptables 2>&1 | more
```

Another way to accomplish the same result but without requiring modification of the firewall code is to issue the command

```
sh -x /etc/rc.d/rc.iptables 2>&1 |more
```

This simple procedure generally enables you to find the problem with the firewall script.

A common cause of the failure of firewalls that perform routing is an improper value of the `ip_forward` kernel option. If this is the case, issue this command:

```
sysctl -w net.ipv4.ip_forward=1
```

If the firewall begins working, add the appropriate line to the `/etc/sysctl. conf` file.

You can generally pinpoint other causes of failure by adding firewall rules that log traffic. For this method to work, you must be able to limit the volume of traffic traversing the firewall to a level that doesn't clog the logs. A good initial plan is to log packets arriving on the `INPUT`, `OUTPUT`, and `FORWARD` chains and log every dropped packet. If packets are being inappropriately accepted or dropped, you should be able to inspect the system log entries and determine the cause.

Summary

This chapter described several tools you can use to test firewalls: Nmap, Nessus, and Firewall Tester. It also provided suggestions for testing and troubleshooting firewalls. Chapter 13 explains how to maintain and administer firewalls.

Chapter 13

Administering a Firewall

IN THIS CHAPTER

- ◆ Logging and log monitoring

- ◆ Network monitoring

- ◆ Network intrusion detection

- ◆ Responding to an incident

A FIREWALL IS NOT A FIRE-AND-FORGET DEVICE that, once deployed, can then be ignored. Recall that a firewall has two major purposes with regard to attacks: prevention and detection. Because novel attacks arise regularly, a neglected firewall is likely to eventually fail to protect its network. Therefore, as explained in Chapter 11, you should keep your firewall host up to date. And, a firewall that is not regularly monitored cannot detect attacks.

This chapter explains the ongoing process of administering a firewall after you've deployed it. The chapter explains in particular how to set up and use system and firewall logs to monitor traffic and how to use several popular network-monitoring and intrusion detection applications. Finally, the chapter presents brief guidelines for responding to an intrusion incident.

Remote Logging

To maximize the value of system logs, you should configure and use

- ◆ Remote logging

- ◆ Logwatch, to monitor logged events

- ◆ Supplementary log-monitoring applications – such as Fwlogwatch, Port Scan Attack Detector, and Swatch – that generate alerts and produce activity reports

It's convenient to store a host's system logs on the host itself so that they can be accessed by the system administrator when logged in to the host. However, system logs are an asset too important to be stored on only one host. Like other important files, they should be backed up so that the loss of the original logs does not result in the loss of their contents.

Moreover, system logs are a common target of computer intruders. An intruder is likely to erase or tamper with a host's system logs in an effort to conceal the compromise of the host. After a host has been compromised, its logs can no longer be trusted.

A simple way of protecting system logs is to employ remote logging. In a remote logging configuration, a host writes the usual system log files but also sends log entries over the network to a central logging host. If the host is compromised and its logs become untrustworthy, administrators can examine the duplicate logs on the central logging host. The duplicate logs may disclose the occurrence of the compromise and give clues to its method.

Of course, an intruder who discovers that a compromised system is logging remotely may attack the logging host. However, a properly configured logging host is likely to present a difficult target. The logging host should generally run no services other than the remote logging service and possibly SSH. Moreover, SSH sessions should be allowed only from a few trusted hosts within the protected network or possibly only from hosts on a private, administrative network. If the logging host is running only these relatively secure services, an intruder finds it difficult to compromise the logging host and erase or tamper with its logs. Doing so almost certainly requires time, during which the original compromise may be detected. Moreover, remote logging can be supplemented by other measures – such as the deployment of a network intrusion detection system – which further decrease the likelihood that a host compromise will go unnoticed.

Configuring Remote Logging

Configuring remote logging is relatively simple. First, set up the host that will receive the log entries. Depending on the number of hosts sending log entries to the logging host, the logging host's logs may quickly become large. An attacker may try to take a remote logging host out of service by overflowing its storage. So, be sure to use a host that has ample disk space.

To configure the host to accept remote log entries, make sure that the firewall accepts UDP datagrams having a destination port of 514. Remote hosts use that port to send log entries to the logging host.

 You should generally configure your firewall to accept only UDP 514 datagrams having source IP addresses from hosts within your network. Otherwise, an attacker can easily disable the remote logging host by sending it many fake log entries.

Next, modify the /etc/sysconfig/syslog file by changing the line

```
SYSLOGD_OPTIONS="-m 0"
```

to read

```
SYSLOGD_OPTIONS="-r -m 0"
```

The `-r` flag specifies that the syslog process should accept remote log entries. The `-m 0` specifies that the syslog process should not write regular timestamps. If you prefer that the log file include timestamps, you can exclude this option. See the syslogd man page for more information on the syslogd options.

After you've configured syslogd, you must enable the reception of remote log entries. To do so, restart the syslogd process by issuing the command

```
service syslog restart
```

To configure a host to send log entries to the logging server, modify the host's `/etc/syslog.conf` file. To send all log entries to the logging server, add a line of this form:

```
*.*          @host
```

where *host* is the host name or IP address of the logging server. Then, restart the host's syslogd process by issuing this command:

```
service syslog restart
```

Testing Remote Logging

To verify that remote logging is working, tail the last several lines of `/var/log/messages` on the logging server. You should see a log entry indicating that logging was restarted on the remote host. If you don't find such a line, the remote host's firewall may be blocking the outgoing UDP 514 datagrams. Examine the firewall log entries on the logging host and the remote host to determine whether either host's firewall is responsible for the problem. If you cannot determine the cause of the problem, use tcpdump to verify that UDP 514 datagrams are being sent by the remote host and received by the logging host.

The Userspace Logging Daemon (ulogd) enables you to send IPTables log output to databases, files, and running processes. Using ulogd, you can create sophisticated IPTables log analysis systems. You can learn more about ulog at `http://freshmeat.net/projects/ulogd`.

Using Logwatch

The Logwatch log analysis program is installed as part of the basic Red Hat Linux installation in some Red Hat Linux releases. If it's not installed on your system, you can install it using the distribution media.

In the default Logwatch configuration, the script `/etc/cron.daily/00-log watch` causes the program to run daily, at 4:00 a.m. Many administrators find that the Logwatch default configuration works well. However, by customizing the Logwatch configuration, even more useful log analysis reports are made available.

The Main Logwatch Configuration File

The file `/etc/log.d/logwatch.conf` is the main file used to specify the Logwatch options. The default configuration is shown in Listing 13-1. Table 13-1 summarizes the configuration options provided in the main configuration file.

TABLE 13-1 THE LOGWATCH CONFIGURATION SETTINGS

Setting	Description
Archives	If the value is Yes, processes log archives in addition to /var/log/messages.
Detail	Specifies the amount of detail to be included in the report. Can be specified as a value or number: Low (0), Med (5), High (10).
LogDir	Specifies the directory containing the log file or files to be analyzed.
Logfile	Specifies the file to be analyzed. By default, Logwatch analyzes a set of files specified in other configuration files.
MailTo	Mails the analysis results to the specified e-mail address.
Print	If the value is Yes, prints the analysis results on stdout.
Range	Specifies the range of dates for which log entries are to be analyzed. Possible values are Yesterday, Today, or All.
Save	The name of a file in which analysis results are saved.
Service	The name of the service for which log entries will be analyzed or the value All, indicating that all log entries will be analyzed.

Listing 13-1: The default /etc/log.d/logwatch.conf

```
# Default Log Directory
# All log-files are assumed to be given relative to this directory.
```

```
# This should be /var/log on just about all systems...
LogDir = /var/log

# Default person to mail reports to.  Can be a local account or a
# complete email address.
MailTo = root

# If set to 'Yes', the report will be sent to stdout instead of being
# mailed to above person.
Print = No

# if set, the results will be saved in <filename> instead of mailed
# or displayed.
#Save = /tmp/logwatch

# Use archives?  If set to 'Yes', the archives of logfiles
# (i.e. /var/log/messages.1 or /var/log/messages.1.gz) will
# be searched in addition to the /var/log/messages file.
# This usually will not do much if your range is set to just
# 'Yesterday' or 'Today'... it is probably best used with
# Archives = Yes
# Range = All

# The default time range for the report...
# The current choices are All, Today, Yesterday
Range = yesterday

# The default detail level for the report.
# This can either be Low, Med, High or a number.
# Low = 0
# Med = 5
# High = 10
Detail = Low

# The 'Service' option expects either the name of a filter
# (in /etc/log.d/scripts/services/*) or 'All'.
# The default service(s) to report on.  This should be left as All for
# most people.
Service = All
# If you only cared about FTP messages, you could use these 2 lines
# instead of the above:
#Service = ftpd-messages    # Processes ftpd messages in /var/log/messages
#Service = ftpd-xferlog     # Processes ftpd messages in /var/log/xferlog
```

Continued

Listing 13-1 *(Continued)*

```
# Maybe you only wanted reports on PAM messages, then you would use:
#Service = pam_pwdb     # PAM_pwdb messages - usually quite a bit
#Service = pam          # General PAM messages... usually not many

# You can also choose to use the 'LogFile' option.  This will cause
# logwatch to only analyze that one logfile.. for example:
#LogFile = messages
# will process /var/log/messages.  This will run all the filters that
# process that logfile.  This option is probably not too useful to
# most people.  Setting 'Service' to 'All' above analyizes all LogFiles
# anyways...
```

Secondary Logwatch Configuration Files

In addition to its main configuration file, Logwatch has several secondary configuration files. These reside in

- ◆ /etc/log.d/conf/logfiles
- ◆ /etc/log.d/conf/services

LOG FILE GROUPS

A set of related log files is a *log file group.* For example, the files /var/log/messages, /var/log/messages.1, and /var/log/messages.2 are part of the messages log file group. The /etc/log.d/conf/logfiles directory contains a configuration file for each log file group to be processed by Logwatch.

These configuration files include one or more LogFile directives and optionally include Archive and ApplyStdDate directives. Each LogFile directive specifies the base name – that is, the name excluding the path – of a log file to be processed by Logwatch.

An Archive directive specifies the base name of a file to be processed by Logwatch if the Archives configuration option has the value Yes. The base name can include regular expression metacharacters that enable matching sets of files. For example, the following directives specify the archive files associated with the messages log file group:

```
Archive = messages.?
Archive = messages.?.gz
```

The ApplyStdDate directive causes Logwatch to filter log entries based on the value of the Range configuration option. The directive has this form:

```
*ApplyStdDate =
```

If the related log entries contain timestamps in a nonstandard location or format, the directive doesn't function properly.

Several additional options are supported, though they're not explained in the Logwatch documentation. For example, here's the log file group configuration file for the messages log file group:

```
# What actual file?  Defaults to LogPath if not absolute path....
LogFile = messages

# If the archives are searched, here is one or more line
# (optionally containing wildcards) that tell where they are...
# Note: if these are gzipped, you need to end with a .gz even if
#       you use wildcards...
Archive = messages.*
Archive = messages.*.gz

# Expand the repeats
*ExpandRepeats =

# Now, lets remove the services we don't care about at all...
*RemoveService = talkd
*RemoveService = telnetd
*RemoveService = inetd
*RemoveService = nfsd
*RemoveService = /sbin/mingetty

# Keep only the lines in the proper date range...
*ApplyStdDate =
```

Notice the use of the ExpandRepeats and RemoveService directives, which are not documented. Fortunately, the Logwatch scripts are well commented. It's generally easy to figure out unfamiliar configuration options.

SERVICES

The files in /etc/log.d/conf/services specify the services whose log entries are analyzed by Logwatch. Each configuration file contains one or more LogFile directives and an indefinite number of additional directives. Unlike the LogFile directive used in configuration files for log file groups, the LogFile directive in a service configuration file specifies the name of a log file group rather than the name of a log file. Additional directives are passed to the executable script that performs the analysis. Each script understands its own set of directives, which can be identified and understood by examining the scripts themselves because they're not documented. Generally, it's not necessary to fully understand the directives; instead, the comments in the service scripts adequately explain their purpose.

Here, for example, is the service configuration file used to analyze log entries made by the IDENTD service:

```
# Which logfile group...
LogFile = messages

# Only give lines pertaining to identd...
*OnlyService = identd
*RemoveHeaders =
```

Notice the OnlyService directive, which restricts the log entries in the messages log file group that are processed by the associated service script. This directive and the accompanying RemoveHeaders directive are frequently used.

CUSTOM ANALYSES

You can write your own analysis script and configure Logwatch to execute it, using log file group and services configuration files. For general guidance in doing so, see the file /usr/share/doc/logwatch-*/HOWTO-Make-Filter.

One shortcoming of Logwatch is that it does not support the analysis of log entries from remote hosts. You can analyze the log files on the central logging host, but the analysis reports aggregate data from all remote hosts, making the reports difficult to interpret and use effectively. You can circumvent this problem in either of two ways:

◆ Run Logwatch separately on each reporting host.

◆ Preprocess files on the central logging host, placing entries from each reporting host into a separate file. Then, run Logwatch on these files.

Other Programs for Auditing and Analyzing Logs

You have, in addition to the Logwatch utility included in the Red Hat Linux distribution, many other options for auditing and analyzing logs. Among the most popular such utilities are

◆ Fwlogwatch

◆ Port Scan Attack Detector (Psad)

◆ Swatch

Fwlogwatch

Written by Boris Wesslowski, Fwlogwatch processes system log entries generated by IPChains or IPTables. In addition, Fwlogwatch supports these log entry formats:

◆ Cisco IOS

◆ Cisco PIX

◆ Ipfilter (BSD, HP-UX, Irix, and Solaris)

◆ Snort

◆ Windows XP firewall

Fwlogwatch is generally run as a Cron job. It can be run in any of three modes:

◆ In *log summary mode,* Fwlogwatch generates a plain text or HTML report that can be e-mailed to specified users or written to a file. By accessing DNS and WHOIS servers, Fwlogwatch can display host name and address block information. Log summary mode supports many options for filtering and sorting data so that customized reports can be easily produced.

◆ In *interactive report mode,* Fwlogwatch generates reports that can be used to notify abuse contacts of attacking networks, incident response teams, or other interested parties. In interactive mode, you can manually revise report contents – for example, you can mask or obfuscate sensitive information. To facilitate incident recordkeeping, Fwlogatch automatically assigns incident tracking numbers.

◆ In *real-time response mode,* Fwlogwatch runs continually rather than as a Cron job. When Fwlogwatch detects a log entry of interest, it can send an e-mail message, revise the firewall configuration, or perform any other action that can be coded as a shell script. Real-time response mode features a Web interface through which you can monitor the Fwlogwatch status.

INSTALLING AND CONFIGURING Fwlogwatch

You can obtain Fwlogwatch from its Web site, `http://cert.uni-stuttgart.de/ projects/fwlogwatch/`. You can download the program as a TAR file or RPM package. To install Fwlogwatch, download the RPM package and issue a command of this form:

```
rpm -Uvh fwlogwatch-0.8.1-1.i386.rpm
```

where `fwlogwatch-0.8.1-1.i386.rpm` is the name of the downloaded file.

To run Fwlogwatch as a Cron job, place a command of the following form in a file named /etc/cron.daily/fwlogwatch:

```
fwlogwatch | /bin/mail -s fwlogwatch user@domain
```

where *user@domain* is the e-mail address to which the generated daily report should be sent. Then, make the file executable by issuing the command

```
chmod u+x /etc/cron.daily/fwlogwatch
```

To run Fwlogwatch in real-time response, mode, issue the command

```
chkconfig fwlogwatch on
```

To immediately start Fwlogwatch, issue the command

```
service fwlogwatch start
```

Fwlogwatch REPORTS

The following example of an Fwlogwatch report shows only the first two log entries:

```
fwlogwatch summary
Generated Tue Aug 06 04:14:18 PDT 2002 by root.

4242 of 14387 entries in the file "/var/log/messages" are packet
logs, 2237 have unique characteristics.

990 entries were excluded by configuration.

First packet log entry: Aug 04 04:16:49, last: Aug 06 04:13:25.

00:00:01:18 bridge IPT (UDP)  - br0 PHYSIN=eth0 5 udp packets from
4.47.54.110 (crtntx1-ar1-4-47-054-110.crtntx1.dsl-verizon.net)
[4.0.0.0/8 NET-SATNET AS1 GTE Internetworking] port 3350 to
192.0.3.27 (cstrike.example.com) port 137 -

00:00:01:17 bridge IPT (UDP)  - br0 PHYSIN=eth0 6 udp packets from
4.47.54.110 (crtntx1-ar1-4-47-054-110.crtntx1.dsl-verizon.net)
[4.0.0.0/8 NET-SATNET AS1 GTE Internetworking] port 3556 to
192.0.3.27 (cstrike.example.com) port 137 -
```

Notice the ISP information, obtained via WHOIS, appearing within square brackets.

CUSTOMIZING Fwlogwatch

You can customize the operation of Fwlogwatch by revising its configuration file, `/etc/fwlogwatch.config`. For information on the configuration directives the program supports, see the program's man page and comments within the sample configuration file distributed with the program.

Port Scan Attack Detector

Port Scan Attack Detector (Psad) works with IPChains and IPTables to detect port scan attacks. Psad can respond to port scans by sending e-mail alerts to administrators. It can also be configured to block IP addresses that are the source of attacks.

You can obtain Psad from its Web site, `http://www.cipherdyne.com/psad/`. From the Web site, you can download it as a TAR file or RPM package. To install the downloaded RPM package, issue a command of this form:

```
rpm -Uvh psad-0.9.2-1rm.i386.rpm
```

where `psad-0.9.2-1rm.i386.rpm` is the name of the downloaded file. To start the psad service, issue the command

```
service psad start
```

Because Psad acquires data from the system logs, your firewall code must log all attacks of interest. Otherwise, Psad cannot analyze them.

Swatch

Simple Watcher (Swatch), written by Todd Atkins and Stephen Hansen, monitors the system logs and generates real-time alerts. The alerts can take any of several forms:

- ◆ Ring the terminal bell.
- ◆ Send an e-mail message.
- ◆ Execute a script.

Swatch is especially useful when used to monitor centralized system logs. It helps prevent important log entries from being lost because of the volume of log traffic.

INSTALLING SWATCH

You can obtain Swatch from its Web site, `http://www.oit.ucsb.edu/~eta/swatch/`. Swatch is distributed as a TAR file. To install Swatch, you must first install several RPMs and one Perl module. The RPMs are shown in this list:

- ◆ perl-Date-Calc-5.0-22.i386.rpm

- ◆ perl-TimeDate-1.10-21.i386.rpm

- ◆ perl-Time-HiRes-1.20-22.i386.rpm

These packages are included in Red Hat Linux 7.3 and later.

You also need the File::Tail Perl module, which you can obtain from the Comprehensive Perl Archive Network (CPAN), at http://www.cpan.org/. The Perl modules contained in the three RPMs mentioned earlier also reside on CPAN. You can download and compile the Perl modules rather than install the RPMs, if you prefer. However, simply installing the RPMs is generally more convenient.

After downloading the TAR file containing the File::Tail module, unpack the contents of the TAR file by issuing a command of the form

```
tar zxf File-Tail-0.98.tar.gz
```

where File-Tail-0.98.tar.gz is the name of the downloaded file. Unpacking the file creates a directory having a name similar to the base name of the file – for example, File-Tail-0.9. Make that directory the current directory and then issue these commands as root:

```
perl Makefile.PL
make
make install
```

If you downloaded other modules from CPAN, you can install them by following a similar procedure.

Now, download the Swatch distribution TAR file. Then, unpack it by issuing a command of the form:

```
tar zxf swatch-3.0.4.tar.gz
```

where swatch-3.0.4.tar.gz is the name of the downloaded file. The tar command creates a directory with a name similar to the base name of the TAR file itself. For example, the directory might be named /swatch-3.0.4. Change the current working directory to the created directory. Then issue these commands:

```
perl Makefile.PL
make
make install
```

SETTING UP THE SWATCH SERVICE

Swatch does not include a SysVInit script, without which it's awkward to stop and stop the Swatch service. However, you can easily code one yourself. Here's an example:

```
#! /bin/sh
#
# chkconfig: 2345 60 20
# description: The swatch service monitors system logs, sending \
#     alerts when specified events occur.
# processname: swatch

# Get config.
. /etc/sysconfig/network

# Get functions
. /etc/init.d/functions


RETVAL=0

start() {
    echo -n $"Starting swatch service: "
    /usr/bin/swatch -c /etc/swatch.conf --daemon
    RETVAL=$?
    echo
    [ $RETVAL -eq 0 ] && touch /var/lock/subsys/swatch
    return $RETVAL
}

stop() {
    echo -n $"Stopping swatch service: "
    killproc swatch
    RETVAL=$?
    echo
    [ $RETVAL -eq 0 ] && rm -f /var/lock/subsys/swatch
    return $RETVAL
}

restart() {
    stop
    start
}

# See how we were called.
case "$1" in
 start)
    start
    ;;
```

```
stop)
    stop
    ;;
status)
    status swatch
    ;;
restart)
    restart
    ;;
condrestart)
    [ -f /var/lock/subsys/swatch ] && restart || :
    ;;
*)
    echo $"Usage: $0 {start|stop|status|restart}"
    exit 1
    ;;
esac

exit $?
```

CONFIGURING SWATCH

Before starting the Swatch service, you should supply the service with a configuration file. The Swatch distribution directory contains sample configurations in its /examples directory. Here is a simple configuration file:

```
ignore /rsync/

watchfor /session opened for user root/
  echo bold
  bell 3

watchfor /authentication failure/
  echo bold
  bell3

watchfor /ANONYMOUS FTP LOGIN/
  echo bold
  bell 3

watchfor /.*/
  echo
```

The file contains two main directives:

- ♦ ignore causes Swatch to ignore log entries matching the following regular expression.
- ♦ watchfor causes Swatch to perform a series of actions when a log entry matches the following regular expression.

Table 13-2 summarizes the actions supported by Swatch. See the man page for the syntax used to specify actions.

TABLE 13-2 SWATCH ACTIONS

Action	Description
bell	Rings the terminal bell.
continue	Causes Swatch to attempt to match subsequent patterns after performing the actions in the current action block.
echo	Prints the matched line to stdout. The directive supports a variety of colors and modes.
exec	Executes a shell command using as arguments the fields extracted from the matched line.
mail	Sends an e-mail message containing the matched line.
pipe	Pipes the matched line into a command.
quit	Causes Swatch to terminate.
throttle	Limits the frequency with which the associated pattern is matched.
write	Uses the write command to send the matched line to specified users.

After creating your configuration file, save it as /etc/swatch.conf for compatibility with the SysVInit script given earlier in this chapter, in the section "Setting Up the Swatch Service." Then, move your SysVInit script to /etc/init.d/swatch, give the root user execute permission to the file, and issue this command:

```
chkconfig --add swatch
```

This command establishes the symbolic links used by the SysVInit facility. After they're established, you can start Swatch by issuing the command

```
service swatch start
```

By default, Swatch monitors the /var/log/messages file. However, you can instruct Swatch to monitor another file by using the -t flag. See the man page for details. To monitor multiple log files, simultaneously run multiple instances of Swatch. Simply tweak the SysVInit file appropriately.

WORKING WITH SWATCH

After starting Swatch, log in as root or perform another action that triggers a rule in the Swatch configuration file. Within a few seconds, Swatch should execute the action associated with the rule.

If Swatch isn't working correctly, stop the service. Then, run Swatch interactively by issuing a command having this form:

```
/usr/bin/swatch -c /etc/swatch.conf -f filename
```

where filename is the name of the log file you want to analyze. Swatch makes a single pass through the file rather than run continuously. You can iteratively tweak the Swatch configuration and issue this command until your configuration is correct.

Network Monitoring

In addition to monitoring system logs, you should more generally monitor the status of networks. The first indication that a host has been compromised may be an unexpected surge in network traffic volume or the unavailability of a host or service. In this section, I describe two tools useful for network monitoring.

NetSaint

NetSaint, a flexible tool for monitoring hosts and networks, is capable of monitoring both the availability of services and the use of resources, such as processor load and disk usage. Via the NetSaint Web-based interface, you can view system status, as shown in Figure 13-1. NetSaint can also generate real-time alerts, which can be delivered by e-mail, pager, or a user-defined method. NetSaint monitoring and notification are customizable, so you can adapt it to meet almost any requirement.

From the NetSaint menu, you can select any of about one to a half-dozen displays and reports. Figure 13-2 shows the display known as the Tactical Overview. This display shows the number of hosts and services in each possible status category. It also shows what flags, notifications, event handlers, and checks are active. Finally, in the Network Health section, colored bars show the overall status of hosts and services at a glance.

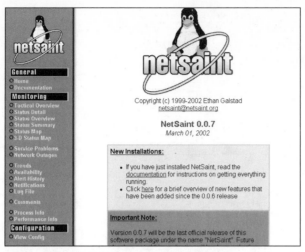

Figure 13-1: The NetSaint main screen and menu

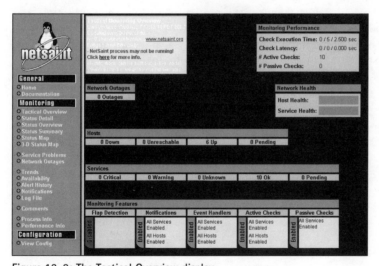

Figure 13-2: The Tactical Overview display

NetSaint can show detailed status information as well as summary status information. Figure 13-3 shows the Status Detail display, which presents the current status of each host and service. The display shows the last time the service was checked for availability and the time during which the service has been available. Names of hosts and services are links that let you drill down to view even more detailed information.

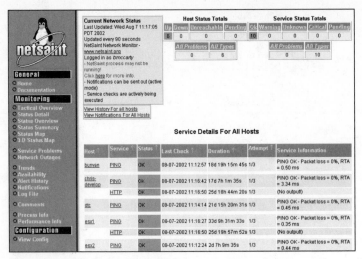

Figure 13-3: The Status Detail display

Figure 13-4 shows the Host Trends display, a bar chart that shows the time and duration of important events affecting a host. The display can be configured to show a time period of particular interest. The display also reports the percentage of time that the host was up, down, unreachable, or in an indeterminate state.

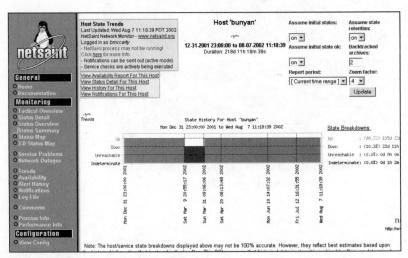

Figure 13-4: The Host Trends display

You can quickly view the uptime records of all the hosts on a network by viewing the Availability display, as shown in Figure 13-5. This display shows the time spent by each host in the state categories up, down, unreachable, and indeterminate. The report period is user selectable, like that of the Host Trends display.

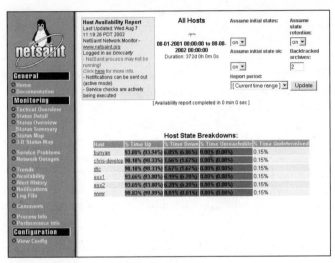

Figure 13-5: The Availability display

The Alert History display, as shown in Figure 13-6, records the alerts issued by NetSaint. You can use the display to verify that you received all the alerts NetSaint generated.

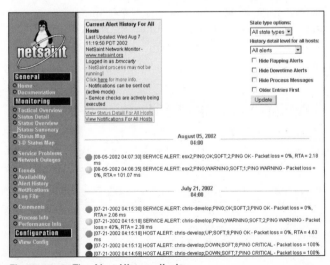

Figure 13-6: The Alert History display

TIP   As mentioned, NetSaint provides several additional displays and options beyond those presented. See the NetSaint Web site, at `http://www.netsaint.org/,` for examples of other displays.

INSTALLING NetSaint

You can obtain the NetSaint RPM files via the NetSaint Web site, which contains a link to the FTP server from which you can download them. You need these packages:

◆ `netsaint`

◆ `netsaint-plugins`

◆ `netsaint-www`

In addition to Netsaint, you should generally install the following packages:

◆ `apache`

◆ `gd`

◆ `gd-devel`

However, if you don't want to view the NetSaint Web-based graphical displays, you can omit installing these packages. In that case, you can also omit downloading and installing the `netsaint-www` package.

You can install the NetSaint packages and related packages in the usual way, by using the `rpm` command or the GnomeRPM tool. However, depending on your system's configuration, you may find that you need additional packages.

CONFIGURING NetSaint

NetSaint uses three main configuration files:

◆ The main configuration file, `/etc/netsaint/netsaint.cfg`

◆ The host configuration file, `/etc/netsaint/hosts.cfg`

◆ The CGI configuration file, `/etc/netsaint/nscgi.cfg`

The main configuration file and CGI configuration file don't generally require any changes. If you want to explore them, you can

◆ Consult the documentation and man page installed with the `netsaint` package.

◆ View the documentation residing on the NetSaint Web site.

◆ Read the comments contained in the default configuration files.

In the host configuration file, you must specify the hosts and services that you want NetSaint to monitor. Follow these general steps:

1. Configure one or more host groups.

2. Configure one or more hosts for each host group.

3. Configure one or more contact groups, each representing a group of persons who receive alerts.

4. Configure one or more contacts for each contact group.

5. Configure one or more services to be monitored for each host.

You'll probably find that the comments and examples in the default configuration file are sufficient to guide you in specifying the proper directives. If not, consult the documentation available on the NetSaint Web site.

After you've revised the configuration files, check the configuration by issuing the command

```
/usr/sbin/netsaint -v /etc/netsaint/netsaint.cfg
```

Fix any errors before starting NetSaint for the first time.

RUNNING NetSaint

To start NetSaint, first ensure that the httpd service is running, starting it if necessary. Then, issue the command

```
service netsaint start
```

You should be able to access NetSaint via the URL http://host.domain/netsaint/, where host.domain is the host name and domain name of the host on which NetSaint is running.

Because NetSaint is a CGI program, it may — and likely does — present security vulnerabilities. You should configure your Web server to forbid access to the NetSaint directory tree by untrusted hosts. You should also use the htpasswd facility to limit NetSaint access to authorized users only.

MRTG

The Multi Router Traffic Grapher (MRTG), which is part of the Red Hat Linux distribution, lets you conveniently visualize the volume of traffic traversing network switches and routers via a Web browser. Figure 13-7 shows the top portion of a typical MRTG Web page. In addition to the daily graph, MRTG provides several additional graphs:

◆ Weekly

◆ Monthly

◆ Yearly

Using MRTG, you can easily spot unexpected spikes in traffic volume. Such spikes may indicate inbound or outbound scanning activity or other conditions relevant to network security.

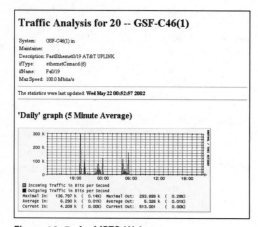

Figure 13-7: An MRTG Web page

CONFIGURING MRTG

The easiest way to configure MRTG is by using the `cfgmaker` program. To do so, issue the command

```
/usr/bin/cfgmaker --global 'WorkDir: /var/www/html/mrtg' \
                  --global 'Options[_]: bits,growright'  \
                  --output /etc/mrtg/conf                \
                  community@router.domain
```

where *community* is a community string that provides read access to your router or switch having the host name *router.domain*.

RUNNING MRTG

Many MRTG users run MRTG as an hourly Cron task. To do so, create a file containing these commands:

```
#!/bin/sh
/usr/bin/mrtg /etc/mrtg/mrtg.conf --logging /var/www/html/mrtg
```

Save the file as `/etc/cron.hourly/mrtg` and give the root user `execute` access to the file.

When the Cron task runs, it places HTML and graphics files in the directory `/var/www/html/mrtg`, which was specified when `cfgmaker` was run. You can view the MRTG reports by using any graphics-capable browser.

 Because MRTG exposes the structure of your network to anyone viewing its reports, secure them from unauthorized access. Configure your Web server to forbid access to the `/mrtg` directory tree by untrusted hosts, and use the `htpasswd` facility to limit MRTG access to authorized users.

Network Intrusion Detection

Reliably detecting network attacks and intrusions is difficult. Two types of error are possible:

- A *false negative* is the failure to report an actual attack or intrusion.

- A *false positive* is a report of an attack or intrusion where none exists.

System logs are prone to both false negatives and false positives. False negatives occur because system logs weren't originally designed to detect attacks and intrusions. You can minimize the number of false negatives by

- Writing firewall code that logs probable attacks and intrusions

- Using log-analysis programs to point out interesting log entries possibly associated with attacks and intrusions

Suppressing false positives in system logs is more difficult because firewall code can examine only packet headers. Often, information in packet headers is sufficient to classify a packet as suspicious but not sufficient to identify an attack with certainty. If you log such a packet, you may generate a false positive. However, if you choose not to log the packet, you may generate a false negative. Either way, your identification is less than fully reliable.

Network monitors, such as NetSaint and MRTG, are even less reliable than system logs as a means of identifying attacks and intrusions. Unavailable services or traffic volume anomalies may or may not be associated with an attack or intrusion. Moreover, many attacks and intrusions cause neither service unavailability nor traffic volume anomalies. Thus, when used to detect attacks and instructions, network monitoring generates a significant level of false positives and false negatives.

Fortunately, other tools designed for detecting attacks and intrusions are available. These tools are known as *network intrusion detectors*. In comparison with system logs and network monitors, network intrusion detectors identify attacks and intrusions more reliably.

However, even network intrusion detectors are imperfect. Network intrusion detection technology is relatively young. Many network intrusion detectors generate a significant number of false positives that an analyst must inspect and manually classify. The better network intrusion detectors enable an analyst to customize an operation to eliminate false positives that occur repeatedly. Over time, an analyst can tune the operation of such a network intrusion detector so that it detects attacks and intrusions quite reliably.

The following sections describe several popular open-source network intrusion detectors.

DShield

DShield is a distributed intrusion detection system, one that collects data from many sources. Network administrators around the globe regularly submit suspicious log entries to the DShield database. Almost 100 million log entries are reported monthly. On the DShield Web site, at `http://www.dshield.org/`, users can view a variety of statistics on attack types and attacking IP addresses. For instance, as shown in Figure 13-8, the DShield home page presents a map of the globe showing the geographical origin of recent attacks and the relative frequency of attacked ports.

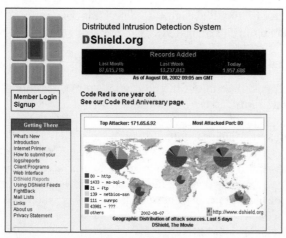

Figure 13-8: The DShield main page

Figure 13-9 shows another useful DShield report, the Top 10 Target Ports. This report shows the ports most frequently probed and attacked. For each port, a graphic shows a one-month history of activity. The report compares the relative threat levels associated with various services.

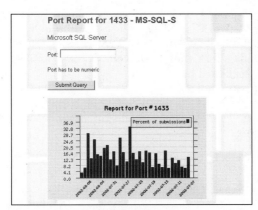

Top 10 Target Ports

This list shows the top 10 most probed ports. You may also want to check the Port of the Day which will discuss a recently active port in more detail. Our Internet Primer explains what these terms mean.

Service Name	Port Number	Activity Past Month	Explanation
http	80		HTTP Web server
ms-sql-s	1433		Microsoft SQL Server
ftp	21		FTP servers typically run on this port
sunrpc	111		RPC, vulnurable on many Linux systems. Can get root
netbios-ssn	139		Windows File Sharing Probe
???	43981		Netware/IP
smtp	25		Mail server listens on this port.
ssh	22		Secure Shell, old versions are vulnerable
ingreslock	1524		
bootps	67		

The Table   Entries for the Top 10 Target Ports table are selected based on the number of accesses to a particular port for the past 5 days. This data was last updated on August 09, 2002 09:01

Figure 13-9: The DShield Top 10 Target Ports page

To obtain more detailed information about a port of interest, view the DShield port report, as shown in Figure 13-10. This report uses a much larger graphic to depict activity. The report also includes daily counts of activity for the specified port, although they are not shown in the figure.

Port Report for 1433 - MS-SQL-S

Microsoft SQL Server

Port: [   ]

Port has to be numeric

[Submit Query]

Report for Port # 1433

Percent of submissions ■

Figure 13-10: A DShield port report

DShield also provides a Web page that lets you query an IP address to determine whether it has been reported as the source of recent attacks. As shown in Figure 13-11, the report generated by DShield includes information about the associated netblock and service provider. DShield automatically queries the problem registry, making DShield quite a bit more convenient than the whois command.

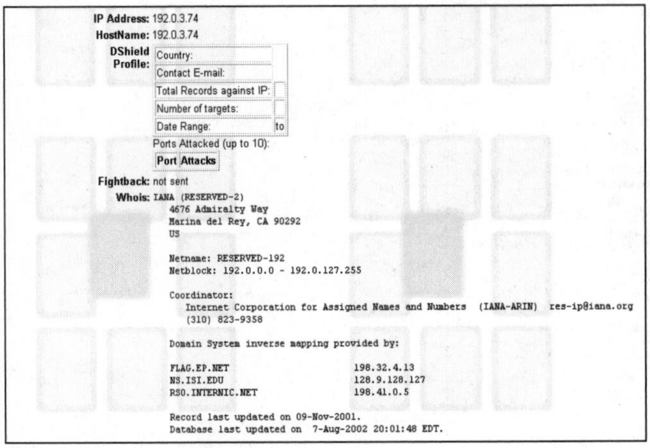

Figure 13-11: A DShield IP report

Other popular DShield reports include a list of the ten IP addresses generating the largest number of reported probes and attacks and a list of IP network addresses that appear to be consistent sources of attacks, referred to as the *block list*. Many administrators configure their firewalls to block all traffic from networks listed in the block list.

ACQUIRING DShield

The DShield Web site lets you enter reports of probes and attacks. However, manually entering this information is quite inconvenient. Instead, most users run an automated script that periodically e-mails information to DShield. DShield provides scripts that process system log entries generated by

- ◆ IPChains

- ◆ IPTables

- ◆ LaBrea

- ◆ Portsentry

- ◆ Snort

DShield supports about one dozen other sources of log entries, including those generated by commercial firewalls.

To acquire DShield for use with IPTables, download the Linux 2.4.*x* IPTables client script from the DShield Web site. The script is distributed as a TAR file, which you can unpack by issuing the command

```
tar zxf iptables.tar.gz
```

where `iptables.tar.gz` is the name of the downloaded file. The command creates a directory named using the base name of the TAR file, `iptables`.

CONFIGURING DShield

Configuring and then installing DShield is easier than installing and then configuring it. And, you should configure DShield in test mode before attempting to configure it in live mode. So, the sequence of the installation and configuration procedure may seem odd.

To configure DShield in test mode, modify the `test.cnf` file to point to your system's log file. As shown in Listing 13-2, the `test.cnf` file points by default to `/var/log/messages`, so you may be able to skip this step.

Listing 13-2: test.cnf

```
log=/var/log/messages
whereto=./output.txt
from=nobody@nowhere.com
userid=0
to=report+hield.org
cc=
bcc=
sendmail=/usr/sbin/sendmail -oi -t
source_exclude=./dshield-source-exclude.lst
target_exclude=./dshield-target-exclude.lst
source_port_exclude=./dshield-source-port-exclude.lst
target_port_exclude=./dshield-target-port-exclude.lst
linecnt=./dshield.cnt
verbose=Y
debug=Y
rotate=N
obfus=N
```

After `test.cnf` correctly points to your log file, run the `test.wrapper.sh` script from within the `/iptables` directory:

```
./test.wrapper.sh
```

Running the script creates the file debug.txt in the /iptables directory. Using a text editor, examine the contents of debug.txt to determine whether the script operated successfully.

After the test script runs successfully, you can install DShield and customize its configuration.

INSTALLING DShield

To install the client, move the files in the /iptables directory to new locations, as specified in Table 13-3. You should also read the contents of the file /usr/local/doc/dshield/README.txt, which explains the installation and configuration processes. (These may have been updated after this book was published.)

TABLE 13-3 DSHIELD CLIENT FILE LOCATIONS

File	Location
changelog.txt	/usr/local/doc/dshield
CVS	/usr/local/doc/dshield
dshield.cnf	/etc
dshield-source-exclude.lst	/etc
dshield-source-port-exclude.lst	/etc
dshield-target-exclude.lst	/etc
dshield-target-port-exclude.lst	/etc
iptables.pl	/usr/local/bin
README.txt	/usr/local/doc/dshield
test.cnf	/etc
test_wrapper.sh	/usr/local/bin

CUSTOMIZING DShield

The main DShield configuration file is /etc/dshield.cnf. You should modify its log directive to point to the system log file, just as you previously modified the same directive in the test.cnf file. Listing 13-3 shows the dshield.cnf file, stripped of explanatory comments. In addition to the log directive, you should modify these directives:

- ◆ from should specify your return e-mail address.

- ◆ userid should specify your DShield userid.

You can obtain a DShield userid by registering via the DShield Web page. If you want to obfuscate the reported IP address information, change the value of the obfus directive from N to Y. Otherwise, DShield may forward your report to the abuse contact of the attacker's ISP, which may publicize your IP addresses more widely than you'd like.

Listing 13-3: dshield.cnf

```
from=nobody@nowhere.com
userid=0
to=report÷hield.org
cc=
bcc=
log=/var/log/messages
sendmail=/usr/sbin/sendmail -oi -t
whereto=MAIL
source_exclude=/etc/dshield-source-exclude.lst
target_exclude=/etc/dshield-target-exclude.lst
source_port_exclude=/etc/dshield-source-port-exclude.lst
target_port_exclude=/etc/dshield-target-port-exclude.lst
obfus=N
linecnt=/tmp/dshield.cnt
verbose=N
debug=N
rotate=N
```

The DShield configuration file identifies four secondary files that affect the DShield operation:

- ◆ dshield-source-exclude.ls

- ◆ dshield-target-exclude.ls

- ◆ dshield-source-port-exclude.lst

- ◆ dshield-target-port-exclude.lst

You can revise these files to filter log entries that would otherwise be reported. You can filter by source IP address, target IP address, source port, or target port. IP addresses and ports can be specified individually, one per line, or as ranges. For further information on the DShield configuration directives, see the comments in the configuration file.

RUNNING DShield

DShield should not be configured to run continuously. Running it as a hourly Cron task is generally ideal. To do so, create the file `/etc/cron.hourly/dshield`, containing these lines:

```
#!/bin/sh

# Send email to dshield.org, summarizing snort alerts from
# /var/log/messages.

#/usr/local/bin/iptables.pl
```

Then, give the root user `execute` access to the file. After an hour has elapsed, log in to the DShield Web site and view your Recent Submissions page. Verify that the page correctly reflects recent system activity, tweaking the configuration file as necessary to resolve problems.

TIP If your browser is configured to cache Web pages, you may need to clear the cache in order to view the most recent version of the Recent Submissions page.

Portsentry

Portsentry is a simple intrusion detection system that can be configured to monitor unused ports. When a remote host accesses a monitored port, Portsentry logs the incident. Optionally, Portsentry can also

- ◆ Add the offending host to the `/etc/hosts.deny` file, thereby configuring TCP wrappers to block access to services protected by TCP wrappers.

- ◆ Reconfigure the firewall to block all traffic from the offending host.

A clever attacker might spoof IP addresses to induce Portsentry to block access from important hosts. The Portsentry configuration options include a file that lets you identify trusted hosts from which apparent attacks are ignored.

CONFIGURING PORTSENTRY

Portsentry requires the `libpcap` RPM package, which is part of the Red Hat Linux distribution. If you have not already installed `libpcap`, you should do so before installing Portsentry. You can download the Portsentry TAR file from `http://www.psionic.com/products/index.html`. After downloading the file, unpack it by issuing a command of the form

```
tar zxf portsentry-2.0b1.tar.gz
```

where *portsentry-2.0b1.tar.gz* is the name of the downloaded file.

 TIP Portsentry was once distributed as part of the Red Hat Powertools distribution. However, it's best that you download the most current version of Portsentry via the Web.

Once you've downloaded the file, change the current working directory to the directory created by the `tar` command. There, you find almost two dozen files. Among them are the ones in this list:

◆ `Makefile` is the makefile used to compile and install Portsentry.

◆ `portsentry.conf` is the Portsentry configuration file.

◆ `portsentry.ignore` identifies hosts and networks that should not be classed as attackers.

◆ `README.install` contains detailed installation instructions.

To prepare to compile and install Portsentry, perform these steps:

1. Edit the makefile, replacing the line

   ```
   CFLAGS = -O -Wall
   ```

   near the top of the file with the line

   ```
   CFLAGS = -O -Wall -I/usr/include/pcap
   ```

2. Edit the `portsentry.conf` file, replacing the line

   ```
   INTERFACE="auto"
   ```

   near the top of the file with the line

   ```
   INTERFACE="ethn"
   ```

   where `ethn` is the network interface on which Portsentry should listen. Also replace the line

   ```
   INTERFACE_ADDRESS="XXX.XXX.XXX.XXX"
   ```

   with a line that specifies the IP address associated with the network interface — for example:

```
INTERFACE_ADDRESS="192.0.34.72"
```

You should also review the values assigned in the TCP_PORTS and UDP_PORTS directives, removing any ports that are associated with services running on the local host.

3. Edit the portsentry.ignore file, adding lines that specify the IP address of any host that you do not want to be considered an attacker and blocked. You can specify entire networks using CIDR notation as explained in Chapter 2, if you like. The portsentry.ignore file should include, at a minimum, lines specifying these elements:

- The local network, 127.0.0.0/24

- The IP addresses associated with local interfaces

- The IP addresses of trusted routers

  If you specify too many entries, your Portsentry may fail to report actual attacks. However, if you specify too few entries, Portsentry may take down your network by erroneously blocking access to important hosts.

BUILDING AND INSTALLING PORTSENTRY
To build Portsentry, issue these commands:

```
make linux
make install
```

RUNNING PORTSENTRY
To launch Portsentry, issue the command

```
/usr/local/psionic/portsentry2/portsentry
```

Tail the /var/log/messages file to determine whether Portsentry is running properly. You should see log entries resembling the following:

```
Aug  8 10:05:38 rhl72 portsentry[882]: adminalert: Monitoring interface eth0 and
address: 192.0.34.33
Aug  8 10:05:38 rhl72 portsentry[882]: adminalert: Initializing PortSentry BPF
filters.
Aug  8 10:05:38 rhl72 portsentry[882]: adminalert: Monitoring TCP ports:
1,11,15,79,111,119,143,515,540,635,666,1080,1524,2000,6667,12345,12346,20034,273
74,27665,31337,32771,32772,32773,32774,40421,49724,54320,54321
Aug  8 10:05:38 rhl72 portsentry[882]: adminalert: Monitoring UDP ports:
1,7,9,69,161,162,513,635,2049,27444,32770,32771,32772,32773,32774,31337,54321
Aug  8 10:05:38 rhl72 portsentry[882]: adminalert: PortSentry is initialized and
monitoring.
```

To verify that Portsentry is operating properly, log in to a host not listed in the `portsentry.ignore` file. Then, telnet to a TCP port on the Portsentry host, specifying a destination port that is being monitored. For example:

```
telnet 192.0.3.74 1
```

Tail the log file. You should see entries such as these:

```
Aug  8 10:33:01 rhl72 portsentry[882]: attackalert: Host 192.0.34.129 has been
blocked via wrappers with string: "ALL: 192.0.34.129"
Aug  8 10:33:01 rhl72 portsentry[882]: attackalert: TCP SYN scan from host
192.0.34.129/192.0.34.129 to TCP port: 1 from TCP port: 35965
Aug  8 10:33:01 rhl72 portsentry[922]: attackalert: Host: 192.0.34.129 is
already blocked - Ignoring
```

If the simulated attack is not logged, check the Portsentry configuration files.

Portsentry provides several options not described in this relatively brief overview. For more information on Portsentry, see the Psionic Web site, `http://www.psionic.com/products/index.html`, and the documentation that accompanies the distribution.

Snort

Snort is a sophisticated open-source network intrusion detection system. Its capabilities and performance rival those of commercial network intrusion detection systems costing thousands of dollars. Like IPTables and other packet filtering programs, Snort can inspect packet headers. But, Snort can also inspect packet payloads. It compares the contents of packet headers and payloads against a database of signatures associated with more than 1,500 attacks and generates alerts when a match is detected. Snort signatures are relatively easy to write, so Snort can be quickly extended to handle new attacks as they become known.

MODES OF OPERATION

Snort can operate in any of three basic modes:

- Sniffer mode
- Packet logger mode
- Network intrusion detection mode

In sniffer mode, Snort prints packets to the screen as they're detected. Sniffer mode is primarily useful for troubleshooting Snort.

In packet logger mode, Snort records packets to disk. Snort can write the packets in any of several formats, including Tcpdump format. Snort can subsequently process a Tcpdump log as input, enabling you to analyze data offline rather than in real time.

In network intrusion detection mode, Snort analyzes traffic and generates alerts whenever a packet or series of packets matches an attack signature. Snort can generate alerts in a variety of ways. It can

◆ Write a log of one-line alerts.

◆ Write a log of multiline alerts.

◆ Send alerts to the Syslog facility.

◆ Send alerts to a UNIX socket.

◆ Generate SNMP traps.

◆ Send alerts via Windows WinPopUp messages.

◆ Send alerts to a database.

 TIP

Tcpdump itself is capable of writing packet to disk. However, Snort can reassemble fragments and perform other operations designed to counteract an attacker's attempts to evade detection. Consequently, you may prefer to log packets via Snort rather than via Tcpdump, particularly if you plan to analyze them for indications of attacks and intrusions.

Snort's one-line alerts resemble the following:

```
09/05/02-16:22:36.933776  [**] [1:1807:1] WEB-MISC Transfer-
Encoding: chunked [**] [Classification: Web Application Attack]
[Priority: 1] {TCP} 211.147.9.26:3954 -> 192.0.34.72:80
```

Snort's multiline alerts resemble the following:

```
 [**] [1:1807:1] WEB-MISC Transfer-Encoding: chunked [**]
[Classification: Web Application Attack] [Priority: 1]
09/05/02-16:22:36.933776 211.147.9.26:3954 -> 192.0.34.72:80
TCP TTL:52 TOS:0x0 ID:51754 IpLen:20 DgmLen:510 DF
***AP*** Seq: 0x8F8E8A34  Ack: 0x7007FF53  Win: 0x8218  TcpLen: 32
TCP Options (3) => NOP NOP TS: 512309340 171021572
[Xref => http://www.securityfocus.com/bid/4474]
[Xref => http://cve.mitre.org/cgi-bin/cvename.cgi?name=CAN-2002-0079]
[Xref => http://www.securityfocus.com/bid/5033]
[Xref => http://cve.mitre.org/cgi-bin/cvename.cgi?name=CAN-2002-0392]
```

As you can see, the multiline alert reports more information, including the TTL, TOS, TCP ID, datagram length, TCP flags, and several other header fields.

Snort can be configured to generate multiple kinds of alerts. However, doing so may affect its ability to keep pace with traffic on a high-speed network. When properly configured and running on a host with adequate resources, Snort can analyze traffic flowing at rates as high as 100 Mbps.

In addition to detecting attacks, Snort can thwart many kinds of attacks by means of its Flexible Response facility, which enables Snort to respond to a detected attack by sending a TCP RST to the attacker, victim, or both the attacker and victim. Alternatively, Flexible Response can send an ICMP unreachable message to the attacker.

INSTALLING SNORT

You can obtain Snort from its Web site, at `http://www.snort.org/`. Snort is distributed as either a TAR file or an RPM package. You're likely to find it more convenient to download and install the RPM package than the TAR file.

Several versions of the Snort RPM package are available:

- A plain version

- A source RPM

- A version supporting SNMP reporting

- A version supporting the Flexible Response facility

- A version supporting the sending of alerts to a MySQL database

- A version supporting the sending of alerts to a Postgresql database

In addition, Snort RPMs combining several characteristics are available. For example, you can download a Snort RPM supporting both SNMP and Flexible Response.

To install Snort, first make sure that your system includes the `libpcap` package, which is part of the Red Hat Linux distribution. Then, download the desired Snort RPM and install it in the usual way — for example:

```
rpm -Uvh snort-1.8.7-1snort.i386.rpm
```

where `snort-1.8.7-1snort.i386.rpm` is the name of the RPM file you downloaded.

CONFIGURING SNORT

The main Snort configuration file is `/etc/snort/snort.conf`. Listing 13-4 shows the contents of the file, with comments deleted to conserve space. You should revise several configuration directives before running Snort:

- In the directive assigning a value to HOME_NET, replace any with the network address of the monitored network. For example:

```
var HOME_NET 192.0.34.0/24
```

◆ In the directive assigning a value to EXTERNAL_NET, replace any with a specifier that excludes the network address of the monitored network. The Snort syntax for doing so consists of an exclamation mark (!) prefixed to a comma-separated list of IP addresses contained within square brackets. The exclamation mark specifies the negation of the list that follows. For example:

```
var EXTERNAL_NET ![192.0.34.0/24,10.0.0.0/8]
```

◆ If desired, modify the directives assigning values to SMTP, HTTP_SERVERS, SQL_SERVERS, and DNS_SERVERS. To do so, use a single IP address or a comma-separated list of IP addresses contained within square brackets. For example:

```
var SMTP 192.0.34.2
var HTTP_SERVERS [192.0.34.3,192.0.34.4]
```

◆ Modify the value of the RULE_PATH directive to correspond to the directory containing the *.rules files, /etc/snort:

```
var RULE_PATH /etc/snort
```

TIP You can disable features and rule sets by prefixing a hash mark (#) to the line containing the corresponding preprocessor or include directive. To learn more about Snort features and how they work, consult the Snort User's Manual, available on the Snort Web site. The sections "Writing Snort Rules" and "Advanced Snort Rules" of this chapter discuss Snort rules.

Listing 13–4: /etc/snort/snort.conf

```
var HOME_NET any
var EXTERNAL_NET any
var SMTP $HOME_NET
var HTTP_SERVERS $HOME_NET
var SQL_SERVERS $HOME_NET

var DNS_SERVERS $HOME_NET
var RULE_PATH ../rules
preprocessor frag2
preprocessor stream4: detect_scans
preprocessor stream4_reassemble
preprocessor http_decode: 80 -unicode -cginull
preprocessor rpc_decode: 111
preprocessor bo: -nobrute
```

```
preprocessor telnet_decode
preprocessor portscan: $HOME_NET 4 3 portscan.log
include classification.config
include $RULE_PATH/bad-traffic.rules
include $RULE_PATH/exploit.rules
include $RULE_PATH/scan.rules
include $RULE_PATH/finger.rules
include $RULE_PATH/ftp.rules
include $RULE_PATH/telnet.rules
include $RULE_PATH/smtp.rules
include $RULE_PATH/rpc.rules
include $RULE_PATH/rservices.rules
include $RULE_PATH/dos.rules
include $RULE_PATH/ddos.rules
include $RULE_PATH/dns.rules
include $RULE_PATH/tftp.rules
include $RULE_PATH/web-cgi.rules
include $RULE_PATH/web-coldfusion.rules
include $RULE_PATH/web-iis.rules
include $RULE_PATH/web-frontpage.rules
include $RULE_PATH/web-misc.rules
include $RULE_PATH/web-attacks.rules
include $RULE_PATH/sql.rules
include $RULE_PATH/x11.rules
include $RULE_PATH/icmp.rules
include $RULE_PATH/netbios.rules
include $RULE_PATH/misc.rules
include $RULE_PATH/attack-responses.rules
include $RULE_PATH/local.rules
```

RUNNING SNORT

The Snort RPM installs a `SysVInit` file for Snort. However, you're likely to need to modify the file before running Snort for the first time. Listing 13-5 shows the contents of the file. Several explanatory comments have been deleted to conserve space.

Listing 13-5: /etc/init.d/snortd

```
#!/bin/sh
#
# snortd        Start/Stop the snort IDS daemon.
#
# chkconfig: 2345 40 60
```

Continued

Listing 13-5 *(Continued)*

```
# description:  snort is a lightweight network intrusion detection \
#         tool that currently detects more than 1100 host and \
#         network vulnerabilities, portscans, backdoors, and more.
#
. /etc/init.d/functions

INTERFACE=eth0

case "$1" in
  start)
    echo -n "Starting snort: "
        cd /var/log/snort
    daemon /usr/sbin/snort -A fast -b -l /var/log/snort -d -D \
        -i $INTERFACE -c /etc/snort/snort.conf
    touch /var/lock/subsys/snort
    echo
    ;;
  stop)
    echo -n "Stopping snort: "
    killproc snort
    rm -f /var/lock/subsys/snort
    echo
    ;;
  restart)
    $0 stop
    $0 start
    ;;
  status)
    status snort
    ;;
  *)
    echo "Usage: $0 {start|stop|restart|status}"
    exit 1
esac

exit 0
```

To prepare to run Snort, follow these steps:

1. If necessary, revise the name of the network interface on which Snort should listen. The interface is identified by the assignment

   ```
   INTERFACE=eth0
   ```

2. Revise the Snort arguments specified in these lines:

```
daemon /usr/sbin/snort -A fast -b -l /var/log/snort -d -D \
   -i $INTERFACE -c /etc/snort/snort.conf
```

Table 13-4 summarizes the arguments that appear in the default `SysVInit` file. See the Snort man page for information about additional arguments you can specify.

3. Consider adding the `-o` flag to the Snort command. This flag changes the order in which Snort processes rules, letting you write rules that ignore specified packets. The flag is not included in the default configuration because a badly written rule can cause all packets to be ignored. However, if you check your rule set before going live, you should avoid this problem.

4. Consider adding the `-s` flag to the Snort command. This flag causes Snort alerts to be sent to the Syslog facility.

TABLE 13-4 SNORT ARGUMENTS USED IN THE DEFAULT CONFIGURATION

Argument	Description
-A	Specifies the Snort alert mode, which can be any of the following: fast (generates one-line alerts), full (generates multiline alerts), unsock (sends alerts to a UNIX socket), or none.
-b	Logs packets in Tcpdump format.
-l	Specifies the directory to which log files are written.
-d	Specifies that the application layer data will be logged.
-D	Specifies that Snort will run as a daemon.
-i	Specifies the interface on which Snort will listen.
-c	Specifies the location of the Snort configuration file.

You can start the Snort service in the usual way:

```
service snortd start
```

When you do so, you should tail the `/var/log/messages` file, looking for messages that indicate a problem has occurred. If Snort failed to start, fix the configuration problem and try again.

WRITING SNORT RULES

As mentioned, writing your own Snort rules is relatively easy. The basic form of a Snort rule is

```
type protocol sip sport -> dip dport
```

where

- ◆ `type` is the rule type: `pass`, `log`, or `alert`.

- ◆ `protocol` is the protocol: `ip`, `tcp`, `udp`, or `icmp`.

- ◆ `sip` is the source IP address.

- ◆ `sport` is the source port number.

- ◆ `dip` is the destination IP address.

- ◆ `dport` is the destination port number.

If a packet matches a Snort rule, the type of the rule determines the action taken. Snort does not attempt to match the packet to subsequent rules. The actions that can be specified are shown in this list:

- ◆ `pass` causes Snort to ignore the packet.

- ◆ `log` causes Snort to log the packet.

- ◆ `alert` causes Snort to generate an alert.

The value `any` can be used to specify the source or destination port, causing the rule to match whatever source or destination port appears in the packet. An IP address can be specified individually or as a list, using the same syntax as in the configuration file. Moreover, a Snort variable defined in the configuration file can be used to specify an IP address. For example, the rule

```
alert tcp $EXTERNAL_NET any -> $HOME_NET 80
```

matches traffic having a source IP address outside the monitored network incoming on port 80 of a host on the monitored network. The symbol -> denotes that the IP address and the port appearing to its left pertain to the source and that the IP address and port appearing to its right pertain to the destination. A rule using the alternate symbol, <>, such as the following:

```
alert tcp $EXTERNAL_NET any <> $HOME_NET 80
```

matches the same packets matched by a combination of the rules:

```
alert tcp $EXTERNAL_NET any -> $HOME_NET 80
alert tcp $HOME_NET 80 -> $EXTERNAL_NET any
```

TIP

If you have difficulty determining whether Snort is generating alerts, you can temporarily add an alert rule that flags common traffic. For instance:

```
alert tcp $EXTERNAL_NET any -> $HOME_NET 80
```

Once you're satisfied that all is well, you can delete the rule.

ADVANCED SNORT RULES

Snort supports more advanced rules that test additional header and payload fields and that customize generated alerts. More than three dozen specifiers are available for use in coding advanced rules. Table 13-5 summarizes the most commonly used specifiers. See the Snort User's Manual to learn about other specifiers and to learn details of the operation of the summarized specifiers. Most Snort rules are defined using only the specifiers summarized in the table. So, you should be able to read and understand most rules by merely referring to the table.

The specifiers are coded within parentheses, at the end of the associated rule. For example, here's a rule that generates an alert in response to outbound activity on TCP port 69, associated with the TFTP service:

```
alert tcp $HOME_NET any -> $EXTERNAL_NET 69 (msg:"Outbound TFTP attempt";
  priority:2)
```

Though the rule occupies two lines on this page, that's merely because of unavoidable line wrap. Snort rules should be written on a single line.

TABLE 13-5 COMMON SNORT SPECIFIERS

Directive	Description
classtype	Specifies an attack category referenced as part of an alert. Snort includes more than two dozen predefined attack categories.
content	Specifies one or more ASCII or binary strings that appear within the packet payload.
dsize	Specifies the packet payload size.
flags	Specifies the value of TCP flags.
icode	Specifies the ICMP code.

Continued

TABLE 13-5 COMMON SNORT SPECIFIERS *(Continued)*

Directive	Description
itype	Specifies the ICMP type.
msg	Specifies a message printed as part of an alert.
priority	Specifies the alert priority as a number from 1 to 3, with 1 representing the highest priority.
reference	Specifies a reference to a standard vulnerability-description database entry associated with an alert.
rev	Specifies the revision number associated with a rule.
sid	Specifies a unique number — the signature ID — associated with a rule.

SnortSnarf

Snort alerts are generally sent to ASCII files. You can view alerts as they're gener-ated by tailing an alert file or view them after the fact by opening the file in read-only mode using a text editor. But, it's awkward to see the big picture because of the volume of alerts, which is typically substantial.

SnortSnarf is an open-source Perl program that produces HTML pages from Snort alert files. Figure 13-12 shows a typical SnortSnarf page. Hyperlinks on a SnortSnarf page let you drill down to view the details of individual alerts of partic-ular interest to you. Other hyperlinks let you view information describing the vul-nerability associated with a standard Snort alert.

INSTALLING SnortSnarf

You can obtain SnortSnarf from the Silicon Defense Web site, at `http://www.silicon defense.com/`. After downloading SnortSnarf, unpack the TAR file into the `/usr/local` directory. Then, copy the files in the following subdirectories to `/usr/lib/perl5/site_perl` or to another directory on the Perl module path:

- `/usr/local/SnortSnarf-*/include`

- `/usr/local/SnortSnarf-*/include/SnortSnarf`

If your Perl installation does not include the Time::JulianDay module, you also need to install it. To do so, issue these commands:

```
cd /usr/local/SnortSnarf-*/Time-modules
perl Makefile.PL
```

```
make
make install
```

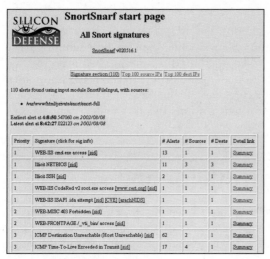

Figure 13-12: A SnortSnarf page

RUNNING SnortSnarf

SnortSnarf supports a variety of run-time arguments, as documented in the file named Usage. Here's a typical command used to run SnortSnarf:

```
/usr/local/snortsnarf/snortsnarf.pl \
  -d /var/www/html/private/snort/snortsnarf.new \
  -homenet 199.107.97.0/32 -dns -rs \
  -refresh=300 -ymd /var/www/html/private/snort/snort-full
```

The flags have the following significance:

- ◆ -d specifies the directory in which SnortSnarf will place the HTML files.

- ◆ -homenet specifies the network address of the monitored network.

- ◆ -dns specifies that SnortSnarf will attempt to resolve IP addresses to host names.

- ◆ -rs causes the highest-priority alerts to be listed at the top of the summary page.

- ◆ -refresh causes the HTML files to include an HTML directive to refresh the page after the specified interval (300 seconds) elapses.

- ◆ -ymd specifies that dates are displayed in year-month-day format.

- ◆ The final argument specifies the name of the Snort alert file to be processed.

SnortSnarf, like many Perl applications, is fairly CPU- and memory-intensive. Therefore, you should generally run it on a host other than the host running Snort. Otherwise, Snort may drop packets when SnortSnarf is running. You may find that it's convenient to use the Rsync utility to periodically transfer the Snort alert file from the network intrusion detection host to the host that runs SnortSnarf. It's fairly simple to set up a Cron job that performs this task every 15 minutes or half-hour.

Responding to an Incident

No matter how much care you devote to network security, you're likely to someday have to respond to a network incident. Follow these guidelines, based on those developed at the Software Engineering Institute's Workshop on Incident Response, to try to recover fully and in a timely manner:

1. **Prepare for potential incidents.** Putting monitoring and detection systems in place is critical to detecting and recovering from incidents. Likewise, having access to known good backups of software and data is generally necessary if complete recovery is to be accomplished.

2. **Detect unauthorized access.** Detection should disclose the existence of the unauthorized access, the means of compromise, and the affected software and data. Host intrusion detection systems, such as Tripwire, are critical to accurately understanding the means and scope of compromise.

3. **Contain the attack and consequent damage.** Generally, a compromised system should be taken offline immediately. Otherwise, the attacker has additional time to conceal the damage and use the compromised system to attack other systems.

4. **Eradicate the cause of the incident and restore affected systems to operational status.** Attackers often install Trojan software or backdoors, surreptitious means of re-entering a compromised system. Therefore, the most reliable way to eradicate the cause of an incident and restore a compromised system to operational status is by reloading to bare metal — that is, to a freshly formatted file system — from a known good backup. Otherwise, the Trojan software or backdoor might make it easy for the attacker to compromise the system again.

5. **Follow up by documenting lessons learned.** You're likely to have to have made some mistakes in responding to the incident or otherwise handled the incident less than perfectly. With the help of knowledgeable, objective outsiders, analyze and assess your performance. Determine and document ways in which your response to subsequent incidents can be improved in comparison with your response to the recent incident.

Summary

This chapter has discussed a variety of tools you can use to more effectively and efficiently administer and monitor your firewall and the network it protects. In protecting networks, remote logging and intrusion detection systems play an important role alongside firewalls. By augmenting your firewall with these and other measures, you bolster your network's defense.

Glossary

abuse contact An e-mail address associated with a registered domain and specifically designated as an appropriate destination for e-mail pertaining to complaints of network abuse.

accept To allow a packet to pass through a firewall.

active mode FTP An FTP mode in which the server opens the data connection.

annualized loss expectancy The expected annual loss due to a specified risk.

annualized rate of occurrence The number, or fractional number, of occurrences of a risk expected in a single year.

append To add an IPChains or IPTables rule to the foot (end)of a chain.

application level The protocol layer that supports messages or services. FTP, SMTP, and HTTP are common application-level protocols.

application protocol A high-level protocol specific to an application. FTP, SMTP, and HTTP are common application protocols.

autorooter A program that scans a host or network for vulnerabilities and launches exploits against any that are identified.

availability A property of data or a computing resource that reflects the relative frequency with which the data can be accessed or the resource used. The term *reliability* is often used when referring to the availability of a computer resource.

backdoor Malicious software that enables an intruder to conveniently re-enter a compromised host as a privileged user.

bastion host A host that is publicly accessible and therefore hardened against attack.

blackhat An attacker having a relatively high degree of expertise.

block To forbid a packet to pass through a firewall.

body The contents of a packet not included in the packet header, including the message itself.

bug An error contained in a computer program. A bug is more formally referred to as a defect. Bugs can lead to vulnerabilities that have security implications.

choke firewall A firewall that sits between a DMZ network and a private network that it protects.

client The host that initiates communication.

confidentiality A property of data that reflects the degree to which the data are kept private.

configuration control Maintaining a record of all changes to a software configuration.

connection (1) An entry in the state table. (2) A state that occurs when two hosts have successfully executed a series of steps preliminary to message exchange.

connection-oriented protocol A protocol that requires communicating hosts to establish a connection before exchanging data.

criminal intent The knowledge of and disregard for the possible harmful consequences of actions.

datagram The unit of data transfer over a TCP/IP network.

default gateway A router that forwards packets to and from the Internet.

default route The host to which packets should be forwarded unless a router table rule specifically identifies an appropriate route.

defect An error contained in a computer program.

denial of service An event or attack that impairs the availability of data or a resource.

destination network address translation (DNAT) A firewall function that modifies the destination IP address of a packet.

DHCP lease A temporary right to use an IP address provided by a DHCP server.

diff (1) A comparison of two text files that indicates differences between them. (2) The act or process of creating such a comparison.

distributed denial of service A denial of service attack launched concurrently from multiple attacking hosts.

DMZ network A network that sits behind a firewall and contains publicly accessible servers.

dotted quad A method of expressing the IP address of a host or network device, in which the 32-bit IP address is written as four numbers, separated by dots. Each of the four numbers gives the value of 8 bits (one octet) of the IP address.

drop To forbid a packet to pass through a firewall, sending no error response to the sender.

dual-homed host A host having two network interfaces.

dynamic NAT Substituting the source or destination address of a packet with a non-fixed value.

egress rule A firewall rule that pertains to outbound traffic.

encapsulation A technique in which a lower-level protocol is used to transport a message encoded using a higher-level protocol. For example, TCP and UDP datagrams are encapsulated within IP datagrams.

ephemeral port A port numbered 1024 or higher.

established (1) A type of connection that has seen traffic flow in both directions. (2) A state that corresponds to the completion of the TCP three-way handshake.

exploit A program or series of actions designed to compromise a host by taking advantage of a system flaw or bug.

exposed host firewall A simple, single-host firewall architecture.

exposure factor The relative loss in financial value of an asset due to a specified risk.

false positive An alert that does not correspond to a significant event.

financial value The monetary value of a business asset.

firewall A device or host that protects a host or network by permitting only authorized communication between hosts.

firewall architecture The topological relationship between network hosts and the firewall or firewalls that protect them.

firewall life cycle A model that identifies and describes temporal phases of a firewall project.

flush To delete the rules associated with an IPChains or IPTables chain.

forward name resolution The resolution of a host name to an IP address.

fragment A portion of a packet that has been divided to decrease its size to avoid exceeding the MTU of a network.

frame The unit of data sent across a physical network.

FTP File Transfer Protocol.

gateway An older term for *router*. Also, any host or device that forwards packets from one network to another.

gateway firewall A firewall that sits between a public network and the private network it protects.

hardened host A host that is the subject of special measures protecting it from attack and compromise.

header Information at the beginning of a packet, giving basic information about the packet contents.

hops The number of transport layer (layer 3) devices and hosts on a path between two devices or hosts.

host address The portion of an IP address that indicates which host within a network the address refers to.

host scan The scanning of a host to determine the services it offers.

HTTP HyperText Transfer Protocol.

ingress rule A firewall rule that pertains to inbound traffic.

insert To add an IPChains or IPTables rule at the head (beginning) of a chain.

integrity A property of data that reflects the degree to which they are free of unauthorized and/or accidental change.

Internet level The protocol layer that supports routing and error messages. ARP, IP, and ICMP are common Internet-level protocols.

IP address A 32-bit number assigned as the network address of a host or network device. The number has two components: a network address and a host address. IPv6 headers include a larger IP address field.

IP spoofing Sending packets containing a fake source or destination IP address.

IPSec Security-enhancing protocol extensions to IPv4, included in IPv6.

LAN host A host that resides on the private network rather than on the public network.

local exploit An exploit that must be run on the local host.

loopback IP address The IP address 127.0.0.1, which refers to the local host.

MAC (media access control) address The hardware address of a host or network device.

mail protocol Any of several protocols used for e-mail communication, such as IMAP, POP, and SMTP.

man in the middle A sophisticated attack in which a host takes the place of a trusted host, enabling the exploitation of the trust relationship.

masquerading A form of source NAT in which multiple hosts share a single public IP address.

maximum transmission unit (MTU) The size of the largest frame that can be sent over a physical network.

multicast A technique whereby a single transmitted packet can be received by multiple destination hosts.

multi-homed host A host that has multiple network interfaces.

multiplication A phenomenon whereby sending a single packet can stimulate multiple responses.

negative scan A scan that confirms a host characteristic by eliciting the absence of a response from the host.

Netfilter Linux kernel hooks that enable packet filtering. IPTables is the primary command-line interface to Netfilter.

network A set of computers than can communicate with one another and the hardware and software facilities that enable the communication.

network address The portion of an IP address that indicates the network the address refers to.

network address translation The translating of the source or destination IP address of packets. Often used to enable hosts on a network to share a single external IP address.

network intrusion detection system A system for identifying, classifying, and reporting attacks directed against a network.

network layer The protocol layer that supports physical access to the network. Ethernet is a common network layer protocol.

network mask (netmask) A value that specifies how an IP address is divided into a network address and a host address.

network scan The scanning of a network to determine what hosts are alive.

noisy scan A scan that's likely to be noticed by network administrators.

non-stateful packet filtering A firewall technology that does not track connection status.

normal mode FTP An FTP mode in which the server opens the data connection.

oracle A record of expected test results. The oracle is compared with actual test results to determine whether a test was successful.

packet Any small unit of data sent over a packet-switching network.

packet forwarding Enabling packets to traverse networks.

passive mode FTP An FTP mode in which the client opens the data connection.

permissive firewall A firewall that accepts novel traffic – that is, traffic not explicitly authorized.

ping An ICMP datagram that requests a host or device to respond by sending a special datagram.

port A number used to distinguish multiple destinations associated with a single host.

port forwarding Substituting the destination port of a packet.

port scan A scan that examines many ports.

portmap or **portmapper** A program used to map remote procedure call (RPC) programs to ports.

positive scan A scan that confirms a host characteristic by eliciting a response from the host.

private addresses An address set aside by the Internet Assigned Numbering Authority (IANA) and Internet Engineering Task Force (IETF) for private use. Private addresses are not routable. They are also known as *RFC 1918 addresses.*

privilege escalation The process of obtaining access privileges beyond those that are authorized.

probing Searching a host or network for vulnerabilities.

protocol A formal description of the rules governing communication between computers.

proxy An intermediary through which hosts communicate.

proxying Communicating through an intermediary.

regression testing Testing performed after a software change, intended to verify that preexisting functions have not been impaired.

reject To forbid a packet to pass through a firewall, sending an error response to the sender.

remote exploit An exploit that can attack a host other than the local host.

reply datagram A datagram flowing from a server to a client.

repudiation The denial of the occurrence of a transaction, especially an e-commerce transaction.

request datagram A datagram flowing from a client to a server.

response datagram A datagram flowing from a server to a client.

restrictive firewall A firewall that blocks novel traffic — that is, traffic not explicitly authorized.

retry packet A packet sent to retry a failed transmission or connection attempt.

reverse name resolution The resolution of an IP address to a host name.

reverse proxy A proxy that protects a server.

RFC 1918 addresses An address set aside by the Internet Assigned Numbering Authority (IANA) and IETF for private use. RFC 1918 addresses are not routable. They are also known as *private addresses.*

rootkit A set of programs that enable an intruder to mask his presence and activities, monitor use of a compromised system, or obtain privileged access after an initial break-in.

router A host or device that forwards packets between or among networks.

router firewall A firewall that forwards packets.

router table The table used by a router to determine the host or network to which a packet should be forwarded.

routing Forwarding packets between connected networks.

routing table A table maintained by a router, which describes the accessible networks.

scanner A program that probes a host or network for vulnerabilities.

scanning Searching a host or network for vulnerabilities.

scenario A set of circumstances considered representative of a class of possible situations, used to characterize risk.

script kiddie An attacker having a relatively low degree of expertise. Script kiddies generally rely on scripts and exploits written by others.

security through obscurity A security measure that depends on the ignorance or inexpertise of the attacker.

segment The unit of TCP data transfer between communicating hosts.

server The host that responds to a client.

service A running program that responds to requests transmitted by clients.

service scan The scanning of a network to determine which hosts, if any, offer a particular service.

single loss expectancy The monetary value associated with an incident of a specified risk.

social engineering An attack that targets the human components of a system. Persuading help desk staff members to disclose a password is a common type of social engineering.

socket The combination of an IP address and port number. A service has one or more associated sockets.

software lifecycle A model that identifies and describes the temporal phases of a software project.

source network address translation (SNAT) A firewall function that modifies the source IP address of a packet.

split-horizon DNS A technique for limiting information disclosure. Split-horizon DNS uses two DNS servers _ one that answers external requests and another that answers internal requests.

split-screened network architecture A sophisticated firewall architecture that includes one or more dual-homed servers.

spoof A falsified source or destination IP address.

standard mode FTP An FTP mode in which the server opens the data connection.

state table The table used by a stateful firewall to track connection status.

stateful packet filtering A firewall technology that tracks connection status.

static network address translation (NAT) Substituting a fixed IP address as the source or destination address of a packet.

stealthy scan A scan that's unlikely to be noticed by network administrators.

subnetting Splitting a single network into two or more smaller networks.

subnetwork (subnet) A network created by subnetting a larger network.

supernetting Joining two or more consecutively numbered networks into a single, larger network.

SYN-FIN scan A TCP scan in which the SYN and FIN flags are both set.

system port A port numbered 1023 or lower.

target The IPChains or IPTables chain or action associated with a rule.

TCP three-way handshake A series of messages exchanged to establish a TCP connection.

three-way firewall architecture A single-host firewall architecture that includes public, DMZ, and private networks.

timeout The interval during which a host sends retry packets before determining that an error condition cannot be circumvented.

traffic direction or **traffic flow** The source and origin of a datagram, which can be inbound, outbound, or internal.

transport level The protocol layer that supports datagram delivery. TCP and UDP are common transport-level protocols.

trojan A hostile program that is designed to appear benign.

tunnel A connection between two networks, such as one established by a VPN.

user chain An IPChains or IPTables chain other than the default, preexisting chains.

vulnerability A software defect that can be exploited to compromise security.

warez Illegal copies of copyrighted software or data.

well-known port A port registered with the Internet Assigned Numbers Authority (IANA).

worm An autorooter that operates without human direction. A worm makes copies of itself on infected target systems and thus spreads much as a virus does.

X client A program that uses an X display.

X server A program that manages an X display.

Appendix A

Firewall and Security Web Sites

This appendix identifies several Web sites and pages potentially useful to readers of this book.

Security Web Sites

- ◆ CERT (Computer Emergency Response Team) Coordination Center:

    http://www.cert.org/

- ◆ CIAC (Computer Incident Advisory Capability):

    http://www.ciac.org/ciac/

- ◆ COAST (Computer Operations, Audit, and Security Technology):

    http://www.cerias.purdue.edu/coast/

- ◆ COAST Internet Firewalls – Resources:

    http://www.cerias.purdue.edu/coast/firewalls/

- ◆ InfoSysSec:

    http://www.infosyssec.org/infosyssec/index.html

- ◆ Internet Engineering Task Force (IETF):

    http://www.ietf.org/

- ◆ Internet Storm Center:

    http://www.isc.org/

- ◆ Linux Security.com:

    http://www.linuxsecurity.com/

- ◆ NIH (National Institutes of Health) Computer Security Information:

    http://www.alw.nih.gov/Security/security.html

- ◆ Packet Storm:

    http://www.packetstormsecurity.org/

- ◆ Red Hat Security Resource Center:

    http://www.redhat.com/solutions/security/

- ◆ SANS Institute:

    http://www.sans.org/

- ◆ Security Focus:

    http://www.securityfocus.net/

Mailing Lists and Online Communities

- ◆ BugTraq:

    http://online.securityfocus.com/archive/1

- ◆ CERT-Advisory Mailing List:

    http://www.cert.org/advisories/

- ◆ Firewalls Mailing List:

    http://www.isc.org/services/public/lists/firewalls.html

- ◆ Firewall Wizard's Mailing List Archive:

    http://honor.icsalabs.com/mailman/listinfo/firewall-wizards

- ◆ ICSA Labs' Firewall Community:

    http://www.icsalabs.com/html/communities/firewalls/index.shtml

Security Tools and Software

◆ Advanced Intrusion Detection Environment (AIDE):

http://www.cs.tut.fi/~rammer/aide.html

◆ COPS:

http://www.ibiblio.org/pub/Linux/system/security/

◆ Crack:

ftp://coast.cs.purdue.edu/pub/tools/unix/libs/cracklib

◆ Firewall Tester:

http://ftester.sourceforge.net/

◆ FreeS/WAN:

http://www.freeswan.org/

◆ Hogwash:

http://hogwash.sourceforge.net/

◆ ICMPInfo:

ftp://coast.cs.purdue.edu/pub/tools/unix/netutils

◆ Ifstatus:

ftp://coast.cs.purdue.edu/pub/tools/unix/sysutils/ifstatus

◆ ISS:

http://iss.net/

◆ John the Ripper:

http://www.openwall.com/john/

◆ Linux Ethernet Bridging:

http://bridge.sourceforge.net/

- ◆ Linux Router Project:

  http://www.linuxrouter.org/

- ◆ Logcheck:

  http://www.psionic.com/products/trisentry.html

- ◆ Nessus:

  http://www.nessus.org/

- ◆ Netcat:

  ftp://coast.cs.purdue.edu/pub/tools/unix/netutils/netcat

- ◆ PortSentry:

  http://www.psionic.com/products/trisentry.html

- ◆ SAINT:

  http://www.wwdsi.com/saint/

- ◆ Snort:

  http://www.snort.org/

- ◆ SOCKS:

  http://www.socks.nec.com/

- ◆ T.REX Proxy-Based Open Source Firewall:

  http://www.opensourcefirewall.com/trex.html

- ◆ Tiger:

  http://www.net.tamu.edu/ftp/security/TAMU/

- ◆ TIS Firewall Toolkit:

  http://www.fwtk.org/main.html

- ◆ Tripwire:

  http://www.tripwire.org/

Articles, FAQs, HOWTOs, and Whitepapers

- ◆ "Anonymous FTP Configuration Guidelines":

  http://www.cert.org/tech_tips/anonymous_ftp_config.html

- ◆ "Computer Security Information Sources For the DOE Community":

  http://www.ciac.org/ciac/documents/CIAC-2302_Computer_
  Security_Information_Sources_For_the_DOE_Community.pdf

- ◆ "Denial of Service Attacks":

  http://www.cert.org/tech_tips/denial_of_service.html

- ◆ "Distributed Denial of Service":

  http://www.ciac.org/ciac/documents/CIAC-
  2319_Distributed_Denial_of_Service.pdf

- ◆ "Electronic Resources for Security Related Information":

  http://www.ciac.org/ciac/documents/CIAC-2307_Electronic_
  Resources_for_Security_Related_Information.pdf

- ◆ "FAQ: Firewall Forensics (What am I seeing?)":

  http://www.robertgraham.com/pubs/firewall-seen.html

- ◆ "Firewall and Proxy Server HOWTO":

  http://www.tldp.org/HOWTO/Firewall-HOWTO.html

- ◆ "How to Eliminate the Ten Most Critical Internet Security Threats":

  http://www.sans.org/topten.htm

- ◆ "Internet Firewalls: FAQ":

  http://www.interhack.net/pubs/fwfaq/

- ◆ "Intruder Detection Checklist":

  http://www.cert.org/tech_tips/intruder_detection_checklist.html

◆ "IPTables Tutorial":

http://people.unix-fu.org/andreasson/iptables-tutorial/
iptables-tutorial.html

◆ "IPTables":

http://www.cs.princeton.edu/~jns/security/iptables/

◆ "IRC On Your Dime":

http://www.ciac.org/ciac/documents/CIAC-2318_IRC_On_Your_
Dime.pdf

◆ "Linux 2.4 NAT HOWTO":

http://netfilter.samba.org/documentation/HOWTO/NAT-HOWTO.html

◆ "Linux 2.4 Packet Filtering HOWTO":

http://netfilter.samba.org/documentation/HOWTO/packet-
filtering-HOWTO.html

◆ "Linux iptables HOWTO":

http://www.linuxguruz.org/iptables/howto/

◆ "Linux netfilter Hacking HOWTO":

http://netfilter.samba.org/documentation/HOWTO/netfilter-
hacking-HOWTO.html

◆ "Packet Filtering for Firewall Systems":

http://www.cert.org/tech_tips/packet_filtering.html

◆ "Securing Internet Information Servers":

http://www.ciac.org/ciac/documents/ciac2308.html

◆ "Securing X Windows":

http://www.ciac.org/ciac/documents/CIAC-2316_Securing_
X_Windows.pdf

◆ "Steps for Recovering from a UNIX or NT System Compromise":

http://www.cert.org/tech_tips/win-UNIX-system_compromise.html

◆ "UNIX Computer Security Checklist (Version 2.0)":

    http://www.cert.org/tech_tips/unix_security_checklist2.0.html

◆ "UNIX Incident Guide How to Detect an Intrusion":

    http://www.ciac.org/ciac/documents/CIAC-
    2305_UNIX_Incident_Guide_How_to_Detect_an_Intrusion.pdf

Appendix B

Protocol Numbers

For a more complete list of protocols, see the file /etc/protocols or the Internet Assigned Numbering Authority (IANA) Web site, at http://www.iana.org/assignments/protocol-numbers. Table B-1 summarizes the most commonly used protocols. The table is organized by protocol number for convenient access.

TABLE B-1 COMMON PROTOCOLS

Protocol Identifier	Protocol Number	Protocol Name	Description
ip	0	IP	Internet protocol, pseudo protocol number
icmp	1	ICMP	Internet control message protocol
igmp	2	IGMP	Internet group management protocol
ggp	3	GGP	Gateway-gateway protocol
ipencap	4	IP-ENCAP	IP encapsulated in IP (officially "IP")
st	5	ST	ST datagram mode
tcp	6	TCP	Transmission control protocol
cbt	7	CBT	CBT, Tony Ballardie <A.Ballardie@cs.ucl.ac.uk>
egp	8	EGP	Exterior gateway protocol
igp	9	IGP	Any private interior gateway (Cisco: for IGRP)
bbn-rcc	10	BBN-RCC-MON	BBN RCC Monitoring

Continued

TABLE B-1 COMMON PROTOCOLS *(Continued)*

Protocol Identifier	Protocol Number	Protocol Name	Description
nvp	11	NVP-II	Network Voice Protocol
pup	12	PUP	PARC universal packet protocol
argus	13	ARGUS	ARGUS
emcon	14	EMCON	EMCON
xnet	15	XNET	Cross Net Debugger
chaos	16	CHAOS	Chaos
udp	17	UDP	User datagram protocol
mux	18	MUX	Multiplexing protocol
dcn	19	DCN-MEAS	DCN Measurement Subsystems
hmp	20	HMP	Host monitoring protocol
prm	21	PRM	Packet radio measurement protocol
xns-idp	22	XNS-IDP	Xerox NS IDP
trunk-1	23	TRUNK-1	Trunk-1
trunk-2	24	TRUNK-2	Trunk-2
leaf-1	25	LEAF-1	Leaf-1
leaf-2	26	LEAF-2	Leaf-2
rdp	27	RDP	"reliable datagram" protocol
irtp	28	IRTP	Internet Reliable Transaction Protocol
iso-tp4	29	ISO-TP4	ISO Transport Protocol Class 4

Protocol Identifier	Protocol Number	Protocol Name	Description
netblt	30	NETBLT	Bulk Data Transfer Protocol
mfe-nsp	31	MFE-NSP	MFE Network Services Protocol
merit-inp	32	MERIT-INP	MERIT Internodal Protocol
sep	33	SEP	Sequential Exchange Protocol
3pc	34	3PC	Third Party Connect Protocol
idpr	35	IDPR	Inter-Domain Policy Routing Protocol
xtp	36	XTP	Xpress Tranfer Protocol
ddp	37	DDP	Datagram Delivery Protocol
idpr-cmtp	38	IDPR-CMTP	IDPR Control Message Transport Proto
tp++	39	TP++	TP++ Transport Protocol
il	40	IL	IL Transport Protocol
ipv6	41	IPv6	IPv6
sdrp	42	SDRP	Source Demand Routing Protocol
ipv6-route	43	IPv6-Route	Routing Header for IPv6
ipv6-frag	44	IPv6-Frag	Fragment Header for IPv6
idrp	45	IDRP	Inter-Domain Routing Protocol

Continued

TABLE **B-1** **COMMON PROTOCOLS** *(Continued)*

Protocol Identifier	Protocol Number	Protocol Name	Description
rsvp	46	RSVP	Resource ReSerVation Protocol
gre	47	GRE	Generic Routing Encapsulation
mhrp	48	MHRP	Mobile Host Routing Protocol
bna	49	BNA	BNA
ipv6-crypt	50	IPv6-Crypt	Encryption Header for IPv6
ipv6-auth	51	IPv6-Auth	Authentication Header for IPv6
i-nlsp	52	I-NLSP	Integrated Net Layer Security TUBA
swipe	53	SWIPE	IP with Encryption
narp	54	NARP	NBMA Address Resolution Protocol
mobile	55	MOBILE	IP Mobility
tlsp	56	TLSP	Transport Layer Security Protocol
skip	57	SKIP	SKIP
ipv6-icmp	58	IPv6-ICMP	ICMP for IPv6
ipv6-nonxt	59	IPv6-NoNxt	No Next Header for IPv6
ipv6-opts	60	IPv6-Opts	Destination Options for IPv6
	61	any host internal protocol	
cftp	62	CFTP	CFTP
	63	any local network	

Protocol Identifier	Protocol Number	Protocol Name	Description
sat-expak	64	SAT-EXPAK	SATNET and Backroom EXPAK
kryptolan	65	KRYPTOLAN	Kryptolan
rvd	66	RVD	MIT Remote Virtual Disk Protocol
ippc	67	IPPC	Internet Pluribus Packet Core
	68	any distributed file system	
sat-mon	69	SAT-MON	SATNET Monitoring
visa	70	VISA	VISA Protocol
ipcv	71	IPCV	Internet Packet Core Utility
cpnx	72	CPNX	Computer Protocol Network Executive
cphb	73	CPHB	Computer Protocol Heart Beat
wsn	74	WSN	Wang Span Network
pvp	75	PVP	Packet Video Protocol
br-sat-mon	76	BR-SAT-MON	Backroom SATNET Monitoring
sun-nd	77	SUN-ND	SUN ND PROTOCOL-Temporary
wb-mon	78	WB-MON	WIDEBAND Monitoring
wb-expak	79	WB-EXPAK	WIDEBAND EXPAK
iso-ip	80	ISO-IP	ISO Internet Protocol
vmtp	81	VMTP	Versatile Message Transport

Continued

TABLE B-1 COMMON PROTOCOLS *(Continued)*

Protocol Identifier	Protocol Number	Protocol Name	Description
secure-vmtp	82	SECURE-VMTP	SECURE-VMTP
vines	83	VINES	VINES
ttp	84	TTP	TTP
nsfnet-igp	85	NSFNET-IGP	NSFNET-IGP
dgp	86	DGP	Dissimilar Gateway Protocol
tcf	87	TCF	TCF
eigrp	88	EIGRP	Enhanced Interior Routing Protocol (Cisco)
ospf	89	OSPFIGP	Open Shortest Path First IGP
sprite-rpc	90	Sprite-RPC	Sprite RPC Protocol
larp	91	LARP	Locus Address Resolution Protocol
mtp	92	MTP	Multicast Transport Protocol
ax.25	93	AX.25	AX.25 Frames
ipip	94	IPIP	Yet Another IP encapsulation
micp	95	MICP	Mobile Internetworking Control Pro.
scc-sp	96	SCC-SP	Semaphore Communications Sec. Pro.
etherip	97	ETHERIP	Ethernet-within-IP Encapsulation
encap	98	ENCAP	Yet Another IP encapsulation
	99		Any private encryption scheme

Protocol Identifier	Protocol Number	Protocol Name	Description
gmtp	100	GMTP	GMTP
ifmp	101	IFMP	Ipsilon Flow Management Protocol
pnni	102	PNNI	PNNI over IP
pim	103	PIM	Protocol Independent Multicast
aris	104	ARIS	ARIS
scps	105	SCPS	SCPS
qnx	106	QNX	QNX
a/n	107	A/N	Active Networks
ipcomp	108	IPComp	IP Payload Compression Protocol
snp	109	SNP	Sitara Networks Protocol
compaq-peer	110	Compaq-Peer	Compaq Peer Protocol
ipx-in-ip	111	IPX-in-IP	IPX in IP
vrrp	112	VRRP	Virtual Router Redundancy Protocol
pgm	113	PGM	PGM Reliable Transport Protocol
	114		any 0-hop protocol
l2tp	115	L2TP	Layer Two Tunneling Protocol
ddx	116	DDX	D-II Data Exchange
iatp	117	IATP	Interactive Agent Transfer Protocol

Continued

TABLE B-1 COMMON PROTOCOLS *(Continued)*

Protocol Identifier	Protocol Number	Protocol Name	Description
stp	118	STP	Schedule Transfer
srp	119	SRP	SpectraLink Radio Protocol
uti	120	UTI	UTI
smp	121	SMP	Simple Message Protocol
sm	122	SM	SM
ptp	123	PTP	Performance Transparency Protocol
isis	124	ISIS	ISIS over IPv4
fire	125	FIRE	
crtp	126	CRTP	Combat Radio Transport Protocol
crdup	127	CRUDP	Combat Radio User Datagram
sscopmce	128	SSCOPMCE	
iplt	129	IPLT	
sps	130	SPS	Secure Packet Shield
pipe	131	PIPE	Private IP Encapsulation within IP
sctp	132	SCTP	Stream Control Transmission Protocol
fc	133	FC	Fibre Channel
rsvp-e2e-ignore	134	RSVP-E2E-IGNORE	
	134-254	Unassigned	
	255	Reserved	

Appendix C

Ports and Services

The Internet Assigned Numbering Authority (IANA) assigns well-known (1–1023), registered (1024–49151), and dynamic ports (49152–65535). Ports are generally registered in TCP/UDP pairs, irrespective of whether the related service uses one or both protocols. Tables C-1 through C-3 describe these ports.

See the IANA Web site, at http://www.iana.org/assignments/protocol-numbers, for more information.

Table C-1 WELL-KNOWN PORTS

Service	Port	Protocol
rtmp	1	ddp
tcpmux	1	tcp
tcpmux	1	udp
nbp	2	ddp
echo	4	ddp
rje	5	tcp
rje	5	udp
zip	6	ddp
echo	7	tcp
echo	7	udp
discard	9	tcp
discard	9	udp
systat	11	tcp
systat	11	udp
daytime	13	tcp
daytime	13	udp
netstat	15	tcp

Continued

445

TABLE C-1 WELL-KNOWN PORTS *(Continued)*

Service	Port	Protocol
qotd	17	tcp
qotd	17	udp
msp	18	tcp
msp	18	udp
chargen	19	tcp
chargen	19	udp
ftp-data	20	tcp
ftp-data	20	udp
fsp	21	udp
ftp	21	tcp
ftp	21	udp
ssh	22	tcp
ssh	22	udp
telnet	23	tcp
telnet	23	udp
smtp	25	tcp
smtp	25	udp
time	37	tcp
time	37	udp
rlp	39	tcp
rlp	39	udp
nameserver	42	tcp
nameserver	42	udp
nicname	43	tcp
nicname	43	udp
tacacs	49	tcp
tacacs	49	udp

Service	Port	Protocol
re-mail-ck	50	tcp
re-mail-ck	50	udp
domain	53	tcp
domain	53	udp
whois++	63	tcp
whois++	63	udp
bootps	67	tcp
bootps	67	udp
bootpc	68	tcp
bootpc	68	udp
tftp	69	tcp
tftp	69	udp
gopher	70	tcp
gopher	70	udp
netrjs-1	71	tcp
netrjs-1	71	udp
netrjs-2	72	tcp
netrjs-2	72	udp
netrjs-3	73	tcp
netrjs-3	73	udp
netrjs-4	74	tcp
netrjs-4	74	udp
finger	79	tcp
finger	79	udp
http	80	tcp
http	80	udp
kerberos	88	tcp

Continued

TABLE C-1 WELL-KNOWN PORTS *(Continued)*

Service	Port	Protocol
kerberos	88	udp
supdup	95	tcp
supdup	95	udp
linuxconf	98	tcp
hostname	101	tcp
hostname	101	udp
iso-tsap	102	tcp
csnet-ns	105	tcp
csnet-ns	105	udp
poppassd	106	tcp
poppassd	106	udp
rtelnet	107	tcp
rtelnet	107	udp
pop2	109	tcp
pop2	109	udp
pop3	110	tcp
pop3	110	udp
sunrpc	111	tcp
sunrpc	111	udp
auth	113	tcp
auth	113	udp
sftp	115	tcp
sftp	115	udp
uucp-path	117	tcp
uucp-path	117	udp
nntp	119	tcp
nntp	119	udp

Service	Port	Protocol
ntp	123	tcp
ntp	123	udp
netbios-ns	137	tcp
netbios-ns	137	udp
netbios-dgm	138	tcp
netbios-dgm	138	udp
netbios-ssn	139	tcp
netbios-ssn	139	udp
imap	143	tcp
imap	143	udp
snmp	161	tcp
snmp	161	udp
snmptrap	162	udp
cmip-man	163	tcp
cmip-man	163	udp
cmip-agent	164	tcp
cmip-agent	164	udp
mailq	174	tcp
mailq	174	udp
xdmcp	177	tcp
xdmcp	177	udp
nextstep	178	tcp
nextstep	178	udp
bgp	179	tcp
bgp	179	udp
prospero	191	tcp
prospero	191	udp

Continued

TABLE C-1 WELL-KNOWN PORTS *(Continued)*

Service	Port	Protocol
irc	194	tcp
irc	194	udp
smux	199	tcp
smux	199	udp
at-rtmp	201	tcp
at-rtmp	201	udp
at-nbp	202	tcp
at-nbp	202	udp
at-echo	204	tcp
at-echo	204	udp
at-zis	206	tcp
at-zis	206	udp
qmtp	209	tcp
qmtp	209	udp
z39.50	210	tcp
z39.50	210	udp
ipx	213	tcp
ipx	213	udp
imap3	220	tcp
imap3	220	udp
link	245	tcp
link	245	ucp
rsvp_tunnel	363	tcp
rsvp_tunnel	363	udp
rpc2portmap	369	tcp
rpc2portmap	369	udp
codaauth2	370	tcp

Service	Port	Protocol
codaauth2	370	udp
ulistproc	372	tcp
ulistproc	372	udp
ldap	389	tcp
ldap	389	udp
svrloc	427	tcp
svrloc	427	udp
mobileip-agent	434	tcp
mobileip-agent	434	udp
mobilip-mn	435	tcp
mobilip-mn	435	udp
https	443	tcp
https	443	udp
snpp	444	tcp
snpp	444	udp
microsoft-ds	445	tcp
microsoft-ds	445	udp
kpasswd	464	tcp
kpasswd	464	udp
smtps	465	tcp
photuris	468	tcp
photuris	468	udp
saft	487	tcp
saft	487	udp
gss-http	488	tcp
gss-http	488	udp
pim-rp-disc	496	tcp

Continued

TABLE C-1 WELL-KNOWN PORTS *(Continued)*

Service	Port	Protocol
pim-rp-disc	496	udp
isakmp	500	tcp
isakmp	500	udp
biff	512	udp
exec	512	tcp
login	513	tcp
who	513	udp
shell	514	tcp
syslog	514	udp
printer	515	tcp
printer	515	udp
talk	517	udp
ntalk	518	udp
utime	519	tcp
utime	519	udp
efs	520	tcp
router	520	udp
ripng	521	tcp
ripng	521	udp
timed	525	tcp
timed	525	udp
tempo	526	tcp
courier	530	tcp
conference	531	tcp
netnews	532	tcp
netwall	533	udp
iiop	535	tcp

Service	Port	Protocol
iiop	535	udp
gdomap	538	tcp
gdomap	538	udp
uucp	540	tcp
klogin	543	tcp
kshell	544	tcp
dhcpv6-client	546	tcp
dhcpv6-client	546	udp
dhcpv6-server	547	tcp
dhcpv6-server	547	udp
afpovertcp	548	tcp
afpovertcp	548	udp
rtsp	554	tcp
rtsp	554	udp
remotefs	556	tcp
nntps	563	tcp
nntps	563	udp
whoami	565	tcp
whoami	565	udp
submission	587	tcp
submission	587	udp
npmp-local	610	tcp
npmp-local	610	udp
npmp-gui	611	tcp
npmp-gui	611	udp
hmmp-ind	612	tcp
hmmp-ind	612	udp

Continued

TABLE C-1 WELL-KNOWN PORTS *(Continued)*

Service	Port	Protocol
gii	616	tcp
ldaps	636	tcp
ldaps	636	udp
acap	674	tcp
acap	674	udp
ha-cluster	694	tcp
ha-cluster	694	udp
kerberos-adm	749	tcp
kerberos-iv	750	tcp
kerberos-iv	750	udp
kerberos_master	751	tcp
kerberos_master	751	udp
passwd_server	752	udp
krb5_prop	754	tcp
krbupdate	760	tcp
webster	765	tcp
webster	765	udp
phonebook	767	tcp
phonebook	767	udp
omirr	808	tcp
omirr	808	udp
supfilesrv	871	tcp
rsync	873	tcp
rsync	873	udp
swat	901	tcp
rndc	953	tcp
rndc	953	udp

Service	Port	Protocol
telnets	992	tcp
telnets	992	udp
imaps	993	tcp
imaps	993	udp
ircs	994	tcp
ircs	994	udp
pop3s	995	tcp
pop3s	995	udp

TABLE C-2 REGISTERED PORTS

Service	Port	Protocol
socks	1080	tcp
socks	1080	udp
kpop	1109	tcp
supfiledbg	1127	tcp
skkserv	1178	tcp
rmtcfg	1236	tcp
h323hostcallsc	1300	tcp
h323hostcallsc	1300	udp
xtel	1313	tcp
ms-sql-s	1433	tcp
ms-sql-s	1433	udp
ms-sql-m	1434	tcp
ms-sql-m	1434	udp
ica	1494	tcp

Continued

TABLE C-2 REGISTERED PORTS *(Continued)*

Service	Port	Protocol
ica	1494	udp
wins	1512	tcp
wins	1512	udp
ingreslock	1524	tcp
ingreslock	1524	udp
prospero-np	1525	tcp
prospero-np	1525	udp
support	1529	tcp
datametrics	1645	tcp
datametrics	1645	udp
sa-msg-port	1646	tcp
sa-msg-port	1646	udp
kermit	1649	tcp
kermit	1649	udp
l2tp	1701	tcp
l2tp	1701	udp
h323gatedisc	1718	tcp
h323gatedisc	1718	udp
h323gatestat	1719	tcp
h323gatestat	1719	udp
h323hostcall	1720	tcp
h323hostcall	1720	udp
tftp-mcast	1758	tcp
tftp-mcast	1758	udp
hello	1789	tcp
hello	1789	udp
radius	1812	tcp

Service	Port	Protocol
radius	1812	udp
radius-acct	1813	tcp
radius-acct	1813	udp
mtp	1911	tcp
mtp	1911	udp
hsrp	1985	tcp
hsrp	1985	udp
licensedaemon	1986	tcp
licensedaemon	1986	udp
gdp-port	1997	tcp
gdp-port	1997	udp
cfinger	2003	tcp
nfs	2049	tcp
nfs	2049	udp
knetd	2053	tcp
zephyr-srv	2102	tcp
zephyr-srv	2102	udp
zephyr-clt	2103	tcp
zephyr-clt	2103	udp
zephyr-hm	2104	tcp
zephyr-hm	2104	udp
eklogin	2105	tcp
ninstall	2150	tcp
ninstall	2150	udp
cvspserver	2401	tcp
cvspserver	2401	udp
venus	2430	tcp

Continued

TABLE C-2 REGISTERED PORTS *(Continued)*

Service	Port	Protocol
venus	2430	udp
venus-se	2431	tcp
venus-se	2431	udp
codasrv	2432	tcp
codasrv	2432	udp
codasrv-se	2433	tcp
codasrv-se	2433	udp
corbaloc	2809	tcp
afbackup	2988	tcp
afbackup	2988	udp
squid	3128	tcp
icpv2	3130	tcp
icpv2	3130	udp
mysql	3306	tcp
mysql	3306	udp
trnsprntproxy	3346	tcp
trnsprntproxy	3346	udp
prsvp	3455	tcp
prsvp	3455	udp
rwhois	4321	tcp
rwhois	4321	udp
krb524	4444	tcp
krb524	4444	udp
fax	4557	tcp
hylafax	4559	tcp
rfe	5002	tcp
rfe	5002	udp

Service	Port	Protocol
sgi-dgl	5232	tcp
sgi-dgl	5232	udp
cfengine	5308	tcp
cfengine	5308	udp
noclog	5354	tcp
noclog	5354	udp
hostmon	5355	tcp
hostmon	5355	udp
postgres	5432	tcp
postgres	5432	udp
canna	5680	tcp
cvsup	5999	tcp
cvsup	5999	udp
x11	6000	tcp
x11-ssh-offset	6010	tcp
ircd	6667	tcp
ircd	6667	udp
afs3-fileserver	7000	tcp
afs3-fileserver	7000	udp
afs3-callback	7001	tcp
afs3-callback	7001	udp
afs3-prserver	7002	tcp
afs3-prserver	7002	udp
afs3-vlserver	7003	tcp
afs3-vlserver	7003	tcp
afs3-kaserver	7004	tcp
afs3-kaserver	7004	udp

Continued

TABLE C-2 REGISTERED PORTS *(Continued)*

Service	Port	Protocol
afs3-volser	7005	tcp
afs3-volser	7005	udp
afs3-errors	7006	tcp
afs3-errors	7006	udp
afs3-bos	7007	tcp
afs3-bos	7007	udp
afs3-update	7008	tcp
afs3-update	7008	udp
afs3-rmtsys	7009	tcp
afs3-rmtsys	7009	udp
xfs	7100	tcp
tircproxy	7666	tcp
http-alt	8008	tcp
http-alt	8008	udp
webcache	8080	tcp
webcache	8080	udp
tproxy	8081	tcp
tproxy	8081	udp
jetdirect	9100	tcp
mandelspawn	9359	udp
sd	9876	tcp
sd	9876	udp
amanda	10080	tcp
amanda	10080	udp
kamanda	10081	tcp
kamanda	10081	udp
amandaidx	10082	tcp

Service	Port	Protocol
amidxtape	10083	tcp
pgpkeyserver	11371	tcp
pgpkeyserver	11371	udp
h323callsigalt	11720	tcp
h323callsigalt	11720	udp
isdnlog	20011	tcp
isdnlog	20011	udp
vboxd	20012	tcp
vboxd	20012	udp
binkp	24554	tcp
binkp	24554	udp
quake	26000	tcp
quake	26000	udp
wnn6-ds	26208	tcp
wnn6-ds	26208	udp
asp	27374	tcp
asp	27374	udp
traceroute	33434	tcp
traceroute	33434	udp

TABLE C-3 DYNAMIC PORTS

Service	Port	Protocol
tfido	60177	tcp
tfido	60177	udp
fido	60179	tcp
fido	60179	udp

Appendix D

ICMP Types and Codes

Table D-1 summarizes the message types and codes used in ICMP messages. The table is organized by message type for convenient access and lists only messages whose descriptions are recognized by IPTables.

TABLE D-1 ICMP MESSAGE TYPES AND CODES

Message Type	Message Code	Description
0		echo-reply
3		destination-unreachable
	0	network-unreachable
	1	host-unreachable
	2	protocol-unreachable
	3	port-unreachable
	4	fragmentation-needed
	5	source-route-failed
	6	network-unknown
	7	host-unknown
	8	source-host-isolated
	9	network-prohibited
	10	host-prohibited
	11	TOS-network-unreachable
	12	TOS-host-unreachable
	13	communication-prohibited
	14	host-precedence-violation
	15	precedence-cutoff

Continued

TABLE D-1 ICMP MESSAGE TYPES AND CODES *(Continued)*

Message Type	Message Code	Description
4		source-quench
5		redirect
	0	network-redirect
	1	host-redirect
	2	TOS-network-redirect
	3	TOS-host-redirect
8		echo-request
9		router-advertisement
10		router-solicitation
11		time-exceeded
	0	ttl-zero-during-transit
	1	ttl-zero-during-reassembly
12		Parameter-problem
	0	ip-header-bad
	1	Required-option-missing
13		Timestamp-request
14		Timestamp-reply
17		Address-mask-request
18		Address-mask-reply

Appendix E

Sample Firewall Scripts

Red Hat's Sample IPChains Firewall (Chapter 7)

Example Firewall Script
Example Firewall Service Script
This script is intended for the home user or small business to set up IP-Masquerading and basic protection for a gateway system using Red Hat Linux.

NO WARRANTY

This script is distributed in the hope that it will be useful, but WITHOUT ANY WARRANTY, without even the implied warranty of MERCHANTABILITY or FITNESS FOR A PARTICULAR PURPOSE. See the GNU General Public License for more details.

```
#!/bin/sh
#
# chkconfig: 2345 11 89
# description: sets up a basic firewall ruleset
#
# This script is setup to use IPCHAINS to protect a small network.   It is
# considered to be 'medium-light' secure.
#
# This script should be saved as /etc/rc.d/init.d/firewallss
#
# to enable the system to run this script at system start and stop, issue
# the command
#      chkconfig --add firewallss --level 2345
# Make sure the script's executable bits are set.  This can be done with
#      chmod u+x firewallss
#
# Thanks go to various people around the office as well as the Trinity OS
# author, David A. Ranch.  To see a more comprehensive firewall example as
# well as other security related topics, please see David's TrinityOS
# document at:
#      http://www.ecst.csuchico.edu/~dranch/LINUX/index-linux.html
```

```
#
# There are three user-configurable sections.  The first is for the network
# values for the firewall.  The second is for CIPE configuration.  The third
# consists of the ipchains commands themselves.  The only thing that should
# need to be changed for the third section is uncommenting the cipe rulesets
# if needed (they are deactivated by default).
#
# Things to watch out for when using this script:
#    a. When starting it by hand it tends to like the network already up.
#       This includes both interfaces.  (When started automatically by
#       init it is started pretty early, there is minimal time for the
#       window to be open. This is medium security, afterall.
#    b. pump, which controls dhcp under Red Hat, isn't very good at picking
#       up a change in address for the interface.  So if the IP addy of the
#       interface changes, the script might need to be start/stopped by hand.
#       You'll loose connectivity and a lot of messages about UDP errors will
#       be logged to /var/log/messages when this happens.
#    c. This script is an example.  It is targeted for a small LAN (a single
#       subnet) and would require work for a more complex network.  It is
#       also not guaranteed to be secure, though it is reasonable.
#
#    NO WARRANTY
# This script is distributed in the hope that it will be useful, but
# WITHOUT ANY WARRANTY, without even the implied warranty of MERCHANTABILITY
# or FITNESS FOR A PARTICULAR PURPOSE.  See the GNU General Public License
# (http://www.gnu.org/copyleft/gpl.html) for more details.
#
#
###### SCRIPT START ########
# ---- these are for the function calls so the script will run as a service
#       only change this if the location on your system is different.  It
#       shouldn't be.
# Source function library.
. /etc/rc.d/init.d/functions

# Source networking configuration.
#       only change this if the location on your system is different.  It
#       shouldn't be.
. /etc/sysconfig/network
. /etc/sysconfig/cipe

# ---- Basic sanity check.  This makes sure that networking is up.  If it
#       isn't, why continue?
# Check that networking is up.
```

```
[ ${NETWORKING} = "no" ] && exit 0


##### USER CONFIGURATION START ######################################
# ---- The device name for the external network interface (in this case "eth1"
#      Change this to match the interface that is your external (WAN) inter-
#      face.  (PPP users would use ppp0, for example).
EXTDEV=eth1
# ---- Don't change the code below.  It uses the ifconfig command and
#      cuts the relevant information out of the display (the IP address) and
#      configures it.  Replacing the code segment with the IP address would
#      result in the same information anyway.  The advantage of using the
#      code below is for DHCP or other dynamic networks.
EXTERNALIP=`ifconfig $EXTDEV | grep "inet addr:" | \
    awk -F: {'print $2'} | cut -d\  -f 1`
if [ -z "${EXTERNALIP}" ]; then
    exit 1
fi


# ---- The device name for the internal network interface (in this case "eth0"
#      See comments above.
INTDEV=eth0
#      See comments above.
INTERNALIP=`ifconfig $INTDEV | grep "inet addr:" | \
    awk -F: {'print $2'} | cut -d\  -f 1`
if [ -z "${INTERNALIP}" ]; then
    exit 1
fi


# ---- The network value for the internal network, in this case it is the
#      reserved block of 192.168.20.xxx  Chance it to match the internal net-
#      work you are using.
INTNET="192.168.20.0"


# ===== End of the first configuration section

# CIPE Configuration section.
# ---- If running CIPE, uncomment these lines.  If you are not running CIPE
#      DON'T mess with any of these.
#CIPEDEV=cipcb0
#CIPE_INET=`ifconfig $CIPEDEV | grep "inet addr:" | \
#    awk -F: {'print $2'} | cut -d\  -f 1`
#if [ -z "${INTERNALIP}" ]; then
#    exit 1
#fi
```

```
#
#CIPE_PTP=`ifconfig $CIPEDEV | grep "P-t-P:" | \
#    awk -F: {'print $3'} | cut -d\  -f 1`
#if [ -z "${INTERNALIP}" ]; then
#    exit 1
# fi
#
# # The internal IPs used for the destination network.
# CIPEINTNET="xxx.xxx.xxx.xxx"
# The real IP network used for Red Hat
# CIPEREALNET="xxx.xxx.xxx.xxx"
# The IP Tunnel Box's IP Addy
# TUNNEL="xxx.xxx.xxx.xxx"
# IMPORTANT NOTE: If using CIPE then the sections below with the same
#                 variables will need to be uncommented.  If you don't
#                 know what CIPE is or don't know how to configure it,
#                 leave it alone.  Variable list: TUNNEL, CIPEREALNET,
#                 CIPEINTNET
# ===== End of CIPE configuration section

echo "EXTDEV: ${EXTDEV} on ${EXTERNALIP}"
echo "INTDEV: ${INTDEV} on ${INTERNALIP}"

# See how we were called.
case "$1" in
  start)
    # Start firewall.
    echo -n "Starting firewall: "

    modprobe ip_masq_ftp
    modprobe ip_masq_irc
    modprobe ip_masq_raudio

# ---- Begin of firewall/ipchain rules.
#  NOTE:  If you have your own firewall script you would rather use, you
#  can replace the below section with it. Replace everything until the ***
#      Don't mess with these unless you know what you are doing.
#    # MASQ timeouts.  Change these only if the timeouts are causing
#                     problems.
#    2 hrs timeout for TCP session timeouts (7200 seconds)
#    10 sec timeout for traffic after the TCP/IP "FIN" packet is
#      received
#    60 sec timeout for UDP traffic (MASQ'ed ICQ users must enable
#      a 30sec firewal
#
```

```
echo "Setting masq timeouts"
ipchains -M -S 7200 10 60


##################################################################
# Forwarding, flush and set default policy of deny. Actually the
# default policy is irrelevant because there is a catch all rule
# with deny and log.

echo "Setting new forward rules"
echo -n "forward..."

# This makes sure that IP forwarding is turned on for networking.
echo 1 > /proc/sys/net/ipv4/ip_forward

# This does the flush
ipchains -F forward
# This sets the default to DENY
ipchains -P forward DENY

# Masquerade from local net on local interface to anywhere.  The
# 255.255.255.0 netmasks out to the last section.  Using the above
# internal network example, it makes it everything in the
# 192.168.20.xxx range to be legal on this interface.
ipchains -A forward -s $INTNET/255.255.255.0 -j MASQ
# Masquerade from local net on local interface to anywhere.  Like the
# above rule, this one says that anything that has the source of the
# internal network should be forwarded to the external device and
# all these packets are to be masquared.  The -d 0.0.0.0/0 indicates
# that the destination of the traffic can be to anywhere.
ipchains -A forward -i $EXTDEV -s $INTNET/24 -d 0.0.0.0/0 -j MASQ

# Backup Rule.  Try this out if forwarding doesn't seem to work with
# the above rule (make sure to comment out the above).  It says that
# any packets are to be masq'd and forwarded to the external device.
# ipchains -A forward -i $EXTDEV -j MASQ

# CIPE Forwarding.  Ignore this unless you need it.
# ipchains -A forward -d $CIPEINTNET/255.255.255.0
# ipchains -A forward -d $CIPEREALNET/255.255.254.0

# catch all rule, all other forwarding is denied and logged. pity
# there is no log option on the policy but this does the job instead.
ipchains -A forward -s 0.0.0.0/0 -d 0.0.0.0/0 -l -j DENY

# These are variations of the uncommented rule above.
```

```
#ipchains -A forward -j DENY -l
#ipchains -A forward -j DENY

### Port Forwarding Operations ################################
#  Uncomment these commands only if port forwarding is needed.
#    this one
# echo "Enabling IPPORTFW Redirection on the external LAN..."
#    this one
# /usr/sbin/ipmasqadm portfw -f
#
# You probably don't have the ipmasqadm package installed.  If
# not, go to http://juanjox.kernelnotes.org/ for the binaries.
# before trying to run these commands.  "rpm -q ipmasqadm" can
# be used to check for the package.
#
#### ---- These Are Examples of Port Forwards
## This one forwards the httpd port from the firewall and
## points it to another machine on the LAN with the IP address of
## 192.168.100.100
# /usr/sbin/ipmasqadm portfw -a -P tcp -L $EXTERNALIP 80 \
#    -R 192.168.100.100 80

## This one forwards a specilized port from the firewall and
## points it at a machine on the LAN with the IP address of
## 192.168.100.100 at port 7000.
# /usr/sbin/ipmasqadm portfw -a -P tcp -L $EXTERNALIP 7000 \
# -R 192.168.100.100 7000


##################################################################
# Incoming, flush and set default policy of deny. Actually the
# default policy is irrelevant because there is a catch all rule
# with deny and log.

echo -n "input..."
echo "Setting new input rules"
# Incoming, flush and set default policy of deny.
ipchains -F input
ipchains -P input DENY

# local interface, local machines, going anywhere is valid
ipchains -A input -i $INTDEV -s $INTNET/24 -d 0.0.0.0/0 -j ACCEPT

# multicasting is valid (xntpd)
ipchains -A input -i $EXTDEV -s $EXTERNALIP/32 -d 224.0.0.0/8 -j ACCEPT
```

```
# remote interface, claiming to be local machines, IP spoofing,
# the rule tells to get lost
ipchains -A input -i $EXTDEV -s $INTNET/24 -d 0.0.0.0/0 -j DENY

# loopback interface is valid.
ipchains -A input -i lo -s 0.0.0.0/0 -d 0.0.0.0/0 -j ACCEPT

# The following are ports that could not be configured to only
# listen on the internal network, thus we firewall the external side.

# Deny access to the backup software port
# These lines are read as "Add to Input, Protocol "tcp", source "all"
# with the destentation
ipchains -A input -p tcp -s 0.0.0.0/0 -d $EXTERNALIP 617 -j DENY

# Deny access to the firewall auth port
ipchains -A input -p tcp -s 0.0.0.0/0 -d $EXTERNALIP 7777 -j DENY

# Deny access to the echo port (used by squid/junkbuster)
ipchains -A input -p udp -s 0.0.0.0/0 -d $EXTERNALIP 7 -j DENY

# Deny access to syslog
ipchains -A input -p udp -s 0.0.0.0/0 -d $EXTERNALIP 514 -j DENY

# remote interface, any source, going to external address is valid
ipchains -A input -i $EXTDEV -s 0.0.0.0/0 -d $EXTERNALIP/32 -j ACCEPT

# IP-IP tunnel.  Use these only if you need them.
# FIXME: limit this to a device (EXTDEV OR CIPEDEV)
# ipchains -A input -p udp -s $TUNNEL $PORT -j ACCEPT
# ipchains -A input -i $CIPEDEV -j ACCEPT

# catch all rule, all other incoming is denied.
# ipchains -A input -j DENY -l
# ipchains -A input -j DENY
ipchains -A input -s 0.0.0.0/0 -d 0.0.0.0/0 -l -j DENY


########################################################################
# Outgoing, flush and set default policy of reject. Actually the
# default policy is irrelevant because there is a catch all rule
# with deny and log.

echo "Setting new output rules"
echo -n "output..."
```

```
# Outgoing, flush and set default policy of deny.
ipchains -F output
ipchains -P output DENY

# local interface, any source going to local net is valid
#ipchains -A output -i $INTDEV -s 0.0.0.0/0 -d $INTNET/24 -j ACCEPT
ipchains -A output -i $INTDEV -s 0.0.0.0/0 -d $INTNET/24 -j ACCEPT

# loopback interface is valid.
# ipchains -A output -i lo -s 0.0.0.0/0 -d 0.0.0.0/0 -j ACCEPT
ipchains -A output -i lo -s 0.0.0.0/0 -d 0.0.0.0/0 -j ACCEPT

# outgoing to local net on remote interface: stuffed routing, deny
ipchains -A output -i $EXTDEV -s 0.0.0.0/0 -d $INTNET/24 -j DENY

# outgoing from local net on remote interface: stuffed masq, deny
ipchains -A output -i $EXTDEV -s $INTNET/24 -d 0.0.0.0/0 -j DENY

# anything else outgoing on remote interface is valid
#ipchains -A output -i $EXTDEV -d 0.0.0.0/0 -j ACCEPT
ipchains -A output -i $EXTDEV -s $EXTERNALIP/32 -d 0.0.0.0/0 -j ACCEPT

# outgoing to IP-IP tunnel for CIPE server is valid.  Use these
# Only if you need them.
# ipchains -A output -i $CIPEDEV -s $CIPE_INET -d $CIPE_PTP/32 -j ACCEPT
# ipchains -A output -i $CIPEDEV -s $CIPE_INET -d $CIPEREALNET/23 \
#    -j ACCEPT
# ipchains -A output -i $CIPEDEV -s $EXTERNALIP -d $CIPEREALNET/23 \
#    -j ACCEPT
# ipchains -A output -i $CIPEDEV -s $CIPE_INET -d 0.0.0.0/0 -j ACCEPT

# catch all rule, all other outgoing is denied.
# ipchains -A output -j DENY -l
# ipchains -A output -j DENY
ipchains -A output -s 0.0.0.0/0 -d 0.0.0.0/0 -l -j DENY


echo "Done with the firewall rulesets"
echo -n "acct..."

# Accounting, flush all entries
ipchains -N acctin
ipchains -N acctout
ipchains -N acctio
# Track traffic just to network, not individual hosts
```

```
      ipchains -I input -j acctio
      ipchains -I input -j acctin
      ipchains -I output -j acctio
      ipchains -I output -j acctout
      ipchains -I forward -j acctout

      echo "done"
      touch /var/lock/subsys/firewall
      ;;

   stop)
      # Stop firewall.
      echo -n "Shutting down firewall: "
      ipchains -F input
      ipchains -A input -j ACCEPT
      ipchains -F output
      ipchains -A output -j ACCEPT
      ipchains -F forward
      ipchains -A forward -j ACCEPT
      ipchains -X acctio
      ipchains -X acctin
      ipchains -X acctout

      rmmod ip_masq_raudio
      rmmod ip_masq_irc
      rmmod ip_masq_ftp

      echo "done"
      rm -f /var/lock/subsys/firewall
      ;;

   restart)
      $0 stop
      $0 start
      ;;

   status)
      status firewall
      ;;

   *)
      echo "Usage: firewall {start|stop|restart|status}"
      exit 1
esac

exit 0
```

Simple IPTables Firewall (Chapter 8)

```
# Replace xxx.xxx.xxx.xxx with IP address of name server
iptables -F
iptables -X
iptables -P INPUT   ACCEPT
iptables -P OUTPUT  ACCEPT
iptables -P FORWARD ACCEPT
iptables -A INPUT -i lo -j ACCEPT
iptables -A INPUT -p udp -s xxx.xxx.xxx.xxx --sport 53 -j ACCEPT
iptables -A INPUT -p tcp --syn -j REJECT
iptables -A INPUT -p udp -j REJECT
```

IPTables Host Firewall (Chapter 9)

```
#!/bin/sh

##################################################################
#  Host firewall 1.0                                             #
#                                                                #
# Firewall for single-homed host, featuring restrictive (blocked by #
# default) input and output rule sets and restrictive ICMP rule set. #
# Includes TCP flag validation and SYN rate limiting.            #
#                                                                #
# Copyright (C) 2002 Bill McCarty                                #
#                                                                #
# This program is free software; you can redistribute it and/or modify #
# it under the terms of the GNU General Public License as published by #
# the Free Software Foundation, version 2 or later.              #
#                                                                #
# WITHOUT ANY WARRANTY, not even implied warranties such as      #
# MERCHANTABILITY or FITNESS FOR A PARTICULAR PURPOSE. See the GNU #
# General Public License for details.                            #
#                                                                #
# You should have received a copy of the GNU General Public License #
# with this program or have been able to obtain it from the program's #
# download site. If not, you can obtain it from the Free Software #
# Foundation's web site, www.gnu.org.                            #
##################################################################
```

```
##############################################################################
# Load kernel modules
##############################################################################

/sbin/modprobe/ip_tables
/sbin/modprobe/ip_conntrack
/sbin/modprobe/iptable_filter
/sbin/modprobe/iptable_mangle
/sbin/modprobe/iptable_nat
/sbin/modprobe/ipt_LOG
/sbin/modprobe/ipt_REJECT
/sbin/modprobe/ipt_limit
/sbin/modprobe/ipt_state
/sbin/modprobe/ip_conntrack_ftp
/sbin/modprobe/ip_conntrack_irc


##############################################################################
# Set kernel configuration options
##############################################################################

sysctl -w net.ipv4.conf.default.rp_filter = 1
sysctl -w net.ipv4.conf.eth0.accept_source_routing = 0


##############################################################################
# Assignments
##############################################################################

# Firewall host IP address
IP="xxx.xxx.xxx.xxx"

# Host lists for inbound services
PING=""
SSH="0.0.0.0/0"
WWW="0.0.0.0/0"

# Rate limits
SYNOPT="-m limit --limit 5/second --limit-burst 10"
LOGOPT="--log-level=3 -m limit --limit 1/second --limit-burst 10"

# The following assignments should not generally need to be changed
BADIP="0.0.0.0/8 10.0.0.0/8 127.0.0.0/8 169.254.0.0/16 172.16.0.0/12 192.0.0/24
192.168.0.0/16 192.0.34.0/24 224.0.0.0/4 240.0.0.0/5 255.255.255.255"
SHUNIP=""
LO="127.0.0.1"
SSH="$SSH $LO"
```

```
WWW="$WWW $LO"
IPT=/sbin/iptables


###########################################################################
# Clear the existing firewall rules
###########################################################################

if [ ! -x $IPTABLES ]
then
  echo "firewall: can't execute $IPTABLES"
  exit 1
fi

$IPT -P INPUT   DROP     # Set default policy to DROP
$IPT -P OUTPUT  DROP     # Set default policy to DROP
$IPT -P FORWARD DROP     # Set default policy to DROP
$IPT -F                  # Flush all chains
$IPT -X                  # Delete all chains

for table in filter nat mangle
do
  $IPT -t $table -F           # Delete the table's rules
  $IPT -t $table -X           # Delete the table's chains
  $IPT -t $table -Z           # Zero the table's counters
done


###########################################################################
# Logging chain
###########################################################################

$IPT -N LDROP
$IPT -A LDROP    -j LOG --log-prefix "IPT Drop:   " $LOGOPT
$IPT -A LDROP    -j DROP

$IPT -N LBADIP
$IPT -A LBADIP   -p tcp --dport 137:139 -j DROP
$IPT -A LBADIP   -p udp --dport 137:139 -j DROP
$IPT -A LBADIP   -j LOG --log-prefix "IPT BAD:   " $LOGOPT
$IPT -A LBADIP   -j DROP

$IPT -N LSHUN
$IPT -A LSHUN    -j LOG --log-prefix "IPT Shun:   " $LOGOPT
$IPT -A LSHUN    -j DROP

$IPT -N LFLOOD
```

```
$IPT -A LFLOOD  -j LOG --log-prefix "IPT Flood:  " $LOGOPT
$IPT -A LFLOOD  -j DROP


$IPT -N LFLAGS
$IPT -A LFLAGS  -j LOG --log-prefix "IPT Flags:  " $LOGOPT
$IPT -A LFLAGS  -j DROP


##############################################################################
# Bad IPs
##############################################################################


$IPT -N BADIP
for ip in $BADIP; do
  $IPT -A BADIP -s $ip -j LBADIP
  $IPT -A BADIP -d $ip -j LBADIP
done


##############################################################################
# Shunned Hosts
##############################################################################


$IPT -N SHUN
for ip in $SHUNIP; do
  $IPT -A SHUN -s $ip -j LSHUN
  $IPT -A SHUN -d $ip -j LSHUN
done


##############################################################################
# SYN Flood Protection (TCP SYN datagrams)
##############################################################################


$IPT -N FLOOD

# Following rule accepting datagram fires at limited rate.

$IPT -A FLOOD $SYNOPT -j RETURN
$IPT -A FLOOD          -j LFLOOD


##############################################################################
# TCP Flag Validation (TCP datagrams)
##############################################################################


$IPT -N FLAGS
$IPT -A FLAGS -p tcp --tcp-flags ACK,FIN FIN              -j LFLAGS
$IPT -A FLAGS -p tcp --tcp-flags ACK,PSH PSH             -j LFLAGS
```

```
$IPT -A FLAGS -p tcp --tcp-flags ACK,URG URG                -j LFLAGS
$IPT -A FLAGS -p tcp --tcp-flags FIN,RST FIN,RST            -j LFLAGS
$IPT -A FLAGS -p tcp --tcp-flags SYN,FIN SYN,FIN            -j LFLAGS
$IPT -A FLAGS -p tcp --tcp-flags SYN,RST SYN,RST            -j LFLAGS
$IPT -A FLAGS -p tcp --tcp-flags ALL ALL                    -j LFLAGS
$IPT -A FLAGS -p tcp --tcp-flags ALL NONE                   -j LFLAGS
$IPT -A FLAGS -p tcp --tcp-flags ALL FIN,PSH,URG            -j LFLAGS
$IPT -A FLAGS -p tcp --tcp-flags ALL SYN,FIN,PSH,URG        -j LFLAGS
$IPT -A FLAGS -p tcp --tcp-flags ALL SYN,RST,ACK,FIN,URG    -j LFLAGS

# Remaining flag combinations considered valid.

##############################################################################
# Input TCP/UDP datagrams
##############################################################################

$IPT -N IN
$IPT -A IN -m state --state INVALID -j LDROP
$IPT -A IN -p tcp --syn -j FLOOD
$IPT -A IN -p tcp        -j FLAGS
$IPT -A IN -m state --state ESTABLISHED,RELATED -j ACCEPT
$IPT -A IN -s $IP -j LDROP

# Accept new inbound connections.

for sip in $SSH; do
  $IPT -A IN -p tcp -s $sip --dport 22 -m state --state NEW -j ACCEPT
done

for sip in $WWW; do
  $IPT -A IN -p tcp -s $sip --dport 80 -m state --state NEW -j ACCEPT
done

# Reject AUTH requests

$IPT -A IN -p tcp --dport 113 -j REJECT --reject-with tcp-reset

# Add additional rules accepting authorized traffic here.
# Traffic not explicitly accepted will be logged and dropped.


##############################################################################
# Output TCP/UDP datagrams
##############################################################################
```

```
$IPT -N OUT
$IPT -A OUT -p tcp -j FLAGS
$IPT -A OUT -s ! $IP -j LDROP
$IPT -A OUT -m state --state ESTABLISHED,RELATED -j ACCEPT
#
# This firewall is configured to block outbound connections by default.
# To allow any output not explicitly blocked, uncomment the following
# line. Place blocking rules here.
#$IPT -A OUT -m state --state NEW                -j ACCEPT

# Accept new outbound connections.

$IPT -A OUT -m state --state NEW -p tcp --dport  21 -j ACCEPT      # ftp
$IPT -A OUT -m state --state NEW -p tcp --dport  22 -j ACCEPT      # ssh
$IPT -A OUT -m state --state NEW -p tcp --dport  25 -j ACCEPT      # smtp
$IPT -A OUT -m state --state NEW -p tcp --dport  43 -j ACCEPT      # whois
$IPT -A OUT -m state --state NEW -p tcp --dport  53 -j ACCEPT      # domain
$IPT -A OUT -m state --state NEW -p tcp --dport  80 -j ACCEPT      # http
$IPT -A OUT -m state --state NEW -p tcp --dport 443 -j ACCEPT      # https
$IPT -A OUT -m state --state NEW -p tcp --dport 873 -j ACCEPT      # rsync

$IPT -A OUT -m state --state NEW -p udp --dport  53 -j ACCEPT      # domain

# Add additional rules accepting authorized traffic here.
# Traffic not explicitly accepted will be logged and dropped.

##############################################################################
# Inbound ICMP messages
##############################################################################

$IPT -N IN_ICMP
for sip in $PING; do
  $IPT -A IN_ICMP  -p icmp --icmp-type echo-request -s $sip -d $IP \
                                                    -j ACCEPT
  $IPT -A IN_ICMP  -p icmp --icmp-type echo-reply   -s $sip -d $IP \
                                                    -j ACCEPT
done
$IPT -A IN_ICMP  -p icmp --icmp-type destination-unreachable  -j ACCEPT
$IPT -A IN_ICMP  -p icmp --icmp-type source-quench            -j ACCEPT
$IPT -A IN_ICMP  -p icmp --icmp-type time-exceeded            -j ACCEPT
$IPT -A IN_ICMP  -p icmp --icmp-type parameter-problem        -j ACCEPT

##############################################################################
# Outbound ICMP messages
##############################################################################
```

```
$IPT -N OUT_ICMP
for dip in $PING; do
  $IPT -A OUT_ICMP -p icmp --icmp-type echo-reply    -d $dip     -j ACCEPT
  $IPT -A OUT_ICMP -p icmp --icmp-type echo-request -d $dip     -j ACCEPT
done
$IPT -A OUT_ICMP -p icmp --icmp-type destination-unreachable  -j ACCEPT
$IPT -A OUT_ICMP -p icmp --icmp-type fragmentation-needed     -j ACCEPT
$IPT -A OUT_ICMP -p icmp --icmp-type source-quench            -j ACCEPT
$IPT -A OUT_ICMP -p icmp --icmp-type parameter-problem        -j ACCEPT


##############################################################################
# Rules for built-in chains
##############################################################################

$IPT -A INPUT -i lo      -j ACCEPT
$IPT -A INPUT            -j BADIP
$IPT -A INPUT            -j SHUN
$IPT -A INPUT -p ! icmp  -j IN
$IPT -A INPUT -p   icmp  -j IN_ICMP
$IPT -A INPUT            -j LDROP

$IPT -A OUTPUT -o lo     -j ACCEPT
$IPT -A OUTPUT           -j BADIP
$IPT -A OUTPUT           -j SHUN
$IPT -A OUTPUT -p ! icmp -j OUT
$IPT -A OUTPUT -p   icmp -j OUT_ICMP
$IPT -A OUTPUT           -j LDROP
```

IPTables Screened Network Firewall (Chapter 10)

```
#!/bin/sh
#
# requirements:
# - sysctls in /etc/sysctl.conf
# - modprobes in /etc/rc./rc.local


#----------------------------------------------------------------------------
#   Screened network firewall
#
#   Copyright (C) 2002 Bill McCarty
#
```

```
# This program is free software; you can redistribute it and/or modify
# it under the terms of the GNU General Public License as published by
# the Free Software Foundation, version 2 or later.
#
# This program is distributed in the hope that it may be useful, but
# WITHOUT ANY WARRANTY, not even implied warranties such as
# MERCHANTABILITY or FITNESS FOR A PARTICULAR PURPOSE. See the GNU
# General Public License for details.
#
# You should have received a copy of the GNU General Public License
# with this program or have been able to obtain it from the program's
# download site. If not, you can obtain it from the Free Software
# Foundation's web site, www.gnu.org.
#-----------------------------------------------------------------------


#-----------------------------------------------------------------------
# Assignments
#-----------------------------------------------------------------------

# Change these assignments to conform to your network architecture
# Weed unneeded variables

EXTDEV=eth0
EXTIP="192.0.34.72"
EXTBASE="192.0.34.0"
EXTBCAST="192.0.34.255"
EXTGATE="192.0.34.254"


INTDEV=eth1
INTIP="10.0.0.1"
INTBASE="10.0.0.0"
INTBCAST="10.0.0.255"
INTNET="10.0.0.0/8"

# IP addresses of hosts and networks authorized to ping firewall
PING="192.0.34.2 $INTNET"

# IP addresses of hosts and networks allowed to SSH into firewall
SSH="192.0.34.2"

# IP address of each public server on internal network
SMTPIP="10.0.0.2"
DNSIP="10.0.0.2"
HTTPIP="10.0.0.2"
POPIP="10.0.0.2"
```

```
AUTHIP="10.0.0.2"
IMAPIP="10.0.0.2"

# IP addresses of hosts and networks not to be communicated with.
SHUN=""

# The following assignments should not generally need to be changed

BADIP="$EXTBASE $EXTBCAST $INTBASE $INTBCAST 0.0.0.0/8 10.0.0.0/8 127.0.0.0/8
169.254.0.0/16 172.16.0.0/12 192.0.2.0/24 224.0.0.0/4 240.0.0.0/5
255.255.255.255"

IPT=/sbin/iptables
LOGOPT="--log-level=3 -m limit --limit 3/minute --limit-burst 3"
SYNOPT="-m limit --limit 5/second --limit-burst 10"

#-------------------------------------------------------------------------------
# Clear the existing firewall rules
#-------------------------------------------------------------------------------

if [ ! -x $IPTABLES ]
then
  die "firewall: can't execute $IPTABLES"
fi

$IPT -P INPUT   DROP      # Set default policy to DROP
$IPT -P OUTPUT  DROP      # Set default policy to DROP
$IPT -P FORWARD DROP      # Set default policy to DROP
$IPT -F                   # Flush all chains
$IPT -X                   # Delete all chains

for table in filter nat mangle
do
  $IPT -t $table -F       # Delete the table's rules
  $IPT -t $table -X       # Delete the table's chains
  $IPT -t $table -Z       # Zero the table's counters
done

#-------------------------------------------------------------------------------
# Bad TCP Flags
#-------------------------------------------------------------------------------

$IPT -N BADFLAGS
$IPT -A BADFLAGS -j LOG --log-prefix "IPT BADFLAGS: " $LOGOPT
$IPT -A BADFLAGS -j DROP
```

```
#-------------------------------------------------------------------------
# TCP Flag Validation
#-------------------------------------------------------------------------

$IPT -N TCP_FLAGS
$IPT -A TCP_FLAGS -p tcp --tcp-flags ACK,FIN FIN               -j BADFLAGS
$IPT -A TCP_FLAGS -p tcp --tcp-flags ACK,PSH PSH              -j BADFLAGS
$IPT -A TCP_FLAGS -p tcp --tcp-flags ACK,URG URG             -j BADFLAGS
$IPT -A TCP_FLAGS -p tcp --tcp-flags FIN,RST FIN,RST         -j BADFLAGS
$IPT -A TCP_FLAGS -p tcp --tcp-flags SYN,FIN SYN,FIN         -j BADFLAGS
$IPT -A TCP_FLAGS -p tcp --tcp-flags SYN,RST SYN,RST         -j BADFLAGS
$IPT -A TCP_FLAGS -p tcp --tcp-flags ALL ALL                 -j BADFLAGS
$IPT -A TCP_FLAGS -p tcp --tcp-flags ALL NONE               -j BADFLAGS
$IPT -A TCP_FLAGS -p tcp --tcp-flags ALL FIN,PSH,URG        -j BADFLAGS
$IPT -A TCP_FLAGS -p tcp --tcp-flags ALL SYN,FIN,PSH,URG    -j BADFLAGS
$IPT -A TCP_FLAGS -p tcp --tcp-flags ALL SYN,RST,ACK,FIN,URG -j BADFLAGS


#-------------------------------------------------------------------------
# SYN Flood Protection
#-------------------------------------------------------------------------

$IPT -N SYN_FLOOD
$IPT -A SYN_FLOOD -p   tcp    --syn $SYNOPT -j RETURN
$IPT -A SYN_FLOOD -p ! tcp               -j RETURN
$IPT -A SYN_FLOOD -p   tcp ! --syn        -j RETURN
$IPT -A SYN_FLOOD -j LOG --log-prefix "IPT SYN_FLOOD: " $LOGOPT
$IPT -A SYN_FLOOD -j DROP


#-------------------------------------------------------------------------
# Bad IP Chain
#-------------------------------------------------------------------------

$IPT -N BAD_IP
$IPT -A BAD_IP -j LOG --log-prefix "IPT BAD_IP: " $LOGOPT
$IPT -A BAD_IP -j DROP


#-------------------------------------------------------------------------
# Shunned Hosts
#-------------------------------------------------------------------------

$IPT -N SHUN
for ip in $SHUN; do
  $IPT -A SHUN -s $ip -j BAD_IP
  $IPT -A SHUN -d $ip -j BAD_IP
done
```

```
#---------------------------------------------------------------------------
# Inbound IP Checks
#---------------------------------------------------------------------------

$IPT -N IN_IP_CHECK
for sip in $BADSIP
do
  $IPT -A IN_IP_CHECK -s $sip -j BAD_IP
done
$IPT -A IN_IP_CHECK -i $EXTDEV -s $EXTIP  -j BAD_IP
$IPT -A IN_IP_CHECK -i $EXTDEV -s $INTNET -j BAD_IP
$IPT -A IN_IP_CHECK -i $INTDEV -s $EXTIP  -j BAD_IP


#---------------------------------------------------------------------------
# Outbound IP Checks
#---------------------------------------------------------------------------

$IPT -N OUT_IP_CHECK
for dip in $BADIP
do
  $IPT -A OUT_IP_CHECK -d $dip -j BAD_IP
done
$IPT -A OUT_IP_CHECK -o $EXTDEV -s $EXTIP  -j RETURN
$IPT -A OUT_IP_CHECK -o $INTDEV -s $INTIP  -j RETURN
$IPT -A OUT_IP_CHECK -j BAD_IP


#---------------------------------------------------------------------------
# Inbound ICMP
#---------------------------------------------------------------------------

$IPT -N IN_ICMP
for sip in $PING; do
  $IPT -A IN_ICMP  -p icmp --icmp-type echo-request -s $sip   -j ACCEPT
  $IPT -A IN_ICMP  -p icmp --icmp-type echo-reply   -s $sip   -j ACCEPT
done
$IPT -A IN_ICMP  -p icmp --icmp-type destination-unreachable  -j ACCEPT
$IPT -A IN_ICMP  -p icmp --icmp-type source-quench            -j ACCEPT
$IPT -A IN_ICMP  -p icmp --icmp-type time-exceeded            -j ACCEPT
$IPT -A IN_ICMP  -p icmp --icmp-type parameter-problem        -j ACCEPT
$IPT -A IN_ICMP -j LOG --log-prefix "IPT In ICMP: " $LOGOPT
$IPT -A IN_ICMP -j DROP


#---------------------------------------------------------------------------
# Outbound ICMP
#---------------------------------------------------------------------------
```

```
$IPT -N OUT_ICMP
for dip in $PING; do
  $IPT -A OUT_ICMP -p icmp --icmp-type echo-request -d $dip     -j ACCEPT
  $IPT -A OUT_ICMP -p icmp --icmp-type echo-reply   -d $dip     -j ACCEPT
done
#
# For a less courteous -- but potentially more secure -- firewall,
# replace destination-unreachable by fragmentation-needed in the
# following rule.
#
$IPT -A OUT_ICMP -p icmp --icmp-type destination-unreachable  -j ACCEPT
$IPT -A OUT_ICMP -p icmp --icmp-type source-quench            -j ACCEPT
#
# For a less courteous -- but potentially more secure -- firewall,
# delete the following parameter-problem rule.
#
$IPT -A OUT_ICMP -p icmp --icmp-type parameter-problem        -j ACCEPT
$IPT -A OUT_ICMP -j LOG --log-prefix "IPT Out ICMP: " $LOGOPT
$IPT -A OUT_ICMP -j DROP


#---------------------------------------------------------------------------
# Destination NAT
#---------------------------------------------------------------------------

if [ "$SMTPIP" != "" ]
then
  $IPT -t nat -A PREROUTING -i $EXTDEV -p tcp -d $EXTIP --dport 25 \
    -j DNAT --to-destination $HTTPIP
fi

if [ "$DNSIP" != "" ]
then
  $IPT -t nat -A PREROUTING -i $EXTDEV -p udp -d $EXTIP --dport 53 \
    -j DNAT --to-destination $HTTPIP
fi

if [ "$HTTPIP" != "" ]
then
  $IPT -t nat -A PREROUTING -i $EXTDEV -p tcp -d $EXTIP --dport 80 \
    -j DNAT --to-destination $HTTPIP
fi
```

```
if [ "$POPIP" != "" ]
then
  $IPT -t nat -A PREROUTING -i $EXTDEV -p tcp -d $EXTIP --dport 110 \
    -j DNAT --to-destination $POPIP
fi

if [ "$AUTHIP" != "" ]
then
  $IPT -t nat -A PREROUTING -i $EXTDEV -p tcp -d $EXTIP --dport 113 \
    -j DNAT --to-destination $HTTPIP
fi

if [ "$IMAPIP" != "" ]
then
  $IPT -t nat -A PREROUTING -i $EXTDEV -p tcp -d $EXTIP --dport 143 \
    -j DNAT --to-destination $IMAPIP
fi


#-----------------------------------------------------------------------------
# Source NAT
#-----------------------------------------------------------------------------

$IPT -t nat -A POSTROUTING -o $EXTDEV          -j SNAT --to-source $EXTIP

#-----------------------------------------------------------------------------
# Inbound traffic to protected network
#-----------------------------------------------------------------------------

$IPT -N IN_NETWORK
$IPT -A IN_NETWORK -p icmp                             -j IN_ICMP
$IPT -A IN_NETWORK -p tcp                              -j TCP_FLAGS
$IPT -A IN_NETWORK -p tcp --syn                        -j SYN_FLOOD
$IPT -A IN_NETWORK -p tcp -m state --state ESTABLISHED,RELATED -j ACCEPT
$IPT -A IN_NETWORK -p udp -m state --state ESTABLISHED,RELATED -j ACCEPT

if [ "$SMTPIP" != "" ]
then
  $IPT -A IN_NETWORK -p tcp --syn -d $SMTPIP --dport 25    -j ACCEPT
fi

if [ "$DNSIP" != "" ]
then
  $IPT -A IN_NETWORK -p udp      -d $DNSIP  --dport 53     -j ACCEPT
fi
```

```
if [ "$HTTPIP" != "" ]
then
   $IPT -A IN_NETWORK -p tcp --syn -d $HTTPIP --dport 80        -j ACCEPT
fi


if [ "$POPIP" != "" ]
then
   $IPT -A IN_NETWORK -p tcp --syn -d $POPIP  --dport 110       -j ACCEPT
fi
#
# If the AUTH service is not running -- which it generally should
# not be -- the TCP/IP stack will respond to clients with a TCP
# RST packet, effectively rejecting the connection. So, it's
# reasonable to open this port even if no service is running.
#
if [ "$AUTHIP" != "" ]
then
   $IPT -A IN_NETWORK -p tcp --syn -d $AUTHIP --dport 113       -j ACCEPT
fi


if [ "$IMAPIP" != "" ]
then
   $IPT -A IN_NETWORK -p tcp --syn -d $IMAPIP --dport 143       -j ACCEPT
fi


#--------------------------------------------------------------------------
# Outbound traffic from protected network
#--------------------------------------------------------------------------

$IPT -N OUT_NETWORK
$IPT -A OUT_NETWORK -p icmp -j OUT_ICMP
$IPT -A OUT_NETWORK -p tcp  -j TCP_FLAGS
$IPT -A OUT_NETWORK -m state --state ESTABLISHED,RELATED -j ACCEPT
#
# The following six rules enable clients running on the protected network
# to connect to remote servers. Add and delete rules to customize the
# authorized services.
#
$IPT -A OUT_NETWORK -m state --state NEW -p tcp --dport  21 -j ACCEPT # ftp
$IPT -A OUT_NETWORK -m state --state NEW -p tcp --dport  22 -j ACCEPT # ssh
$IPT -A OUT_NETWORK -m state --state NEW -p tcp --dport  25 -j ACCEPT # smtp
$IPT -A OUT_NETWORK -m state --state NEW -p tcp --dport  80 -j ACCEPT # http
$IPT -A OUT_NETWORK -m state --state NEW -p tcp --dport 443 -j ACCEPT # https

$IPT -A OUT_NETWORK -m state --state NEW -p udp --dport  53 -j ACCEPT # domain
```

```
#-------------------------------------------------------------------------------
# Inbound traffic to firewall host
#-------------------------------------------------------------------------------

$IPT -N IN_FIREWALL
$IPT -A IN_FIREWALL -p icmp                              -j IN_ICMP
$IPT -A IN_FIREWALL -p tcp                               -j TCP_FLAGS
$IPT -A IN_FIREWALL -p tcp --syn                         -j SYN_FLOOD
$IPT -A IN_FIREWALL                                      -j IN_IP_CHECK
$IPT -A IN_FIREWALL -m state --state ESTABLISHED,RELATED -j ACCEPT
$IPT -A IN_FIREWALL -m state --state ESTABLISHED,RELATED -j ACCEPT
for sip in $SSH
do
   $IPT -A IN_FIREWALL -p tcp -s $sip --dport 22 -m state --state NEW -j ACCEPT
done
#
# Add additional rules authorizing traffic inbound to firewall
# host here.
#
$IPT -A IN_FIREWALL -j LOG --log-prefix "IPT IN_FIREWALL: " $LOGOPT
$IPT -A IN_FIREWALL -j DROP


#-------------------------------------------------------------------------------
# Outbound traffic from firewall host
#-------------------------------------------------------------------------------

$IPT -N OUT_FIREWALL
$IPT -A OUT_FIREWALL -p icmp                              -j OUT_ICMP
$IPT -A OUT_FIREWALL -p tcp                               -j TCP_FLAGS
$IPT -A OUT_FIREWALL -m state --state ESTABLISHED,RELATED -j ACCEPT
$IPT -A OUT_FIREWALL                                      -j OUT_IP_CHECK
#
# The following six rules enable clients running on the firewall host to
# connect to remote servers. Add and delete rules to customize the
# authorized services.
#
$IPT -A OUT_FIREWALL -m state --state NEW -p tcp --dport  21 -j ACCEPT  # ftp
$IPT -A OUT_FIREWALL -m state --state NEW -p tcp --dport  22 -j ACCEPT  # ssh
$IPT -A OUT_FIREWALL -m state --state NEW -p tcp --dport  25 -j ACCEPT  # smtp
$IPT -A OUT_FIREWALL -m state --state NEW -p tcp --dport  80 -j ACCEPT  # http
$IPT -A OUT_FIREWALL -m state --state NEW -p tcp --dport 443 -j ACCEPT  # https

$IPT -A OUT_FIREWALL -m state --state NEW -p udp --dport  53 -j ACCEPT  # domain

$IPT -A OUT_FIREWALL -j LOG --log-prefix "IPT OUT_FIREWALL: " $LOGOPT
$IPT -A OUT_FIREWALL -j DROP
```

```
#----------------------------------------------------------------------------
# Main Firewall Rules
#----------------------------------------------------------------------------

$IPT -A FORWARD                -j SHUN
$IPT -A FORWARD -i $EXTDEV -j IN_NETWORK
$IPT -A FORWARD -i $INTDEV -j OUT_NETWORK
$IPT -A FORWARD                -j LOG --log-prefix "IPT FORWARD: " $LOGOPT
$IPT -A FORWARD                -j DROP

$IPT -A INPUT                  -j SHUN
$IPT -A INPUT    -i lo         -j ACCEPT
$IPT -A INPUT                  -j IN_FIREWALL
$IPT -A INPUT                  -j LOG --log-prefix "IPT INPUT: "   $LOGOPT
$IPT -A INPUT                  -j DROP

$IPT -A OUTPUT                 -j SHUN
$IPT -A OUTPUT -o lo           -j ACCEPT
$IPT -A OUTPUT                 -j OUT_FIREWALL
$IPT -A OUTPUT                 -j LOG --log-prefix "IPT OUTPUT: "  $LOGOPT
$IPT -A OUTPUT                 -j DROP
```

Appendix F

Virtual Private Networks (VPNs)

Virtual private networks (VPNs) enable secure communications between private networks, using the Internet or another insecure network as the means of communication. VPNs are especially useful for connecting remote offices and users to central computing resources. For example, a business having offices in New York, Los Angeles, and London might establish a VPN to enable secure, transparent communication between the offices. The same organization might also configure VPNs enabling staff to securely access the organization's private network from home offices or by using mobile computers, such as laptops.

As the word *virtual* suggests, a VPN can be considered a network implemented in software. Although VPN traffic must traverse a real, physical network, it is encrypted to protect it from eavesdropping and tampering. A VPN is not generally as secure as an actual private network, but a well-designed and -administered VPN provides a high level of security for traffic flowing across it.

Because a VPN uses a public network for transport, VPN traffic crosses the network perimeter of an organization using a VPN. Therefore, organizations that deploy both VPNs and firewalls must configure their firewalls to interoperate with VPNs they operate. Consequently, most commercial firewall offerings support VPNs.

Linux IPTables does not directly support the use of VPNs. However, open-source VPNs are available, and IPTables firewalls can be configured to screen VPN traffic. This appendix briefly introduces VPN technology and explains the installation and configuration of FreeS/WAN, an open-source VPN that was developed by using, and is compatible with, Red Hat Linux.

 Red Hat Linux 7 and later have shipped the CIPE open-source VPN. For more information on CIPE, see `http://sites.inka.de/sites/bigred/devel/cipe.html`.

VPN Technology

Modern VPNs are based on IP Security (IPSec), a standard intended to provide secure communication over IP. IPSec supports

491

- Access control

- Authentication

- Data encryption

- Data integrity

- Nonrepudiation

To provide data integrity, authentication, and non-repudiation, IPSec includes a protocol known as Authentication Header (AH). The second main IPSec protocol, Encapsulating Security Payload (ESP), provides data encryption.

The basic connection provided by IPSec is a Security Association (SA). An SA is a one-way connection, so two-way communication requires a pair of SAs. Each SA supports either AH or ESP, but not both. Therefore, a typical two-way IPSec connection requires four SAs – an AH and ESP SA in each of two directions. SAs are identified by a 32-bit number called the Security Parameter Index (SPI) and the destination IP address associated with the connection.

IPSec has two modes of operation:

- *Transport* mode encrypts the IP data but not the IP header.

- *Tunnel* mode encrypts both the IP header and data.

Transport mode interoperates transparently with IP. However, because the IP header is not encrypted, it is vulnerable to tampering. For instance, transport mode communication is subject to eavesdropping via man-in-the-middle attacks. Moreover, NAT operations – which modify source or destination IP addresses – can disrupt the connectivity of transport mode connections.

Because tunnel mode encrypts both the IP header and data, this mode is more secure. Moreover, tunnel mode can interoperate with NAT. Because IP devices cannot process encrypted packet headers, tunnel mode adds a new IP header to each packet, pointing to the VPN gateway rather than to the actual destination. The VPN gateway decrypts the original IP header and forwards the packet to the proper destination.

IPSec relies on public key cryptography to ensure communication security. IPSec protocols are used to provide the secure exchange of keys:

- Internet Security Association and Key Management Protocol (ISAKMP) defines the steps used to accomplish key exchange.

- Secure Key Exchange Mechanism (SKEME) defines a secure key-exchange mechanism.

- Oakley defines the modes of operation used in establishing a secure connection.

Together, this suite of protocols is referred to as the Internet Key Exchange (IKE) protocol.

Originally, VPN implementations did not interoperate effectively. However, the Secure Wide Area Network (S/WAN) initiative, which promotes interoperability between VPN implementations, has gained significant support. Most leading VPN products can now interoperate in basic modes.

FreeS/WAN

FreeS/WAN is a sophisticated, open-source VPN product that requires significant knowledge and skill to install and configure. It is available from its Web site, `http://www.freeswan.org`. However, it's relatively easy to install and configure FreeS/WAN to support a simple VPN.

This section describes a straightforward application of FreeS/WAN, joining two networks via a VPN running over the Internet. FreeS/WAN supports much more complicated applications consisting of perhaps dozens of discrete VPNs. For more information on FreeS/WAN, see the documentation available on the FreeS/WAN Web site, especially the *FreeS/WAN Quick Start Guide*.

Installing FreeS/WAN

You can download FreeS/WAN as a source distribution or as RPMs. Using RPMs is generally much more convenient. The FreeS/WAN Web site does not host RPMs, but it provides links to sites that do:

- `ftp://ftp.xs4all.nl/pub/crypto/freeswan/RedHat-RPMs`

- `http://rpms.steamballoon.com/freeswan/`

FreeS/WAN is implemented as a kernel module, so it's important that you download a version that matches the version of your installed kernel. You can determine the version of the installed kernel by issuing the command

```
uname -a
```

You should download two FreeS/WAN packages:

- freeswan

- freeswan-module

If your kernel version is older than any available version of FreeS/WAN, update the kernel by using an RPM obtained from the Red Hat Web site or mirror. Be sure to install the kernel using the RPM `-i` flag rather than the `-U` flag:

```
rpm -ivh kernel-2.4.9-34.i386.rpm
```

The `-i` flag causes the new kernel to be installed alongside the older one, whereas if you specify the `-U` flag, the new kernel overwrites the existing one. If something goes awry with installation and you've retained the older kernel, you can use the older kernel to boot the system and recover. If you overwrite the older kernel, you may be unable to recover from an error.

A new kernel version may require an updated version of the modutils package or other packages. If so, install these packages by using the `-U` flag before installing the new kernel. The tux package, a kernel-based HTTP accelerator, sometimes conflicts with new kernel versions. If you're not using tux, the simplest way to resolve this type of problem is to delete tux:

```
rpm -e tux
```

FreeS/WAN also requires `libpcap`, which is included in the Red Hat Linux distribution. If you haven't installed `libpcap`, do so before attempting to install FreeS/WAN.

After you've established the necessary prerequisites, you can install the FreeS/WAN packages:

```
rpm -Uvh freeswan-1.98b_2.4.9_34-0.i386.rpm \
   freeswan-module-1.98b_2.4.9_34-0.i386.rpm
```

To link two sites via a FreeS/WAN VPN, you must install FreeS/WAN on a pair of gateways, one at each site. After you've done so, you can configure FreeS/WAN.

Configuring FreeS/WAN

The main FreeS/WAN configuration file is /etc/ipsec.conf. FreeS/WAN also uses /etc/ipsec.secrets, which contains a public-private key pair used to identify the host. The configuration on each host must include the public key of its counterpart. You can extract this key from the /etc/ipsec.secrets file, as the data following the directive #pubkey=. Because of line wrapping, the data may appear to occupy multiple lines; however, the public key is entirely contained within a single line. If you've worked with SSH keys, you're familiar with this phenomenon.

After extracting the public key of each gateway host, send the key to the counterpart host via a secure method. If the key is compromised in transit, the security of your VPN is easily breached. So, you may prefer to use an offline method of exchange, such as a floppy disk.

After each host has available the public key of its counterpart, you're ready to configure the VPN. Listing F-1 shows a typical site-to-site VPN configuration you can use as a starting point. The file has three main sections:

- ◆ `config setup` specifies the interface used and several processing options.

- ◆ `conn %default` specifies defaults pertaining to all connections.

◆ `conn head-branch` specifies options pertaining to a VPN connection named head-branch.

Listing F-1: Sample /etc/ipsec.conf

```
config setup
        interfaces="ipsec0=eth0"
        klipsdebug=none
        plutodebug=none
        plutoload=%search
        plutostart=%search

conn %default
        keyingtries=0
        authby=rsasig

conn head-branch
        leftid=@head.example.com
        leftrsasigkey=<left public key goes here>
        left=192.0.34.72
        leftnexthop=192.0.34.1
        leftsubnet=10.0.0.0/8
        rightid=@branch.example.com
        rightrsasigkey=<right public key goes here>
        right=192.0.35.72
        rightnexthop=192.0.35.1
        rightsubnet=192.168.1.0/24
        auto=start
```

The configuration directives have these meanings:

◆ `interfaces` specifies the IPSec and actual network interfaces associated with the VPN.

◆ `klipsdebug` specifies the amount of debugging information generated by KLIPS, the FreeS/WAN kernel interface.

◆ `plutodebug` specifies the amount of debugging information generated by Pluto, the FreeS/WAN component responsible for key exchange.

◆ `plutoload` specifies which connections are automatically loaded when the IPSec service starts. The `%search` token causes all defined connections to be loaded at start-up.

- ◆ `plutostart` specifies which connections are automatically started when the IPSec service starts. The `%search` token causes all defined connections to be started.

- ◆ `keyingtries` specifies the number of connection retries permitted. The value 0 permits unlimited retries.

- ◆ `authby` specifies the method used to authenticate connections. The value `rsasig` specifies the use of an RSA key pair.

- ◆ `leftid` assigns a name to the left gateway. The gateways participating in a VPN are arbitrarily designated left and right. The symbol @ is used to identify the name as a fully qualified domain name.

- ◆ `leftrsasigkey` gives the public key of the left gateway. The value copied from the `/etc/ipsec.secrets` file should be pasted here.

- ◆ `left` gives the IP address of the external interface of the left gateway.

- ◆ `leftnexthop` gives the IP address of the default router used by the left gateway.

- ◆ `leftsubnet` gives the IP network address of the private network located behind the left gateway.

- ◆ `rightid` assigns a name to the right gateway.

- ◆ `rightrsasigkey` gives the public key of the right gateway. The value copied from the `/etc/ipsec.secrets` file should be pasted here.

- ◆ `right` gives the IP address of the external interface of the right gateway.

- ◆ `rightnexthop` gives the IP address of the default router used by the right gateway.

- ◆ `rightsubnet` gives the IP network address of the private network located behind the right gateway.

- ◆ `auto` specifies whether the connection can be automatically loaded or loaded and started. The value `start` specifies that the connection can be automatically loaded and started.

You should insert into the configuration file the public keys for the gateway hosts and revise all IP addresses appropriately. The same configuration file can be used on each gateway host if both use the same name for their external network interface. Otherwise, the value assigned to interfaces must differ in each configuration. For full information on each configuration directive used and additional configuration directives supported by FreeS/WAN, see the online documentation.

Starting and Controlling the VPN

If you installed a new kernel, you must reboot your gateway systems before starting the VPN. Be sure to select the updated kernel from the boot menu. If the system boots properly, you can revise /etc/grub/grub.conf to specify the new kernel as the default by changing the value associated with the default directive.

Before starting the VPN for the first time, ensure that the ip_foward kernel option has the value 1 and the rp_filter kernel option has the value 0 for any interface used by the VPN. You can add directives to /etc/sysctl.conf to establish these values:

```
net.ipv4.ip_forward = 0
net.ipv4.conf.eth0.rp_filter = 0
net.ipv4.conf.ipsec0.rp_filter = 0
```

To give immediate effect to these directives, issue the sysctl command:

```
sysctl -p
```

> **TIP**   After your VPN is working, experiment by enabling the rp_filter option. You may find that the VPN operates properly with the option enabled, thereby providing additional security.

The freeswan RPM package configures the IPSec service to start automatically when the system enters run level 3. Therefore, your VPN should start up during the system boot. To manually start the VPN, issue this command on each gateway:

```
service ipsec start
```

As you might expect, you can shut down the VPN by issuing the complementary command

```
service ipsec stop
```

After the IPSec service starts, tail the /var/log/messages file to determine whether the VPN was successfully established. If you find error messages, revise your configuration as necessary. Then, restart the IPSec service on each gateway host.

Testing the VPN

After the VPN has been established, hosts on each private network should be able to access hosts on the other. If your hosts are configured to respond to ping requests, try pinging a host on one private network from a host on the other. After ping confirms that VPN connectivity is working, you can try to access services such as SSH or HTTP.

Firewalls and VPNs

In effect, a VPN provides a back door into your private network. Consequently, protecting your network against unauthorized VPN access is important. Using RSA authentication is one means of doing so. However, the principle of layered defense implies that you should not be content to rely merely on cryptographic authentication or any other single means of protection.

You should generally supplement strong authentication by using RSA keys with other security measures, such as a firewall. To interoperate with a VPN, a firewall must accept the following traffic:

◆ Inbound and outbound traffic on UDP port 500 (IKE)

◆ Inbound and outbound traffic using protocol 50 (ESP)

◆ Inbound and outbound traffic using protocol 51 (AH)

Listing F-2 presents a simple firewall script that accepts only VPN traffic. You can adapt the script to suit your own purposes. However, be sure to revise the IP addresses that appear near the top of the script. The environment variable IP should hold the IP address of the external interface of the VPN gateway, and the environment variable LAN should hold the network address of the private network screened by the VPN gateway.

Listing F-2: A sample firewall script that accepts only VPN traffic

```
#!/bin/sh
IPT=/sbin/iptables
# Change the following two IP addresses
IP=192.0.34.72
LAN=10.0.0.0/8

$IPT -F FORWARD
$IPT -F INPUT
$IPT -F OUTPUT

$IPT -P FORWARD DROP
$IPT -P INPUT DROP
$IPT -P OUTPUT DROP

$IPT -A INPUT -i lo -j ACCEPT
$IPT -A INPUT -p udp -d $IP --dport 500 -j ACCEPT
```

```
$IPT -A INPUT -p 50  -d $IP -j ACCEPT
$IPT -A INPUT -p 51  -d $IP -j ACCEPT

$IPT -A OUTPUT -o lo -j ACCEPT
$IPT -A OUTPUT -p udp -s $IP --dport 500 -j ACCEPT
$IPT -A OUTPUT -p 50  -s $IP -j ACCEPT
$IPT -A OUTPUT -p 51  -s $IP -j ACCEPT

$IPT -A FORWARD -s $LAN -d $LAN -j ACCEPT
```

The host that serves as a VPN gateway could provide other services. However, the more services a host exposes, the more vulnerable the host. Consequently, it's good practice to run only VPN-related services on a VPN gateway.

You can further increase the security of a VPN gateway by limiting the hosts that are allowed to access it. Listing F-3 presents a firewall script that includes a list of authorized VPN gateway IPs. Only hosts having IP addresses appearing on the list are allowed to use the gateway.

Listing F-3: A firewall script that limits VPN access

```
# Change the following IP addresses
VPN_IPS="192.0.35.1 192.0.36.1 192.0.37.1"

for vpn_ip in $VPN_IPS; do
   $IPT -A INPUT  -p udp -s $vpn_ip -d $IP --dport 500 -j ACCEPT
   $IPT -A INPUT  -p 50  -s $vpn_ip -d $IP -j ACCEPT
   $IPT -A INPUT  -p 51  -s $vpn_ip -d $IP -j ACCEPT
   $IPT -A OUTPUT -p udp -s $IP -d $vpn_ip --dport 500 -j ACCEPT
   $IPT -A OUTPUT -p 50  -s $IP -d $vpn_ip -j ACCEPT
   $IPT -A OUTPUT -p 51  -s $IP -d $vpn_ip -j ACCEPT
done
```

Summary

VPNs are an important tool for securely exchanging data between remote sites and users. FreeS/WAN is a sophisticated VPN product compatible with Red Hat Linux. Configuring simple VPNs using FreeS/WAN is relatively straightforward.

Index

Symbols

<> alternate symbol (Snort), 412–413

-> arrow symbol (Snort), 412

@ sign, 42–43

! mark, 202, 203, 237

A

-A flag

with `ipchains` command, 206, 210

with `iptables` command, 254

in Snort configuration, 411

abuse contact, 419

`ACCEPT` target, 205, 250

`accept_redirects`, 324

`accept_source_route`, 324

accepting packets, 82, 419

access, compromise versus, 5–6

accidents, 5

accuracy of data, 4

`ACK` flag

with active mode FTP, 91, 92

fraudulent, 84

function, 33, 81

with passive mode FTP, 90–91

role in closing server connection, 35–36

role in establishing server connection, 34, 35

`ACK` scans

IPChains vulnerability to, 185, 195

IPTables firewall resistance to, 186

acknowledgment number, 33

actions of firewalls, 82–83, 190

active mode FTP

defined, 419

passive mode versus, 93–94

protocol summary, 91–93

Address Resolution Protocol (ARP), 14

address-mask (ICMP message type), 205, 464

administration and maintenance

disconnecting host from network for, 289

as firewall life cycle step, 180

Logwatch log analysis, 376–380

remote logging, 373–375

administrative privileges, 6

Advanced Intrusion Detection Environment (AIDE) site, 431

`alert`, in Snort rules, 412

Alert History display (NetSaint), 391

alternate (<>) symbol (Snort), 412–413

anacron, 338

analysis of attacks, 7

annualized loss expectancy (ALE) value, 181, 419

annualized rate of occurrence, 181, 419

appending rules

defined, 419

`ipchains` command, 206

`iptables` command, 254

appliances, firewall, 8

application layer, 18–19, 80

application level, 419

application protocols

AUTH, 95–96

database services, 114–116

defined, 419

DHCP, 106–107

DNS, 96–97, 107–108

file- and printer-sharing services, 116–120

FTP, 88–94

ICMP, 110–113

low-level protocols versus, 14

mail, 97–99

messaging and user information services, 120–123

multimedia, 100–101

NNTP, 99–100

NTP, 108–109

remote user services, 124–128

RPC-based, 128–130

RSYNC, 101–102

"small" services, 130–136

SSH, 86–88

system and network administration services, 136–138

Traceroute, 109

WHOIS, 105

World Wide Web, 102–105

X Window, 139–141

application-based security measures, 11

application-level proxies, 157–158

`ApplyStdDate` directive (Logwatch), 378

architecture. *See* firewall architecture

`Archive` directive (Logwatch), 378

Archives setting (Logwatch), 376

`arpwatch` utility, 334

501

continued